D1413286

EDUCATIONAL MEDIA AND TECHNOLOGY YEARBOOK

EDUCATIONAL MEDIA AND TECHNOLOGY YEARBOOK

Robert Maribe Branch and Mary Ann Fitzgerald, Editors

1999 VOLUME 24

Published in Cooperation with the
ERIC® Clearinghouse on Information & Technology
and the
Association for Educational Communications
and Technology

1999
Libraries Unlimited, Inc. • Englewood, Colorado

LIBRARIES UNLIMITED, INC.
P.O. Box 6633
Englewood, CO 80155-6633
1-800-237-6124
www.lu.com

Library of Congress Cataloging-in-Publication Data

Suggested Cataloging:

Educational media and technology yearbook, 1999 volume 24 /
    Robert Maribe Branch and Mary Ann Fitzgerald, editors —
Englewood, Colo.: Libraries Unlimited, 1999.
    xii, 281 p. 17x25 cm.
    ISBN 1-56308-636-0
    ISSN 8755-2094
    Published in cooperation with the ERIC Clearinghouse on Information
& Technology and the Association for Educational Communications and
Technology.
    1. Educational technology—yearbooks. 2. Instructional materials
centers—yearbooks. I. ERIC Clearinghouse on Information & Technology.
II. Association for Educational Communications and Technology.
III. Branch, Robert Maribe. IV. Mary Ann Fitzgerald.
LB 1028.3.E372   1999   370.778

VD208

Contents

Part Four
LEADERSHIP PROFILE

Part Five
ORGANIZATIONS AND ASSOCIATIONS
IN NORTH AMERICA

Part Six
GRADUATE PROGRAMS

**Part Seven
MEDIAGRAPHY
Print and Nonprint Resources**

Preface

The purpose of this 24th volume of the *Educational Media and Technology Yearbook* is to highlight multiple perspectives about educational technology and media development. *EMTY* continues to provide information to help media and technology professionals practice their craft in a changing, expanding field. This volume maintains the belief that technology represents tools that act as extensions of the educator. Further, the contention of the editors and contributors is that various media serve as delivery systems for educational communications. The intent of this *Yearbook* is to inform readers about the purposes, activities, programs of study, and accomplishments of organizations and associations dedicated to the advancement of educational communications and technology.

Technology does not refer simply to machines and hardware but includes techniques and procedures derived from scientific research about ways to promote change in human performance, as a way of organizing thought, science, art, and human values. The evolution of educational media and advancements in information delivery technology are requiring educators to reconsider the traditional concept of audiovisual aids and to consider the concept of multimedia applications. This volume of the *Yearbook* reflects current thinking in the field. It includes essays from respected authors about technology trends in education and training, teaching methods and curricular issues, electronic publishing and the state of the profession, and Internet resources.

The *Educational Media and Technology Yearbook* is an active forum for scholarly exchange about processes for developing media and appropriate applications of instructional technology. The fundamental tenet is that educational media and technology should be used to

1. achieve authentic learning objectives,

2. situate learning tasks,

3. negotiate the complexities of guided learning,

4. facilitate the construction of knowledge,

5. support skill acquisition, and

6. manage diversity.

Over the years, the *Educational Media and Technology Yearbook* has become a standard reference in many libraries and professional collections. This volume contains sections devoted to Trends and Issues, Current Developments, The Profession, Organizations and Associations in North America, Graduate Programs, and a Mediagraphy of print and nonprint resources. The topics herein allow this volume to remain consistent with most standard references that contain elements that readers expect to find in each new edition. The editors, publishers, and professionals dedicated to the field know it is important to chronicle the events associated with educational technology through reviews of the profession, generations of leadership, and the influence of culture on the use of educational media and technology.

Robert Maribe Branch

Contributors to
Educational Media and Technology Yearbook 1999

Alex J. Angulo, Graduate Student
Department of Instructional Technology
University of Georgia
604 Aderhold Hall
Athens, GA 30602

Robert Maribe Branch, Ed.D.,
    Associate Professor
Instructional Technology
University of Georgia
604 Aderhold Hall
Athens, GA 30602
Senior Editor

John K. Burton, Ph.D., Professor
College of Education
Virginia Polytechnic Institute and
    State University
220 War Memorial Hall
Blacksburg, VA 24061-0313

Jacquelyn Carll
Instructional Computing Specialist
Mohawk Regional Information Center
Madison-Oneida BOCES
4937 Spring Road
Verona, NY 13478-0168

Costas Criticos, Senior Lecturer
Department of Education
University of Natal
P.O. Box 51304
Durban, South Africa

Jared A. Danielson, Graduate Assistant
College of Education
Virginia Polytechnic Institute and
    State University
220 War Memorial Hall
Blacksburg, VA 24061-0313

Donald P. Ely, Ph.D., Senior Associate for
    Educational Technology
ERIC® Clearinghouse on Information
    & Technology
Professor Emeritus
Instructional Design, Development,
    and Evaluation
Syracuse University
4-194 Science & Technology
Syracuse, NY 13244-4100

Mary Ann Fitzgerald, Assistant Professor
Instructional Technology
University of Georgia
604 Aderhold Hall
Athens, GA 30602
Associate Editor

J. Thomas Head, Ph.D., Director
Media Services
Virginia Polytechnic Institute and
    State University
Old Security Building
Blacksburg, VA 24061-0232

Alan Januszewski, Associate Professor
SUNY Potsdam Education
State University of New York at Potsdam
218 Satterlee Hall
Potsdam, NY 13676

Nancy Nelson Knupfer, Ph.D., Professor
Educational Computing, Design, and
    Telecommunications
Department FAE
College of Education
Kansas State University
363 Bluemont Hall
1100 Mid-Campus Drive
Manhattan, KS 66506-5305
nknupfer@ksu.edu

Bernard Lee
Graduate Student
School of Information Studies
Syracuse University
Syracuse, NY 13244

Barbara B. Lockee, Ph.D., Assistant
    Professor
College of Education
Virginia Polytechnic Institute and
    State University
220 War Memorial Hall
Blacksburg, VA 24061-0313

David R. Moore, Ph.D.
Faculty Development Specialist
Portland State University
Smith Memorial Center
18 SMC
Portland, OR 97207-0751

John F. Moore, Ph.D., Director
Instructional Technologies
Virginia Polytechnic Institute and
    State University
Old Security Building
Blacksburg, VA 24061-0232

Eric Plotnick, Assistant Director
ERIC® Clearinghouse on Information &
    Technology
Syracuse University
4-194 Science & Technology
Syracuse, NY 13244-4100

Arthur Recesso
Technology Planning Specialist
Mohawk Regional Information Center
Madison-Oneida BOCES
4937 Spring Road
Verona, NY 13478-0168

Lynne Schrum, Ph.D., Associate Professor
Department of Instructional Technology
University of Georgia
604 Aderhold Hall
Athens, GA 30602

Ruth V. Small, Ph.D., Associate Professor
School of Information Studies
Syracuse University
4-194 Science & Technology
Syracuse, NY 13244-4100

Lonnie Turbee
Online Content Specialist
Syracuse Language Systems
4314 Wetzel Road, Apt A8
Liverpool, NY 13090

Part One
Trends and Issues

Introduction

New technological applications are usually preceded by trends. Resources dedicated to media development are usually proportionate to the importance attached to the prevailing issues. This is also true of trends and issues in educational communications. While trends do not necessarily predict the future, there is logic in tracing the trends of educational media and technology to determine *indicators* for the future of the field. Soothsaying notwithstanding, Art Recesso and Jackie Carll of the Madison-Oneida New York Board of Cooperative Educational Services have provided some ideas about ways to incorporate technology into the K–12 environment. Dr. Lynne Schrum, Associate Professor of Instructional Technology at the University of Georgia and the President of the International Society for Technology in Education (ISTE), shares practical lessons about trends in distance learning. Dr. John Moore and Dr. Tom Head at Virginia Tech present an instructional development initiative that sets a trend in large-scale efforts to improve teaching excellence, productivity, and effectiveness through appropriate uses of instructional technology. Professor Nancy Nelson Knupfer of Kansas State University and recent Fulbright Scholar presents descriptions about balancing issues related to gender, technology, and instructional design.

Robert Maribe Branch

Integrating Technology into the K–12 Educational Setting

Arthur Recesso
Technology Planning Specialist
Mohawk Regional Information Center

Jacquelyn Carll
Instructional Computing Specialist
Mohawk Regional Information Center

CONCEPTUAL FRAMEWORK

Technological ability in students has been identified as an important factor in student entry into the workforce. *A Nation at Risk* (1983) and other study reports have clearly delineated the need for students to enter the job market with the ability to use technology (Center on Education and the Economy 1990). Technology has come to be recognized as an indispensable tool. People who do not possess technology skills are liable to be resigned to menial work.

Research related to innovations has ranged from diffusion theory, the study of how the use of innovations spreads, to a concern for the hardware components of the innovation. In the past 25 years attention has focused on the administrative procedures and policies related to innovation diffusion and implementation (Trice 1978, Hoffman & Roman 1984, Rogers & Van de Ven 1988, Rogers & Valente 1995). According to Rogers (1983, 1988, 1995), innovations can be discussed in the context of adoption, adaptation, and implementation; stages and/or levels of implementation; and the conditions of the local environment.

A clear distinction between the terms *adoption* and *adaptation* is made in the literature. Rogers (1988) defines adoption as the decision to use an innovation. Davis (1994) defines adaptation in terms of change. Implementation, not adoption or adaptation, is actually putting the innovation to use (Rogers & Van de Ven 1988). The distinction is important. When an innovation is adopted, it is subject to distortion or replacement. It is when an innovation is adapted that there is change. The assumption is that schools that regard change as positive are more likely to adapt an innovation and successfully implement it. Therefore, the focus of this article is on a process of guiding adaptation and implementation.

BACKGROUND

In working with more than 50 school districts in central/northern New York State for the past six to eight years as those districts strove to find cost-effective ways of getting computer technology into the hands of their students, it has become apparent that there are more effective and less effective ways for a district to work through this process. This article is written in the hopes that other districts may benefit from situations and experiences we have encountered. By avoiding some of the pitfalls that have delayed or derailed districts that want to bring computer technology to their students, districts about to embark on this great adventure will be able to save themselves time, aggravation, and money.

WHY USE COMPUTER TECHNOLOGY
IN THE K–12 CLASSROOM?

Everywhere our students turn they encounter computer technology: at home in the form of stand-alone units, laptops, or play stations; at the public library as they reserve materials or search for and borrow books; at supermarket checkout counters; and at drugstores in the card departments. As the children grow more conscious of their surroundings and the work world around them, they become increasingly aware that computer technology underpins the world we live in, controlling climate, turning out products on the production line, and intertwining with the worlds of medicine, sports, entertainment, and industry. As was pointed out in *School Reform in the Information Age* (1996), technology is used extensively outside of school; by using technology within schools it will be possible to make the conditions of school more authentic.

A 1993 study supported by the U.S. Department of Education pointed out capabilities that computer technology can provide to both students and teachers. To students, the technology offers powerful support for learning skills through inquiry and problem solving. For teachers, technology supports functions that are fundamental if teachers are to provide authentic, active learning experiences that are demanded by the educational reform movement. These experiences include developing and tailoring instructional materials, conducting ongoing assessment of student learning, expanding teachers' content and instructional knowledge, and making the crucial home-school connection with parents.

As Sylvia Wier (1992) pointed out in "Electronic Communities of Learners: Fact or Fiction?," networked computers can provide a framework for encouraging change within a complex social, interactional setting. Network projects in which students participate can serve as instructive models of how to use technology to provide continuing teacher support while achieving widespread dissemination of innovative ways of encouraging classroom learning. It is wise, however, for any district contemplating the start of (or continuation of) a computer initiative to be very clear that technology can invite change but cannot ensure that this change will be successful. According to Fullan (1982), educational change involves a number of components, among them possible use of new or revised materials, possible use of new teaching approaches, and possible alteration of beliefs.

Infusion of Technology—Where to Start?

There are a number of areas to consider when designing the technology implementation process. Unfortunately, the trend lately has been for school staff involved in the design process to be too broad in their approach. Each school district has improvement initiatives such as learning standards, goals, benchmarks, and state and national mandates that affect curriculum. Questions to be asked include "Does technology fit in here as a tool? Will it provide support for core curriculum? Will it be a tool to enhance and extend student learning?" In order to avoid being overwhelmed by the implementation process, there must be focus during the planning process. This focus should be on a specific educational benchmark, learning episode, or content area (e.g., English Language Arts standards, Math/Science/Technology standards). The stakeholders involved in the technology innovation should center their efforts on a particular standard or issue.

Form an Effective District-Wide Technology Planning Committee

To develop a thoughtful and comprehensive district-wide technology plan that will equitably serve the needs of district students, it is necessary to gather a broad base of informed opinion from the decision-makers who represent all aspects of the learning community. The district technology planning team should invite these people to serve: teachers who are content area specialists to represent pre-K–12; department chairs, staff and curriculum developers, administrators, board of education members, parents, and PTO/PTA members; community businesspeople; and area technology planning specialists.

Staff Development—An Important Consideration

As the plan shapes up, staff development must be foremost in the minds of the key decision-makers in the school. For technology to be truly integrated, change must take place. Putting computers into a room where all the learning that takes place is teacher-directed, didactic, and compartmentalized will result in neither educational reform nor effective integration of computer technology within that classroom. For reform to take place, the classroom must be a place where students can explore, where they have interactive modes of instruction, and where they have sufficient time to pursue authentic and multidisciplinary work within collaborative groups. District administrators need to review staff development provided during the past three years. In order to plan for successful future staff development related to technology, an assessment of training already provided to teachers needs to be conducted. This review will accomplish several things. First, it will help the group see the "big picture" of where the district has been headed. Second, key elements of successful staff development programs can be used to help teachers bridge the gap from old to new concepts that they will encounter as they take their first steps toward integrating technology into their classes. To protect the monetary and time investment the district has already made in successful staff development, and to move forward with a cohesive plan that takes the best from the past to build upon for the future, a thoughtful analysis of past successful staff development must precede future planning.

Visitations

In conjunction with the formation of an inclusive Technology Planning Committee and assessment of past successful staff development, other initiatives must go forth. Selected groups of teachers, particularly those who will be involved in the first wave of technology infusion in the district, need to visit other school districts that have already begun to bring computer technology into their schools. This tactic works best when elementary teachers visit classrooms at their own grade level and when middle, junior, and high school teachers visit classrooms where teachers of the same subject content area are using networked computers with students. These visits need to be carefully arranged so that both the visiting and the visited teachers are clear about expectations and about what will happen during the visit. The host schools should make it possible for the visitors to have time alone with the teachers after their classes have been observed. That way, the visitors can ask questions about what was observed and request explanations of what preceded the lesson and what will follow. They can also communicate some of the stress and anxiety they expect as their district moves forward with its technology integration initiative—stress and anxiety that those visited have already lived through and mastered.

CONSIDERING THE SOFTWARE ISSUE

Visitations can also allow teachers to view software packages with which they may be unfamiliar, and can provide opportunities for questions about how well a particular package aligns with grade level or subject area curriculum; how well it ties in to the district, state, or national standards; and how readily it lends itself to the authentic assessment process.

Determining the expected student performance outcomes establishes benchmarks by which to evaluate the software and hardware required to complete the job. Educators working with content they previously taught without the benefit of technology will look for software to enhance or even redevelop an existing lesson. Educators developing new lessons, learning units, or learning experiences will want software that will provide either new curriculum content or practice in new strategies/skills that students will need to master (see Figure 1). In either situation there are several questions that need to be answered in order for the teacher to effectively use the software as a tool in the classroom.

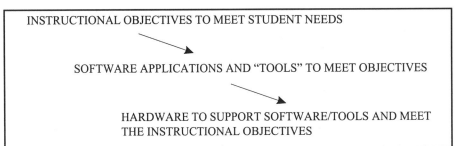

INSTRUCTIONAL OBJECTIVES TO MEET STUDENT NEEDS

SOFTWARE APPLICATIONS AND "TOOLS" TO MEET OBJECTIVES

HARDWARE TO SUPPORT SOFTWARE/TOOLS AND MEET
THE INSTRUCTIONAL OBJECTIVES

Figure 1.

How well does the software meet the demands of the learning environment?
The software must meet several criteria for the teacher:

- ease of use for the teacher and the student so that both are able to concentrate on meeting objectives of the learning episode and are not hindered by struggling to make the software work

- accessibility of student work (in file format) and ease of evaluation by both student and teacher

- flexibility of use with a variety of learning style methodologies

Network software versions run over a local area network (LAN) with multiple individual computers connected to a server. The network versions of software support a learning environment where educators and students enjoy:

- file sharing: access to assignments created by the teacher, access to student work for teacher review, student group access to the same files

- multiple access to the same software package

Passwords and other security measures provide privacy for students' and teachers' work. For every piece of software an educator intends to use with students, the two questions to be answered are: "What strand of the curriculum does this software support or tie into?" (including the issue of how software will assist students in meeting more stringent performance standards) and "Will this software package run with the current computer workstations in my classroom and the current network in my building?" Instructional and technical—those are the issues concerning software that must be dealt with, regardless of the hype put out by software manufacturers.

What are the system requirements of the software? This important question must be answered before selecting a package. If the software is to be installed on computers already in the classroom, then existing hardware must be reviewed to determine if:

- processor speeds are adequate

- there is enough hard drive space

- there is enough memory (amount of RAM required)

- the computer(s) are connected to the network (LAN)

- the computers must have sound capabilities (and speakers or headsets)

- a CD-ROM drive is available

- a microphone is attached and installed

This checklist will assist educators at any level. If the existing computers in the classroom do not meet the software requirements, one of three actions must be taken: Upgrade the existing hardware (if possible), replace the existing hardware completely (which, in some cases, can be more cost-effective in the long run), or select an alternative software package. Software programs that are graphically oriented (e.g., many pictures, complex images, motion) and require sound must have computers with enough power to make them work effectively. Attempting to shortcut on the system requirements of the software only leads to student and teacher frustration and disenchantment with the technology. Working with the checklist above not only ensures that the software will work, but that it will meet the teacher's need to deliver instruction to students. The instructional process can only be enhanced by technology when that technology actually works.

THE HARDWARE ISSUE

It is easy to become mired in the debate of platform and hardware to be used in the classroom. If the school district has first identified the expected outcomes and the software to be used to meet those outcomes, then the hardware decision should be less painful and take less time. The hardware selected should run the software and instructional tools identified during the planning process. The hardware requirements of the software are clearly listed by the software/device developer. In situations where the product is offered on multiple platforms, then the decision must be based on comfort level of the educator. Technically there is no advantage of one hardware platform over another. It has been our experience that teachers with a higher level of comfort and familiarity with their computer technology make better use of it.

There are other concerns the planning group should consider when planning for technology implementation. Many structural and environmental conditions within a school can affect the success of a technology implementation process. There should be specific attention to the following:

- Will the existing wiring throughout the building support additional technology?
  Power and computer wiring should be checked. Do not assume there is enough energy to make the computers work. There should be at least one dual-capacity outlet per computer.

- Is there furniture available to house the computer hardware?
  A good rule of thumb is a 3-foot-by-3-foot space per computer.

  > Are tables the correct height for the students?
  > Will students have to reach over equipment to access the printer?
  > Does the furniture provide for wiring trays?

- Is there space for printers?

- Are computers situated away from chalkboards, heating units, windows, and water?

- Have existing network capabilities been reviewed? Will they need to be expanded?

- Who will support the software and hardware chosen?

- What kind of personnel resources will the district be able to identify and train as part of its on-site maintenance of equipment?

- What is the initial cost of each workstation?

- What is the cost to maintain and support each workstation?

If attention is paid to these items, selecting hardware, estimating costs, and planning for implementation will be more effective.

Selecting New Hardware

Purchasing new hardware to operate the software selected for instruction makes the hardware decision much easier in some cases and very difficult in others. The hardware purchased must be compatible with existing networks and operating systems in the school. Therefore, if the school has very little or no equipment, the decisions are easier. Everything is new and will certainly work together if a district buys all of the same equipment or at least plans compatible systems. However, for schools that are upgrading or adding to an existing inventory of equipment, there are problem areas to be avoided.

Software and operating systems being used by educators and students (e.g., Windows 3.11) change constantly (e.g., Windows 95/98). This presents a special problem for the classroom. Students at the same grade level across the district should have access to identical resources. Incompatible software or hardware causes accessibility and ease-of-use issues that can harm the learning process and morale. A school district that engages in thoughtful planning will make a concerted effort to determine the implications of introducing new technology or upgrading software.

There are instructional as well as technical problems inherent in mixing computer equipment in the classroom. In our experience we have found it more beneficial to the learner and the teacher to keep hardware and software consistent in each classroom. If, however, a mixed-age hardware situation must exist within a school district because of financial constraints, then clear boundaries must be set. It is more effective to consider the instructional needs and the age of the learners before designating which grade levels will operate on which systems and software. As an example of instruction driving the hardware implementation process, in 1997 one of our school districts wanted to upgrade classroom computers in three elementary schools. The purchases, as initially planned, would have placed one newer Pentium 200 multimedia computer in the K–5 classrooms alongside three networked 486 computers. However, because of the need of teachers and students to share files, to use identical software, and to share a printer among the four computers in the classroom, the mixing strategy would not work. The solution was to transfer all the existing computers from the middle school and high school (requiring them to buy new machines) to complete the computer clusters in the elementary classrooms. Then every elementary classroom had the same equipment, software, and network components. The resources the school district had invested in training and redesigning instruction would be put to further use by providing the elementary teachers with consistency of platform and software. The middle school and high school teachers had to start over, but the tradeoff for them was newer equipment to meet their needs. It should be stressed that the entire process was driven by teachers. It was their instructional planning and design and their input in Technology Planning Committee meetings that allowed us to work together to find a technical solution.

One caution: It should not be assumed that older equipment satisfies the needs of teachers and students, especially in elementary schools. New products for the primary grades are just as demanding, or even more demanding, as the programs used in high school. Moving older computers into elementary classrooms may not be feasible because of the software selected to help students meet curricular objectives. The concern should not only be for compatibility of equipment but also for the compatibility of the technology with the demands of the students' learning environment. The challenge is to balance the students' needs with technological functionality. In this respect, purchasing a computer for the classroom is very different from purchasing a computer for the home or office.

A DISCUSSION OF WHAT WORKS

Thus far this article has discussed technology from the theoretical to the practical perspective. The literature says technology as an innovation is affected by the administrative procedures of an organization. The steps toward creating an effective implementation plan have been presented. The final step is to discuss what happens when technology is implemented in the classroom. Once the implementation takes place, does having computers in the classroom make a difference? Many studies have investigated the answer to that question. A number of studies were reviewed and reported here in brief as to their findings.

<u>Computer integration and writing instruction</u>

- Marcia Hailo (1990) found that students made more revisions and had a better attitude toward writing, but the students "play with the fonts."
- Lucy Calkins (1990) discovered that computers encourage student revisions of deeper structure of writing; students are more likely to become involved in serious revision; and they made a greater total number of revisions.
- Tonja Caster (1983) found that students were more likely to create original stories using a computer.
- Johnston & Olson (1989) found that children quickly learn to use word processing software and often do better writing than with pencil and paper.
- Cheever (1987) found that using word processing results in fewer grammatical, punctuation, and capitalization errors, especially among students with low abilities.
- Riel (1989) found that authentic writing with computers is an effective way of learning language mechanics. When combined with the use of telecommunications, such as a cooperative development project, improvements show up on both holistic assessments and standardized tests.
- MacArthur et al. (1990) discovered that when children use a computer to study spelling, they are more engaged and, as a result, achieve higher spelling scores.
- Kirkwood & Gimblett (1992) found that computers help elementary students of all ability levels to learn science content and to increase their logical thinking and problem-solving skills.
- Phillips & Soule (1992) saw that students show greater achievement on standardized tests after using computers for math problem solving.
- Char (1993) discovered that children can use a computer-based manipulative math environment that provides more control and flexibility than hands-on materials, helping to integrate objects and symbols in a visual approach where real manipulatives are not feasible.
- Vacc (1991) found that children using computers in math are more independent learners.

John Crandler (1997), in *Summary of Current Research and Evaluation Findings in Technology in Education*, reported on a number of outcomes for students related to their use of technology within the curriculum when content and strategies are determined to meet accepted education standards. In such cases, research shows that technology, according to these quotations from Crandler:

- increases performance when interactivity is prominent
- increases opportunities for interactivity with instructional programs
- is more effective with multiple technologies (video, computer, telecommunications, etc.)
- improves attitude and confidence, especially for at-risk students.
- provides instructional opportunities otherwise unavailable
- increases opportunities for student-constructed learning
- increases student collaboration on projects

- increases mastery of vocational and workforce skills
- helps prepare students for work when emphasized as a problem-solving tool
- significantly improves problem-solving skills of learning-disabled students
- improves writing skills and attitudes about writing for urban LEP students
- improves writing skills as a result of using telecommunications

SUMMARY

The intent of this article is to provide an overview of the technology integration process. It begins with a theoretical foundation of pursuing the integration of technology into K–12 schools. From that point we move toward the practical implications for implementing technology. The software and hardware issues are presented based on the experiences of the authors and their colleagues and the wide range of information that is available. In a final stage, studies related to the implementation and use of technology are reviewed. They are presented to inform the reader of what can and cannot be expected as a result of the planning and implementation process. Collectively, the information that was provided within this article is meant to inform the practitioner of the issues and practices that exist when addressing technology planning and integration into K–12 schools.

REFERENCES

Calkins, L. (1990). *The art of teaching writing.* Portsmouth, NH: Heineman.

Caster, T. (1983). *The use and effectiveness of computers in the classroom.* Paper presented at the Annual Study Conference of the Georgia Association for Childhood Education International, Athens, GA.

Char, C. (1993). *Computer graphic feltboards: New software approaches to children's mathematical exploration.* MA: Education Development Center.

Cheever, M. S. (1987). *The effects of using a word processor on the acquisition of composition skills by the elementary student.* Doctoral dissertation, Northwest University.

Crandler, J. (1997). *Summary of current research and evaluation findings on technology in education.* Internet page at URL: http://www.fwl.org.

Davis, O. L., Jr. (1994). Don't adopt, adapt: A reminder for every year. *Journal of Curriculum and Supervision 9* (4), 403–5.

Fine, C. (1991). *Research on the national geographic kids network.* Oak Brook, IL: North Central Regional Educational Laboratory.

Fullan, M. (1982). *Implementing educational change: Progress at last.* Paper Presented at the National Invitation Conference, National Institute of Education, Warrenton, VA.

Hailo, M. (1990). Student writing: Can the machine maim the message? *NYPC Magazine*, January, 19–24.

Johnston, J., and Olson, K. (1989). *The use of the computer as a writing tool in a kindergarten and first grade classroom.* CIEL Pilot Year Final Report, Part 2. Ann Arbor, MI: University of Michigan and Apple Computer.

Kirkwood, J. J., and Gimblett, R. R. (1992). Expert systems and weather forecasting in the 4th and 5th grades. *Journal of Computing in Childhood Education 3* (3–4), 323–33.

Lichenstein, N. (1996). *The effect of word processing on writing achievement.* Master's thesis, Kean College.

MacArthur, C. A., et al. (1990). Computer instruction with learning disabled students: Achievement, engagement, and other factors that influence achievement. *Journal of Computing Research 6* (3), 311–28.

Mehlinger, H. D. (1996). School reform in the information age. *Phi Delta Kappan 77* (6), 400–477.

Newman, D., et al. (1989). Computer mediation of collaborative science investigations. *Journal of Educational Computing Research 5* (2), 151–66.

Phillips, J., and Soule, H. (1992). *A comparison of fourth graders' achievement: Classroom computers versus no computer.* Paper presented at MidSouth Educational Research Association.

Riel, M. (1989). The impact of computers in the classroom. *Journal of Research on Computing in Education 22*, 180–90.

Rogers, E. M. (1983). *Diffusion of innovations.* New York: Free Press.

Rogers, E. M., and Valente, T. M. (1995). The origins and development of the diffusion of innovations paradigm as an example of scientific growth. *Science Communication 16* (3), 242–73.

Rogers, E. M., and Van de Ven, A. H. (1988). Innovations and organizations: Critical perspectives. *Communication Research 15* (5), 632–51.

U.S. Department of Education. (1983). *A nation at risk: A report to the nation from the secretary of education.* National Commission on Excellence in Education, Washington, DC.

Vacc, N. N. (1991). A comparison using a microcomputer precision teaching, and worksheets to master basic multiplication facts. *Journal of Educational Technology System 20* (30), 179–98.

Trends in Distance Learning
Lessons to Inform Practice

Lynne Schrum
Department of Instructional Technology
University of Georgia

INTRODUCTION

This article offers a look at distance learning, which is now in practice throughout the United States and around the world. The rapid development of information technologies has changed the manner in which distance education is conducted, but it may also serve to give distance education an equal status with more traditional education. It is timely to reflect on previous distance learning experiences and the current evolution of the discipline, so that we may make wise decisions in the future.

For purposes of this article, distance education represents a way of communicating with geographically dispersed individuals and groups. Distance learning is above all the process of teaching and learning in which learners "just happen to be physically separate from a teacher" (Garrison & Shale 1990). The possibility of learning that is free of time and place constraints is an overriding desire of many educators and potential learners.

First, this article will define and briefly review the history of distance learning. Next, it will look at pertinent research that informs practice. Then, the article will explore the development of online distance. Finally, it will offer some practical suggestions for the development of online educational experiences.

A GLIMPSE OF THE HISTORY OF DISTANCE LEARNING

As early as 1728, regular mail service was used to aid traditional education. Although this model did not become widespread for many years, it did demonstrate that individuals do take responsibility for their learning when it is important to them. For the last 150 years, correspondence education was used to accomplish the goal of delivering instruction to place-bound individuals or nontraditional students. This was accomplished primarily by mailing print forms of class lectures and assignments. As other media and technologies became available, they were incorporated into distance education, including newspapers, radio, television, telephones, satellite transmission, electronic publishing, and computer-mediated communication (CMC).

Since World War I, distance education has spread rapidly and is now known in some form all over the world. The British Broadcasting Corporation (BBC) used radio for adult education, primarily for individuals to improve their lives, without credit or degrees. Australia has had its Radio School of the Air to reach school-age children living on remote stations for decades. Schools at all levels in the United States also used radio, for self-enrichment or credit.

Television brought new dimensions to the world of distance education. In 1957, the Sunrise Semester began throughout the United States and continues in one form or another today. Up until the 1960s, most education at a distance was part of traditional educational institutions, either four-year universities or community colleges. In 1963, the University of the Air in the United Kingdom was granted a charter and began teaching in 1971. The Open University, as it came to be named, is now one of the most well known of the institutions specifically devoted to distance learning, and its model has been duplicated in many similar institutions worldwide.

RESEARCH IN THE FIELD

Throughout the literature, little evidence exists that any one technology provides the "one best means" to accomplish all the goals of distance education. In an extensive review of the research on distance delivery systems, McClelland and Saeed (1986) found that there were no substantive differences in achievement or cost-effectiveness among the various media. They suggested that for distance education it is, first, important to reconceptualize instruction and, second, to focus the research on instructional design, learning tasks, and the learner. Herschback (1984) similarly summed up his work by concluding that studies indicate little or no difference in learner outcomes when various media are compared (cited in McClelland & Saeed 1986). And Smith (1984) found in her review of the research that telecourses are at least as good as traditional on-campus lecture format courses.

More recent research tends to support similar conclusions. One study (Beare 1989) compared five delivery systems, from traditional to telecourse, and found no differences in student achievement or course evaluations. Other studies (Boone 1995, McDevitt 1995) investigated the use of two-way television, and results indicated that the students and their professors felt the technology provided appropriate experiences and discussions, even when the technology repeatedly broke down.

Schrum (1996), in an investigation of compressed video for course instruction and professional development workshops, found that participants viewed such video as an appropriate manner in which to provide staff development to rural educators and to offer classes to distant locations. Similar results and responses have been reported by others using compressed video systems (Hakes et al. 1993; Lyons, MacBrayne, & Johnson 1994). Overall, learners and instructors in these studies rated distance education as useful and appropriate.

THE DEVELOPMENT OF
ONLINE DISTANCE EDUCATION

Recent developments in network and communication technologies offer geographically and physically separated individuals access to courses and instruction in a timely and more interactive manner through increased communication, interactivity among participants, and incorporation of collaborative pedagogical models. Distance education via these technologies has unique characteristics (speed, interactivity, multiple locations, and a variety of communication techniques), so that for the first time we can provide experiences that allow teacher and learner to interact over distance in almost traditional ways.

The literature reports an increasing number of courses and degrees delivered entirely online. Some courses are traditional undergraduate subject matter courses. In some circumstances the technology is only a repository and merely holds the materials (Boston 1992), and in others there is evidence that the technology itself assists in a paradigm shift so that it becomes the environment for learning (Dede 1995).

Harasim (1990) summarized the characteristics of online courses as place and time independence, many-to-many communication that fosters real collaborative learning, and dependence on text-based communications to promote thoughtful and reflective commentary. Other advantages to using this type of distance learning are instantaneous (synchronous) and asynchronous communication, access to and from geographically isolated communities, multiple participation within activities, and cultural sharing of diversity and recognition of similarities among the people of our world.

Development of an online educational environment is not a trivial task. Wiesenberg and Hutton (1996) identified three major challenges for the designer to consider: taking into account increased time for delivery of the course (they estimated two or three times what is necessary for a traditional course), creating a community online, and encouraging students to become independent learners.

Reid and Woolf (1996) discuss the benefits of integrating online components into traditional classes, such as accessibility, learner control, heightened communication, access to worldwide resources, and the potential for a student-centered environment. Heeren and Lewis (1997) suggest matching the media with the task to keep lean media for tasks that do not require much interaction (e.g., electronic mail), and reserve rich media for things that require more interaction and a broader spectrum of activity (e.g., face-to-face).

Learners report greater control and responsibility toward their learning. Students also find that the act of writing demands greater reflection than speaking (Harasim 1990; Rohfeld & Hiemstra 1994). Berge (1996) also identified the significant changes that occur in the role of the teachers of an online course. Several research and anecdotal studies have looked at online components of traditional courses and have concluded that these components substantially increase the communication between the teacher and the students, and among the students, when compared with similar writing classes without the computer communication component (Hiltz 1990; Schrum 1995; Schrum & Lamb 1996).

CONSIDERATIONS IN DESIGNING ONLINE INSTRUCTION

The data gathered from personal experience, interviews, and the literature suggested two significant considerations. First, online courses meet the needs of some students: those unable to attend a university or whose university does not offer a desired course, those in remote locations or in gridlocked urban areas, those already comfortable with computers, and those who prefer to work individually or without time and location constraints. Students identify themselves as successful when they had strong reasons for signing up for this type of course, moved through the lessons fairly rapidly, had support from their family, were independent learners, and began with a certain level of technological knowledge and experience. It is also reported that real ongoing change in practice and students' continued use of information technology is dependent on the ease and cost of access, time available for practice and experimentation, and support for risk taking. These changes must be taken into consideration when designing an online educational experience.

Second, it is evident that an individual instructor may not succeed without certain issues having been considered before launching an online course. The characteristics and questions that have emerged help construct guidelines for making decisions about the creation of other courses. These can be divided into the areas of pedagogical, organizational, and institutional issues.

Pedagogical Concerns

Pedagogical issues include identification of learning goals, recognition of philosophical changes in the teaching and learning process, reconceptualization of the teacher's role, evaluation of student and instructor, and creating interactivity within learning activities (between teacher and student and among the students).

Before any decisions can be made about delivery or models, each instructor must make pedagogical decisions about the fundamental goals of a course. The salient questions when creating an educational experience have always been, "What is the purpose of this course?" and "What are the instructional and personal goals of this course for all students?" These are questions that all educators must ask themselves when designing courses, and, in general, educators have become comfortable and adept at this task.

Once instructional goals are determined, educators must examine the philosophical changes that online learning requires. The course designer may choose to redesign an existing course or create a new one, but it is unwise to simply transport an old course to this new medium. The structure of the course, the planning for educational and personal needs, and the teacher's role must all be reconceptualized. It is clear that active and independent learning must take place, but the designer will also have to determine what will promote this type of learning. Further, from adult learning theory we know that authentic learning, relevant materials, and negotiated assignments are required to ensure the participation, involvement, and action necessary to meet these goals.

The nature of online teaching requires the instructor to rethink the evaluation process as well. The evaluation component must be ongoing and continual; just leaving everything to one midterm and a final paper would put everyone at a disadvantage. The instructor must become familiar with each student's work, and the only way to accomplish that is through many instructional activities. Additionally, without visual cues the instructor might not be aware of a student's confusion or total misunderstanding of subject matter or what is required. The feedback loop becomes more important, so perhaps it is wise to include specific times when students fill out an anonymous questionnaire regarding the progress of the course. For example, the teacher could include one question each week to focus students' consideration of the content, interaction, and effective reaction to the online environment.

Organizational Issues

Organizational issues revolve around timing, inclusion of face-to-face components (if possible), structure of group interactions, and minimum prerequisites for taking the course.

Once the pedagogical questions are answered, the instructor can turn to the organizational questions. First, a decision must be made to determine how much of the course will be online. In other words, is this to be a Web-enhanced course or a Web-only course? The online component may range from occasional electronic assignments that supplement traditional class meetings, to a course that is basically online with two or three physical class meetings, to a course that is held entirely online. Some of the structures of these courses include those that are entirely online, those that combine online and face-to-face activities, and those that have some combination of models. Obviously, many factors may be predetermined and out of the instructor's control; for example, if the course is intended for a distant audience, then meeting face-to-face may not be an option.

Another question concerns the timing of the course. Will it begin and end on a schedule—perhaps to coincide with the school or university calendar? Or will it be conducted as a completely independent study? Many students benefit from the routine and structure that accompany a traditional course schedule, while others are frustrated by the need to move either more quickly or more slowly than they would prefer. Recently one educator asked if he should allow a student to proceed through lessons and activities at her own pace or to force her to stay with the rest of the class. Whatever decision is made, it is important that the participants be informed of their responsibilities for the course.

Interaction is now supported and facilitated in many ways. "Groupware," a new class of software, assists in instruction and collaboration. Groupware refers to software that supports and augments group work, particularly those capabilities useful in educational and social psychological research settings. The use of networks and groupware as instructional tools has potential to enhance the nature and perceptions of interaction in online courses (Schrum & Lamb 1996).

Other organizational issues have emerged. Group size may influence the communications patterns but also may affect the life of the teacher. Teaching online courses requires a great deal of time—to answer mail, manage data, and respond to postings. While instructors may feel that 15–20 students is manageable, some institutions may plan for many times that number. Are extra tutors available to assist? Or is it possible to team-teach this type of course? One instructor decided that the team approach allowed the widest possible flexibility and the best support for students.

Institutional Issues

Institutions must address issues of faculty incentives, access and equity, credit decisions, ongoing evaluation, and continual support for students and teachers.

Institutional issues must be considered and discussed as an educational organization begins to focus on online education, particularly as many institutions may see it as an avenue to raise revenues (Phelps et al. 1991). Recognition in the promotion and tenure process is essential for faculty who create and teach online courses. Institutional support for innovative practices requires that time be allowed for design and development.

Other institutional issues concern the amount and types of credit offered for online courses and the students' ability to use the credit for graduate or undergraduate degrees, salary increments, or other types of certification. Will students of an online course be supported in registration, transcripts, and the like in the same ways as traditional students on campus? Who will bear the expense of additional access and connections necessary? Will modems or computers be loaned to students who cannot afford them? How do students at a distance gain access to official or research materials? Many access questions can now be answered more easily by archiving resources online, but the issues still exist when long-distance calls are involved.

Last, it is essential that system-wide evaluation components be included. Is the course pedagogically sound? Is the organizational structure appropriate and equitable? Did the institution offer the support necessary for students and for the educator? Did unique problems arise from the nature of the online course or components? Additionally, most instructors are currently evaluated by the students; however, in an online environment a professor's love of subject, commitment to students, sense of humor, and willingness to adapt might not come through, which will call for a more substantial and perhaps collaborative evaluation of the instructor by all stakeholders.

CONCLUSION

This chapter has presented a perspective on the growing and evolving nature of distance learning, its history, and the research that has informed the practice. It focused more specifically on online distance learning, which has become the most significant growth area in conjunction with the rapid development of, and access to, information technologies. It is essential that educators take the lead to ensure that this aspect of education will remain in the domain of pedagogical and instructional specialists as more institutions move into this arena.

REFERENCES

Beare, P. L. (1989). The comparative effectiveness of videotape, audiotape, and telelecture in delivering continuing teacher education. *American Journal of Distance Education 3* (2), 57–66.

Berge, Z. L. (1996). Changing roles in higher education: Reflecting on technology. *Collaborative Communications Review*. McLean, VA: International Teleconferencing Association, 43–53.

Boone, W. J. (1995). Science teacher preparation with distance education technology. *Journal of Technology and Teacher Education 3* (1), 93–104.

Boston, R. L. (1992). Remote delivery of instruction via the PC and modem: What have we learned? *American Journal of Distance Education 6* (3), 45–57.

Dede, C. (1995, July). The transformation of distance education to distributed learning. *InTRO*. Internet page at URL: http://129.7.160.78/InTRO.html. Fulford & Zhang, 1993.

Garrison, D. R., and Shale, D. (Eds.). (1990). *Education at a distance: From issues to practice*. Malabar, FL: Krieger Publishing.

Hakes, B., et al. (1993). The burgeoning interest in compressed video. *TechTrends 38* (1), 16–21.

Harasim, L. M. (1990). Online education: An environment for collaboration and intellectual amplification. In *Online education: Perspectives on a new environment*, ed. L. M. Harasim. New York: Praeger, 39–64.

Heeren, E., and Lewis, R. (1997). Selecting communication media for distributed communities. *Journal of Computer Assisted Learning 13* (2), 85–98.

Herschback, D. (1984). *Addressing vocational training and retraining through educational technology: Policy alternatives* (*Information Series* No. 276): Columbus, Ohio.

Hiltz, R. S. (1990). Evaluating the virtual classroom. In *Online education: Perspectives on a new environment*, ed. L. M. Harasim. New York: Praeger, 133–84.

Lyons, C. M., MacBrayne, P., and Johnson, J. L. (1994). Interactive television as a vehicle for the delivery of higher education to rural areas. *Journal of Educational Technology Systems 22* (3), 205–11.

McClelland, J., and Saeed, F. (1986). *Adult education and vocational education: Implications for research on distance delivery* (ED 276852). Minneapolis, MN: University of Minnesota.

McDevitt, M. A. (1995). Two-way television: Linking preservice teachers to real world schools. *Journal of Technology and Teacher Education 3* (1), 81–92.

Phelps, R. H., et al. (1991). Effectiveness and costs of distance education using computer-mediated communication. *American Journal of Distance Education 5* (3), 7–19.

Reid, J. E., and Woolf, P. (1996). *Online curriculum development at Shorter College: A report from the field.* Internet page at URL: http://www.caso.com/iu/articles/reid02.html.

Rohfeld, R. W., and Hiemstra, R. (1994). Moderating discussions in the electronic classroom. In *Computer mediated communication and the online classroom*, ed. Z. L. Berge and M. P. Collins. Cresskill, NJ: Hampton Press, 91–104.

Schrum, L. (1995). On-line education: A study of pedagogical, organizational and institutional issues. In *An international survey of distance education and teacher training: From smoke signals to satellite—II*, ed. R. A. Cornell and K. Murphy. Orlando, FL: University of Central Florida and Paris: International Council for Educational Media, 157–63.

Schrum, L. (1996). *Compressed video: Strategies for collaboration and interactivity.* Paper presented at the FSU/AECT Conference on Distance Education, Tallahassee, FL.

Schrum, L., and Lamb, T. A. (1996). Groupware for collaborative learning: A research perspective on processes, opportunities, and obstacles. *Journal of Universal Computer Science 2* (10). Available online at URL: http://www.iicm.edu/jucs.

Smith, J. (1984). An evaluation of telecourse achievement at Saddleback College. *Technological Horizons in Education 11* (1), 94–96.

Wiesenberg, F., and Hutton, S. (1996). Teaching a graduate program using computer-mediated conferencing software. *Journal of Distance Education 11* (1), 83–100.

Breaking the Mold
Virginia Tech's Instructional Development Initiative

John F. Moore and J. Thomas Head
Virginia Polytechnic Institute and State University

Virginia Tech, a major research university of 1,500 faculty and 25,000 students, faced a serious challenge in 1991–1993 as it grappled with a series of severe budget cuts amid calls for improving undergraduate education. To cope with the sudden loss of budget and positions, the university restructuring plan recognized faculty as a core asset and cited investment in faculty development as a way to recover and regain momentum. A primary goal was to enhance student learning and improve instruction. To reach this goal, a plan was developed and implemented in 1993 for a university-wide Instructional Development Initiative (IDI) that would make significant use of instructional technology.

Between 1993 and 1997, the university invested more than $10 million in the first phase of the IDI. As a result of this commitment, more than 1,400 of the faculty participated in workshops designed to support course transformation and received modern computer technology for their offices. More than 500 student-access computers, each multimedia equipped and networked, were installed in public labs and computer-intensive classrooms. Fifty presentation classrooms and seven distance learning classrooms were developed. Faculty from every college received more than $1 million in course development grants. Several hundred courses now have online components. These and other parallel activities represent a substantial commitment to improving instruction across the university. To our knowledge, the IDI remains the only large-scale continuing program of its kind in the nation. In this article, we will outline the rationale, components, and activities of the Initiative, then describe several major outcomes, and conclude by sharing some insights we have gained.

INSTRUCTIONAL DEVELOPMENT INITIATIVE

The Instructional Development Initiative is a large-scale effort to improve teaching excellence, productivity, and effectiveness through appropriate uses of instructional technology. It has four functional areas: 1) the Faculty Development Institute, 2) course development resources and support, 3) student access to computing resources, and 4) classroom facilities. The IDI project emanates jointly from the Office of the Provost and the Vice President for Information Systems. Management responsibility rests in the Instructional Services division of Information Systems, with planning and implementation chiefly through the Educational Technologies group of Instructional Services. Staff from all areas of Information Systems collaborate on various aspects of the IDI project. The consolidation and coordination of these areas under one vice president enables a common project focus that is instrumental in achieving overall goals.

FACULTY DEVELOPMENT INSTITUTE

The Faculty Development Institute (FDI) provides faculty with the knowledge and resources to use instructional technology to enhance the quality of their teaching and to transform courses. The FDI provides the opportunity for all faculty over a four-year period to participate in an intensive workshop centered on the reexamination of the curriculum, the culture of teaching, and the integration of instructional technology. In these three-day and four-day summer workshops, groups of 20 faculty investigate alternative instructional strategies designed to improve the productivity of the teaching-learning process. While attending the workshops, faculty participants receive a state-of-the-art computer and a suite of appropriate software applications. About 360 different faculty participate each summer.

Selection and sequencing of workshop participants is a college and department decision, based on a four-year plan developed by the Provost. Every four years, faculty can elect to participate again, attending another workshop and receiving a new computer and software. This recurring contact is important because it ensures that all faculty have access to up-to-date knowledge, skills, and technology. In addition, this periodic updating facilitates user support by standardizing a widely used set of software tools and a purposely limited range of computer hardware.

While faculty often perceive the FDI as a "computer workshop" prior to participation in the sessions, that perception tends to shift toward a course improvement orientation as they become involved in a workshop. While actively participating in the workshop, faculty spend several days away from their office so they can rethink their teaching options, see how others are using technology, and apply what they are learning by developing a personal, course-related project. A very effective feature of FDI is a series of presentations by past faculty participants who demonstrate how and why they have changed their courses. These presentations provide credible responses to questions about effects on student learning and attitude, productivity, student-faculty communication, development time, and similar concerns of faculty.

The content of FDI workshops has evolved each year. In 1993–1994, the core skills being taught were E-mail, introduction to multimedia, developing classroom presentations, and principles of computer-based instruction. As the effects of FDI have spread across the campus, and in recognition of the increased importance of the Internet, the workshop focus and organization now reflects more sophisticated and varied uses of instructional technology among the participating faculty. Many workshops have also focused on strategic, discipline-specific software like Mathematica. In all workshops, the use of open lab time is important so that faculty get the opportunity to apply what they learn to the development of new course materials they will take with them.

The design of workshops is aided by the feedback received in previous years, by surveys of forthcoming participants, and by steering groups. It is clear that with changing technology and the evolving needs of faculty, the content of FDI needs to be continually updated and evaluated for effectiveness. The FDI summer workshops, by providing introductions to instructional tools and methods, set the stage for more extensive follow-up workshops that continue throughout the year.

Evaluation of the workshops by the faculty attendees is positive. Evaluations are conducted every 90 minutes using a Web-based form, providing rapid reports to workshop facilitators. Changes can be made expeditiously because of this feedback system. We have found that participants are more likely to provide richer responses if they can type their comments on a Web form, rather than make handwritten comments on a survey sheet. Faculty clearly value the opportunity to explore instructional issues with their colleagues and to discover the potential of technology for enhancing their teaching. They have indicated that IDI resources are critical if they are to adapt to the needs of their students.

SUPPORTING COURSE DEVELOPMENT

Faculty who seek assistance in course development have several avenues available. The Educational Technologies unit of Instructional Services provides consulting, design, assessment, project management, and a variety of technical support services to faculty engaged in the development and implementation of Web-based and CD-ROM software. Departmental and building-based support staff are particularly instrumental in assisting faculty engaged in course transformation activities.

More than $1 million in university funding to support 50 course development projects was awarded in 1997–1998 by the Center for Innovation in Learning and the Center for Excellence in Undergraduate Teaching. Summer faculty stipends, faculty release time, wages for student programmers and other technical personnel, equipment, and software are provided. The strategic focus of many initial grants was for high-enrollment core curriculum courses. An ongoing evaluation effort is examining the effects of these projects on student attitudes, enhancements in learning outcomes, and increases in faculty and student productivity.

Another support service is the New Media Center (NMC), which was established in 1994. The NMC provides access to up-to-date multimedia software and high-end computers in an open-lab environment staffed with expert tutors. The facility is free and open to all segments of the university and community on a walk-in basis to support development of multimedia and Web projects. A large variety of workshops are conducted in the NMC, including many FDI sessions, community-oriented programs, in-service workshops for primary and secondary school teachers, and professional development courses for lifelong learning. During 1996–1997, there were more than 13,000 users of the NMC.

STUDENT COMPUTER ACCESS AND CLASSROOM UPGRADES

Computer labs for student access were installed by the IDI project in 12 locations on campus, providing more than 500 computing stations for accessing the Internet and computer-based courseware. Creating these multimedia-capable, networked facilities was especially important at the start of the IDI project. Faculty needed assurances that if they made homework assignments requiring access to computers, those students who did not own a computer would have access. The labs remain heavily used as faculty develop network-based materials for their students. Nevertheless, providing universal access for all students at any time is problematic. Therefore, a requirement for universal student computer ownership will be phased in, starting with the freshman class in August 1998. Over the next several years, this ownership requirement will redefine the strategic value of centrally managed computer labs.

Since the summer of 1993, more than 50 classrooms have been upgraded with computer-aided teaching stations (CATS). These stations provide faculty and students with the capability for displaying a wide array of computer-generated presentations, including scientific visualization and other complex graphic displays. All of the stations have a network connection that provides access to the Internet for downloading information during class sessions. These equipped classrooms are in great demand by faculty across all colleges and departments in the university.

OUTCOMES

Faculty in every academic department are clearly committed to improved teaching and enhanced learning. Examples include redesigned course objectives and assessment methods, shifts toward active learning strategies, increased use of online student writing, increased use of feedback to students, asynchronous interaction with course content, and collaboration of faculty in the design and teaching of courses that expand student learning into areas not feasible without instructional technology. Other effects of this Initiative consist of inclusion of distance learners in on-campus classes and an online summer school.

Student enthusiasm about the changes in courses helps to motivate and reinforce faculty. Students like having improved access to course materials and the flexibility and convenience that asynchronous methods offer. Many students express initial concerns that technology might depersonalize a course, but they actually find higher levels of interaction and connectedness and feel less alienation than in many traditional courses. Of particular interest, students report they are more challenged by being active learners, and they often respond positively by engaging in learning at a higher level.

Cyberschool

One of the most significant outcomes during the early stages of the IDI was the development of Cyberschool. Starting as a grassroots movement of early adopters, the Cyberschool movement is the leading example of faculty making substantive transformations in their teaching. The faculty meet to share techniques, insights, and concerns and sometimes to collaborate in teaching online courses. Cyberschool faculty incorporate a fusion of computer-interactive classroom and asynchronous learning methodologies, traditional classroom practice, advanced multimedia, and networks. The intent is to give students and faculty more options over the time, place, and pace of learning.

As they gained experience teaching online, the Cyberschool faculty collectively advocated changes in university policies regarding faculty roles and institutional barriers impeding asynchronous courses and degree programs. For example, they were a central force in instituting the freshman computer requirement. The teaching innovations of faculty in the Cyberschool movement have been instrumental in demonstrating the potential of large-scale uses of networked instructional technology. Their work continues to help faculty, students, parents, administrators, legislators, and granting agencies understand new ways to enhance the quality of undergraduate teaching.

ACCESS

As a result of Cyberschool, a deeper examination of instructional technology's strategic value was initiated. The ACCESS project started in 1995 with partial underwriting from the Sloan Foundation. The project studied the effects of shifting introductory, high-enrollment, lower-division courses away from the standard credit-for-contact model and toward an online mode. Of particular interest, the ACCESS project examined the incorporation of online components into large lecture classes and the effects of this new paradigm on faculty and student productivity. Using a combination of quantitative and qualitative research methods, the study found that asynchronous learning techniques helped overcome some problems of the large-class lecture model. Faculty roles moved toward facilitation and away from repetitively dispensing information. In one course, up to 15 percent of classroom time was regained by simply shifting all class announcements onto a Web page. Enhanced visual materials appeared to generate a greater degree of interest and understanding of course content. Student access to online course notes helped improve preparation and studying. Problems of alienation, common in large classes, diminished through increased contact and interaction that occurred by use of online discussion groups, listservs, and E-mail. Students also reported that they worked harder and completed projects more thoroughly because of increased peer contact and collaborative group projects.

New Initiatives

Other parallel projects likewise are extending the IDI into the long-term focus of the university. First, distance learning is now increasingly recognized to be strategically important to the university and its constituents, and an Institute for Distributed and Distance Learning is being developed. Second, Net.Work.Virginia, a statewide ATM network managed by Virginia Tech, provides economical and scaleable high-bandwidth connectivity for voice, video, and data. It is facilitating the rapid and cost-effective expansion of educational services across the state and beyond. Third, a new building, the Advanced Communications and Information Technology Center, will create a test bed for investigating and evaluating teaching and learning in the twenty-first century. This facility will bring together faculty and students doing research on learning, instructional technology, distance learning, digital libraries, human-computer interaction, virtual reality, scientific visualization, wireless communication, networks, and evolving technologies.

WHAT WE HAVE LEARNED

The IDI has demonstrated that a significant long-term impact on the culture of the university can be brought about by providing faculty with time and resources to conduct course transformations that use instructional technologies effectively. We have observed that many faculty in a research university have a considerable, often latent enthusiasm for teaching that can be unleashed by a sustained IDI effort. When faculty are given appropriate resources and support, many commit to learning how to use technology to improve teaching and enhance learning.

Providing sustained and accessible ongoing support after the summer workshops is critical to maintaining faculty efforts. This support should be as accessible as possible, ideally at a department or building level, to maximize efficiency and minimize faculty frustration. Follow-up workshops during each semester can provide a high degree of customization for faculty who wish to expand their knowledge and skills.

An overarching goal is to help faculty construct a personal linkage between instructional technologies and their pedagogy. Workshops need to stay focused on teaching, learning, curriculum, and the needs and accomplishments of faculty and students. They should not focus on technology for its own sake. The successful implementation of this goal is at the heart of the Initiative's long-term strategic value to the faculty and the university.

In less than five years, the IDI has enabled the university to reach the goals of enhancing student learning and improving instruction. FDI workshops, research studies, continuing campus-wide discussions, course development support, assessment, and new initiatives are all facilitating substantive changes in the teaching and learning culture of the university. They continue to illuminate the process by which hundreds of faculty have made significant changes in their teaching methods, course dynamics, and expectations for student learning. The Instructional Development Initiative continues to serve as a catalyst for change and to help the faculty advance the university into the twenty-first century.

Gender, Technology, and Instructional Design
Balancing the Picture

Nancy Nelson Knupfer, Ph.D.
College of Education, Kansas State University

ABSTRACT

Educational practice reflects both obvious and subtle societal messages. The visualization and passive acceptance of gender stereotypes is tremendously influential. These stereotypes appear in seemingly endless situations, ranging from work to home to entertainment, across all social levels, and from the older technologies to the new technologies. Decision-makers often ignore the need to seek input about school practice from the teachers who are responsible for implementation; this is evident in the new distance education technologies. We must take stock of the pervasive messages of gender stereotypes, their tremendous influence on children and adults, and be aware of how these stereotypes can perpetuate biased value systems into otherwise innovative environments. Instructional designers and teachers have tremendous influence on students, so they have the power and responsibility to help add balance.

INTRODUCTION

At first glance the common theories and practice of instructional design do not reflect any obvious pattern in relation to cultural pluralism and gender, yet a closer analysis of the historical practice of instructional design reveals the "one size fits all" approach. A close examination of instructional design and gender reveals a clear, consistent, and pervasive relationship that has deep historical roots and winds throughout our daily lives while perpetuating itself through its interweavings with society. Perhaps the interweavings have become even more complex and influential as more emphasis is placed on the visual communication offered by the new technologies. Changing economics, workforce patterns, and social roles clearly call for instructional designers to become more aware of gender equity and take steps to provide a more equitable balance.

Over the years, society has carried messages to the public that are laden with gender stereotypes. These messages reach people through many forms of communication, including the spoken word, print-based and electronic text, still images, full-motion images, auditory channels, and various combinations of these forms. The stereotypes permeate our educational materials, mass media, and entertainment resources, and influence school practices, work environments, and interpersonal contacts. They affect our child-rearing practices, choices of products and activities, fashion design, attitudes, value systems, aspirations, self-concepts, opportunities, access to information, social contacts, and wage-earning potential. The stereotypes are so deeply ingrained into our society that even when people recognize the discriminations, they accept them as *the way things are.*

Somehow these practices get passed along into the educational system, and opportunities for school and work are influenced by gender. Part of what influences educational practice is the persistent visualization of gender stereotypes throughout our society in various forms, ranging from the older technologies to the new ones. Further, the imagery of computer technology itself as male turf has now been solidified (Turkle & Papert 1990) and extended to the World Wide Web (WWW) through general style and explicit graphic advertisements (Knupfer 1998a). We must take stock of the pervasive messages of gender stereotypes and their tremendous influence on instructional design, schooling, and society.

SOCIETY AND GENDER ROLE CONSTRUCTION

Mass media images of our society reflect the stereotypes and the realities of gender tracking, often separating males from females and perpetuating specific caricatures (Knupfer, Kramer, & Pryor 1997). The roles are defined, and the images are engraved in people's minds through various forms of artwork, entertainment, advertisements, productions, and educational materials.

The cultural messages of gender separation begin early and are perpetuated throughout society in many ways. For example, the television commercials surrounding popular children's programs feature the gratuitous sequence of two commercials for boys and two for girls, not necessarily in any specific order, but certainly distinctive in gender imaging (Courtney & Whipple 1983; Downs & Harrison 1985; Kilbourne 1990; Lovdal 1989; Macklin & Kolbe 1984). The boys' commercials are fast-paced, outdoors, and rugged; usually involve something on wheels; often depict aggression; employ music with a fast tempo and distinctive beat; and use camera angles that slant up, placing the boys in a dominant position within the picture. The girls' commercials typically are slower-paced, indoors, and tender; involve dolls or fashion messages; often depict emotion and caring for others; employ musical, sweet, calm undertones; and use camera angles that slant down, placing the girls in the less dominant portion of the picture. This becomes more serious when one realizes that the stereotypes reinforced by television carry over into daily life (Berry & Asamen 1993; Berry & Mitchell-Kerman 1982; Bretl & Cantor 1988; Fidell 1975).

Why does the mass media perpetuate gender stereotypes? Why do the stores line aisles with gender-laden, color-coded toys? Why do preschools post rosters separated by gender rather than classroom? All of these factors reinforce stereotypes that begin at an early age and lead to separation by gender throughout life. At what point and for what reasons do the genders mix in the visual images depicted in advertising and in real life? As more emphasis is placed on using the visual media in schools, what implications does this separation have for males and females? What messages are given to males and females about turf, not mixing, and why? Where is the common ground, and why is it not more frequently visited? How can we balance good education about personal and family values, caring, and nurturing, without perpetuating gender stereotypes?

GENDER STEREOTYPES

Girls and boys seem to mix well until they reach preschool age, when there begins a distinct emphasis on activities and treatment of children by gender. By the time they are five years old, there is a distinct value system at work within them that clearly specifies values that they pick up from messages within our culture, its fairy tales, media imagery, and so on. The effect of the value system can be seen in the toys that the children ask for, their hobbies, and the gender separation that evolves into things like birthday parties that are segregated by gender at the tender age of six (Chen 1994).

While this is not true for all girls and all boys, it is a pattern that is evident in our schools, homes, and society. If you doubt for one moment that it is true, then watch patterns of socialization as students walk to and from school or ask yourself if you have ever heard of the comment, "He plays like a girl" or "He runs like a girl" in reference to any sports activity. This familiar comment certainly is not flattering to anyone and does not recognize the achievement of women athletes, but instead seems to perpetuate the attitude of sports being a male domain. The media, schools, parents, and adults who encounter children in personal care and community life all contribute to the gender messages. Images in advertisements within print-based, televised, and WWW format continue to portray men and women in stereotyped roles (Knupfer 1998b). Males continue to dominate the computer culture, cyberspace, clip art, and the advertising about using technology professionally and productively (Knupfer, Rust, & Mahoney 1997).

The socially constructed meaning, expectations, and opportunities based on gender begin with differing expectations for people, depending upon their sex at birth (Stern & Karraker 1989). They are revealed in the way:

- we groom boys for leadership positions while we teach girls to be submissive

- we emphasize the importance of male-dominated sports

- teachers respond to boys differently than to girls (Olivares & Rosenthal 1992)

- girls are labeled as second-class citizens (Knupfer 1997a)

- stereotypes are perpetuated in the media (Kilbourne 1990; Schwartz & Markham 1985)

- we recruit for jobs (Bem & Bern 1973; Fidell 1975; Rowe 1990)

- we provide examples, exercises, and meaningful educational opportunities that boys can often relate to better than girls

- we groom boys for entire categories of jobs involving science, math, medicine, politics, and leadership (Knupfer 1996).

Girls can achieve equally well in the aforementioned areas but have not been encouraged to do so until recently. Now the attempts are filled with remaining hurdles and barriers that must be overcome (Top 1991). Meaningful instructional design practice must do more to attend to these matters and take an active role in encouraging girls (Van Nostrand 1991). While not enough has been done, and it is too late for many, instructional designers can renew efforts to provide experiences that girls can relate to, offer instructional opportunities that are not gender biased, and encourage teachers to actively attend to issues of gender equity (Turkle & Papert 1990).

CULTURE, GROUPS, AND SCHOOLING

Let us examine some ideas about groups, territory, and belonging. Community is the joining together or grouping of individuals in society. People tend to seek out others that have something in common with themselves and to whom they can relate to comfortably. People form communities based upon both natural and constructed situations. Natural communities are those that happen as a result of nature, such as being born a certain race, with a certain hair color, or as a male or female. Constructed communities are defined by boundaries that humans set by beliefs and interests. Examples of constructed communities are those defined by chosen areas of beliefs and interests, such as religious beliefs and resulting congregations, areas of study, professional occupations, hobbies, leisure activities, participation in clubs, and so on. People join communities based on comfort and a sense of identity with a common link (Knupfer & Rust 1997).

Communities play a large and significant role in society. They not only define where individuals fit into society but also help people to establish identities. They provide continuity and a sense of belonging to something greater than an individual realm. Communities provide people with focus and purpose; therefore, they can be tremendously important in terms of providing a sense of belonging or not belonging, which in turn can inspire or discourage individual participation and success in specific activities. Thus, to neglect, omit, or separate people on the basis of any natural community categorization, including gender, can have grave consequences in terms of the constructed communities in which they can identify. Certainly segregation of educational or social opportunities on the basis of gender has long-term consequences.

While it might be true that boys and girls are in the same classes at school, it is also true that some teachers do a very efficient job of separating them within classroom groups. For example, "Preschool X," a well-established and popular preschool located in a Midwest university town, seems to have wonderful teachers who make sense when they talk about balancing gender perceptions in school, but despite their spoken awareness, the teachers continue to separate the children by gender. When children break into groups it is by gender, and even on field trips, parents are assigned groups of children to supervise by gender. The roster that is hung in the hallway and distributed to parents does not specify which room a child is assigned to, but is only classified according to gender. All of the boys' names are listed at the top and all of the girls' names listed at the bottom, but there is no way to tell which children are assigned to which teacher. Thus, parents have a difficult time determining which children are in their child's classroom but can fall easily into grouping the children by gender for social activities outside of the school situation.

This gender separation is not limited to preschools. I recently viewed a set of popular educational videotapes that were being used both for teacher training and by teachers within their classrooms. I was appalled at the gender messages being mass-marketed through these subtle means. In the tapes, three different teachers conducted different lessons as follows:

- A female teacher conducted a classroom game in which boys were pitted against girls.

- A female teacher conducted a competitive exercise and introduced it by claiming that girls were more "long-winded" than boys; therefore, roles were assigned based on who was likely to take less time giving explanations.

- A male teacher told girls that females were good at determining bargains in grocery pricing and told boys that they would not be able to understand whether the price of a sack of potatoes reflected a sale or not, obviously suggesting that females shop for groceries and males do not. This was part of a math lesson, but the underlying gender message was quite clear.

How do these materials get produced, marketed, and used with our teachers and children? Why do adults not see the subtle messages about gender stereotypes that are being passed along to our children?

Society offers opportunities to mix, yet at some point during our childhood years those opportunities are changed by parents and teachers who promote segregation by gender. By the teenage years, males and females are strongly discouraged from intermingling by parents who fear sexual encounters. Are we to believe that males and females cannot interact in platonic ways? If this is a common belief, then perhaps it is a result of the way the media continues to influence people through its portrayal of men and women in stereotypical ways (Roberts & Maccoby 1985). Certainly the media plays a complex role in this entire scenario.

IMAGES OF MALES AND FEMALES

In the midst of the Information Age, or Digital Revolution as it is sometimes called, access to digitized media has become important to personal achievement within school and careers. As computers replace typewriters, telecommunications and multimedia become more prominent in educational settings, and personal computing assumes greater importance in more homes, females have gained more access to the technology than ever before. Yet advertisements still portray females in supportive, nondescript roles while males are shown using the technology in productive ways that benefit their careers. For example, clip art and advertisements in various media, ranging from print to television to the WWW, show males in dominant positions, being in control, and gaining power as a result of using the technology, while females are depicted in submissive or helping roles that tend to emphasize being sexually attractive and beautiful (Knupfer 1998a).

Little is different about the advertisements concerning technology and the advertisements about other types of products, and little has changed concerning gender representation in advertising over the last 20 years. A classic example from which to begin examining the messages depicted through gendered advertising was offered by Erving Goffman (1976). Goffman's work clearly states that what may seem "natural" in advertising illustrations usually is not natural at all and is, in actuality, politically loaded. Goffman further warns that if we accept these gender-laden messages as natural reflections of reality and model our own attitudes and behavior on them, then the messages also become personally and socially destructive.

Many of the characteristic gender-role scenarios that Goffman identified can be seen in advertisements across the various media formats today, thus typifying and extending today's mass-media messages to include the new areas of technological access (Knupfer 1998a). For example, when women use cellular telephones at work they call home, whereas men use the phones to attend to business or finances. Also, when using computers, boys are shown in confident poses using computers to gain knowledge and win, while girls are shown sitting at computers for decorative purposes, often posed in sexually attractive positions to call attention to the computer as an object, but not what they are using it for (Knupfer 1997a). What does this say about the messages we give males and females about using technology in general, and computers in particular?

These persistent patterns continue to influence public perception of gender stereotypes and perpetuate attitudes that clearly favor male technology users. Instructional practice is influenced by these messages, which constantly feed the old system and all but strangle attempts to pay serious attention to gender equity (Gornick & Moran 1972; McCormick 1994). It is important to look beyond the female role and see that is happening to males as well. Mass media sets up expectations for male stereotypical behavior and places males in the position of identifying themselves with work and success at the expense of emotion and family involvement (Knupfer 1997b). Materials developed for use in public, private, and military schools as well as images delivered to the public through advertising, television, and public service messages continue to portray women and men in stereotypical ways, thus trapping everyone into media-determined gender roles (Knupfer 1996).

The consequences of this portrayal are evident in our schools. Research reveals that among high school students there are consistent, significant gender differences related to interest and confidence about using computers as well as gender-stereotyped views about computer users (Martin, Heller, & Mahmoud 1992; Shashanni 1994). The low confidence among girls in working with computers, and their lack of interest in computers, can be explained as a product of the social institution in which their individual self-concepts are built (Shashanni 1994).

Many women who work with computer technology believe that the environment is hostile toward them (Turkle & Papert 1990). Yet gender differences in attitudes toward technology begin in the way that males and females are raised, thus reflecting the social expectations of individuals, family, friends, and society (Canter 1979; Davies & Kandel 1981; Eccles 1987). To correct the problem of neglect and omission of women from the computer culture is no small thing; there must be a change in the attitude and behavior of society toward women and technology.

Despite attempts to correct this situation over many years, progress is slow to come, and it is obvious that gender bias continues concerning use of the new media. For example, a study of computer clip art images available for business, school, and home use revealed that the stereotypes have invaded the desktop computing environment, with images of men depicted in leadership and authority roles, and those of women depicted in subordinate roles (Binns & Branch 1995). When people rely on clip art for presentations, they simply pass on the stereotypes due to the limited selection available, or they avoid using art that portrays people. Do we really want to be in a situation of sanitizing our use of visuals because we cannot find suitable clip art that represents gender without stereotypes?

INCREASING EQUITY THROUGH GOOD INSTRUCTIONAL DESIGN

Inequities that result from the practice of instructional design often go unrecognized because they emerge not just as a result of what has been done but also as a result of what has been left undone. The neglect and omission of the female population can be subtle on an individual basis, but collectively appear throughout society as artifacts of something that begins in the home and perpetuates itself throughout schooling and employment practices. If that was not the case, then there would be no need for recent efforts to attract girls into the study of math and science (Kable & Meece 1994), and the number of distressing stories about females succeeding despite the myriad of obstacles (Aisenberg & Harrington 1988; Clark & Corcoran 1986; Frenkel 1990; Gornick 1990) would no longer be told. Logically, then, we should ask what instructional designers can do to help promote gender equity.

The relationship between gender equity and instructional design is complex. Instructional designers can attend to creating better balance in the curriculum and educational practices that translate into lifetime effects. They must first be alert to the signs of gender bias and recognize its great importance on people's lives. More than 25 years ago, lawmakers recognized the need for reform within a system that perpetuated gender bias. Although improvements have been made to a certain degree, legislation has failed to address gender bias in a deep and meaningful way. Instructional designers can help by attending to the messages that people receive through instructional, entertainment, advertising, and public service channels. If gender balance is to be achieved in schools and daily life, instructional designers will need to take a more proactive role.

Efforts to create gender balance must recognize that gender differences have been socially constructed, and some of those differences will always remain. Not all gender differences are negative, yet some of them can be extremely harmful. Evidence of these differences appear at different ages, in different ways, and in differing intensities among individual situations. Gender-sensitive instructional designers can encourage teachers to eliminate bias in classroom language, learning materials, instructional activities, and interactions so that equal opportunities are provided for each sex, regardless of ingrained societal prejudices. They can encourage people who work with children or develop educational materials to take gender into account only when it will increase equity or prevent discrimination.

Forcing people to change value systems will not help; it would be more productive to seek the common ground on which males and females can work together. One way of helping to establish this common ground is through imagery portrayed to the general public. Imagery that shows regular women in productive roles using technology in powerful ways, or men in nurturing situations with home and family, would help. Instructional designers can help to put such imagery into materials used for public messages and instructional situations.

Removing the gender bias that has permeated our lives over the years is a difficult task that cannot be isolated to formal school situations alone. With persistent and relentless effort, instructional designers can continue to draw attention to the current inequities and goals of gender-balanced education and extend their consideration to all areas, including new situations made possible by technological delivery systems. As technology offers different educational opportunities, such as the possibility of education via the Internet, the importance of educating society beyond the formal school setting presents great challenge and potential.

Yet the role of girls and women in relation to the new media has made little progress beyond that depicted with the now-traditional media forms. The Internet is clearly an environment that was structured by and for males. Now that the Internet has evolved to heavy usage of the WWW, will this visually rich communications environment remain as male turf? What societal factors will influence the outcome? So far, messages within our society that are reinforced by the mass media emphasize that youth and attractiveness are good, sex is important, and males and females have certain roles to play that are separate and distinct.

These biases continue to support instructional design in its historical sense by constantly feeding the old system while all but strangling attempts to pay serious attention to gender equity (Gornick & Moran 1972; McCormick 1994). Materials developed for use in public, private, and military schools as well as instructional messages delivered to the public through advertising, television, and public service messages continue to portray women and men in stereotypical ways. Perhaps awareness is the first step toward improvement—that is, helping educators recognize subtle gender bias so that they are able to intentionally produce instructional materials with a more balanced perspective.

Through mass education, our country has experienced successful educational campaigns targeted at changing attitudes about smoking, preventive health care, birth control, and racial prejudice. The forces working against gender balance are great, and it will take sustained efforts of at least the same magnitude to change attitudes toward women in this society. As the medical field brought about changes in public policy by educating the masses about the harmful effects of secondhand smoke, instructional designers will need to educate the public about the negative effects of current attitudes and instructional practices on females. Through proactive and relentless efforts, instructional designers can help educate society as whole, not just teachers. An informed society will be the catalyst to bring about continued social changes leading to gender equity.

REFERENCES

Aisenberg, N., and Harrington, M. (1988). *Women in academe: Outsiders in the sacred grove*. Amherst, MA: University of Massachusetts Press.

Bem, S. L., and Bern, D. J. (1973). Does sex-biased job advertising "aid and abet" sex discrimination? *Journal of Applied Social Psychology 3* (1), 6–18.

Berry, G., and Mitchell-Kerman, C. (Eds.). (1982). *Television and the socialization of the minority child*. New York: Academic Press.

Berry, G. L., and Asamen, J. K. (1993). Children and television: Images in a changing sociocultural world. Newbury Park, CA: Sage Publications.

Binns, J. C., and Branch, R. C. (1995). Gender stereotyped computer clip-art images as an implicit influence in instructional message design. In *Imagery and visual literacy*, ed. D. G. Beauchamp, R. A. Braden, and R. E. Griffin. Rochester, NY: International Visual Literacy Association, 315–24.

Bretl, D. J., and Cantor, J. (1988). The portrayal of men and women in U.S. television commercials: A recent content analysis and trends over 15 years. *Sex Roles 18* (9/10), 595–609.

Canter, R. J. (1979). Achievement-related expectations and aspirations in college women. *Sex Roles 5* (4), 453–59.

Chen, M. (1994). *The smart parent's guide to KIDS' TV*. San Francisco, CA: KQED Books.

Clark, S. M., and Corcoran, M. (1986, Jan./Feb.). Perspectives on the professional socialization of women faculty: A case of accumulative disadvantage? *Journal of Higher Education 57* (1), 20–43.

Courtney, A. E., and Whipple, T. W. (1983). *Sex stereotyping in advertising*. Lexington, MA: Lexington Books.

Davies, M., and Kandel, D. B. (1981). Parental and peer influences on adolescents' educational plans: Some further evidence. *American Journal of Sociology 87* (2), 363–83.

Downs, A. C., and Harrison, S. K. (1985). Embarrassing age spots or just plain ugly? Physical attractiveness stereotyping as an instrument of sexism on American television commercials. *Sex Roles 13* (1/2), 9–19.

Eccles, J. S. (1987). Gender roles and women's achievement-related decisions. *Psychology of Women Quarterly 11* (2), 135–72.

Fidell, L. S. (1975). Empirical verification of sex discrimination in hiring practices in psychology. *American Psychologist 25* (12), 1094–98.

Frenkel, K. A. (1990, Nov.). Women and computing. *Communications of the ACM 33* (11), 34–46.

Goffman, E. (1976). *Gender advertisements*. New York: Harper & Row.

Gornick, V. (1990). *Women in science: 100 journeys into the territory*. New York: Touchstone/Simon & Schuster.

Gornick, V., and Moran, B. K. (Eds.). (1972). *Woman in sexist society: Studies in power and powerlessness*. New York: Basic Books.

Kable, J. B., and Meece, J. (1994). Research on gender issues in the classroom. In *Handbook of research on science teaching and learning*, ed. D. L. Gabel. New York: Macmillan, 542–57.

Kilbourne, W. E. (1990). Female stereotyping in advertising: An experiment on male-female perceptions of leadership. *Journalism Quarterly 67* (1), 25–31.

Knupfer, N. N. (1996). Technology and gender: New media with old messages. In *Beeldenstorm in Deventer: Multimedia education in Praxis*, selected papers of the 4th International Summer Research Symposium of Visual Verbal Literacy, sponsored by the International Visual Literacy Association (IVLA) and Rijkshogesschool Ijselland, ed. T. Velders. Deventer, The Netherlands: Rijkshogesschool Ijselland, 94–97.

Knupfer, N. N. (1997a). Gendered by design. *Educational Technology 37* (2), 31–37.

Knupfer, N. N. (1997b). New technologies and gender equity: New bottles with old wine. In *19th annual conference proceedings of selected research and development presentations at the 1997 national convention of the Association for Educational Communications and Technology (AECT)*, sponsored by the Research and Theory Division of AECT, ed. O. Abel, N. J. Maushak, and K. E. Wright. Albuquerque, NM, 115–24.

Knupfer, N. N. (1998a, Winter). Gender Di*Visions* across technology advertisements and the WWW: Implications for educational equity. *Theory into Practice 37* (1), 54–63.

Knupfer, N. N. (1998b). Targeting technology in television advertisements: Social symbols, cultural codes, and gender messages. In *Connecting with the community: Exploring resources for visual learning and expression*, ed. R. E. Griffin, C. B. Schiffman, and W. J. Gibbs. Rochester, NY: International Visual Literacy Association, 295–302.

Knupfer, N. N., and Rust, W. J. (1997). Technology, mass media, society, and gender. In *19th annual conference proceedings of selected research and development presentations at the 1997 national convention of the Association for Educational Communications and Technology (AECT)*, sponsored by the Research and Theory Division of AECT, ed. O. Abel, N. J. Maushak, and K. E. Wright. Albuquerque, NM, 125–32.

Knupfer, N. N., Kramer, K. M., and Pryor, D. (1997). Gender equity on-line: Messages portrayed with and about the new technologies. In *Vision quest: Journeys toward visual literacy*, ed. R. E. Griffin et al. Pittsburgh, PA: Omni Press, 391–99.

Knupfer, N. N., Rust, W. J., and Mahoney, J. E. (1997). Out of the picture, out of the club: Technology, mass media, society, and gender. In *Vision quest: Journeys toward visual literacy*, ed. R. E. Griffin et al. Pittsburgh, PA: Omni Press, 373–80.

Lovdal, L. T. (1989). Sex role messages in television commercials: An update. *Sex Roles 21* (11/12), 715–24.

Macklin, M. C., and Kolbe, R. H. (1984). Sex role stereotyping in children's advertising: Current and past trends. *Journal of Advertising 13* (2), 34–42.

Martin, D. C., Heller, R. S., and Mahmoud, E. (1992). American and Soviet children's attitudes toward computers. *Journal of Educational Computing Research 8* (2), 155–85.

McCormick, T. M. (1994). *Creating the nonsexist classroom: A multicultural approach.* New York: Teachers College Press.

Olivares, R. A., and Rosenthal, N. (1992). *Gender equity and classroom experiences: A review of research.* Minneapolis, MN: University of Minnesota. (ED 366701).

Roberts, D. F., and Maccoby, N. (1985). Effects of mass communication. In *Handbook of social psychology* (3d ed.), ed. G. Lindzey and E. Aaronson. New York: Random House.

Rowe, M. P. (1990). Barriers to equality: The power of subtle discrimination to maintain unequal opportunity. *Employee Responsibilities and Rights Journal 3* (2), 153–63.

Schwartz, L. A. and Markham, W. T. (1985). Sex stereotyping in children's toy advertisements. *Sex Roles: A Journal of Research 12* (1–2), 157–70.

Shashanni, L. (1994). Socioeconomic status, parent's sex-role stereotypes, and the gender gap in computing. *Journal of Research on Computing in Education 26* (4), 433–51.

Stern, M., and K. H. Karraker (1989). Sex stereotyping of infants: A review of gender labeling studies. *Sex Roles: A Journal of Research 20* (1), 501–22.

Top, T. J. (1991). Sex bias in the evaluation of performance in the scientific, artistic, and literary professions: A review. *Sex Roles: A Journal of Research 24* (1/2), 73–106.

Turkle, S., and Papert, S. (1990). Epistemological pluralism: Styles and voices within the computer culture. *Signs: Journal of Women in Culture and Society 16* (1), 128–57.

Van Nostrand, C. H. (1991). *Gender-responsible leadership: Do your teaching methods empower women?* New York: Sage Publications.

Part Two
The Profession

Introduction

Alan Januszewski, Associate Professor at the State University of New York at Potsdam, has a thought-provoking synopsis of the history of educational technology. Costas Criticos, Senior Lecturer at the University of Natal in South Africa and international learning spaces design consultant, presents his clockwork paradigm of technology that epitomizes the ingenuity of media development through existing technologies and available educational resources. Jared Danielson and Professor John Burton, from the Department of Instructional Technology in the College of Human Resources and Education at Virginia Tech, share an actual case illustrating how a support system for instructional technology can be implemented in higher education.

Robert Maribe Branch

Forerunners to Educational Technology

Alan Januszewski
Associate Professor
State University of New York at Potsdam

An interesting but overlooked question by those studying the history and conceptual development of educational technology is, "If it's true that educational technology is a process, then why do the most notable historical accounts of the field all seem to focus on the visual and audiovisual movements as the basis for the field? Does this not just further the stereotype that educational technology is merely hardware or gadgets or things?" It seems that if you want to conceive of educational technology as a process, then you must focus on the history and concepts that are essential to the process if you want to understand why educational technology is the way it is.

In this chapter the case is made that we can explore the idea that educational technology is a process by looking at the development of the field through two distinct yet related filters or screens. The first of these filters was the effort to professionalize the audiovisual field. Many members of the audiovisual field were interested in professionalizing and gaining status for the field, but James D. Finn spearheaded this movement (Finn 1953). He wrote and spoke extensively about the need for audiovisual specialists to become professionals. He identified six criteria that had to be met in order for a field of practice to be called a profession. The two that were most important to the development of a process of educational technology were an intellectual technique and a body of intellectual theory expanded by research. Finn saw that the intellectual technique of the field needed to be based on research and theory.

Finn was instrumental in obtaining large amounts of funding to conduct conceptual and theoretical studies of the field, including the Technological Development Project, which funded the effort to write the 1963 definition of educational technology. Finn also sought the funding to create an organization analogous to the "French Academy" for the preservation of the language inside the professional organization of the field (Ely 1994). The efforts to increase the prestige of the audiovisual field were political in the broad meaning of that term. The concepts and ideas central to the field of educational technology were affected by these politics. As such, politics and political overtones are likely to be an undercurrent to any historical or conceptual study of educational technology.

The second of these filters, the influence of science and engineering on the audiovisual education movement, is intertwined with the two criteria for a profession identified by Finn and included above. Intellectual technique and theory and research are concepts fundamental to science and engineering. This filter is somewhat less political, at least on the surface. But the political connotations are there. Science and engineering influenced the interpretation of many of the concepts and ideas that were central to the field of educational technology and were included in later formal definitions of educational technology (AECT 1972; AECT 1977). In some instances the desire to gain professional status gave reason to some involved in the field to adopt particular conceptions of science and engineering in education. But there were many instances when the idea of gaining status for the field was not a concern. Many practitioners simply adopted a particular conception of science or engineering based on their belief systems or academic backgrounds. Politics were still involved in these latter cases, but there was much less conscious effort on the part of those involved at this level. In general, however, the two primary factors in the development of educational technology as a process—the drive to professionalize the audiovisual field and the influence of science and engineering—have a political undercurrent.

EARLY TECHNOLOGY

No one really knows who coined the phrase *educational technology*. The historian of educational technology, Paul Saettler (1990), admitted having difficulty identifying the source of the term. Saettler documented the use of "educational engineering" in the 1920s, and "educational technology" and "instructional technology" in the late 1940s. But he was unable to say with certainty who first used the term "educational technology," nor was he able to provide a precise date for its initial use. Because we cannot pinpoint the linguistic beginning of educational technology, it would be helpful to get a handle on how the word *technology* got into modern American English and what it has meant.

Historian David Noble (1977) credits Jacob Bigelow, a physician who lectured at Harvard in 1829, with popularizing the term *technology* in the United States.

> There has probably never been an age in which the practical applications of science have employed so large a portion of talent and enterprise of the community, as in the present. To embody . . . the various topics which belong to such an undertaking, I have adopted the general name of Technology, a word sufficiently expressive, which is found in some of the older dictionaries, and is beginning to be revived in the literature of practical men of the present day. Under this title is attempted to include an account . . . of the principles, processes, and nomenclatures of the more conspicuous arts, particularly those which involve applications of science, and which may be considered useful, by promoting the benefit of society, together with the emolument of those who pursue them (Bigelow, as quoted in Noble, 1977, 3–4).

Noble's discussion of Bigelow's treatise on industrial technology included the following points: The "overriding imperative" of the development and use of technology was increasing efficiency for "profitable utility" (p. 4); technology included the "scientific investigation and the systematic application of scientific knowledge to the process of commodity production" (p. 5); and technology was the result of extensive "research and development" (p. 5) rather than the direct and obvious applications of science alone to the mass production of standardized products. "From the start," Noble surmised, "modern technology was nothing more nor less than the transformation of science into a means of capital accumulation, through the application of discoveries in physics and chemistry to the processes of commodity production" (p. 4).

Noble's analysis of industrial technology raises questions about the field of educational technology. What is the relationship, if any, of educational technology to industrial technology? Why was an educational technology desirable? What does a technologically based education program look like?

Strong ties and parallels between industrial technology and educational technology were established early in this century (Finn 1957; Heinich 1984). These ties were linguistic and conceptual. This was because the predecessors of educational technology borrowed terminology and images from industrial technology. Concepts that were used in industrial technology, such as efficiency, standardization, and production, were introduced into the field of education early in the twentieth century. These ties can be thought of as conceptual bonds that link industrial technology and educational technology.

To demonstrate the existence of these bonds we must look at the ideas that influenced those who contributed to the development of educational technology as a field of study. Three major ideas seemed to be most influential: engineering (Bern 1961; Szabo 1968), science (Finn 1953; Ely 1970; Jorgenson 1981; Saettler 1990; Shrock 1990), and the development of a professional audiovisual education movement (Ely 1963; Ely 1970; Jorgenson 1981; Saettler 1990; Shrock 1990). The way in which these ideas influenced the field of educational technology were both related and interdependent.

Engineering

The concept of engineering was at the heart of Noble's (1977) thinking regarding industrial technology in the United States in the late nineteenth and early twentieth centuries. The term *engineering* described certain acts of research and development and/or the efforts to put the resulting technology into common industrial practice.

Shortly after the initial surge of technology into modern industry, the concept of engineering began to play a part in certain circles of education. Saettler (1990) stated that Franklin Bobbitt and W. W. Charters were among the first to use the phrase "educational engineering" in the 1920s, primarily as an approach to developing the curriculum. But prior to their work, the principles of scientific management were being applied to the educational system in the United States (Callahan 1962). The theme of the *Twelfth Yearbook of the National Society for the Study of Education, Part I* (1913) was scientific management applications in the schools. The rationale for the introduction of scientific management in education was brought about by the skyrocketing enrollment in the public schools in the United States due to the effect of immigration and industrialization (Callahan 1962; Kliebard 1987).

Scientific management was developed as an industrial technique, primarily through the work of Frederick Taylor, in the early part of the twentieth century (Taylor 1911). Scientific management was grounded in the application of measurement techniques from the newly developing sciences to the management of industrial plant production. Soon after the introduction of scientific management in industry, educators began to take hold of the concept (Callahan 1962). Three individuals played key roles in its introduction: Frank Spaulding, the superintendent of schools in Newton, Massachusetts; William Allen, the director of the New York City Bureau of Municipal Research; and James Munroe, an industrialist educator and secretary of the Corporation of the Massachusetts Institute of Technology (Callahan 1962).

James Munroe (1912) made the conceptual tie between scientific management in educational settings and educational engineering. He provided the reasoning for its implementation in education. He argued that "we need *educational engineers* [my italics] to study this huge business of preparing youth for life, to find out where it is good, where it is wasteful, where it is out of touch with modern requirements, where and why its output fails" (p. 20).

Munroe also described the duties of these educational engineers and used an industrial analogy to explain how he envisioned the operation of the schools:

> Such engineers would make a thorough study of (1) the pupils who constitute the raw materials of the business of education; (2) the building and other facilities for teaching, which make up the plant; (3) the school boards and the teaching staff, who correspond to the directorate and the working force; (4) the means and methods of instruction and development; (5) the demands of society in general and of industry in particular upon boys and girls—this corresponding to the problem of markets; and (6) the question of the cost, which is almost purely a business problem (Munroe 1912).

Years after Munroe (1912) advocated an assembly line notion of education, W. W. Charters (1945, 1951) refined the concept of educational engineering, specifically as it applied to the means and methods of instruction. Charters's writing underscored the rich conceptual bonds that united technology, engineering, and education.

Wary of skeptics and critical comments, Charters was cautious about his use of the engineering analogy for education. In the introduction to "Is There a Field of Educational Engineering?" he wrote:

> For twenty years, the writer has been playing with an affirmative answer to the question posed in the title of this article. On occasion, he has spoken informally of curriculum "engineering." Curriculum planners carry out activities and have ideals that

parallel those of engineering, but caution has always prevailed against the public use of the term. Always present has been the fear that educators might be accused of borrowing the prestige of the engineer (Charters 1945).

This article explored the parallels between education and engineering. Charters employed a definition of engineering from *The Engineering Profession* by T. J. Hoover and J. C. L. Fish (1941) that stated that "engineering is the professional and systematic application of science to the efficient utilization of natural resources to produce wealth" (Charters 1945). Each of the elements of this definition was used as a basis for comparing engineering and education.

Charters's analysis of education and engineering served an important purpose for modern educational technology. It identified the basic characteristics of engineering and associated them with curriculum development activities. The concept of engineering discussed by Charters and the concept of technology outlined by Noble were similar in four ways: they were systematic; they were applications of science; they emphasized the efficient utilization of resources; and their goal was the production of wealth. The conceptual ties between engineering and technology in education became more apparent as educational engineering evolved from curriculum development into educational technology.

Charters explained how each of these four characteristics related to developing instructional methods and products. He argued that "the word, *systematic*, implies 'the thoroughness and impartiality with which the truth is pursued.' " While he admitted that there were few perfected techniques in education in 1945, he stated that "substantial beginnings have been made," and he further argued that continued efforts to thoroughly organize these successful techniques of instruction would inevitably result in their application in the schools.

Charters believed *systematic* implied *thorough*. Years earlier, Munroe had used the word *thorough* to describe the analysis required in order to successfully "engineer" the schools. The word *systematic* frequently appears in the literature of modern educational technology. Although its use therein may be derived from industrial technology, its meaning was not always consistent in the literature of the field. In some instances *systematic* meant *thoroughness*, but in others it was merely a step-by-step procedure.

Charters further stated that "the *applications of science* to problems" was an essential trait of engineering. He considered physics, chemistry, and mathematics to be the sciences basic to industrial engineering and said that "[educational engineering's] basic areas are psychology, sociology, and mathematics." Charters knew that the sciences that he considered basic to education were not the same as those of engineering. He believed that this difference was because sociology and psychology were newer sciences and had yet to develop the quantitative rigor of physics and chemistry. However, Charters did believe that educational engineering, like industrial engineering, should derive its methods based on research from its own "basic sciences."

Charters then focused on the notion of efficiency. He argued that efficiency "is the pride of the engineer. . . . Whenever the engineer eliminates friction, invents shortcuts, increases manpower output, or decreases costs, he increases efficiency" (Charters 1945). He believed that educators should strive to be more efficient and charged them to develop methods that would enable students to learn more in a shorter period.

Charters also believed that "engineering operates to produce wealth. This ultimate objective is widely conceived by the engineer. It does not imply money alone." He considered wealth to be "all those things which serve a useful purpose" and argued that "education also moves toward wealth as its objective," but admitted that educators used other terms to represent the idea of wealth. "They speak of satisfaction or growth or values of similar import." Charters concluded that "both professions have identical objectives; the resources used to achieve the ends are different."

Unlike Munroe (1912), who was interested in engineering the overall schooling process, the central tenet of educational engineering for Charters was the systematic development of instructional methods and products. It is important to note that Charters's discussion of educational engineering, while certainly different from Munroe's, was not in opposition to Munroe. In fact, the two views of educational engineering are complementary. Charters provides details for one of the areas of education that Munroe identified as being an important subject of analysis for the educational engineer: the means and methods of instruction and development.

Charters (1951) provides a description of how the educational engineer goes about the task of engineering instructional methods and materials. It consisted of five major activities:

> The engineer will identify the idea to be worked upon, analyze it, and select promising hypotheses concerning its practical uses. He will experimentally play with plans for building a structure that will use the full value of the idea. He will build a unit, an operational technique, an instructional method. He will operate the tool and try it out in practice. He will test the results to measure the efficiency and practicality of what he has constructed.[1]

Charters (1945) emphasized the attitude of engineering while describing the difference between the educational engineer and what he called "the idea man." He stated:

> The core of engineering is an attitude. The engineer has a passion for building things and making them run. . . . His happiness lies in devising a method, a structure, or a program that he hopes will work. The educational engineer, too, loves to plan, to organize, and to operate. In the administrative field, he is known as the organizer; in the laboratories, he builds instruments, sets up procedures, and puts them into operation; in the curriculum field, he starts with the function of an area and happily analyzes it, collects materials, organizes them, and tries them out. . . . To him the program is the thing. He gets pleasure not from merely savoring an idea but from building a structure and experiencing the satisfaction that comes from efficient operation. While the idea man says, "This is a grand idea," the educational engineer says, "These are masterly methods for carrying out the idea." One loves to play with theories; the other loves methods. One enjoys argument; the other loves production.

This attitude, the passion for action, contributed to the way that educational technologists interpreted some of the concepts that were important to their field of study, specifically those of science and engineering, which were viewed in ways that would make them easy to apply in educational settings.

Charters anticipated four other ideas or issues that would be addressed frequently in the literature of educational technology: the prestige of the profession (Ely 1963; Finn 1965); educational engineering (or educational technology) as solving problems in education (Finn 1960a; AECT 1977); the pattern of the scientific method (Banathy 1968; Jorgenson 1981); and the idea that many individuals in education might be considered part of this new field (educational engineering or educational technology) because they perform some of the same tasks (AECT 1972; AECT 1977; Ely 1982).

Finally, Charters argued that the engineering concept is a natural model for all people to adapt.

> An engineer is a builder. He builds structures to fulfill functions. He is a solver of problems. . . . This is the essence of human intelligence—the formal steps of reflection. It is the pattern followed in the scientific method and is the heart of the engineering method. It is the common possession of all people, the native pattern of intelligent life (Charters 1945, 34).

Two key concepts in this engineering analogy of education are reflection and scientific method. It is likely that Charters's discussion of these concepts was influenced by the writings of his contemporary, John Dewey. It is important to note the differences between Dewey and other scholars. Dewey was frequently cited as the source of ideas in order for the other scholars to gain a certain level of credibility, although he was frequently misinterpreted. Educational technologists are as guilty of this as other specialists in education are.

In 1929, Dewey argued "that, in concrete operation, education is an art, either a mechanical art or a fine art is unquestionable." He further said that engineering is "in actual practice, an art. But it is an art that progressively incorporates more and more science into itself. It is the kind of art it is precisely because of a content of scientific subject-matter which guides it as a practical operation." But Dewey also cautioned educators about the dangers of developing an engineering mentality. While he felt that the engineering conception of education should not be immediately discarded, he argued that if "the psychologist or observer and experimentalist in any field reduces his findings to a rule which is uniformly adopted, then, only, is there a result which is objectionable and destructive of the free play of education as an art."

Dewey was concerned about rigidity and standardization in the schools. Many proponents of science and engineering in education sought to identify and develop standardized rules for education. Dewey was concerned about the problems associated with the development of standardized rules of teaching based on science. Dewey warned educators that

> . . . this happens not because of scientific method but because of departure from it. It is not the capable engineer who treats scientific findings as imposing upon him a certain course which is to be rigidly adhered to: it is the third- or fourth-rate man who adopts this course. Even more, it is the unskilled day laborer who follows it. For even if the practice adopted is one that follows from science and could not have been discovered or employed except for science, when it is converted into a uniform rule of procedure it becomes an empirical rule-of-thumb procedure—just as a person may use a table of logarithms mechanically without knowing anything about mathematics (Dewey 1929).

There are two major differences between Dewey and Charters on their views of science and engineering in education. First, Charters sought to engineer the systemization of instruction through a science that was intended to standardize processes and outcomes. Dewey opposed this algorithmic approach to a science and engineering of education. Second, Charters (1945) equated the steps of scientific method and reflection with the method of engineering. While Dewey (1929, 1933) and Charters (1945) agreed that there are five distinct stages in reflective thinking, Charters felt that reflective thinking (as articulated in his engineering method) was a linear process, a procedure with definite starting and ending points. Dewey disagreed with this idea:

> The five phases, terminals, or functions of thought that we have noted *do not follow one another in set order* [my italics]. On the contrary, each step in genuine thinking does something to perfect the formation of a suggestion and promote its change into a leading idea or directive hypothesis. It does something to promote the location and definition of the problem. Each improvement in the idea leads to new observations that yield new facts or data and help the mind judge more accurately the relevancy of facts already at hand. The elaboration of the hypothesis does not wait until the problem has been defined and an adequate hypothesis has been arrived at; it may come in at any intermediate time. And . . . any particular overt test need not be final (Dewey 1933).

In addition to saying that there was no set order to the stages in thinking, he further argued that "no set rules can be laid down on such matters" (1933). He believed that reflective thinking "may be introductory to new observations and new suggestions, according to what happens in consequence of it." For Dewey, reflective thought and the scientific method were open processes that allowed the problem under consideration or the hypothesis being tested to be revised based upon a preliminary consideration of data.

Dewey also opposed the educational engineering advocated by Munroe (1912). He thought Munroe's "plant model" of education put practitioners in the role of industrial plant workers to use the methods generated by science and scientific management. Dewey wanted to have practitioners use reflective thought, as exemplified in his interpretation of the scientific method, to avoid falling into the trap of using standardized procedures in situations where they were not warranted.

Over the years educational technologists have used the term "reflective thinking," but they were not often clear about what they meant by it. Many of the early educational technology leaders were interested in generating "scientific" principles that would lead to replicable procedures that could be used in developing instructional methods and materials (e.g., Finn 1960; Sturlorow 1961; Lumsdaine 1964). The standardization of procedures is contrary to Dewey's conception of education as a "mechanical art" or engineering. In this regard, the early leadership of the field seemed to be more influenced by Charters's view of educational engineering than by Dewey's view of engineering in education or education as a mechanical art.

Science

The second major influence on modern educational technology was the use of science in education. There was more than one view of science in education because modern technology, and subsequently educational technology, is so closely associated with science. As such, it is important to understand which view of science had the most affect on the field of educational technology.

Educational historian and curriculum scholar Herbert M. Kliebard (1987) identifies three distinct views that were held by early-twentieth-century educators regarding the purpose of science as it related to education. The first purpose is to identify and study the "natural order of development in the child." This view of science, espoused primarily by G. Stanley Hall, posited that for curriculum decisions to be better informed, the educator should study children in their natural environment, collect and analyze data about them, and prescribe activities for their education.

The second view of science in education was "Dewey's idealization of scientific inquiry as a general model of reflective thinking" (Kliebard 1987). Dewey was interested in using the scientific method as a model for teaching thinking skills (broadly conceived) to students. Science was to be both a basis for a method of instruction and the primary subject matter to be taught.

The third view "was a science of exact measurement and precise standards in the interest of maintaining a predictable and orderly world" (Kliebard 1987). No single person acted as the primary advocate for this view of science; many scholars contributed to it. In this instance science in education was a series of laboratory and experimentally derived methods that were used to screen and place students, establish the curriculum, determine the proper instructional methods, and test students in an effort to predict and control learning outcomes. The object was to assure that learning had occurred in an efficient and effective manner.

Arguments can be made that modern educational technology has, at one time or another, incorporated ideas and practices from all three of these views of science. Some might argue that certain learning theories or instructional practices can be traced to Hall's "developmental science." Others might argue that the systems approach or the instructional development process is, in fact, a manifestation of John Dewey's view of the scientific method.

But the view of science most evident in the workings of modern educational technology is the science of "exact measurement and precise standards in the interest of maintaining a predictable and orderly world" (Kliebard 1987). This view is most evident in the practice and research in the field. Specific examples from the field include the systems models, behavioral objectives, and task analysis used in front-end analysis; the use of mastery learning techniques and criterion-referenced testing; and the highly quantitative nature and the design of experiments conducted by many researchers. Because the purpose of science in education here is one in which outcomes could be predicted in advance so as to minimize waste, the role of science in education begins to resemble the concept of educational engineering.[2]

Most individuals involved in the formulation of educational technology have held that the purpose of science in education is based on prediction, control, and standardization. This view of science was exemplified by the writings of James D. Finn, one of the acknowledged early leaders of the field. Finn came to prominence at the University of Southern California (USC), where he had taken a faculty position in 1949 after completing his doctoral work at Ohio State University under Edgar Dale. At USC, Finn played a key role in shaping the future of the field in at least four ways: 1) by leading the first academic department officially designated "Instructional Technology" in the United States; 2) by supervising the doctoral work of candidates, many of whom would go on to be influential leaders in the field; 3) by acting as a consultant to the U.S. Office of Education, from which he received funding to direct several major projects; and 4) by serving as a consultant to major national corporations.

Finn was also a prominent national speaker. In a speech that he delivered to the John Dewey Society (1962), he argued for the desirability of science in education. Finn used the example of W. W. Charters's work to respond to philosophical critiques of scientism[3] in education:

> Scientism in those days was Charters and educational engineering and activity analysis; scientism today is B. F. Skinner and pigeons and programmed learning. Charters was demolished for inventing a system of curriculum-making designed—so it was charged—to preserve the social status quo, and the measurement movement was subjected to blast after blast. . . .
>
> For those of you who follow Dewey, Bode and Kilpatrick, whose god was the method of science, this is, indeed a strange attitude. It was strange when they had it; it is stranger now. . . .
>
> Take . . . Charters' theories of analysis . . . today, those theories are being used for identical problems by psychologists who never heard of Charters. . . . Analysis is needed in all sorts of programming, in the statement of objectives, and throughout the developing technology of instruction. . . .
>
> Analysis, in the sense that Charters used it and as it is being used today in a hundred ways, is, in part at least, the discrimination of details. . . . I suggest that because of a social bias characteristic of the 30's, the great exponents of the scientific method in education successfully struck down one of the great educational scientists of that generation and prevented a generalized scientific technique from becoming more effective in education (Finn 1962).

Finn is really arguing from the assumption that a technology of instruction is desirable. Given his professional background, this is to be expected. But the reason that Dewey, Bode, and Kilpatrick opposed the use of theories of analysis was that they did not believe that science, as represented by activity analysis, was equipped to determine educational goals (Bode 1927; Saettler 1990). They believed that goal setting in education was a philosophical and moral consideration. Although the scientific method is the basis for Dewey's conception of reflective thinking and he viewed philosophy as reflective thought, Dewey stands apart from using a "scientific" procedure to determine educational goals.

In his writing Finn seemed to miss the point that there is, or was, more than one view of science in education. He accused Dewey, Bode, and Kilpatrick, "the great exponents of the scientific method," of striking down "one of the great educational scientists [Charters] of that generation." Here lies the importance of realizing that there are multiple views of science in education. Finn did differentiate between "exponents of the scientific method" and "educational scientists," but he does not account for the possibility that the view of science held by Dewey was much different from that held by Charters. In fact it was, as outlined earlier in this essay.

Finn was partially correct when he argued that a 1930s social bias opposed activity analysis as a way to build the curriculum. However, to attribute any disagreement about the role of science in education solely to social bias, excluding legitimate disagreements about "what science is," is to offer an incomplete and poorly constructed argument.

Further, Finn seemed oblivious to the fact that answering the question "What is science?" is a legitimate intellectual pursuit. He ridiculed the U.S. Congress and the National Science Foundation for promoting the study of the philosophy of science:

> As an amusing sidelight, the NSF has a brochure offering certain kinds of rewards to personnel in the various sciences and the "scientific" side of certain social sciences, for example, mathematical economics. Included, with approval, in the "scientific" studies is the subject of philosophy of science! To be fair, the NSF itself is probably not to blame. Congress and the conditions surrounding the use of funds have set these boundaries. The point, however, is still valid [4](Finn 1960b).

Finn's writing is used here as an example. The purpose of the previous discussion is not to deride him. Rather, the point is to show that individuals such as Finn, who were extremely influential in the early educational technology movement and in the formulation of the definitions of educational technology, held a limited and very specific conception of science and its role in education. To Finn, science was a given. It did not have to be interpreted; it simply had to be discovered and directed toward practical tasks. The results then had to be tested and revised as necessary.

Audiovisual Education

The rise of the audiovisual education movement was the third major influence on the field of educational technology. Historically, the concept of "audiovisual education" had not been interpreted as widely as the concepts "engineering" and "science." Even for those individuals who called for the development of an educational technology, audiovisual education was a concept that was initially based on hardware and equipment (e.g., Finn 1960a). Much of the equipment for classroom use became readily available after World War II (Lange 1969). Consequently, educational technology is popularly believed to have been the result of an evolution of the audiovisual education movement and primarily a post–World War II idea (Lange 1969; Saettler 1990). This interpretation occurred in spite of the fact that the formal definitions of educational technology provided by the DAVI and the AECT were process definitions and had their roots in the educational practice of the progressive era.

One example of the belief that educational technology was an outgrowth of the audiovisual education movement is the work of the 1963 Commission on Definition and Terminology, which was part of the Technological Development Project directed by James Finn. This group, led by Donald Ely, produced a definition of the field, then called "Audiovisual Communications," that later became the first definition of educational technology published by the DAVI (later the AECT). In the second chapter of the monograph (Ely 1963) the Commission argued that "this analysis must begin with a consideration of the audiovisual field since it was here that the initial developments in the technology of instruction were largely concentrated. Audiovisual personnel were the first technologists in education" (Ely 1963).

In his book *The Evolution of American Educational Technology* (1990), Paul Saettler provides a detailed description of the effect of the audiovisual education movement on modern educational technology. His account of the audiovisual movement highlights the shift in the emphasis from the machine-based concept of the field to a systematic approach for improving instruction.

Although visual aids had been used frequently in the nineteenth century (Anderson 1962), the literature of educational technology states that the audiovisual education movement began in earnest in the early 1930s (AECT 1977; Ely 1963; Saettler 1990). In 1932, several professional organizations merged into the Department of Visual Instruction (DVI) of the National Education Association (Ely 1963; Saettler 1990). This organization was primarily concerned with the promotion and use of visual aids in the schools. In the 1930s, visual aids were seen primarily as teaching aids, as enrichment for teachers' use in the classroom (Jorgenson 1981).

The concept of the field as one of "teaching aids" gradually shifted toward "audiovisual techniques to improve instruction" (McBeath 1972). Charles F. Hoban, Jr., and Edgar Dale are generally credited as being two of the most important contributors to this shift in orientation (Ely 1970; Jorgenson 1981; Saettler 1990). Hoban received his doctorate under Edgar Dale's supervision at Ohio State University. Hoban's 1937 text, *Visualizing the Curriculum* (written with his father, Charles F. Hoban, Sr., and Samuel Zisman), "was the most important textbook in the field in the 1930s because of its systematic treatment of the relationship between the concrete materials of teaching and the process of learning" (Ely 1970, 84). Ely also provided an often-cited definition of visual aids:

> A visual aid is any picture, model, object, or device which provides concrete visual experience to the learner for the purpose of (1) introducing, building-up, enriching, or clarifying abstract concepts, (2) developing desirable attitudes, and (3) stimulating further activity on the part of the learner. . . . Visual aids are classified according to general types along a scale of concreteness and abstraction.

Hoban promoted a curriculum that included concrete learning experiences that were based on the use of visual aids. He provided many creative ideas for teachers to use in the classroom and also included a detailed discussion of how to integrate the materials of instruction into the curriculum. It is this integration with instruction that supports a process view of educational technology.

Edgar Dale advanced the case for diverse learning experiences in the classroom (Jorgenson 1981). Dale originally came to the University of Chicago to study with Ralph Tyler. After several years he took a position on the faculty at Ohio State University where he worked alongside W. W. Charters and Sidney L. Pressey. In the first edition of his textbook, *Audio-Visual Methods in Teaching* (1946), Dale explained his now-famous "cone of experience." The cone, he argued, served as a visual analogy for demonstrating the levels of "concreteness" of different teaching techniques and instructional materials (Dale 1946). Dale believed that abstract symbols and ideas could be more easily understood and retained by the learner if they were built on a more concrete experience. "A well-educated person has a mind stacked with a rich variety of concepts, grounded in concrete personal experiences. And such experiences are classifiable through a pictorial device— a metaphorical 'cone of experience' " (Dale 1946). The purpose of the cone was to represent a range of learning potentials from direct experience to symbolic communication, a concrete-to-abstract scale.

Dale's cone of experience was a tool that melded the educational theory of John Dewey and the ideas on learning posited by Donald Durrell (Dale 1946). This was one of the first attempts by individuals in the audiovisual movement to build a model of instruction that involved learning theory and the use of audiovisual materials and equipment.

The cone of experience became one of the most influential conceptual contributions to the growth of the audiovisual movement (Saettler 1990). The cone was "perhaps one of the most useful, simple tools for media selection" (Briggs 1980). Dale's discussion of the interaction between experience, in which he included teaching methods and materials, provided a basis for investigating ways to help the learner attain increasingly abstract concepts. This discussion opened the door for further study of methods of instruction by members of the audiovisual field. It also signaled a movement away from the view that the field was solely concerned with "things" or equipment and production of instructional materials.

The work of Hoban and Dale did much to validate and promote the use of audiovisuals to improve instruction. Their efforts represent the beginnings of a subtle shift from the view of the audiovisual field as teaching aids to a field involved in an integrated and systematically derived approach to the use of materials and methods in the classroom setting. Finn joined Dale and Hoban to produce an article for the 1949 Yearbook of the National Society for the Study of Education, *Audio-Visual Materials of Instruction*. They stated that "audiovisual materials and devices should not be classified exclusively as 'eye' and 'ear' experiences. They are modern *technological* means of providing rich, concrete experiences for students" [my italics] (Dale, Finn, & Hoban 1949). In the 1950s, Dale, Hoban, and Finn continued to steer the audiovisual education movement toward an emphasis on the means and processes involved in instruction.

CONCLUSION

By the 1950s, certain ideas of engineering, science, and the audiovisual education movement had begun to come together in both linguistic and conceptual ways. The writings of Dale, Hoban, and Finn had interpreted the audiovisual concept as a technological means for improving instruction. This technological orientation was grounded in the production-oriented attitude of educational engineering and a science of education that focused on standardization and control. The attempts to establish a science of education gave rise to measurement and prediction-based methods and outcomes that could easily be adapted to a procedural concept of educational engineering.

The influence of engineering and science and the rise of the audiovisual education movement helped to shape the assumptions and goals of modern educational technology. This influence was further strengthened by attempts to bring status to the audiovisual field by trying to make it a profession.

NOTES

1.   For a detailed discussion of his engineering method in education see Charters, 1945, specifically pp. 36–37 and 56.

2.   For specific examples see Mager, 1962; Banathy, 1968; Bloom, 1968; and Saettler, 1990.

3.   It is unclear if Finn is aware that "scientism" is a perjorative. He does not acknowledge this at any point in his text. Nor does he define his meaning of the term. However, to be fair, this article is based on a speech and there may have been something in the delivery that is absent in the text.

4.   It is interesting to note that while Finn disapproved of the NSF providing funding for the study of the philosophy of science, he himself was not above using federal money, through the Technological Development Project, to fund the work of the Commission on Definition and Terminology that created the first formal definition of educational technology. It is not a long stretch to think that the entire conceptual study that was undertaken by the Commission might fall under the rubric of the philosophy of technology! What is important here is that Finn must have believed that everyone knew what science was but not enough people knew what technology was.

REFERENCES

Anderson, C. (1962). *Technology in American education 1650–1900*. Washington, DC: U.S. Department of Health, Education and Welfare/U.S. Government Printing Office.

Association for Educational Communications and Technology (1972). The field of educational technology: A statement of definition. *Audiovisual Instruction 17*, 36–43.

Association for Educational Communications and Technology (1977). *The definition of educational technology*. Washington, DC: Association for Educational Communications and Technology.

Banathy, B. (1968). *Instructional systems*. Palo Alto, CA: Fearon.

Bern, H. (1961). Audiovisual "engineers?" *Audiovisual Communications Review 9*, 186–94.

Bode, B. (1927). *Modern educational theories*. New York: Macmillan.

Callahan, R. (1962). *Education and the cult of efficiency: A study of the forces that have shaped the administration of the public schools*. Chicago: University of Chicago Press.

Charters, W. W. (1945). Is there a field of educational engineering? *Educational Research Bulletin 24* (2), 29–37, 53.

Charters, W. W. (1951). The era of the educational engineer. *Educational Research Bulletin 30* (12), 233–46.

Dale, E. (1946). *Audio-visual methods in teaching*. New York: Dryden Press.

Dale, E., J. D. Finn, and C. F. Hoban (1949). Research on audio-visual materials. In *Audio-visual materials of instruction*. Forty-Eighth Yearbook of the National Society for the Study of Education. Chicago: University of Chicago Press.

Dewey, J. (1916). *Democracy and education*. New York: Macmillan.

Dewey, J. (1929). Education as a science. In *Intelligence in the modern world: John Dewey's philosophy*, ed. J. Ratner. New York: Modern Library, 631–40.

Dewey, J. (1933). *How we think*. New York: Macmillan.

Ely, D. P. (1963). The changing role of the audiovisual process: A definition and glossary of related terms. *Audiovisual Communication Review 11* (1), supplement 6.

Ely, D. P. (1970). Toward a philosophy of instructional technology. *British Journal of Educational Technology 1* (2), 81–94.

Ely, D. P. (1982). The definition of educational technology: An emerging stability. *Educational Considerations 10* (2), 2–4.

Ely, D. P. (1994). *Personal conversations*. Syracuse, NY: Syracuse University Press.

Finn, J. D. (1953). Professionalizing the audio-visual field. *Audio-Visual Communications Review 1* (1), 6–17.

Finn, J. D. (1957). Automation and education: General aspects. *Audio-Visual Communications Review 5* (1), 343–60.

Finn, J. D. (1960a). Automation and education: A new theory for instructional technology. *AV Communications Review 8* (1), 5–26.

Finn, J. D. (1960b). Teaching machines: Auto-instructional devices for the teacher. *NEA Journal 49* (8), 41–44.

Finn, J. D. (1962). A walk on the altered side. *Phi Delta Kappan 44* (1), 29–34.

Finn, J. D. (1965). The marginal media man. Part 1: The great paradox. *Audiovisual Instruction 10* (10), 762–65.

Heinich, R. (1984). The proper study of instructional technology. *Educational Communications and Technology Journal 32* (2), 67–87.

Hoban, C. F. , C. F. Hoban, Jr., and S. B. Zisman (1937). *Visualizing the curriculum*. New York: Dryden Press.

Hoover, T. J., and Fish, J. C. L. (1941). *The engineering profession*. Stanford, CA: Stanford University Press.

Jorgenson, S. (1981). *A conceptual analysis of the assumptions and aspirations of instructional development*. Unpublished Doctoral dissertation. Ann Arbor, MI: University Microfilms International.

Kliebard, H. M. (1987). Curriculum theory: Give me a "for instance." *Curriculum Inquiry 6* (4), 257-69.

Lange, Phil C. (1969). *History and principles of instructional media, educational communications, and technology*. Unpublished manuscript. New York: Teachers College, Columbia University.

Lumsdaine, A. (1964). "Educational technology, programmed learning, and instructional science." In *Theories of learning and instruction*. Sixty-third Yearbook of the National Society for the Study of Education, ed. E. Hilgard. Chicago: University of Chicago Press.

McBeath, R. J. (Ed.). (1972). *Extending education though technology: Selected writings by James D. Finn on instructional technology*. Washington, DC: Association for Educational Communications and Technology.

Munroe, J. P. (1912). *New demands in education*. New York: Macmillan.

Noble, D. (1977). *America by design*. New York: Oxford University Press.

Saettler, P. (1990). *The evolution of American educational technology*. Englewood, CO: Libraries Unlimited.

Shrock, S. (1990). A brief history of instructional development. In *Instructional technology past, present, and future*, ed. G. Anglin. Englewood, CO: Libraries Unlimited, 11–19.

Sturlorow, L. M. (1961). *Teaching by machine*. Washington, DC: U.S. Department of Health, Education, and Welfare/U.S. Government Printing Office.

Szabo, W. (1968). Introduction to audio-visual engineering. *Audiovisual Communications* (6).

Taylor, F. W. (1911). *The principles of scientific management*. New York: Harper & Brothers.

Clockwork Courage!*

Costas Criticos
University of Natal, Durban, South Africa

INTRODUCTION

The peaceful demise of apartheid and the country's first democratic election is one of the twentieth century's social miracles. Nelson Mandela, affectionately known as Madiba, is the hero often associated with this miracle. Mandela often casts his "Madiba magic" to resolve political crises and to spur national sports teams to victory. One area where even the "Madiba magic" has had no power is education.[1] Education is in a crisis, teachers are dispirited, and pupils are disillusioned as the revolutionary fervor of Peoples Education has evaporated. Evidence of parents' impatience with the government's efforts to replace apartheid education is evident in the growth of private schools and colleges.

In part, the slow pace of change in education is due to the monumental challenge of dismantling the apartheid education system and replacing it with a nonracial and equitable system. Great progress has been made with policies that provide an equitable and appropriate education. But *implementing* the blueprint to resolve the "education crisis" and undo the apartheid legacy is proving more difficult than formulating the plans.

Curriculum, resources, and *learning spaces* can each be regarded as crucial components in the implementation of the new post-apartheid education system. In my report I will highlight some of the landmark developments and principal features that characterize these components of education. The common response to our crisis has been to abandon hope or look for some outside intervention such as foreign aid or a wonder technology (like the Internet). The courageous and less common response has been to find solutions in the teachers and pupils and in local and everyday resources.

So, my report is a story about courage—it is about people who have declared war on inappropriate education and who have relied on their wits and basic resources as weapons. They have few allies, and they cannot afford to use sophisticated technological weapons in the education battle.

THE CLOCKWORK PARADIGM OF TECHNOLOGY

I have brought along a South African invention that illustrates the paradigm of educational technology that is taking root at home. This wind-up radio is an ingenious combination of low and high technologies that span many centuries. It is now possible to use radio communication in areas without electricity or where people cannot afford batteries. Sixty turns of the handle will store enough energy to give you over an hour of listening. UNESCO and other agencies make extensive use of this radio in relief and development projects.

The clockwork radio offers us a tangible metaphor for technology that we can apply in most applications of development and technology transfer in education. A few months ago I attended a conference that attempted to envision education in South Africa in the twenty-first century. A paper[2] presented by a development consultant, Philip Christensen, sketched the need for a dual-character technology for our region (1997). He described two different types of educational technology to suit the wide diversity of need in the country—a high-tech strategy and a low-tech strategy.

---

*This paper was originally presented at the 1998 AECT Convention, St. Louis, Missouri, February 1998.

I have taken Christensen's dual technology and identified it as a paradigm (Clockwork Paradigm) that has an emerging influence in South African education.

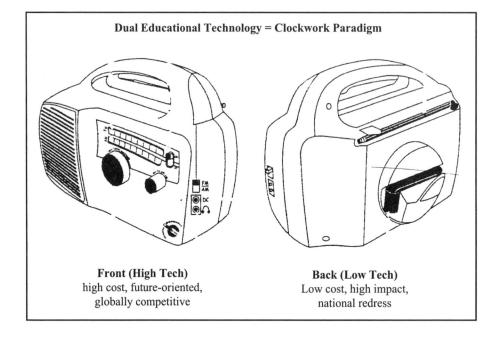

Dual Educational Technology = Clockwork Paradigm

Front (High Tech)
high cost, future-oriented,
globally competitive

Back (Low Tech)
Low cost, high impact,
national redress

The following is a summary of the key features of this "Clockwork Paradigm" of educational technology arranged as answers to the questions What?, How?, and When?

What?

- appropriate for specific needs;
- cost-effective;
- environmentally and socially responsible;

How?

- uses old, new, low, and high technologies in combinations of side-by-side and leverage relationships; and is

When?

- just-in-time.

I will now illustrate how this paradigm of educational technology has manifested itself in South Africa in relation to the three crucial components that I have identified in the educational crisis. (In each case I will describe the challenge and a solution associated with the Clockwork Paradigm.)

CURRICULUM

The Challenge

Khretsi Lehoko, Chief Director of Adult and Distance Education in the Department of Education, sees the new national Outcomes Based Education program of Curriculum 2005 as presenting new challenges for educators (1997). The new curriculum includes:

- a focus on outcomes and not on content
- an integrated curriculum—between "old" subject divisions and between school and "life"
- a learner-centered pedagogy
- "open" classrooms, spaces for learning, timetables, and collaborative arrangements
- a cooperative community of learners who use the surrounding community as a resource.

The implementation of the curriculum is behind schedule and this year we have seen its introduction limited to grade 1. Each year, additional grades will be added until the year 2005 when it is anticipated that all grades would have incorporated the new curriculum. Common wisdom would seek additional funds to accelerate the publishing of textbooks and increase the pace of in-service training to cope with the challenges of Curriculum 2005.

A Clockwork Solution

Rather than wait for an unreliable supply of textbooks for the new curriculum (*Natal Mercury* 10 February 1998, 3), a number of teacher and nongovernmental organizations have helped teachers and learners develop their own materials. Many teachers are now starting to use indigenous knowledge and local communities and environments as their laboratories. One such example is the School Water Action Project (SWAP). Children in the SWAP program develop skills associated with ecology and environmental responsibility while they undertake an audit of water resources. SWAP coordinator Rob O'Donoghue reaches remote schools and river areas on his bicycle, which is equipped with a laptop, GPS system, and a cellular telephone. Field data recorded by students on a spreadsheet is uploaded to the SWAP home page on the Internet.

In this project the students are starting to develop some of the skills of citizenship and local action at the same time as they refine their biological skills.

RESOURCES

The Challenge

With most provincial departments of education short of funds, books and other essential materials have not been supplied to all schools. The worst hit by these shortages are schools in rural and poor areas (*Natal Mercury* 10 February 1998, 3). These shortages have been identified by many analysts as the major reason for the worst school results that we have had in South Africa. However, there is no simple causal relationship between resources and achievement.

The common explanation of the link between poor performance and poor resources is frequently contradicted. Some well-resourced schools perform poorly and some underresourced schools perform well. This was strikingly evident in the rating of South Africa's top 100 schools (*Sunday Times* 11 January 1998). More than one-third of the top schools come from disadvantaged communities where the schools are poorly equipped and underresourced. Most notable in this list is a school in my province, KwaZulu-Natal, where endemic violence is still smoldering, and students have one of the lowest educational budgets in the country. In spite of this, the school secured a 100 percent pass rate in the national examinations and 60 percent at the level for acceptance into university. The school has no telephone, fax machine, electricity, or water. What it does have in common with the other schools in the "Top 100" is a teaching staff that has the courage to be resourceful and committed to promoting learning. Resourcefulness is not about simply using resources; it is about selecting, discerning, and constructing resources in any context. The following examples illustrate this quality.

A Clockwork Solution

Using inexpensive items such as newspapers and household chemicals, students and their resourceful teachers are able to develop valuable learning resources. In the SWAP project students use an inexpensive microbiological field kit for conducting water tests normally reserved for the high-tech laboratory.

Other equally innovative low-cost resources include the diazo poster printing device, which uses a plastic pipe, a bicycle pump, and a plastic bottle to reproduce large-size posters without the use of electricity. This type of resourcefulness is not only restricted to low-tech resources. There are many high-tech and high low-tech innovations that are very encouraging to the education community.

Africa has a big backlog in information infrastructure. While our continent has only 1 percent of all telephones in the world, we constitute 10 percent of its population (*Natal Mercury* 9 February 1998, 4). Most of these telephones are clustered in southern Africa so the picture is particularly bleak for our northern neighbors.

Cell phone and satellite technology are likely to be used to accelerate the rate of delivery because of the lack of land-line infrastructure. One such proposal for educational delivery is the use of "webcasting"[3] technology. A "webcasting" project currently under development uses a mix of low and high technology to allow schools without sophisticated PCs or communication to benefit from Web and other resources. Schools, teachers' centers, and learning centers are increasingly moving toward "thin-client network servers," which use recycled 286/386 machines[4] in a network with one high-speed server. At certain times of the day, satellite broadcasts (webcasting) will transmit digital data for later access from the local server. In this way we will be able to leapfrog two major problems that we experience in South Africa: bandwidth limitations and a poor postal service (Butcher 1998, 20).

This project is of particular relevance for the future macro-plan that will locate schools in a clustered educational precinct. Webcasting technology can benefit from the economy of scale in the new clustered schools. Ideally, a communication system should be provided as part of the building utilities in this precinct. Rather than retrofitting the trunking and cables, a communication system should be installed during the construction stage in anticipation of a wide area network linking all the schools to the webcast server.

LEARNING SPACES

The Challenge

According to Luis Crouch (1997), a consultant economist to the Department of Education, we can expect that the operating expenses of a classroom will amount to approximately 30 times more than the construction costs. These estimates seem to check out with the current situation in some provinces that are using up to 98 percent of their education budget on teachers' salaries. With such a small slice of the budget left uncommitted, it is not surprising that there are insufficient classrooms, and many of the existing classrooms are unsuitable for education. An audit of school buildings a few years ago revealed that:

- 1 out of every 10 schools is in need of major repairs, and 1 out of every 20 is not fit for education;

- almost half of all schools (38 percent) have no telephones;

- almost half of all schools (43 percent) have no electricity;
- more than half of all schools have no water on-site and a significant number are not within walking distance of a water source;
- and 13 percent of schools had no toilets (Bot 1997; Mona 1997).

A Clockwork Solution

One option is the clustering of schools as a serious attempt to transform the quality of education and allow learners of different race and socioeconomic groupings to interact and share common facilities. Neville Alexander, a key advocate of clustering, defends the idea like this:

> At a time when scarcity of resources is a major consideration, it is clear that the sharing of resources between schools and between the schools and the surrounding communities is an attractive and decisive feature of our proposal (Alexander, Smit et al. 1995).

The first major school building scheme that is going to draw on these ideas is the Cato Manor housing development in Durban. The scheme is using development funds and other provincial grants to transform a squatter area into a high-density housing complex. Part of the scheme involves the establishment of 75 schools in a clustered arrangement. Architectural researcher and planner Jennifer Whitehead describes the rationale of the project as follows:

> What we have proposed in Cato Manor is a co-operation between the various delivery agents to enable facilities to be shared. Schools will be ideally located in "Social Facilities Precincts," along with a public library, community hall, and sports fields. The public library will be stocked with books required by the schools, the library will use school classrooms to enable it to operate as a Community Learning Centre, the school will use the community hall for functions, and the sports fields will be a community resource accessed by the schools during times when most adults are otherwise engaged (Whitehead 1995).

Appropriate Learning Spaces

The development of learning spaces are framed by our assumptions of education. Traditional teaching and classroom arrangements dominate our view of education. In the end, it is these views that have stifled more creative approaches to the design of schools.

I can illustrate the exaggerated value of the traditional classroom with an incident that occurred a few years ago at a school in rural KwaZulu-Natal. The school that is bursting at the seams always has one class that finds itself without a classroom. These classes have to go out to the dusty playing field for their lessons. You might expect—as I did—that the teacher and class would seek out one of the few shady trees as a refuge from the harsh sunlight. Instead of this, the class filed out to an area in the middle of the playground where a classroom was marked out with neat rows of stones. The "classroom" even had a break in the wall for a doorway.

The "Virtual Classroom."

The children stood along the wall of their "classroom" while the teacher, who was standing at the "doorway," waited patiently for them to get into a straight line before she gave the command to "go in." The class didn't walk through the "virtual wall," but instead turned in through the "doorway" and made their way to their neatly arranged rows of "virtual desks." By this time, the teacher was in the front of the "room" where she greeted the children and then sat down on the dusty floor.

The lesson then proceeded in much the same way as in the school's real classrooms. What is so attractive about the classroom and its rituals that teachers and pupils regard them as normal? Why does the classroom become the organizing unit on which development proposals and architectural designs are based? *Surely the learner and the curriculum would be better starting points for design and planning?* School architecture that starts with learning rather than the classroom as the point of departure is starting to take root.

The earliest evidence of this radical perspective was in the mid-eighties. Farouk Cassim, who is now in Parliament, made a major effort to establish a revolutionary school inspired by Toffler's future scenarios of an information society. In Cassim's school the classroom gave way to the Infosphere—a resource center devoted to related disciplines (Cassim 1987). At any one time the resource center would house a few teachers and a number of learners of different ages engaged in individual and collaborative learning tasks. In this way the resource-based modular program dispensed with the strict subject specialization, formal divisions of time, and the lack of integration of school knowledge with the world of work. In the end, the project was abandoned because of lack of support; it represented an educational vision that was far too radical for the pre-Internet era.

Infosphere—typical resource center for the proposed Parklands Private School. The media and book collections of each resource center are captured on a common library catalog that can be accessed from any one of the seven resource centers.

More recently the school for pediatric patients at the new Academic Hospital has based its design on a learning center rather than the classroom-based school. In this learning center a variety of learning activities for patients with different medical conditions and different learning needs can be supported. If the learner is the point of departure in planning curricula, learning spaces, and resources, then we are more likely to achieve effective solutions.

CONCLUSION

Our state departments of education are not unaware of the need for more systemic approaches to technology. In the last major ministerial commission on technology, the Technology Enhanced Learning Commission, a caution was issued about the uncritical implementation of technology. They advocated an integrated approach and one in which technology is used to augment existing learning nodes. In summary:

> The investigation shows that technology can be used to improve the quality of education. When introduced on the basis of poorly considered decision making, however, it can also reduce the quality of education. Technology can be used to redress imbalances of the old system and help in developing new teaching and learning strategies, but it can also entrench those imbalances. Technology can empower learners for participation in a democratic process, but it will do so only if suitable organisational, curricular, and instructional decision making processes are put in place (Butcher 1996).

This is a sober reminder that every problem is unique and context bound—there is no silver bullet, quick fix, or grand theory in educational delivery. However, paradigms of education that frame an approach to educational problems in a creative, appropriate, strategic, and responsible manner have a strong chance of providing a range of solutions to a variety of problems. The "Clockwork Paradigm" in this report is an attempt to identify some of the characteristics of such a paradigm. In this case, the paradigm is not a prescriptive theoretical vision but a descriptive account of courageous responses to educational problems.

NOTES

1.   In President Mandela's last opening address to parliament before his retirement and forthcoming 1999 elections, he said we were an over-governed country and he announced a drastic reduction of the civil service. Savings in government are likely to be routed to some of the priority areas such as education.

2.   The paper subtitled "Lessons for South Africa" could just as well have been "Lessons from South Africa."

3.   Webcasting involves the broadcast of a substantial number of Websites in digital data form via satellite—local servers linked to a receiver and decoder then download the data steams and act as a proxy server for a number of preselected Websites, which users in a LAN/WAN can access at very high speeds.

4.   The SWAP project has equipped schools with recycled 286 PCs.

REFERENCES

Bot, M. (1997). School register of needs: A provincial comparison of school facilities. *EduSource Data News 17* (August 1997), 1–4.

Butcher, N. (1996). Considering the use of technology in education and training: A brief summary of the TELI report. *Open Learning: Newsletter of SAIDE 2* (4), 1–3.

Butcher, N. (1998). "Exploring the use of Internet and satellite technologies to support the professional development of teachers." Unpublished report of the South African Institute of Distance Education. Johannesburg: SAIDE.

Cassim, F. (1987). Design of learning spaces: Parklands private school. In *Design of Learning Spaces*, ed. C. Criticos and M. Thurlow. Durban: Media Resource Centre, University of Natal, 133–42.

Christensen, P. R. (1997). *Educational technology and educational reform: Lessons for South Africa.* Paper presented at the conference Future World—Educating for the 21st Century, Cape Town, 2 December.

Criticos, C. (1997a). *Designing learning spaces for the future.* Paper presented at the Learning Spaces for the Future, RDP Culture of Learning and Schools Building Programme Conference, Pretoria: Dept. of Education, 22–23 April.

Criticos, C. (1997b). *Curriculum, resources and learning spaces—Synergy or discord in the 21st century?* Paper presented at the conference Future World—Educating for the 21st Century, Cape Town, 2 December.

Crouch, L. A. (1997). *International perspectives on planning and finance for classroom construction.* Paper presented at Learning Spaces for the Future, RDP Culture of Learning and Schools Building Programme Conference, Pretoria: Dept. of Education, 22–23 April.

Halloran, J. D. (1990). *Developments in communication and democracy.* Paper presented at 17th Conference of the International Association of Mass Communication Research, Bled, Yugoslavia.

Lehoko, K. (1997). *The implication for Curriculum 2005 on the learning space: Organising education for effective learning.* Paper presented at Learning Spaces for the Future, RDP Culture of Learning and Schools Building Programme Conference, Pretoria, Dept. of Education, 22–23 April.

Mona, V. (1997). SA schools in shocking condition. *The Teacher,* 3.

Seeking the big African link-up. In *Natal Mercury* (9 February 1998), 4.

Smit, W., and Hennessy, K. (1995). *Taking South African education out of the ghetto: An urban planning perspective.* Rondebosch, South Africa: UCT Press.

Still no stationery or books for pupils. In *Natal Mercury* (10 February 1998), 3.

Sunday Times (11 January 1998). Editorial: Name those schools which fail their pupils, 14.

Whitehead, J. (1995). *The Cato Manor challenge: A quest for appropriate standards in learning spaces.* Learning Spaces Development in Southern Africa. Durban: University of Natal, Department of Education, UND.

A Support System for
Instructional Technology in Higher Education
The Housecalls Program of Virginia Tech's College
of Human Resources and Education

Jared A. Danielson and John K. Burton
Virginia Polytechnic Institute and State University

The housecalls program at Virginia Tech's College of Human Resources and Education provides a useful, practical example of an effort that, while supplying a support structure for instructional technology (IT), also leads to the effective implementation of IT in higher education. This chapter describes the context for and the workings of the housecalls program and shows how it promotes innovation in IT within a hierarchy reminiscent of Abraham Maslow's (1970)—a hierarchy of faculty technical and instructional support needs. The chapter will also address innovation theory (Rogers 1971; Ely 1990) and demonstrate how the housecalls program has been consistent with Ely's eight conditions that facilitate the implementation of educational technology.

CONTEXT

Virginia Tech and the Faculty Development Initiative

Virginia Polytechnic and State University is a land-grant university in southwest Virginia. It is a large school, boasting an enrollment of approximately 25,000 students. Virginia Tech has tended to focus heavily on engineering and technical trades, and the administration at Virginia Tech has long valued the importance of remaining abreast of emerging technologies. Therefore, as new tools (e.g., desktop computers) that might be useful in a university setting have emerged, administrators have been eager to supply faculty and students with the opportunity to use them.

With the availability of affordable, easy-to-use, and relatively powerful desktop computers in the early 1990s, accompanied by the availability of funds for their purchase from the State Council of Higher Education in Virginia (SCHEV) equipment trust fund, Virginia Tech administrators decided to provide professors with this powerful, new, and little-understood tool. The program, which would provide professors with computers and, hopefully, give them the tools necessary to use them effectively, became known as the Faculty Development Initiative (FDI).

The goal of FDI was twofold. First, FDI would place a computer on each faculty member's desk every five years. Second, FDI would provide faculty with the knowledge and skills necessary to use their computers for developing courseware. In exchange for receiving a new computer, each faculty member would be required to attend a series of three to five all-day workshops aimed at teaching them how to use their new computers effectively. In general, while the FDI program has succeeded in placing computers on the desks of most faculty members in the university, it has not resulted in many faculty using their computers for any substantial efforts at course development.

FDI and the College of Human Resources and Education

Shortly after the advent of FDI, the College of Education at Virginia Tech was forcibly merged with the College of Human Resources. While all colleges had participated in FDI and been recipients of SCHEV money, this merger illustrated the disparity in the way particular colleges and departments had chosen to allocate those resources. The education "side" had generally used their SCHEV money to maintain and build on what was initiated with FDI. Computers had been replaced when outdated, and efforts had been made to keep software up-to-date. The Human Resources "side," however, had tended to allocate their SCHEV money in other ways, leaving faculty with old systems (both in terms of hardware and software) that were unreliable and difficult to maintain and support. Many faculty rarely or never used their computers for everyday tasks, much less to create and maintain courseware.

This situation illustrated several of the shortcomings of the FDI initiative. First, while resources were allocated to provide faculty with initial training, in many cases that training was not immediately useful for the faculty, and it was quickly forgotten. In other cases, while the training might have been considered useful by the faculty member, it was frequently not easily implemented. For example, the first several groups of faculty receiving FDI training learned how to do E-mail at a time when there were very few others to correspond with. Finally, while FDI provided for initial training, it did not provide for follow-up training. As a result, many faculty failed to use what had been taught in their FDI training and quickly forgot what had been learned.

Those faculty who made an effort to use their new equipment and skills soon discovered other problems. While FDI had provided them with computers and training, it did not provide for follow-up support to deal with the myriad of technical problems associated with computer use. Some professors, frustrated by incessant system crashes, inability to network correctly, inability to print reliably, and the like, abandoned the thought of using their computers for course development. Some professors abandoned their computers altogether and found vacancies for them on the floors of their offices.

THE COLLEGE OF HUMAN RESOURCES
AND EDUCATION AND A "MASLOWIAN" HIERARCHY
OF FACULTY TECHNICAL NEEDS

The situation in which so many post-FDI faculty members found themselves reveals a set of requirements that must be met for faculty to effectively implement new technologies in teaching endeavors. This set of requirements can well be understood when arranged hierarchically, in a pyramid reminiscent of Abraham Maslow's hierarchy of human needs. Maslow's hierarchy illustrates the theory that meeting certain fundamental human needs is prerequisite to meeting others. In his hierarchy, the need for food and shelter is fundamental and is prerequisite to meeting higher needs such as that for human affection.

In our analogy to the implementation of educational technology, certain basic technological needs precede and are prerequisite to others. Our version of the hierarchy of faculty needs when adopting technology in education appears in Figure 1 below. As can be seen, the most basic of all requirements (if faculty are to use these tools effectively) is that of having properly functioning equipment. The highest-level requirement is that of creating good, theory-based instructional products. Clearly, while the latter is the ultimate and certainly more glamorous goal, it will not happen until the requirements below it have been met. It is our contention (and experience) that the needs that require the most time to address are those found at the top and the bottom of the pyramid. Therefore, any endeavor that strives to meet these requirements must have the ability to spend a great deal of time and resources "at the bottom" before moving its way up. Furthermore, we argue that it is futile to "sit at the top" of the pyramid and wait for faculty to come ask for assistance with weighty and important matters of theory and development. This is the case because without support at the bottom, most faculty will never arrive at the top, and those faculty who have had the drive to arrive to the top unaided are unlikely to solicit help once there.

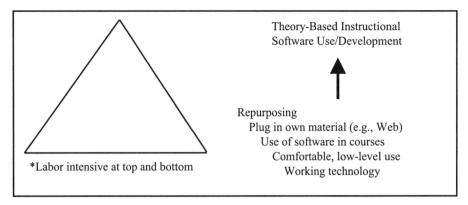

Figure 1. The Hierarchy of Implementation of Instructional Technology Requirements.

THE HOUSECALLS PROGRAM AS AN ATTEMPT TO HELP FACULTY MOVE UP THE HIERARCHY

The merger of the College of Education with the College of Human Resources found a group of somewhat disconnected departments suddenly affiliated with each other. Most of these departments suffered many basic technology-related problems, and in none of them was there a formal, organized method for dealing with such problems. The Department of Teaching and Learning from the Education "side" was the only department with the knowledge and skills to deal with such problems on their own. The Department of Teaching and Learning is a large department, composed of about 50 faculty, 14 staff, and 40 graduate assistants (GAs). These people use approximately 120 computers. The department also houses the Education Technology Lab, where there are an additional 70 computers. Two technologically savvy programs, Educational Technology and Technology Education, are both housed in the department. Through faculty and students in these two programs, the Department of Teaching and Learning was traditionally able to resolve its own computer-related technical problems, and faculty in that department were generally enabled to use their FDI-provided equipment in their daily professional lives.

The Birth of the Housecall Operation

In an attempt to resolve the myriad of technical problems plaguing the college, while at the same time taking advantage of the resources to be found within the newly formed college, administrators at the college level and within the Department of Teaching and Learning determined to create a service that would provide technical support for the college, provide a venue for training and supporting graduate students, and support faculty in their efforts to use their computers as educational tools (i.e., move faculty up the hierarchy). With this decision, the housecalls program (housecal@vt.edu) was created.

The initial and primary focus of the housecalls program was to provide reliable, prompt (contact within the hour), and personal technical assistance to faculty within the college. Housecalls was not to be merely a technical service, however. It was to provide "human contact" (95 percent of housecalls' calls are dealt with face-to-face), advice and on-the-spot training for technical and instructional questions, and in-service training for technical and instructional issues.

Overview of the Housecalls Service

1. Scope

    Housecalls serves the College of Human Resources and Education, including approximately 170 faculty and 65 staff using about 400 machines (Mac and IBM-compatible).

2. Financial Commitment

    Housecalls employs six GAs (at approximately $15,000.00/yr. = $90,000.00), one staff member (approximately $21,000.00/yr.), and other wage employees (approximately $10,000.00/yr.). Operating and inventory costs are approximately $15,000.00/yr. The total costs reach approximately 135,000.00/yr.

3. Time and Expertise Commitment

    Housecalls handles on average between 120 and 140 calls per month. Fewer than 5 percent are not handled in person, and fewer than 5 percent are referred to another level of maintenance. Time per call ranges from two minutes to seven-plus hours. Technical difficulty of calls ranges from wiggling a wire to reformatting the hard drive and reinstalling all software. Level of difficulty of training-type calls ranges from teaching someone how to change the margins on a page to helping someone design an effective course Web page or design an effective course strategy for asynchronous communication. Level of difficulty of calls increases as clients learn and become more sophisticated.

4. Scalability of Housecalls

    Housecalls was piloted with just the Department of Teaching and Learning. It has scaled well to the entire college.

5. Portability of Housecalls

    Colleges in the Appalachian College Association are building support structures for their colleges patterned after the housecalls service. None of them have been functioning long enough to assess their overall effectiveness yet.

The Future of Housecalls—Continued Movement up the Hierarchy

Thus far, much of the housecalls program's resources have gone to meeting needs at the bottom of the hierarchy. However, the service is changing more and more to help faculty as their need for support in instructional technology broadens and becomes more sophisticated. Specifically, housecalls plans to continue and expand in the following areas:

1. Providing training for those approaching the top of the hierarchy, including regularly scheduled training sessions in the lab and continued on-site training by appointment.

2. Providing training at the bottom of the hierarchy, including regularly scheduled training in the lab and taking advantage of opportunities to teach faculty and staff basic maintenance skills while on housecalls. In this way, faculty and staff are becoming more and more self-sufficient in dealing with basic technical problems.

3. Continuing to meet needs as they arise, including taking advantage of occasional on-demand consulting opportunities and formal teaching opportunities. This behavior refers to an interesting phenomenon seen through the housecalls program. Because faculty and staff are learning to trust the GAs who support them, they are turning to them for more and more advice on instructional design issues. For example, faculty members are turning to lab staff for training in using software and for advice on issues such as how to best arrange teaching spaces or how best to use E-mail to promote on-line interaction in a class.

HOUSECALLS AND THEORIES OF INNOVATION

Our experience thus far with the housecalls program and its context have lent support to research and theory done previously in the area of diffusion and implementation in educational technology. Rogers (1971) was one of the pioneers in the field of diffusion research and introduced five attributes of innovations: relative advantage, compatibility, complexity, trialability, and observability. Ely (1990) built on the work of Rogers and others and identified eight conditions that facilitate the implementation of educational technology. We will briefly examine each of Ely's conditions, providing examples from our context that demonstrate the presence of these conditions.

1. Dissatisfaction with the Status Quo

    Clearly, most faculty and staff in the College of Human Resources were dissatisfied with a situation in which they were expected to use computers without technical support. The housecalls service addressed this dissatisfaction. Increasingly, dissatisfaction in other areas is leading to other kinds of implementation as well. For example, at Virginia Tech more and more students are demanding the luxury of having notes, outlines, and the like online. This is causing some faculty to change in ways that they probably would not have otherwise.

2. Knowledge and Skill Exist

    It seems unlikely that the housecalls program could prove successful without the knowledge and skills provided by faculty and staff in the Educational Technology program.

3. Resources Are Available

    Without the availability of SCHEV money, most faculty and staff would not be able to support the original purchase or continued upgrading of equipment and software. In the Department of Teaching and Learning, all faculty and staff are provided with a computer to take home and work/play on. The department also provides a modem and pays the monthly Internet access fee for faculty and staff.

4. Time Is Available

    It is not clear that faculty at Virginia Tech have any more time to spend adopting new technologies than faculty anywhere else.

5. Rewards or Incentives Exist for Participation

    Faculty members receive new computers for participating in FDI. Increasingly, there is anecdotal evidence to suggest that faculty are rewarded for adopting emerging technologies and effective instructional design strategies in the form of higher approval from students. There are formal incentive structures that encourage adopting emerging technologies in instruction as well. The university supports a grant program that awards money for an "innovations in learning with technology" program. Similarly, the College of Human Resources and Education has an Associate Dean of Innovations, who allocates money for the implementation of instructional technology.

6. Participation Is Expected and Encouraged

    Faculty members are required to participate in FDI. Various innovations (such as the use of E-mail) are also required on a department-by-department basis.

7. Commitment by Those Who Are Involved

    Because the housecalls program was started at the college level, and because FDI was started at the university level, there is commitment to the success of each from administrators. Similarly, in the case of the housecalls program, because the services provided are so universally required, there is general commitment to its continued success. The fact that the housecalls program continues to be funded, in spite of the nontrivial costs involved, is perhaps the surest indication of commitment on the part of decision-makers.

8. Leadership Is Evident

    Various leaders are supportive of the housecalls program and in the adoption of emerging technologies in the College of Human Resources and Education. At the university level, the Provost has stressed the importance of using new technologies as much as possible. At the college level, the Dean of Innovations has consistently supported and funded initiatives to integrate technology in teaching and learning endeavors. The chair of the Department of Teaching and Learning has also been instrumental. He introduced and championed the housecalls program and has consistently pushed the department toward adoption of new technologies. He has also stressed the importance of thoughtful application of technology, acknowledging the weaknesses of using technology for technology's sake and stressing the need to support faculty wherever they may find themselves on the "hierarchy" of instructional technology needs.

CONCLUSION

By attempting to meet basic needs first and move up the hierarchy of educational technology needs with faculty and staff, the housecalls program has been able to promote educational technology and build a successful service organization while at the same time providing technical service to the College of Human Resources and Education. The success and longevity of housecalls and FDI and their correlation to theories of innovation suggest that their future is secure as long as the prevailing attitudes and resources in Virginia Tech's College of Human Resources and Education continue. Our experience with housecalls also suggests that if institutions are to successfully adopt new technologies for instruction, they must provide support for faculty, from the most basic technical support to sophisticated instructional support.

REFERENCES

Ely, D. P. (1990). Conditions that facilitate the implementation of educational technology innovations. *Journal of Research on Computing in Education 23* (2), 298–305.

Maslow, A. H. (1970). *Motivation and personality*, 2d ed. New York: Harper & Row.

Rogers, E. M. (1971). *Communication of innovations*. New York: Free Press.

Part Three
Current Developments

Introduction

One of the goals of the *Educational Media and Technology Yearbook* is to present up-to-date information on new developments in the field. This year's volume focuses on developing Web-based resources for instructional planning, principles to guide practice in the delivery of distance education, motivation in design, and the most frequently asked questions. While this section attempts to be comprehensive in its review of current developments, the range of topics is not exhaustive.

The authors in this part represent teachers, students, professors, network information specialists, virtual librarians, and administrators from a variety of educational institutions. The following researchers and practitioners contributed to this part:

Ruth V. Small

Bernard Lee

David R. Moore

Barbara B. Lockee

Donald P. Ely

Lonnie Turbee

Eric Plotnick

Robert Maribe Branch

Web-Based Resources
for K–12 Instructional Planning

Ruth V. Small
Associate Professor
School of Information Studies, Syracuse University

Bernard Lee
Graduate Student
School of Information Studies, Syracuse University

Jack Cooper has taught elementary science for the past 14 years. Jack is preparing to teach a unit on the solar system to the fourth-grade classes in his school. Although he has taught this unit several times before, Jack is looking for instructional planning information—new ways to present the content, more challenging student activities, and different methods for assessing learning. After exhausting the resources of his school library and those available through his district's interlibrary loan service, Jack uses one of the major Internet search engines to look for relevant sites on the World Wide Web. To his delight, the search engine lists 200 sites that contain information on the solar system, but Jack soon realizes that he has to look at each site individually to identify which resources might be useful and then must look at each item to ascertain if it is appropriate for fourth-grade students. After reviewing more than 30 Websites, Jack finds only three that fit his criteria, with only one of sufficient quality to be useful. Since he has no more time to wade through the remaining 170 sites or to use another search engine, Jack ends his search, discouraged and frustrated.

Any educator who has searched the Internet for instructional planning resources knows what an overwhelming experience it can be. Because of the explosion of resources on the Internet/World Wide Web and the lack of one comprehensive, consistent index to those resources, information searching becomes a cumbersome and lengthy activity, often causing the searcher to prematurely end the search process before determining if the most relevant and useful resources have been located (Rivera, Singh, & McAlister 1994).

THE INTERNET AND WORLD WIDE WEB

The Internet had its origins in the 1960s as a U.S. Department of Defense network called the ARPANET (Sterling 1993). This network was initially intended as a decentralized military communication network, but by the 1980s it had become a global computer network, connecting thousands of smaller computer networks in colleges and universities, government agencies, and corporate scientific laboratories. The Transmission Control Protocol/Internet Protocol (TCP/IP), a common set of rules, enabled computer users operating different types of computer platforms in different parts of the world to access the Internet and interact with each other. By the 1990s, Internet access had expanded to anyone with a computer and a modem—schools, libraries, small businesses, and homes around the world.

Currently, the fastest growing part of the Internet is the World Wide Web (usually referred to as "the Web"). Before the development of the Web, the Internet was solely a text-based medium. Since the introduction in the early 1990s of relatively easy-to-use graphical browsers such as Mosaic and Netscape Navigator, millions of people have been able to access all types of data in a unified format on any computer platform. In recent years the Web has transformed the

Internet from a text-based to a multimedia network containing text, pictures in full color, graphics, sound, and even video clips.

Another value-added feature of the Web is its use of "hyperlinks" that allow users to simply click on highlighted text or objects and automatically jump to other relevant information (e.g., definitions). The hyperlink feature allows users to navigate between related sites as well as to pursue topics of interest in depth.

THE WEB AND INSTRUCTIONAL PLANNING

The Internet allows educators to combat isolation, exchange ideas, and obtain information for improving and enhancing their instruction (Honey & Henriquez 1993). It stores hundreds of collections of educational materials containing thousands of documents freely available to teachers.

The number of educational Websites is already enormous and "as time goes by, there will be an ever-increasing pool of electronic online resources providing multifaceted, multicultural, in-depth information" (Rademann 1998). Educational Websites include everything from individual activities to lesson plans, to unit plans containing several lessons to curriculum guides, to state and national education standards mapping. These resources reside in a variety of home sites, including "Ask-an-Expert" services, large federally funded sites, state sites (typically created and maintained by state education departments), sites of individual educators, and commercial sites usually containing both free and fee-based materials.

Ask-an-Expert Services

Digital "Ask-an-Expert" reference services, also known as "Ask-A" services, are the nearly 70 Internet-based question-and-answer services serving the K–12 education community (Lankes 1997). These services, handling education-related questions with a broad scope (e.g., AskERIC) or within a narrowly defined subject area (e.g. Ask-a-Volcanologist), are intended to meet the specific reference needs of their users by providing information with a reasonable turnaround time. "The Virtual Reference Desk," a project of the ERIC Clearinghouse on Information and Technology and the National Library of Education, will establish a single national cooperative digital reference service that incorporates the various Ask-an-Expert services for the K–12 education community. Some examples of current Ask-an-Expert services are:

- AskERIC (http://ericir.syr.edu), developed as a project of the ERIC Clearinghouse on Information and Technology at Syracuse University, is a personalized Internet-based service that provides answers to education-related questions from students, teachers, librarians, and administrators. AskERIC's human intermediaries, using ERIC databases and digests as well as Internet resources, respond to most questions within 48 hours.

- Ask-a-Volcanologist (http://volcano.und.nodak.edu/vwdocs/ask_a.html) is operated out of the University of North Dakota and is staffed by three professional volcanologists located in different parts of the world. The site also features lesson plans and activity ideas for teachers, a keyword-searchable list of frequently asked questions (FAQs) on volcanology, and information on volcanoes throughout the world.

- Ask Dr. Math (http://forum.swarthmore.edu/dr.math/dr-math.html) is a question-and-answer service that originated at Swarthmore College for K–12 (and beyond) math students and teachers. Typical questions posed to Ask Dr. Math come from various branches of mathematics (e.g., geometry, algebra, trigonometry) and include those on exponents, infinity, polynomials, etc. Ask Dr. Math archives its answers in a searchable database organized both by grade level and topic. It also links to other sites containing lesson plans and other instructional materials.

Government Sites

There are a number of large databases funded through various U.S. federal government departments and agencies (e.g. Department of Education, National Library of Education) that include a range of K–12 educational materials for instructional planning. Some examples of national database sites:

- The Eisenhower National Clearinghouse (http://www.enc.org), established by Ohio State University, provides links to lesson plans and classroom-based activities on a variety of math and science topics aimed primarily toward the K–12 community. Topics covered are quite diverse (e.g., "The Africanized Honey Bee," "Fractal Units for the Elementary School Math Student").

- AskERIC Virtual Library (http://ericir.syr.edu/Virtual) contains hundreds of selected educational resources such as lesson plans, InfoGuides, materials related to educational television programs, archives of education-related listservs (e.g., LM_NET, K12ADMIN), other special projects affiliated with AskERIC, and links to other sources of lesson plans. AskERIC InfoGuides are online pathfinders that point educators to Internet, ERIC, and traditional print resources dealing with specific educational topics (e.g., "Reading Motivation," "Guidelines for Writing Lesson Plans," "Integrating the Internet into Classroom Instruction").

- The Smithsonian Education Website (http://educate.si.edu/lessons/start.html) emphasizes inquiry-based, active learning with primary sources and museum collections. It offers lesson plans, teaching and study guides, activities, posters, and slides designed for teachers of upper elementary and middle school students and covering the fields of art, language arts, science, and social studies. This site's educational resources are rich and often feature photographs and reproductions of art and other objects from the various collections of the Smithsonian Institution.

State-Based Sites

A growing number of state-based Websites are offering educators a host of materials provided largely by K–12 teachers in their state. Some examples of state-based Websites:

- Tried *n* True Dynamite Lesson Plans (http://www.ofps.dpi.state.nc.us/OFPS/tc/ TNT/ index.html) is a site created by the North Carolina Department of Public Education. T*n*T offers model lesson plans for teachers by teachers. The lesson plans are organized by grade level and subject area and are mapped to North Carolina education standards. This site also includes a Rubric for Content Criteria, providing eight categories for evaluation of lesson plans.

- TENET or the Texas Education Network (http://www.tenet.edu), a nationally recognized collaborative effort of Texas education organizations, promotes excellence in education in the state of Texas by providing a transparent communications infrastructure linking students, parents, educators, and administrators. Through TENET's Resource Center, educators may access a wealth of materials for curriculum support and development in a range of subject areas, as well as information on professional development for educators.

- UtahLINK (http://www.wce.wwu.edu/necc97/poster2/UtahLink/WebWhacker/WW1.html) is part of the Utah Education Network. Its goal is to provide Utah public schools with Internet connectivity, training, resources, and collaboration opportunities between classrooms across the state. UtahLINK offers lesson plans that are specific to the state's core curriculum, covering a wide range of subjects from fine arts to physical education.

Individual Sites

There are a myriad of grassroots Websites, developed and maintained by individual educators throughout the country, that offer high-quality, useful K–12 educational resources to their colleagues. Some examples of individual sites:

- Kathy Schrock's Guide for Educators (http://www.capecod.net/schrockguide) is a compilation of Internet sites organized by subject headings that are useful for curriculum design and professional development. This site includes original material to help teachers understand basic Internet concepts, more than 1,400 annotated links to other Websites, and a set of tools for evaluating Web pages.

- Carol Hurst's Children's Literature Site (http://www.carolhurst.com), created by Carol Otis Hurst and Rebecca Otis, contains curriculum development resources and ideas for integrating literature with a range of content areas. It features a collection of children's book reviews as well as a newsletter and professional products for teachers. In addition, the site offers ideas, activities, games, and lesson plans on how to incorporate children's literature into the curriculum.

- The Weather Dude (http://nwlink.com/~wxdude), authored by Nick Walker, a Seattle meteorologist, offers information about weather and meteorology on topics such as hurricanes, air quality, and climate change. The site links to lesson plans and classroom activities for teaching about weather to students in grades K–12.

Commercial Sites

There are many commercial educational sites on the Web, offering a combination of free and fee-based resources. Some examples of commercial sites for K–12 educators:

- Microsoft's Encarta Online (http://encarta.msn.com/schoolhouse/lessons/default.asp) offers a collection of tested lesson plans for the K–12 community. These lesson plans are organized by topic and link to Encarta's electronic encyclopedia, as well as a host of related Websites. Lesson plans cover a wide range of topics from fine arts to computers and information technology.

- Discovery Channel School Online (http://school.discovery.com/importantinformation/index.html), a service of Discovery Communications, offers a wide range of instructional resources for grade K–12 educators. Its Index to Lesson Plans provides a list of lesson plans related to Discovery Channel video programs. Lesson plans are geared primarily toward science, social studies, language arts, and the humanities. They are organized by subject area, topic, and title and linked to the Mid-Continent Regional Educational Laboratory (McREL) curriculum standards, utilizing an easy-to-use index.

- Classroom Connect (http://www.classroom.net) offers a variety of information and services, such as a searchable database of K–12 educational products, including videos, books, training systems, conferences, and newsletters; featured monthly links to lesson plans to copy and use; online instructional materials; and a guide to searching the Internet.

LIMITATIONS OF THE WEB

"While the potential of the Internet is quite vast, it can be problematic to access its rich information and communication (educational) resources" (Milheim 1997). The explosive growth of the Internet and the Web and a lack of a centralized organizational structure to the Internet has made searching for information a difficult and complicated task. The amount of time and effort required, the lack of searching precision, and the information overload that results severely limit the usefulness of the Internet/Web as a resource for instructional planning (Tomaiuolo & Packer 1996).

Each of the Websites described above operates as a separate "library collection" of information, often with different access features that require the user to tailor each search differently in response to that site's unique vocabulary and access mechanisms. The various search engines (an Internet program that searches through some defined data set) facilitate Web navigation but lack overlap, are inconsistent, often retrieve irrelevant documents, and are by no means complete or authoritative (Dong & Su 1997; Tomaiuolo & Packer 1996).

EDUCATORS' INFORMATION LITERACY

Today's teachers often lack experience in using the Web and "have no idea of the broadness of information accessible via this network" (Rademann 1998). Information literacy (effective information searching and retrieval skills [e.g., use of Boolean operators] and information-seeking strategies) is becoming as important for teachers as it is for their students. These skills include 1) being able to form an appropriate search strategy, 2) understanding the capability and limitations of each search engine in order to select the most appropriate one for their search, 3) being thoroughly familiar with the unique search features of that search engine, and 4) identifying, locating, evaluating, organizing, and effectively using electronic information. Possessing effective information literacy skills will help educators solve their information problems and satisfy their information needs.

Although there has been some research on the information needs and search patterns of specific groups of educators (e.g., Degge 1982; Grunwald 1986), little is known about the general information-seeking skills of K–12 educators, or what factors contribute to easy and successful searching. Feld (in Mendels 1998) found that 78 percent of teachers reported using the Internet to find information or conduct research. In a study of teachers' Internet use, Small et al. (1998) found that 85 percent (221) of all respondents reported using the Internet sometimes or often for designing their lessons. The study also revealed a set of essential elements (e.g., grade level, teaching method, grouping of learners) that teachers use to define and describe the educational materials they seek. These elements formed the basis of GEM, a project whose mission is to organize and provide educators with quick and easy access to educational materials on the Internet.

GEM: THE GATEWAY TO
EDUCATIONAL MATERIALS

The National Library of Education (NLE) Advisory Task Force articulated the need to improve the organization and accessibility of the substantial, but uncataloged, collections of educational materials available on various federal, state, university, nonprofit, and commercial Internet sites. The Gateway to Educational Materials (GEM) Project of the ERIC Clearinghouse on Information and Technology, sponsored by the NLE and the U.S. Department of Education, teams a variety of public and private information providers, national and state educators' organizations, regional education laboratories, and state education departments to develop a common gateway that provides the nation's teachers with "one-stop, any-stop access" to the thousands of lesson plans, curriculum units, and other Internet-based educational resources. In essence, GEM is intended to alleviate educators' "needle in a haystack" Internet search experiences.

GEM users can enter the Gateway (the union catalog of resources) through any of the online educational resource collections within the GEM system (e.g., the AskERIC Virtual Library, Eisenhower National Clearinghouse, Smithsonian), specify the parameters of their information need (e.g., "high-quality fourth-grade unit plans on the solar system"), receive a rich set of records describing only those resources that meet the specified criteria, and obtain direct access to any or all of those resources, plucked from multiple databases and Websites. The GEM system uses a common vocabulary and searching features that filter out information that does not meet the user's specific requirements and provides quick and easy access to many educational collections simultaneously rather than one at a time. Each resource is described by a simple, standardized metadata record (i.e., a set of descriptive terms that are "more informative than an index entry but less complete than a formal cataloging record" [Weibel 1995]). The metadata record points the user to the actual resource. GEM provides a central organization of and access to the educational materials on the Internet that educators have needed and wanted for so long.

Jack Cooper is again preparing to teach his annual fourth-grade science unit on the solar system. This time he uses the GEM catalog by first navigating to a "host" site—any of the dozens of Internet sites participating in the project. Jack can choose to browse through the GEM catalog or explore the contents of the catalog by using a Web search engine that searches not only the host site but also all other participating GEM sites. The catalog allows Jack to describe his specific information need on the basis of a number of access points (e.g., topic, subject area, grade level, quality level, state and national curriculum standards), thereby assuring a more precise retrieval of resources that meet Jack's criteria. The resources retrieved may come from any or all of the participating GEM sites. Once he decides which resources are most appropriate, Jack can access each full-text document by simply clicking on a link. He can then print out any document he wishes to have in hard copy. Within minutes, Jack walks away with dozens of great teaching ideas to use and share with colleagues.

REFERENCES

Degge, R. M. (1982). The classroom art teacher as inquirer. *Studies in Art Education 24* (1), 25–32.

Dong, X., and Su, L. T. (1997, Apr.). Search engines on the World Wide Web and information retrieval from the Internet: A review and evaluation. *Online & CD-ROM Review 21* (2), 67–82.

Grunwald, K. A. (1986). *An information needs analysis of Colorado vocational educators.* Doctoral dissertation, Colorado State University.

Honey, M., and Henriquez, A. (1993). *Telecommunications and K–12 educators: Findings from a national survey.* Bank Street College of Education (ED 59923).

Lankes, R. D. (1997). "Virtual Reference Desk: Briefing Packet" (1998, Feb.). Internet page at URL: http://www.vrd.org.

Mendels, P. (1998, Mar. 15). Teachers see benefits of Internet, but drawbacks raise concerns. *Technology Cybertimes* (Internet journal at URL: http://www.nytimes.com/library/tech/98/03/ cyber/articles/15poll. html).

Milheim, W. D. (1997, Mar.). Instructional utilization of the Internet in public school settings. *TechTrends 42* (2), 19–23.

Rademann, T. (1998). Information unlimited: Employing Internet resources in education. Internet page at URL: http://www.isoc.org/inet97/proceedings/D3/D3_1.HTM).

Rivera, J. C., Singh, S. K., and McAlister, K. (1994). Mosaic: An educator's best friend. *T.H.E. Journal 22* (3), 91–94.

Small, R. V., et al. (1998). *An investigation of preK–12 educators' information needs and search behaviors on the Internet.* Paper presented at the Annual Conference of the Association for Educational Communications & Technology, St. Louis, MO.

Sterling, B. (1993, Feb.). Short history of the Internet. *The Magazine of Fantasy and Science Fiction.* Internet page at URL: http://www.forthnet.gr/forthnet/isoc/short.history.of.internet.

Tomaiuolo, N. G., and Packer, J. G. (1996, June). An analysis of Internet search engines: Assessment of over 200 search queries. *Computers in Libraries*, 58–62.

Weibel, S. (1995, July). Metadata: The foundations of resource description. *D-Lib Magazine*, 1–6. Internet journal at URL: http://www.dlib.org/dlib/July95/07weibel.html.

A Taxonomy of Bandwidth
Considerations and Principles to Guide Practice in the
Design and Delivery of Distance Education

David R. Moore
Portland State University

Barbara B. Lockee
Virginia Polytechnic Institute and State University

ABSTRACT

Often, distance teaching technologies are chosen for reasons of availability rather than necessary capacity. Instructors are challenged with designing events that take advantage of the abilities of delivery technologies without exceeding their transmission capacity. Therefore, an understanding of bandwidth and its role in distributed learning systems is necessary for the creation of appropriate distance education activities. The goal of this chapter is to assist distance educators in making wise instructional development choices to maximize the effectiveness of available bandwidth by making tradeoffs between applicable variables.

Distance education is the most rapidly growing form of instruction in the world (McIsaac & Gunawardena 1996). Its popularity is due in part to its distributed nature, its ability to bring learning opportunities to the student who may otherwise not be able to participate. As distance education evolves to serve its clientele in more convenient ways, instructional providers have developed a strong reliance upon the Internet as a delivery mechanism (Markwood 1994), increasing and localizing course availability to a degree unattainable by previous communication channels.

The movement of distance education to the desktop computer reflects the growing demand for instruction that is time- and place-independent, addressing the needs of the individual student (Brown & Brown 1994). The convergence of audio, video, text, and graphics in a networked, readily accessible virtual space has prompted a variety of instructional packaging solutions, from asynchronous (occurring at different times) text-based interactions to real-time desktop videoconferencing, enhanced by a never-ending array of peripherals such as electronic whiteboards and application sharing capabilities. While room-based videoconferencing also continues to grow in popularity, Web-based instruction extends the reach of traditional distance education to locations and hours beyond such systems. Learners with an Internet connection can participate in coursework at their convenience without having to go to a given location at a designated time, the constraints imposed by two-way large group conferencing.

While networked instruction to the desktop offers a variety of possibilities for course delivery, it is not without flaw. Slow download time, delayed audio, and jerky video images are the result of such a system's primary limitation—bandwidth. As distance educators seek to take advantage of the power of desktop computing for distributed learning, bandwidth constrains potentialities by putting a limit on the information transfer capabilities of various teaching technologies.

Instructional providers encounter challenges maximizing the instructional potential of this confined resource. Unfortunately, the task is not always easy, as distance educators often inherit a media infrastructure and typically are not in a position to increase the physical capability of their systems. Instead, they must choose appropriate instructional and media attributes that are effective and yet use the existing bandwidth wisely. Different instructional strategies require different levels of bandwidth. While the physical infrastructure of available bandwidth places constraints on the possibilities, a course designer has complete flexibility working under that ceiling.

Bandwidth is a volume measure of information flow. On a digital network it is the number of bits that can be transported in a certain period of time. Digital networks are composed of a number of pieces that may include a sender's computer, a connection from the sender's computer to a router's, a connection from the router's to the receiver's computer, and the receiver's computer. The slowest link in that path will define the system's available bandwidth.

When planning network use, one should keep in mind that effective bandwidth is determined by the weakest link in a system. An instructor may have access to a high-speed network connection. However, if the students do not have this same luxury, the rate at which they receive data will be dependent upon their connection, not the instructor's connection. Chances are that the lowest common denominator for most situations will be the telephone line and modem speed.

Instructional design theories recommend that instruction be designed before a medium is chosen. Unfortunately, in the practice of distance education programs, such procedures are rarely possible. Designers usually will have some idea of the system in which they will be expected to present. One instructional parameter that is usually fixed is available bandwidth.

Distance educators must recognize the limitations that their bandwidth capability provides and attempt to maximize this resource to its highest instructional possibilities. One of the goals of designing distance instruction is to reduce cognitive load by eliminating redundant or superfluous information. The goal of this chapter is to assist potential distance educators in making wise instructional development choices to maximize the effectiveness of available bandwidth by making informed tradeoffs between applicable variables.

RATIONALE: WHAT IS THE BANDWIDTH/INSTRUCTION PROBLEM?

The first step in maximizing the use of bandwidth is to identify how much bandwidth is available to the sender and receivers. This assessment involves taking an inventory of the originating network and the network to which students have access. Network technology ranges from regular low bandwidth telephone lines to relatively high bandwidth dedicated fiber lines (see Figure 1). For technical descriptions of how these network technologies operate, see Portway and Lane 1994.

Communication Service	Transmission Rate
OC-3 (Optical Carrier-level 3)	155 Mbps
DS-3 (Digital Signal-level 3)	45 Mbps
T-1	1.544 Mbps
ISDN (Integrated Services Digital Network)	128 to 384 kbps
POTS (Plain Old Telephone Service)	9.6 to 19.2 hbps

Figure 1. Transmission Rates for Different Communications Services (adapted from Portway & Lane 1994).

Stretching a Fixed Resource

The problem of bandwidth has been framed in the context of dealing with a fixed resource. Once it is recognized that working with fixed bandwidth is a zero-sum game, that one instructional variable may be changed as long as another is correspondingly manipulated, tradeoffs can begin to be made that enhance and focus on instructional goals and objectives. A simple algebra formula describes this efficiency:

$$\text{Fidelity}(b1) + \text{Time}(b2) + \text{Interaction}(b3) + \text{Realism}(b4) = (B)\text{andwidth}$$

These variables are explained in the following section. Each variable consumes bandwidth. This algebraic representation allows the reduction of one variable and, thus, the ability to increase another. Unfortunately, this formula is only a heuristic to guide practice. There is not a one-to-one correspondence of bandwidth consumption between the variables. The designer must keep an eye on the degree to which manipulating a particular variable affects available bandwidth. Adjustments to one variable could have large effects on other variables and how the remaining transmission capacity can be used.

These variables should be manipulated until an optimal combination is reached for instructional goals to be achieved under the given circumstances. In many cases, this process will provide an incentive to refocus efforts on what truly are the instructional goals and discard those elements that do not further these ends. The result is distance education that assists the learner by reducing cognitive load. What follows is a review of variables that can be manipulated to reduce the consumption of bandwidth and a description of the resulting instructional effect.

Time/Place

Distance education often is referred to in terms of time and place. One of the strongest advantages of distance education is the ability to break the constraints of both to provide educational opportunities to those who may otherwise not participate. With regard to bandwidth usage, different instructional strategies tend to reflect different bandwidth demands because of the nature of the end-user media capabilities. The timing, or synchronicity, of student access to instructional events or resources will affect the rate at which the data are received. For example, a synchronous activity such as two-way videoconferencing requires a significant amount of bandwidth because two channels of information are being sent and received simultaneously. The location of access to instructional events or resources will also influence the types of information and activities in which students can participate, simply due to the nature of bandwidth availability at prospective venues. Figure 2 illustrates examples of time and place conditions that are applicable to distance education. The conditions in each quadrant will be discussed in terms of the amount of bandwidth likely needed. Consider the difference between using the Internet at school and at home. Chances are that many educational institutions have at least T-1 access (1.5 Mbps), while most home Internet access occurs through a 14.4 to 56.6 kbps modem.

		Time	
		Same	*Different*
Place	*Same*	Traditional Classroom	Conferencing Applications
Place	*Different*	Lab-Based Instruction	Web-Based Instruction

Figure 2. Examples of Time/Place Instruction (adapted from Johansen et al. 1991).

Same Time/Same Place

Instruction occurring in this quadrant is often referred to as the "traditional classroom" approach, although most would find such a generalization problematic. This model of instruction is typically seen as nondistributed and thus needing little or no bandwidth. Web uses in the classroom will, of course, need Internet access and at least some lower level of connectivity such as a standard telephone modem. Broader uses of bandwidth will be analyzed in the remaining three quadrants.

Same Time/Different Place

Synchronous distance education usually relies on video-based forms of instruction, although alternative methods of desktop collaboration, such as audio conferencing and application sharing, are quickly becoming popular. Synchronous video-delivered distance education can be very bandwidth-intensive, especially if the originating site is connected and interacting with many different sites. In this case, one connection port is handling both an outgoing and an incoming signal, therefore doubling the amount of data being carried through the system. This type of instruction thus needs more bandwidth to accommodate the two-way flow of information. Examples of higher bandwidth activities in this model are two-way room-based videoconferencing or desktop videoconferencing through dedicated networks. However, same time/different place events can also occur through lower bandwidth channels such as Web chat forums using the Internet as the communication device.

Different Time/Same Place

This model of distance education usually occurs in a campus-based lab setting, where many students may access specialized instructional materials, such as curriculum-specific software sent over a local network. This model has the advantage of maintaining more control of the elements that could decrease bandwidth (i.e., ensuring that all the students have access to the same network that the instructor does). Additionally, that network does not have to compete with traffic beyond itself. Instruction conducted in this quadrant typically takes advantage of the larger capacity dedicated networks to which institutions have access, such as T-1 or higher. The Virginia Tech Math emporium is an example of such a setting. In this 500-seat computer lab, freshmen work at their own pace through software developed by the math faculty. Students can access courseware 24 hours a day, seven days a week.

Different Time/Different Place

This model is the fastest growing approach to distance education due to the advent of the Internet as an instructional delivery tool. The increase in Web-based instruction has led to the creation of "virtual universities," or program offerings that are completely time- and place-independent. Regarding bandwidth, the more distributed over time and place the instructional delivery system is, the less bandwidth-intensive it tends to be. Therefore, the advantage of asynchronous use of such networked instruction over the previous model is the lack of time and place constraints for the student. Because learners access network-based courseware at different times in this model, the load on the originating server is thus dispersed. Because this model benefits largely from place-independence, students can engage in coursework from a variety of settings at any time, from the higher-capacity access found in an institutional or workplace computer lab to the lower-bandwidth, but more convenient, connection from home.

Fidelity

Fidelity is the degree to which original data is accurately reproduced (i.e., the quality of transmission). Digital technologies allow reproductions with almost 100 percent accuracy. In order to do this, network protocols have been created to ensure that errors are not accepted as valid transmissions. Each time the system encounters an error it rejects it and requests the data again, ensuring validity. "Noise" delays this verification process and results in reducing the available bandwidth level.

This process is particularly burdensome when the original source contains extraneous data. For example, if an audio file has been recorded in a room with halogen lights, small background buzz will also exist on the track. If this file is sent through the network, the buzz takes as much bandwidth to deliver as a track without the incidental noise. Unfortunately, the extraction of relevant information will be much more difficult from the track with the buzz. Remember: Garbage in equals garbage out. Networks can only transfer at the initial quality state or less. One may not be able to increase a network's capacity, but one can ensure that the state of the initial data is served to clientele in a preferable condition.

Degree of Realism

Graphic information is a flexible attribute that may be adjusted to reduce data and yet retain instructional meaning. Effective instructional graphics are often those that are midway between realistic and rudimentary (Dwyer 1978). By changing photographs to line drawings, one can minimize the data transmitted while maintaining or increasing instructional value. Many standard graphics can be converted into vector graphics (i.e., illustrations that are defined by mathematical equations) that are translated and redrawn by the student's computer. Vector graphics are dramatically smaller in file size than raster graphics (i.e., photographs), which have specific pixels assigned to specific positions, therefore producing a larger file size and using more bandwidth (Rieber 1994).

Color is another attribute that can often be reduced without sacrificing instructional value. Modern computer monitors can display millions of color variations. However, often this extra color information does not add value to the instructional presentation. A black-and-white graphic may be just as effective as an instructional cue if color is not necessary to understand the concept or to recognize image elements (Dwyer 1978). Remember that by reducing the bandwidth a graphic is consuming, one can put the bandwidth to work elsewhere in the course design. Those color elements that are critical to the instructional message should be emphasized, while others may be altered to black and white.

As with any instructional event, information can be represented through a variety of mechanisms. A concept may be conveyed by a simple graphic image or perhaps may require more realistic visual detail in order to promote learning. Just as in Dale's Cone of Experience (see Figure 3), where media content moves from the abstract to the concrete presentation (Dale 1969), images can also range from less realistic line drawings (lower bandwidth) to extremely realistic displays, such as color photographs or digital video (higher bandwidth).

Bandwidth is highly correlated with the degree of realism associated with information, as closer approximations of reality demand higher bandwidth. For example, a Web-based course consisting of primarily textual data and some supplemental static images would require far less bandwidth than two-way videoconferencing, or even desktop videoconferencing, simply because of the amount of data necessary to depict motion. To some extent, the degree of realism can also be altered to reflect constraints on the instructional delivery system. If learners are accessing course materials from home through a modem, then a process may possibly be depicted through a series of still photographic images instead of a more bandwidth-intensive digital movie.

Streaming technologies allow for the transmission of audio and video representations of information by delivering small amounts of data at a time, thus decreasing the amount of bandwidth necessary for the acquisition of such typically large data files. Figure 4 illustrates the requirements of various levels of information and the relative amount of bandwidth needed.

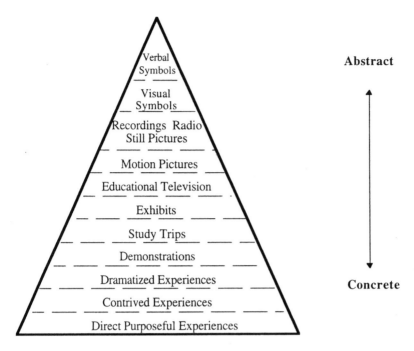

Figure 3. Dale's Cone of Experience.

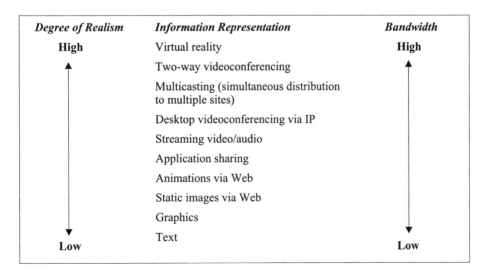

Figure 4. Realism, Information, and Bandwidth.

Level of Interaction

Another variable that has an impact on the amount of bandwidth needed is the level of inter-action inherent within an instructional event. Older forms of distance education focused on the "one-to-many" model, where the teacher was the originator of information and the remote site students were merely receivers. Communication with the instructor was done largely outside of class time, either through the mail or telephone office hours. As instructional models have evolved to become more student-centered, so have the technologies used for distance teaching and learning. While labeling a course "interactive" seems almost a necessity, developers must realize that building in interaction also requires a payment in bandwidth. Simultaneous two-way communication cuts available bandwidth by half, begging the questions "When is interaction necessary?" and "What are some alternatives?" Can the learning outcomes be achieved through the one-way presentation of information, or will discussion, collaboration, or role-playing be an integral part of such achievement? If interaction is a necessary component of the instructional event, then is a high degree of realism necessary in such an interaction? Is a video image really important, or can ideas be effectively communicated through audio or text? Figure 5 illustrates the level of bandwidth needed for various types of interaction strategies.

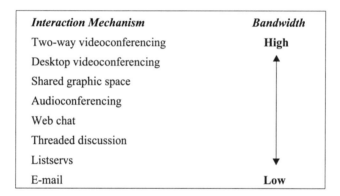

Figure 5. Types of Interaction and Bandwidth.

CONSIDERATIONS AND PRINCIPLES TO GUIDE PRACTICE

The goal of this chapter was to assist distance educators in making wise instructional strategy choices to maximize the effectiveness of available bandwidth by making tradeoffs between available instructional variables. A number of areas have been delineated that may be examined to ensure that instruction stays focused on goals and objectives while working within the constraints that bandwidth resources impose. These suggestions are presented under the assumption that bandwidth, in the short-term, is not easily changed. Unfortunately, even though an instructional designer can manipulate available variables, sometimes instructional goals may not be attainable within a given system. At some point, a decision must be made whether to compromise goals or change or cancel the instructional event. Sometimes it is better to consider a completely different instructional strategy. However, the opportunities within distance education are varied enough that in most cases, with enough planning and consideration, an instructor will be able to use available resources to communicate effectively with students.

Designing instruction and maximizing available bandwidth is not a linear process that can be followed step-by-step. The internal conversation of looking at design goals and accounting for resources, such as the amount of bandwidth the instruction will take, is often neglected in instructional design models. Hopefully, these suggestions on integrating bandwidth have demonstrated the importance of designing instruction not only for instructional effectiveness but also to fit within the limitations of available resources.

Designing for bandwidth involves making tradeoffs and possibly altering the instructional design process. The opportunities for tradeoffs are particularly clear with computer-mediated education, but the same ideas can be applied to instructional design as a practical, real-world activity.

REFERENCES

Brown, F. B., and Brown, Y. (1994). Distance education around the world. In *Distance education: Strategies and tools*, ed. B. Willis. Englewood Cliffs, NJ: Educational Technology Publications, 3–39.

Dale, E. (1969). *Audiovisual methods in teaching*, 3d ed. New York: Holt, Rinehart & Winston.

Dwyer, F. M. (1978). *Strategies for improving visual learning*. State College, PA: Learning Services.

Johansen, R., et al. (1991). *Leading business teams: How teams can use technology and group process tools to enhance performance*. Reading, MA: Addison-Wesley.

Markwood, R. (1994). Computer tools for distance education. In *Distance education: Strategies and tools*, ed. B. Willis. Englewood Cliffs, NJ: Educational Technology Publications, 199–211.

McIsaac, M., and Gunawardena, C. (1996). Distance education. In *Handbook of research for educational communications and technology*, ed. D. Jonassen. New York: Simon & Schuster/Macmillan, 403–37.

Portway, P., and Lane, C. (1994). *Teleconferencing and distance education*, 2d ed. Livermore, CA: Applied Business Telecommunications.

Rieber, L. (1994). *Computers, graphics & learning*. Dubuque, IA: Wm. C. Brown.

The Field of Educational Technology:
Update 1997
A Dozen Frequently Asked Questions

Donald P. Ely
Senior Associate for Educational Technology
ERIC Clearinghouse on Information & Technology
Professor Emeritus
Instructional Design, Development & Evaluation
Syracuse University

Reprinted from ERIC® Digest, December 1997, EDO-IR-97-09

Educational technology is a term widely used in the field of education (and other areas), but it is often used with different meanings. The word technology is used by some to mean hardware—the devices that deliver information and serve as tools to accomplish a task—but those working in the field use technology to refer to a systematic process of solving problems by scientific means. Hence, educational technology properly refers to a particular approach to achieving the ends of education. Instructional technology refers to the use of such technological processes specifically for teaching and learning.

Other terms, such as instructional development or educational media, which refer to particular parts of the field, are also used by some to refer to the field as a whole.

1. WHAT IS EDUCATIONAL TECHNOLOGY?

The most recent definition of the field (which uses the term, instructional technology) has been published by the Association for Educational Communications and Technology (AECT):

> *Instructional Technology is the theory and practice of design, development, utilization, management, and evaluation of processes and resources for learning.*

The complete definition, with its rationale, is presented in the AECT publication:

- Seels, B. B., and Richey, R. C. (1994). *Instructional technology: The definition and domains of the field.* Washington, DC: Association for Educational Communications and Technology.

An overview of the field can be found in:

- Gagne, Robert M. (Ed.). (1987). *Instructional technology: Foundations.* Hillsdale, NJ: Lawrence Erlbaum.

- Anglin, Gary J. (Ed.). (1995). *Instructional technology: Past, present, and future* (2nd ed.). Englewood, CO: Libraries Unlimited.

2. WHAT ARE THE ROOTS OF EDUCATIONAL TECHNOLOGY?

The field is essentially a 20th century movement with the major developments occurring during and immediately after World War II. What began with an emphasis on audiovisual communications media gradually became focused on the systematic development of teaching and learning procedures which were based in behavioral psychology. Currently, major contributing fields are cognitive psychology, social psychology, psychometrics, perception psychology, and management. The basic history of the field was written by Saettler.

- Saettler, Paul E. (1990). *The evolution of American educational technology.* Englewood, CO: Libraries Unlimited.

A briefer history may be found in:

- Reiser, Robert. (1987). Instructional technology: A history. In Robert M. Gagne (Ed.), *Instructional technology: Foundations* (pp. 11–48). Hillsdale, NJ: Lawrence Erlbaum.

3. WHAT IS A GOOD SOURCE OF RESEARCH FINDINGS?

- Thompson, Ann, Simonson, Michael, and Hargrave, Constance. (1996). *Educational technology: A review of the research* (2nd ed.). Washington, DC: Association for Educational Communications and Technology.

- Kozma, Robert. (1991). Learning with media. *Review of Education Research 61* (2), 179–211.

4. WHAT DO EDUCATIONAL TECHNOLOGISTS DO?

Most educational technologists carry out one or a few of the functions performed in the field. For example, some design instruction, some produce instructional materials, and others manage instructional computing services or learning resources collections. The competencies for instructional development specialists and material design and production specialists are published in:

- Hutchison, Cathleen. (1993). *Instructor competencies: The standards.* (Vol. 1). Batavia, IL: International Board of Standards for Training Performance and Instruction.

A comprehensive description of the functions of education technology personnel is given in:

- Silber, Kenneth. (Ed.). (1979). *The definition of educational technology* (pp. 55–79). Washington, DC: Association for Educational Communications and Technology.

5. WHERE ARE EDUCATIONAL TECHNOLOGISTS EMPLOYED?

Until recently, most educational technologists were employed in schools and colleges as directors of resource centers and developers of curriculum materials. Many are still employed in such positions, but increasing numbers are being employed by training agencies in business, industry, government, the military, and the health professions. Colleges and universities employ individuals who are involved in instructional improvement programs that use a variety of technologies.

6. WHERE DO EDUCATIONAL TECHNOLOGISTS OBTAIN PROFESSIONAL EDUCATION?

Professional programs are offered mostly at the graduate level, although there are a few two-year postsecondary programs in junior and community colleges. Lists of programs are found in:

- Branch, Robert M., and Minor, Barbara B. (Eds.). (1997). Doctoral programs in instructional technology (pp. 233–44), and Master's degree and six year programs in instructional technology (pp. 244–66). In Robert M. Branch & Barbara B. Minor (Eds.). (1997). *Educational media and technology yearbook.* Englewood, CO: Libraries Unlimited.

- Johnson, Jenny K. (Ed.). (1995). *Degree curricula in educational communications and technology: A descriptive directory* (5th ed.). Washington, DC: Association for Educational Communications and Technology.

7.   WHAT FIELDS OFFER GOOD PREPARATION FOR EDUCATIONAL TECHNOLOGY?

Many people enter the field following an undergraduate program in teacher education. More people come from the basic disciplines of the arts and sciences—English, sociology, communications, psychology, the physical sciences, and mathematics. Although there seldom are prerequisites for study in the field, persons who have good preparation in psychology and mathematics seem to have a head start. Formal course work and experience in human relations are helpful.

8.   WHAT ARE THE MAJOR PROFESSIONAL ORGANIZATIONS?

In the United States, most educational technologists would be a member of one or more of the following associations:

- American Educational Research Association (AERA)
  1230 17th Street NW, Washington, DC 20036-3078

- American Society for Training & Development (ASTD)
  1630 Duke Street, Box 1443, Alexandria, VA 22313

- Association for Educational Communications & Technology (AECT)
  1025 Vermont Avenue NW, Suite 820, Washington, DC 20005-3547

- International Society for Performance Improvement (ISPI)
  1300 L Street NW, Suite 1250, Washington, DC 20005

- International Society for Technology in Education (ISTE)
  1787 Agate Street, Eugene, OR 97403-1923

- Society for Applied Learning Technology (SALT)
  50 Culpepper Street, Warrenton, VA 22186.

Major organizations in other parts of the world include:

- Association for Media & Technology in Education in Canada (AMTEC)
  3-1750 The Queensway, Suite 1318
  Etobicoke, Ontario M9C 5H5, Canada

- Association for Educational & Training Technology (AETT)
  Centre for Continuing Education
  The City University, Northampton Square
  London EC1V 0HB, U.K.

9.   WHAT PUBLICATIONS DO EDUCATIONAL TECHNOLOGISTS READ?

The most frequently read journals include:

- *British Journal of Educational Technology*, published by the National Council for Educational Technology, Sir William Lyons Road, Science Park, University of Warwick, Coventry CV4 7EZ, U.K.

- *Learning and Leading with Technology*, published by ISTE.

- *Innovations in Education and Training International*, published by AETT, Kogan Page Ltd., 120 Pentonville Rd., London N1 9JN, U.K.

- *Educational Technology*, published by Educational Technology Publications, 700 Palisade Avenue, Englewood Cliffs, NJ 07632.

- *Educational Technology Research and Development*, published by AECT.

- *Journal of Research on Computing in Education*, published by ISTE.

- *TechTrends*, published by AECT.

10. WHAT ARE THE COMPREHENSIVE REFERENCES FOR THE FIELD?

There are two major encyclopedias:

- Plomp, T., and Ely, D. P. (Eds.). (1996). *The international encyclopedia of educational technology* (2nd ed.). New York: Elsevier Science.

- Unwin, Derek, and McAleese, Ray (Eds.). (1988). *The encyclopedia of educational media communications and technology* (2nd ed.). Westport, CT: Greenwood Press.

There are two major yearbooks which offer articles on current issues and extensive lists of people, organizations, literature, and other resources:

- Branch, R. M., and Minor, Barbara B. (Eds.). (1997). *Educational media and technology yearbook.* Englewood, CO: Libraries Unlimited.

- Osborne, Christopher W. (Ed.). (1993). *International yearbook of educational training and technology.* London: Kogan Page, and NJ: Nichols Publishing Co.

11. WHAT TEXTBOOKS ARE COMMONLY USED?

There are dozens of books used in educational technology courses. Selection of titles depends upon the content of the course, the primary audience, and the instructor's objectives. General textbooks that have been used in a variety of courses are:

- Heinich, Robert, Molenda, Michael, Russell, James, and Smaldino, S. (1996). *Instructional media and technologies for learning* (5th ed.). New York: Macmillan.

- Dick, Walter, and Carey, Lou. (1996). *The systematic design of instruction* (4th ed.). Harper Collins College. Glenview, IL: Scott, Foresman and Co.

12. WHERE CAN MORE SPECIFIC INFORMATION ABOUT EDUCATIONAL TECHNOLOGY BE FOUND?

The ERIC (Educational Resources Information Center) system sponsored by the Office of Educational Research and Improvement of the U.S. Department of Education has been selecting documents on educational technology since 1966 and indexing articles from key journals since 1969. Abstracts of the documents can be found in:

- *Resources in Education*, published monthly by the U.S. Government Printing Office and available in more than 3,500 libraries throughout the world.

Selected articles which have been indexed from educational technology journals are listed in:

- *Current Index to Journals in Education*, found in many libraries or available from Oryx Press, 4041 North Central at Indian School Road, Suite 700, Phoenix, AZ 85012-3397. (800-279-6799)

ERIC Database. Computer searching of the ERIC database is available in many academic and some public libraries. The ERIC database can also be searched over the Internet and on some commercial networks. Specific questions can be addressed to:

- ERIC Clearinghouse on Information & Technology (ERIC/IT)
  4-194 Center for Science and Technology
  Syracuse University, Syracuse, NY 13244-4100
  (315) 443-3640; (800) 464-9107
  URL: http://ericir.syr.edu/ithome

There are World Wide Web sites that focus on discussion of issues in educational technology. The addresses are:

> http://www.aect.org/
> http://h-net.msu.edu/~edweb
> http://www.askeric.org

The ERIC/IT Clearinghouse has a publications list of monographs and digests about current issues and developments in the field and publishes a newsletter, *ERIC/IT Update*, twice each year. Both items are available without charge.

Educational MOO
Text-based Virtual Reality for Learning in Community

Lonnie Turbee
Online Content Specialist
Syracuse Language Systems

Reprinted from ERIC® Digest, March 1997, EDO-IR-97-01

WHAT IS A MOO?

MOO stands for "**M**ulti-user domain, **O**bject-**O**riented." Early multi-user domains, or "MUDs," began as net-based dungeons-and-dragons type games, but MOOs have evolved from these origins to become some of cyberspace's most fascinating and engaging online communities. These are social environments in a text-based virtual reality where people gather to chat with friends, meet new people, and help build the MOO.

Users (sometimes called players or characters) connect from anywhere in the world and are able to communicate with others in real time (as opposed to the delayed communication of e-mail). Users can create rooms, objects, and programs that recreate in text anything the user might imagine. For example, "Gregor" at schMOOze University created a monkey that hands out dry towels to swimmers. This program causes lines of text describing the monkey's actions to appear at regular intervals on the screens of all the users in the same "room."

WHAT IS AN EDUCATIONAL MOO?

An educational MOO has an academic theme and uses a variety of MOO communication tools such as internal e-mail, newspapers, documents, blackboards, and classrooms to accommodate a variety of teaching styles. Teachers can use these tools in harmony with the goals for the class while exploiting the nature of MOO as a student-centered learning environment.

Most MOOs are not designed with specific academic purposes in mind, and some are simply not appropriate for young people. The following successful educational MOOs, however, are suitable for learners of high school age and older.

- **Diversity University, Inc.** http://www.du.org/ —a nonprofit organization providing MOO environments for innovative approaches to learning. Click on "Visit DU MOO" to access the MOO, or see their web gateway: http://moo.du.org:8888/.

- **Virtual Educational Environment (VEE)** http://www.athena.edu/ —at Virtual Online University, Inc., a nonprofit corporation providing computer-mediated distance education classes and services.

- **MundoHispano** http://web.syr.edu/~lmturbee/mundo.html —a well-populated, virtual representation of dozens of cities in the Spanish-speaking world, written entirely in Spanish, for learners, teachers, and native speakers.

- **MOOfrancais** http://www.teleport.com/~dispatch/moofrancais.html —modeled after Paris, a well-organized MOO for learners, teachers, and native speakers of French, entirely in French.

- **schMOOze University** http://www.cc.rim.or.jp/~awaji/schMOOze/ —built to resemble a small college, learners can practice English and socialize with other learners as well as native speakers of English.

- **PennMOO** http://dept.english.upenn.edu/~afilreis/88/moo-home.html —the virtual class-room site in the English Department of the University of Pennsylvania.

WHAT CAN DIFFERENT KINDS OF USERS DO ON A MOO?

Those who first connect to a MOO are called *guests*. Guests have the ability to "talk," send messages across the MOO by "paging," use MOOmail for sending messages, and move around the MOO. They cannot make any permanent changes in their guest "character," nor can they create objects.

Those who want a permanent character with password access need to request this, usually by sending e-mail or MOOmail to the registrar (often the owner) of the MOO. Permanent characters can name themselves, describe themselves, and set their gender. Users come to know one another, forming friendships and a sense of community. These relationships can be one of the most reward-ing aspects of the MOO experience.

Builders are users that have programming permissions for creating rooms, exits, and objects which they can describe in any way that is consistent with the MOO's theme. They can also write customized, durable "messages" that automatically appear when certain commands are used. For example, when a user pages "MariLuz" at MundoHispano, that user will see a line of text in Span-ish stating that a kangaroo puts the message in its pocket and carries it to MariLuz.

Those who learn the MOO programming language can become *programmers* who create more elaborate features such as Gregor's monkey. The ability to create objects, "messages," and programs gives the user a sense of ownership, an outlet for creative writing, and motivation to return.

The *wizards* are at the top of the hierarchy. They create new characters, monitor connec-tions, teach new users, and deal with problems, often with the help of teacher-administrators. They also do deep-level programming and uniquely have access to information such as the users' e-mail addresses. In most MOOs, the *archwizard* is the one who founded the MOO, is the systems opera-tor of the MOO server (computer on which the MOO resides), and is considered the director and ultimate decision-maker.

WHAT DIFFICULTIES CAN I EXPECT WHEN USING A MOO?

Some teachers are uncomfortable with the loss of control over student behavior that inevita-bly occurs. Teachers should help students create personally meaningful tasks before the MOO is accessed, to be followed up with an assessment of outcomes. As an example, language learners might decide what topics they want to discuss with native speakers, then later report to the class what they learned, who taught it to them, and what web sites support their findings.

Some MOO users have quite an emotional response, positive or negative, to the experiences they have. Students have been known to fall in love with or be very offended by other users. While the sense of place and permanence that is achieved on MOO can contribute to the meaningfulness of the learning experience, some users simply have difficulty adjusting to having a virtual self (their "character") somewhere in cyberspace. Teachers need to regularly schedule in-class discus-sions that focus on student reaction to MOO use.

Finally, some students come with poor keyboarding skills and others are uncomfortable with using technology in general. These students need extra attention and time to use the MOO. Pairing them up with a more technically savvy partner during MOO homework time is a good idea.

HOW DO I GET STARTED?

Teachers should spend several weeks becoming familiar with the technology and the psycho-sociological experiences associated with MOO before introducing it to their students. Us-ing a MOO can be like going to a foreign country, and students need to count on their teacher to be a knowledgeable guide.

Technical considerations must be handled first: connecting to the MOO via telnet, and doing it in a user-friendly way using a MUD client program. Given that MOO is a program that runs on a remote computer, it is accessed by opening a telnet program, typing in the server name and port number, and then connecting at the log-in screen of the MOO. An example: open telnet on your own machine. Type in **schmooze.hunter.cuny.edu** where the host name is requested, and type in **8888** where the port number is requested. This will take you to the log-in screen of schMOOze University. At that point, you can type **connect guest** or, if you already have a permanent character, you can type **connect <name > <password>**.

If you connect without using a MUD client, you will find that the lines of text you are writing are interrupted by incoming text from others. This can be most disconcerting. MUD clients, which can be downloaded for free, have a variety of features. The most useful is one which prevents others' text from interrupting yours.

TO ENSURE A POSITIVE MOO EXPERIENCE FOR YOU AND YOUR STUDENTS:

- Become familiar with the technology and the social dynamics of MOO use. Read web sites about educational and social MOOs and provide appropriate web addresses to your students.

- Work the MOO into your class schedule, planning for at least three in-lab MOO training sessions.

- Facilitate in-class design of tasks to be completed in the MOO for homework. Decide how these tasks will be assessed.

- Have your students write journals about their MOO experiences and plan for regular in-class discussions.

- Expect your students to teach you. Many MOO wizards are under age 15!

WHERE CAN I FIND MORE INFORMATION ON EDUCATIONAL MOO?

- **How to connect to a MUSH/MOO/MUD: telnet and client programs**
  http://fly.ccs.yorku.ca/mush/con-intro.html

- **Chaco Communications** http://www.chaco.com/ (download the excellent **Pueblo** MUD client here)

- **Educational VR (MUD) sub-page**,
  http://tecfa.unige.ch/edu-comp/WWW-VL/eduVR-page.html

- **DU Journal of Educational Moos**
  http://tecfa.unige.ch/edu-comp/DUJVRE/vol1/DUJVRE.1.1.text

- **Journal of MUD Research** http://mellers1.psych.berkeley.edu/~jomr/

- **MOO Teachers Tip sheet** http://www.daedalus.com/net/MOOTIPS.html

- **MOOing in a foreign language: how, why, and who?**
  http://web.syr.edu/~lmturbee/itechtm.html

- **MUDs, MOOs, MUSHs** http://www.itp.berkeley.edu/~thorne/MOO.html

- **NETEACH-L MOO Sessions Information**
  http://spot.colorado.edu/~youngerg/moodates.html

- **freya's list 'o moos** http://www.teleport.com/~autumn/moo.html

- **The Palace, Inc. Virtual World Chat Software**
  http://www.thepalace.com/index.html (2-D MOO-like environment)

SUGGESTED READING

Turbee, L. (1995). MundoHispano: A text-based virtual environment for learners and native speakers of Spanish. In Mark Warschauer, (Ed.), *Virtual connections* (pp. 233–34). Manoa, HI: Second Language Teaching and Curriculum Center, University of Hawaii at Manoa.

Turbee, L. (1995). What can we do in a MOO?: Suggestions for language teachers. In Mark Warschauer, (Ed.), *Virtual connections* (pp. 235–38). Manoa, HI: Second Language Teaching and Curriculum Center, University of Hawaii at Manoa.

Warschauer, M., Turbee, L., and Roberts, B. (1996). Computer learning networks and student empowerment. *SYSTEM, 24* (1), 1–14. (EJ 527 752).

Concept Mapping
A Graphical System for Understanding the Relationship Between Concepts

Eric Plotnick
Assistant Director
ERIC Clearinghouse on Information & Technology
Syracuse University

Reprinted from ERIC® Digest, June 1997, EDO-IR-97-05

This ERIC Digest is adapted from WWW documents prepared by Jan W. A. Lanzing, Department of Educational Instrumentation, Faculty of Educational Science and Technology, University of Twente, The Netherlands.

WHAT IS CONCEPT MAPPING?

In the 1960s, Joseph D. Novak (1993) at Cornell University began to study the concept mapping technique. His work was based on the theories of David Ausubel (1968), who stressed the importance of prior knowledge in being able to learn about new concepts. Novak concluded that "Meaningful learning involves the assimilation of new concepts and propositions into existing cognitive structures." A concept map is a graphical representation where nodes (points or vertices) represent concepts, and links (arcs or lines) represent the relationships between concepts. The concepts, and sometimes the links, are labeled on the concept map. The links between the concepts can be one-way, two-way, or non-directional. The concepts and the links may be categorized, and the concept map may show temporal or causal relationships between concepts.

PURPOSE OF CONCEPT MAPPING

Concept mapping is a type of knowledge representation. Jonassen and Grabowski (1993, p. 433) state that structural knowledge may be seen as a separate type of knowledge. "Structural knowledge provides the conceptual basis for why. It describes how prior knowledge is interconnected. . . . Structural knowledge is most often depicted in terms of some sort of concept map that visually describes the relationships between ideas in a knowledge domain." Representing knowledge in the visual format of a concept map allows one to gain an overview of a domain of knowledge. Because the nodes contain only a keyword or a short sentence, more interpretation is required of the reader, but this may be positive. Concept mapping can be used for several purposes:

- To generate ideas (brainstorming);
- To design complex structures (long texts, hypermedia, large web sites);
- To communicate complex ideas;
- To aid learning by explicitly integrating new and old knowledge; and
- To assess understanding or diagnose misunderstanding.

ADVANTAGES OF CONCEPT MAPPING

Visual representation has several advantages:

- Visual symbols are quickly and easily recognized;

- Minimum use of text makes it easy to scan for a word, phrase, or the general idea; and

- Visual representation allows for development of a holistic understanding that words alone cannot convey.

APPLICATIONS OF CONCEPT MAPPING

- **Creativity Tool**—Drawing a concept map can be compared to participating in a brainstorming session. As one puts ideas down on paper without criticism, the ideas become clearer and the mind becomes free to receive new ideas. These new ideas may be linked to ideas already on the paper, and they may also trigger new associations leading to new ideas.

- **Hypertext Design Tool**—As the World Wide Web becomes an increasingly powerful and ubiquitous medium for disseminating information, writers must move from writing text in linear fashion to creating hypertext documents with links to other documents. The structural correspondence between hypertext design and concept maps makes concept mapping a suitable tool for designing the conceptual structure of hypertext. The structure of both a hypertext document and a concept map can be seen as a directed graph or a knowledge graph (Conklin, 1987). A concept map placed on the Web in hypertext may also serve as a Web navigational tool if there are clickable areas on the concept map that take the user immediately to indicated parts of the hypertext document.

  Designing hypertext is an activity with inherent problems. Botafogo, Rivlin and Schneiderman (1992) describe a dilemma faced by designers of hypertext authoring systems. In order to stimulate authors to write clearly structured hypertext (usually hierarchical), they have to decide when to force authors to reflect upon the structure of their work. Imposing a hierarchical structure from the beginning may result in too many restrictions for the author, while any effort to stimulate hierarchy afterwards is too late, and it may even be impossible for authors to restructure the jungle of nodes and relationships. Concept mapping may be a good intermediate step for authors to use to reflect upon their work when developing hypermedia.

- **Communication Tool**—A concept map produced by one person represents one possible way to structure information or ideas. This is something that can be shared with others. A concept map produced by a group of people represents the ideas of the group. In either case, concept mapping can be used as a communication tool for people to use to discuss concepts and the relationships between the concepts. They may try to agree on a common structure to use as a basis for further action.

- **Learning Tool**—Novak's original work with concept mapping dealt with learning. Constructivist learning theory argues that new knowledge should be integrated into existing structures in order to be remembered and receive meaning. Concept mapping stimulates this process by making it explicit and requiring the learner to pay attention to the relationship between concepts. Jonassen (1996) argues that students show some of their best thinking when they try to represent something graphically, and thinking is a necessary condition for learning. Experiments have shown that subjects using concept mapping outperform non-concept mappers in longer term retention tests (Novak, et al, 1983).

  Concept mapping is also gaining inroads as a tool for problem-solving in education. Concept mapping may be used to enhance the problem-solving phases of generating alternative solutions and options. Since problem-solving in education is usually done in small groups, learning should also benefit from the communication enhancing properties of concept mapping.

- **Assessment Tool**—Concept maps can also be used as assessment tools. The research team around Joseph Novak at Cornell found that an important by-product of concept mapping is its ability to detect or illustrate the "misconceptions" learners may have as explanations of content matter. The conceptions students may have are often incomplete and deficient leading to misunderstanding of instruction. Concept maps drawn by students express their conceptions (or their misconceptions) and can help the instructor diagnose the misconceptions that make the instruction ineffective (Ross & Munby, 1991).

ADVANTAGES OF COMPUTER SUPPORT FOR CONCEPT MAPPING

Jonassen (1990) proposes that few of the computer tools used today for learning have been designed as learning tools. Usually educators use existing tools for teaching purposes. According to Jonassen, concept mapping computer tools belong to the rare category of computer tools that were designed specifically for learning. Some of the advantages of computer support for concept mapping include:

- **Ease of Adaptation and Manipulation**—Once you have a concept map on paper, try to fit in those forgotten concepts or the ideas you came up with overnight and you will know the advantages of computer assisted concept mapping. Anderson-Inman and Zeitz (1993) compare the use of the concept mapping program "Inspiration" (see below) with the paper-and-pencil approach and found that using this program "encourages revisions to the concept map because deletions, additions, and changes are accomplished quickly and easily."

- **Dynamic Linking**—Most computer assisted concept mapping tools allow the user to point and drag a concept or group of concepts to another place on the map and automatically update all the appropriate links.

- **Conversion**—Once a concept map is created using a computer, the program usually allows the user to convert the map to different electronic formats. These can be vector or bitmapped images, a text outline, or even a hypertext structure. These electronic formats can then be stored, sent, manipulated, used, printed, and deleted just like any computer file.

- **Communication**—Advantages of digital communication are speed, high fidelity, and reliability. Having a concept map in digital format allows the user to send concept maps as attached files with e-mail messages, or include them in World Wide Web pages. Digitizing enhances the possibilities of using concept maps as communication tools.

- **Storage**—Computer assisted concept mapping allows for digital storage of concept maps. Digital storage takes less space, makes retrieval easier, and is especially important if concept maps will be used on a large scale.

COMPUTER TOOLS—AN EXAMPLE

- **Inspiration**—*Inspiration* <http://www.inspiration.com/> is currently one of the most popular computer software programs for creating concept maps. Organization of concepts, and brainstorming and mapping of ideas are mentioned in the User's Manual (Inspiration Software, 1994) as primary functions of this program. The graphical capabilities of *Inspiration* make it an outstanding program for creating graphs for presentation purposes.

Nodes may be shown in many different useful preset and user-defined shapes. Links may be straight or curved and may be labeled. Arrowheads may be placed on any side, and everything may be set to any color.

Anderson-Inman and Zeitz (1993) describe the classroom use of *Inspiration* and find that it encourages users to revise or change the maps (compared to maps drawn with paper and pencil). The graphical capabilities of *Inspiration* help users personalize concept maps. These capabilities also provide an incentive for users to manipulate concepts and revise conceptual relationships.

SUMMARY

Concept mapping is a technique for representing the structure of information visually. There are several uses for concept mapping, such as idea generation, design support, communication enhancement, learning enhancement, and assessment. A wide range of computer software for concept mapping is now available for most of the popular computers used in education.

REFERENCES

Anderson-Inman, L., and Zeitz, L. (1993, August/September). Computer-based concept-mapping: Active studying for active learners. *The Computing Teacher, 21* (1), 6–8, 10–11. (EJ 469 254).

Ausubel, D. (1968). *Educational psychology: A cognitive view.* New York: Holt, Rinehart, and Winston.

Bitner, B. L. (1996). *Interactions between hemisphericity and learning type, and concept mapping attributes of preservice and inservice teachers.* Paper presented at the Annual Meeting of the National Association for Research in Science Teaching (St. Louis, MO, March 31–April 4, 1996). (ED 400 196).

Botafogo, R. A., Rivlin, E., and Schneiderman, B. (1992). Structural analysis of hypertexts: Identifying hierarchies and useful metrics. *ACM Transactions on Information Systems, 10,* 142–80.

Conklin, E. J. (1987). Hypertext: An introduction and survey. *Computer, 20* (9), 17–41.

Inspiration Software. (1994). *Inspiration for Windows: User's manual* [computer program manual]. Portland, OR: Author.

Jonassen, D. H. (1990, July). What are cognitive tools? In P. A. M. Kommers, D. H. Jonassen, and J. T. Mayes (Eds.), *Proceedings of the NATA advanced research workshop "Cognitive tools for learning"* (pp. 1–6). Enschede, The Netherlands: University of Twente.

Jonassen, D. H. (1996). *Computers in the classroom: Mindtools for critical thinking.* Englewood Cliffs, NJ: Merrill/Prentice Hall.

Jonassen, D. H., and Grabowski, B. L. (1993). *Handbook of individual differences: Learning & instruction.* Hillsdale, NJ: Lawrence Earlbaum Associates. ISBN: 0-8058-1412-4/0-8058-1413-2.

Lanzing, J. W. A. (1996, July 4). *Everything you always wanted to know about . . . concept mapping.* Internet WWW page at URL at: http://utto1031.to.utwente.nl/artikel1/ (version current at March 1997).

Novak, J. D. (1993). How do we learn our lesson? Taking students through the process. *The Science Teacher, 60* (3), 50–55.

Novak, J. D., Gowin, D. B., and Johansen, G. T. (1983). The use of concept mapping and knowledge vee mapping with junior high school science students. *Science Education, 67,* 625–45.

Ross, B., and Munby, H. (1991). Concept mapping and misconceptions: A study of high-school students' understanding of acids and bases. *International Journal of Science Education, 13* (1), 11–24. (EJ 442 063).

Survey of
Instructional Development Models

Eric Plotnick
Assistant Director
ERIC Clearinghouse on Information & Technology
Syracuse University

Reprinted from ERIC® Digest, September 1997, EDO-IR-97-07

DEFINITION OF INSTRUCTIONAL DEVELOPMENT

In *Survey of Instructional Development Models, Third Edition*, Gustafson & Branch (1997) define instructional development (ID) in terms of four major activities.

- Analysis of the setting and learner needs;

- Design of a set of specifications for an effective, efficient, and relevant learner environment;

- Development of all learner and management materials; and

- Evaluation of the results of the development both formatively and summatively.

A TAXONOMY OF ID MODELS

A taxonomy of ID models can help clarify the underlying assumptions of each model, and help identify the conditions under which each might be most appropriately applied. Gustafson's (1981, 1991) schema contains three categories into which models can be placed. Placement of any model in one of the categories is based on the set of assumptions that its creator has made, often implicitly, about the conditions under which both the development and delivery of instruction will occur. The taxonomy has three categories indicating whether the model is best applied for developing: individual classroom instruction; products for implementation by users other than the developers; or large and complex instructional systems directed at an organization's problems or goals.

I. Classroom Orientation ID Models

Classroom ID models are of interest primarily to professional teachers who accept as a given that their role is to teach, and that their students require some form of instruction. Teaching personnel usually view an ID model as a general road map to follow. Typically, a classroom ID model outlines only a few functions, and simply provides a guide for the teacher. The developer who works with teachers would do well to employ any ID model with caution because teachers are not likely to be familiar with the concepts or processes of systematic instructional development.

(This Digest is based on *Survey of Instructional Development Models, Third Edition* by Kent L. Gustafson & Robert M. Branch.)

Gustafson and Branch select and discuss four models to represent the variety of ID models most applicable in the classroom environment:

- Gerlach and Ely (1980). Teaching and media: A systematic approach.

- Kemp, Morrison, and Ross (1994). Designing effective instruction.

- Heinich, Molenda, Russell, and Smaldino (1996). ASSURE.

- Reiser and Dick (1996). Instructional planning: A guide for teachers.

II. Product Orientation ID Models

Product development models typically assume that the amount of product to be developed will be several hours, or perhaps several days, in length. The amount of front-end analysis for product oriented models may vary widely, but it is usually assumed that a technically sophisticated product will be produced. Users may have no contact with the developers. Product development models are characterized by four key features:

- Assumption that an instructional product is needed.

- Assumption that something needs to be produced, rather than selected or modified from existing materials.

- Considerable emphasis is placed on tryout and revision.

- Assumption that the product must be usable by a variety of managers of instruction.

Gustafson and Branch select and discuss three models to represent the variety of ID models that have a product orientation:

- Van Patten (1989). What is instructional design?

- Leshin, Pollock, and Reigeluth (1992). Instructional design: Strategies and tactics for improving learning and performance.

- Bergman and Moore (1990). Managing interactive video/multimedia projects.

III. System Orientation ID Models

System oriented ID models typically assume that a large amount of instruction, such as an entire course or entire curriculum, will be developed, and that substantial resources will be made available to a team of highly trained developers. Assumptions as to whether original production or selection of materials will occur vary, but in many cases original development is specified. Assumptions about the technological sophistication of the delivery system vary, with trainers often opting for more technology than classroom teachers. The amount of front-end analysis is usually high, as is the amount of tryout and revision. Dissemination is usually quite wide, and typically does not involve the team that did the development.

Systems oriented ID models usually begin with a data collection phase to determine the feasibility and desirability of developing an instructional solution to a "problem." Systems models, as a class, differ from product development models in the amount of emphasis placed on analysis of the larger environment before committing to development. Systems models also typically assume a larger scope of effort than product development models. However, in the design, development, and evaluation phases, the primary difference between systems models and product models is one of magnitude, rather than type of specific tasks to be performed.

Gustafson and Branch select and discuss six models to represent the variety of ID models most applicable in the systems environment:

- Instructional Development Institute (IDI) (National Special Media Institute, 1971). IDI model.

- Branson (1975). Interservices Procedures for Instructional Systems Development (IPISD).

- Diamond (1989, 1997). Designing and improving courses and curricula: A practical guide.

- Smith and Ragan (1993). Instructional design.

- Gentry (1994). Introduction to instructional development process and technique.

- Dick (1996). The systematic design of instruction.

CONCLUSIONS

Gustafson and Branch suggest that developers need to acquire a working knowledge of several instructional development models, and ensure that all three categories in their taxonomy are represented in that knowledge. As new and different models are encountered, the new models can then be compared to those with which the developers are familiar. Gustafson and Branch also suggest that developers maintain a repertoire of examples of ID models that can be presented to clients along with varying levels of detail. Such a repertoire will allow developers to introduce the ID process to uninformed clients easily. Developers should always be in the position of selecting an appropriate model to fit a situation, rather than forcing the situation to fit a model.

There has been little substantive change in the general conceptual framework of ID models in recent years that suggest any trend. While some recent models (e.g., Bergman & Moore, 1990) focus on new delivery systems, these models do not represent new conceptions of the ID process. The only safe forecast based on the past would be that little change is likely to occur in the next few years. Gustafson and Branch believe that all the instructional development models they reviewed and discussed will survive well into the next century, and will be able to accommodate new developements in theory and technology.

REFERENCES

Bergman, R., and Moore, T. (1990). *Managing interactive video/multimedia projects*. Englewood Cliffs, NJ: Educational Technology Publications.

Branson, R. K. (1975). Interservice procedures for instructional systems development: Executive summary and model. Tallahassee, FL: Center for Educational Technology, Florida State University. (National Technical Information Service, 5285 Port Royal Rd., Springfield, VA 22161. Document Nos. AD-A019 486 to AD-A019 490).

Diamond, R. M. (1989). *Designing and improving courses and curricula in higher education*. San Francisco, CA: Jossey-Bass. (ED 304 056).

Diamond, R. M. (1997). *Designing and assessing courses and curricula: A practical guide*. San Francisco, CA: Jossey-Bass. In press.

Dick, W. (1996). The Dick and Carey model: Will it survive the decade? *Educational Technology Research and Development, 44* (3), 55–63. (EJ 532 854).

Gentry, C. G. (1994). *Introduction to instructional development: Process and technique*. Belmont, CA: Wadsworth Publishing Company.

Gerlach, V. S., and Ely, D. P. (1980). *Teaching and media: A systematic approach* (2nd ed.). Englewood Cliffs, NJ: Prentice-Hall Incorporated.

Heinich, R., Molenda, M., Russell, J., and Smaldino, S. (1996). *Instructional media and technologies for learning* (5th ed.). New York: Macmillan.

Kemp, J. E., Morrison, G. R., and Ross, S. M. (1994). *Designing effective instruction*. New York: Merrill.

Leshin, C., Pollock, J., and Reigeluth, C. (1992). *Instructional design: Strategies and tactics for improving learning and performance*. Englewood Cliffs, NJ: Educational Technology Publications.

National Special Media Institute. (1971). *What is an IDI?* East Lansing, MI: Michigan State University Press.

Reiser, R., and Dick, W. (1996). *Instructional planning: A guide for teachers* (2nd ed.). Boston: Allyn & Bacon.

Smith, P. L., and Ragan, T. J. (1993). *Instructional design*. New York: Macmillan.

Van Patten, J. (1989). What is instructional design? In K. A. Johnson and L. K. Foa (Eds.), *Instructional design: New alternatives for effective education and training*. New York: Macmillan.

Motivation in Instructional Design

Ruth V. Small
Associate Professor
Information Studies
Syracuse University
Syracuse, New York

Reprinted from ERIC® Digest, July 1997, EDO-IR-97-06

INTRODUCTION

Developing life-long learners who are intrinsically motivated, display intellectual curiosity, find learning enjoyable, and continue seeking knowledge after their formal instruction has ended has always been a major goal of education. Early motivational research was conducted primarily in the workplace, and centered on ways to motivate industrial workers to work harder, faster, and better.

More recent motivational research focuses on the identification of effective techniques for enhancing instructional design, improving classroom management, and meeting the needs of diverse student populations (Wlodkowski 1981). Learning-motivation researchers are applying some of the same theories and concepts found to be effective in industry to the development of motivational models that enhance the teaching-learning environment. One such model is the ARCS Model of Motivational Design developed by John M. Keller of Florida State University (Keller 1983, 1987). ARCS is a systematic model for designing motivating instruction. This digest will describe the ARCS Model, and will outline some of the ways in which ARCS components may be applied to instructional design.

THE ARCS MODEL OF MOTIVATIONAL DESIGN

The ARCS Model of Motivational Design is a well-known and widely applied model of instructional design. Simple, yet powerful, the ARCS Model is rooted in a number of motivational theories and concepts, (see Keller 1983) most notably expectancy-value theory (e.g., Vroom 1964; Porter & Lawler 1968).

In expectancy-value theory, "effort" is identified as the major measurable motivational outcome. For "effort" to occur, two necessary prerequisites are specified—(1) the person must value the task and (2) the person must believe he or she can succeed at the task. Therefore, in an instructional situation, the learning task needs to be presented in a way that is engaging and meaningful to the student, and in a way that promotes positive expectations for the successful achievement of learning objectives.

The ARCS Model identifies four essential strategy components for motivating instruction:

- [A]ttention strategies for arousing and sustaining curiosity and interest;

- [R]elevance strategies that link to learners' needs, interests, and motives;

- [C]onfidence strategies that help students develop a positive expectation for successful achievement; and

- [S]atisfaction strategies that provide extrinsic and intrinsic reinforcement for effort (Keller 1983).

Keller (1987) breaks each of the four ARCS components down into three strategy sub-components. The strategy sub-components and instructionally relevant examples are shown below.

Attention

- *Perceptual Arousal:* provide novelty, surprise, incongruity, or uncertainty. Ex. The teacher places a sealed box covered with question marks on a table in front of the class.

- *Inquiry Arousal:* stimulate curiosity by posing questions or problems to solve. Ex. The teacher presents a scenario of a problem situation and asks the class to brainstorm possible solutions based on what they have learned in the lesson.

- *Variability:* incorporate a range of methods and media to meet students' varying needs. Ex. After displaying and reviewing each step in the process on the overhead projector, the teacher divides the class into teams and assigns each team a set of practice problems.

Relevance

- *Goal Orientation:* present the objectives and useful purpose of the instruction and specific methods for successful achievement. Ex. The teacher explains the objectives of the lesson.

- *Motive Matching:* match objectives to student needs and motives. Ex. The teacher allows the students to present their projects in writing or orally to accommodate different learning needs and styles.

- *Familiarity:* present content in ways that are understandable and that are related to the learners' experience and values. Ex. The teacher asks the students to provide examples from their own experiences for the concept presented in class.

Confidence

- *Learning Requirements:* inform students about learning and performance requirements and assessment criteria. Ex. The teacher provides students with a list of assessment criteria for their research projects and circulates examples of exemplary projects from past years.

- *Success Opportunities:* provide challenging and meaningful opportunities for successful learning. Ex. The teacher allows the students to practice extracting and summarizing information from various sources and then provides feedback before the students begin their research projects.

- *Personal Responsibility:* link learning success to students' personal effort and ability. Ex. The teacher provides written feedback on the quality of the students' performance and acknowledges the students' dedication and hard work.

Satisfaction

- *Intrinsic Reinforcement:* encourage and support intrinsic enjoyment of the learning experience. Ex. The teacher invites former students to provide testimonials on how learning these skills helped them with subsequent homework and class projects.

- *Extrinsic Rewards:* provide positive reinforcement and motivational feedback. Ex. The teacher awards certificates to students as they master the complete set of skills.

- *Equity:* maintain consistent standards and consequences for success. Ex. After the term project has been completed, the teacher provides evaluative feedback using the criteria described in class.

MOTIVATION ASSESSMENT INSTRUMENTS

Since the ARCS Model was introduced in the early 1980's, several instruments have been developed for assessing the motivational quality of instructional situations. The Instructional Materials Motivation Survey (IMMS) (Keller 1987) asks students to rate 36 ARCS-related statements in relation to the *instructional materials* they have just used. Some examples are:

- "These materials are eye-catching." (Attention)

- "It is clear to me how the content of this material is related to things I already know." (Relevance)

- "As I worked on this lesson, I was confident that I could learn the content." (Confidence)

- "Completing the exercises in this lesson gave me a satisfying feeling of accomplishment." (Satisfaction)

Keller and Keller (1989) developed the Motivational Delivery Checklist, a 47-item ARCS-based instrument for evaluating the motivational characteristics of an instructor's *classroom delivery*. Examples of items related to each ARCS component are:

- "Uses questions to pose problems or paradoxes." (Attention)

- "Uses language and terminology appropriate to learners and their context." (Relevance)

- "Provides feedback on performance promptly." (Confidence)

- "Makes statements giving recognition and credit to learners as appropriate." (Satisfaction)

The Website Motivational Analysis Checklist (WebMAC) (Small 1997) is an instrument used for designing and assessing the motivational quality of World Wide Web sites. WebMAC builds on Keller's work (1987a; 1987b; 1989), Taylor's Value-Added Model (1986), and the research on relevance and information retrieval (e.g., Schamber 1994). Still in development and testing, WebMAC identifies 60 items that are categorized according to four general characteristics: Engaging, Meaningful, Organized, and Enjoyable. Some examples of items are:

- "Eye-catching title and/or visual on home page." (Engaging)

- "User-controlled type of information accessed." (Meaningful)

- "Logical sequence of information." (Organized)

- "Links to other websites of interest." (Enjoyable)

SUMMARY

The ARCS Model of Motivational Design is an easy-to-apply, heuristic approach to increasing the motivational appeal of instruction. ARCS provides a useful framework for both the design and improvement of the motivational quality of a range of informational entities—from classroom instruction to Internet resources—and increases the likelihood that these entities will be used and enjoyed.

REFERENCES AND RELATED READINGS

Chemotti, J. T. (1992, June). From nuclear arms to Hershey's kisses: Strategies for motivating students. *School Library Media Activities Monthly, 8* (10), 34–36. (EJ 446 223).

Keller, J. M. (1983). Motivational design of instruction. In C. M. Reigeluth (Ed.), *Instructional design theories and models: An overview of their current status*. Hillsdale, NJ: Erlbaum.

Keller, J. M. (1987a, Oct.). Strategies for stimulating the motivation to learn. *Performance and Instruction, 26* (8), 1–7. (EJ 362 632).

Keller, J. M. (1987b). *IMMS: Instructional materials motivation survey.* Florida State University.

Keller, J. M., and Keller, B. H. (1989). *Motivational delivery checklist.* Florida State University.

Porter, L. W., and Lawler, E. E. (1968). *Managerial attitudes and performance.* Homewood, IL: Dorsey Press.

Schamber, L. (1994). Relevance and information behavior. *Annual Review of Information Science and Technolgy.* Medford, NJ: Learned Information, Inc. (EJ 491 620).

Small, R. V. (1992, Apr.). Taking AIM: Approaches to instructional motivation. *School Library Media Activities Monthly 8* (8), 32–34.

Small, R. V. (1997). *Assessing the motivational quality of world wide websites.* ERIC Clearinghouse on Information and Technology. (IR 018 331).

Taylor, R. S. (1986). *Value-added processes in information systems.* Norwood, NJ: Ablex, 273–75.

Vroom, V. H. (1964). *Work and motivation.* New York: Wiley.

Wlodkowski, R. J. (1981). Making sense our of motivation: A systematic model to consolidate motivational constructs across theories. *Educational Psychologist, 16* (2), 101–10.

Part Four
Leadership Profile

Introduction

The purpose of this section is to profile individuals who have made significant contributions to the field of educational media and technology. Leaders profiled in the *Yearbook* have either held prominent offices, written important works, or made significant contributions that influenced the contemporary vision of the field. They have often been directly responsible for mentoring individuals who themselves became recognized for their contributions. There is no formal survey or popularity contest to choose the persons for whom the profiles are written, but those selected are usually emeritus faculty that remain active in the field or were particularly influential during their association with the profession. The following are the names of those previously profiled in earlier volumes of the *Yearbook*:

James D. Finn	Charles Francis Schuller
James W. Brown	Harry Alleyn Johnson
Wilbur Schramm	Robert M. Morgan
Robert E. De Kieffer	Paul Saettler
Jean E. Lowrie	Donald P. Ely
Robert Morris	James Okey
William Travers	Constance Dorothea Weinman
Robert Mills Gagné	Castelle (Cass) G. Gentry
Robert Heinich	

There are special reasons to feature people of national and international renown, and the editors of this volume of the *Educational Media and Technology Yearbook* believe Thomas F. Gilbert is worthy of such distinction.

You are welcome to nominate individuals to be featured in this section. Your nomination must also be accompanied by the name of the person who would compose the leadership profile. Please direct any comments, questions, and suggestions about the selection process to the Senior Editor.

Robert Maribe Branch

Thomas F. Gilbert
The World According to Gaps, 1927–1995

Alex J. Angulo*
Department of Instructional Technology
University of Georgia

Educational media developers should consider becoming acquainted with Thomas F. Gilbert's work. In the 1950s, Gilbert emerged as one of the pioneer researchers working with machines for teaching. Instructional designers are also likely to find his work of interest because he was one of the first designers of instruction to closely examine the implications of effective and efficient processes in the teaching and learning enterprise. And, of course, performance technologists should become intimately acquainted with his work, for he is often cited as a founder of the field. In the rapidly changing and evolving fields of media, instructional, and performance technologies, however, the past sometimes becomes elusive. Therefore, the task of this biographical tribute is to introduce professionals in these fields to a singular individual who was a creative innovator, a leader, and a decorated contributor to the theory and practice of education, training, and performance improvement.

Gilbert was born in 1927. He grew up in a small town near Columbia, South Carolina, where he was the first in his family to graduate from high school. As an early, avid reader, Gilbert became interested in philosophy and continued his interest at the University of South Carolina, where he completed an undergraduate degree in the discipline. However, young Gilbert, instead of seeking graduate work in philosophy, took a more pragmatic approach to his studies and entered a master's program in psychology at the same institution. Although he later pursued advanced studies in psychology at the University of Tennessee, where he was awarded a doctorate in both clinical psychology and psychometrics, he became disillusioned with his field and dismissed it as largely ineffective. By encouraging this skepticism, Edward E. Curuton, a psychometrician by training, had a significant influence during Gilbert's doctoral studies, inspiring Gilbert to further question the fundamental assumptions and validity of psychology. Curuton's influence later provided Gilbert with insights into challenging the assumptions of learning and performance theory.

After receiving his doctorates, Gilbert's first teaching appointment was at Emory University. But before long, in the early 1950s, Gilbert left Atlanta for Athens to teach at the University of Georgia. As a professor and researcher at Georgia, he read two works that, arguably, most influenced his research: *The Behavior of Organisms: An Experimental Analysis* (1938) and "The Science of Learning and the Art of Teaching" (1954), both by B. F. Skinner. These publications supported Gilbert's belief that there indeed existed a technology of education; and after reading the two studies, he immediately found himself building machines for teaching. Skinner's research inspired him to turn his laboratory into a teaching machine development center. Much of what Gilbert was attempting in Athens reflected what Skinner was doing in Cambridge at Harvard.

*I would like to give special thanks to Robert C. Barber for not only sharing his hard-to-find Thomas Gilbert sources but also in sharing his personal experiences from working with "Tom" on various projects.

In 1958, their paths finally crossed when a paper Gilbert wrote, entitled "Fundamental Dimensional Properties of the Operant," won him an invitation from Skinner to lead the Harvard laboratory. While at Harvard, Gilbert became closely involved with behavioral experimentation and struggled with ways to improve the newly developed principles for teaching and learning. But as he observed countless experiments, Gilbert came to believe that behaviorism was not just for the birds. In fact, Gilbert grew impatient in the laboratory; he was anxious to apply the discoveries in the real world.

During the same period, Gilbert also assisted Bell Laboratories with a teaching machine effort in New Jersey. In the research he conducted at Bell, he began to shape and distill principles for instructional design, regardless of the machines that delivered the instruction. These principles became some of the essential processes of instructional design that are still in use today. Gilbert synthesized his influential theories of teaching and learning in a work titled "An Early Approximation to the Principles of Programming Continuous Discourse, Self-Instructional Materials," a precursor to his technology of education—"Mathetics."

"Principles of Programming" is cited as having coined the term and furthered the theory of "programmed instruction," later to become recognized as a founding concept in the early instructional technology movement. In addition, Gilbert's influence is described in A. J. Romiszowski's *Designing Instructional Systems: Decision Making in Course Planning and Curriculum Design* (1981), where Gilbert is depicted as having significantly influenced Robert Gagné's theories of instruction:

> The earliest [work that distinguished between the processes (theories) and the products (hardware)] is Gilbert's (1962) "Mathetics" system. Gagné's original classic *The Conditions of Learning* (1968) outlines a technology for the development of teaching/learning experiences (events) based very much on the same scientific principles as Gilbert's (Romiszowski 1981, p. 13).

Before leaving the Harvard and Bell laboratories, Gilbert made another important discovery: Marilyn Bender Ferster, Gilbert's future wife and lifetime collaborator, who was also working with Skinner at the time.

Gilbert came closer to applying the new principles in the real world when a group of his colleagues invited him to the University of Alabama. There he led a behavioral research and development center, partially funded by the National Institute of Mental Health. During his tenure at Alabama, Gilbert made a significant contribution to scholarship in founding the short-lived but seminal *Journal of Mathetics*. In the journal, he published further refined statements on the application of behaviorist principles to improving efficiency in education and training.

In addition to directing the center and disseminating his scholarship, Gilbert also began to develop the principles as a practitioner. At the Center for Disease Control, for example, he applied an efficiency model of instruction to reduce the training time for a particular disease diagnosis from 100 hours to 1 or 2 hours. He witnessed similar success with a Morse code training program. Some of his courses won national honors, such as the ASTD annual award, and by 1962 he became the first honorary lifetime member of the National Society for Performance and Instruction (now called ISPI).

His contributions were further rewarded in business and industry training. Consequently, after an influential academic career, he decided to leave academia to become a full-time practitioner. The first in a series of Gilbertarian ventures was called Educational Design Incorporated, later renamed as TOR Education, in 1962. Soon after this firm was purchased by Bell and Howell, Gilbert founded the Energy Conservation Training group. Although not as successful as the TOR firm, it led Gilbert to his next significant and influential venture with Geary Rummler—the Praxis Corporation. This training outfit, founded in 1966, became a major influence in training and development for more than a decade.

During the Praxis years, as he drew from his various experiences with the firm and theories from his earlier research, Gilbert published *Human Competence: Engineering Worthy Performance* in 1978. As is true in almost any body of literature, some of the most powerful and enduring works are slow to catch on in popularity. A brief review of the 47 mini-tributes at the beginning of the 1996 reissue of *Human Competence* may indicate that this is one such classic work. Therein, he laid much of the foundation for a technology of performance. For example, two of his most recognized contributions were in developing the distinction between behavior and accomplishment and advancing the concept of the gap. A problem, he argued, whether in learning or performance, would be more productively viewed as a gap between the accomplishments of an average performer and the exemplary performer. And as Gilbert began to apply his concepts in the contexts he examined, gaps became a way of looking at the world of performance (hence the subtitle for this tribute, "The World According to Gaps").

In 1979, Praxis was acquired by Kemper-Tregoe, launching Gilbert into his last phase as a private consultant with his wife, Marilyn. Throughout the 1980s and early 1990s, their primary interests were in instructional design consulting as well as in various book and editing projects they had under way. However, in 1995, philosopher, psychologist, professor, researcher, instructional technologist, instructional designer, performance engineer, consultant, businessperson, author, and decorated award-winner Thomas F. Gilbert passed away.

Today Gilbert's methods continue to live on, although many instructional designers and performance technologists are unaware of the influence he had on the principles currently in use. In education, he had an impact on Gagné as well as other prominent leaders. In business, his influence can be seen among training luminaries such as Joe Harless and Geary Rummler. His work also continues to receive high acclaim from, and is actively used by, Timm J. Esque of the Intel Corporation. In addition, the 1997 publications *Instructional Design* and *The Performance Technologist* by the International Society for Performance Improvement cite Gilbert as having a lasting influence on current research. Before his death, Gilbert's many exemplary accomplishments were recognized when he was entered in *Training* magazine's HRD Hall of Fame in 1985 and was honored with the Association for Behavior Analysis Outstanding Lifetime Achievement Award. Likewise, in 1991, Gilbert was awarded the first Distinguished Professional Achievement Award from the National Society for Performance and Instruction. It is clear, then, that he was a pioneer and influential leader in educational media and instructional technology. And he very well may be remembered as the "Father of Performance Technology."

REFERENCES

Dean, P. (1992). Allow me to introduce: Thomas F. Gilbert. *Performance Improvement Quarterly 5* (3), 83–95.

Dean, P. (1997). Thomas F. Gilbert, Ph.D.: Engineering performance improvement with or without training. In *Performance improvement pathfinders: Models for organizational learning systems*, ed. P. Dean and D. Ripley. Washington, DC: International Society for Performance Improvement, 45–64, 218–21.

Dixon, G. (1988). An exemplary performer: Tom Gilbert delivers a message that is insistent, caustic, clear. In *What works at work: Lessons from the masters*, ed. G. Dixon. Minneapolis, MN: Lakewood Books, 22–24.

Gilbert, M., and Gilbert, T. (1991). What Skinner gave us. *Training 28* (9), 42–48.

Gilbert, T. (1958). Fundamental dimensional properties of the operant. *Psychological Review 65* (5), 272–82.

Gilbert, T. (1959). An early approximation to the principles of programming continuous discourse, self-instructional materials. In *Psychological problems and research methods in mathematics training*, ed. R. Feierabend and P. Du Bois. St. Louis, MO: Washington University, 76–107.

Gilbert, T. (1962a). Mathetics: The technology of education. *The Journal of Mathetics 1* (1), 7–73.

Gilbert, T. (1962b). Mathetics II: The design of teaching exercises. *The Journal of Mathetics 1* (2), 7–56.

Gilbert, T. (1979). Human incompetence: The autobiography of an educational revolutionist. *NSPI 18* (6), 15–21.

Gilbert, T. (1996). *Human competence: Engineering worthy performance, tribute edition.* Washington, DC: International Society for Performance Improvement, and Amherst, MA: HRD Press.

Gilbert, T. F. (1978). *Human competence: Engineering worthy performance.* New York: McGraw-Hill.

International Society for Performance Improvement. (1997a). *Instructional design.* Washington, DC: International Society for Performance Improvement.

International Society for Performance Improvement. (1997b). *The performance technologist.* Washington, DC: International Society for Performance Improvement.

Romiszowski, A. (1981). *Designing instructional systems: Decision making in course planning and curriculum design.* New York: Nichols Publishing.

Skinner, B. F. (1938). *The behavior of organisms: An experimental analysis.* New York: Appleton-Century-Croft.

Skinner, B. F. (1954). The science of learning and the art of teaching. *Harvard Educational Review 24* (2), 86–97.

Zemke, R. (1984). Tom Gilbert: The world is his laboratory. *Training 21* (12), 110–13.

Part Five
Organizations and Associations in North America

Introduction

Part Five includes annotated entries for associations and organizations headquartered in the United States and Canada whose interests are in some manner significant to the fields of instructional technology and educational media. For the most part, these organizations are associations of professionals in the field or agencies that offer services to the educational media community. Entries are separated into sections for the United States and Canada. The U.S. section begins with a classified list designed to facilitate location of organizations by their specialized interests or services. The Canadian section is small enough not to need such a list.

Information for this section was obtained by direct communication with each organization in early 1998. Several organizations (marked by an asterisk) did not provide updated information, and their entries contain information from the 1998 edition. Several new organizations are listed as well. Readers are encouraged to contact the editors of this volume with names of unlisted media-related organizations for investigation and possible inclusion in the 2000 edition.

Figures quoted as dues refer to annual amounts unless stated otherwise.

United States

CLASSIFIED LIST

Adult and Continuing Education
(ALA Round Table) Continuing Library Education Network and Exchange (CLENERT)
Association for Continuing Higher Education (ACHE)
Association for Educational Communications and Technology (AECT)
ERIC Clearinghouse on Adult, Career, and Vocational Education (CE)
National Education Telecommunications Organization & Education Satellite Company (NETO/EDSAT)
National University Continuing Education Association (NUCEA)
Network for Continuing Medical Education (NCME)
PBS Adult Learning Service (ALS)
University Continuing Education Association (UCEA)

Children- and Youth-Related Organizations
Adjunct ERIC Clearinghouse for Child Care (ADJ/CC)
American Montessori Society
Association for Childhood Education International (ACEI)
Association for Library Service to Children (ALSC)
(CEC) Technology and Media Division (TAM)
Children's Television International, Inc.
Close Up Foundation
Computer Learning Foundation
Council for Exceptional Children (CEC)
ERIC Clearinghouse on Disabilities and Gifted Education (EC)
ERIC Clearinghouse on Elementary and Early Childhood Education (PS)
National Association for the Education of Young Children (NAEYC)
National PTA
Young Adult Library Services Association (YALSA)

Communication
Association for Educational Communications and Technology (AECT)
ERIC Clearinghouse on Information & Technology (IR)
ERIC Clearinghouse on Languages and Linguistics (FL)
ERIC Clearinghouse on Reading, English, and Communication Skills (CS)
Health Science Communications Association (HeSCA)

International Association of Business Communicators (IABC)
Lister Hill National Center for Biomedical Communications of the National Library of Medicine
National Communication Association (NCA)
National Council of the Churches of Christ

Computers
(AECT) Division of Interactive Systems and Computers (DISC)
Association for Computers and the Humanities (ACH)
Association for the Advancement of Computing in Education (AACE)
Computer Learning Foundation
Computer-Using Educators, Inc. (CUE)
International Society for Technology in Education (ISTE)
Online Computer Library Center (OCLC)
Society for Computer Simulation (SCS)

Copyright
Association of American Publishers (AAP)
Association of College and Research Libraries (ACRL)
Copyright Clearance Center (CCC)
Hollywood Film Archive
International Copyright Information Center (INCINC)
Library of Congress

Distance Education
Community College Satellite Network (CCSN)
Instructional Telecommunications Council (ITC)
International Society for Technology in Education (ISTE)
International Telecommunications Satellite Organization (INTELSAT)
National Education Telecommunications Organization & EDSAT Institute (NETO/EDSAT)

Education—General
American Society of Educators (ASE)
Association for Childhood Education International (ACEI)
Association for Experiential Education (AEE)
Council for Basic Education
Education Development Center, Inc.
ERIC Clearinghouse for Science, Mathematics, and Environmental Education (SE)
ERIC Clearinghouse for Social Studies/Social Science Education (ERIC/ChESS)

ERIC Clearinghouse on Counseling and Student Services (CG)
ERIC Clearinghouse on Disabilities and Gifted Education (EC)
ERIC Clearinghouse on Educational Management (EA)
ERIC Clearinghouse on Elementary and Early Childhood Education (PS)
ERIC Clearinghouse on Rural Education and Small Schools (RC)
ERIC Clearinghouse on Teaching and Teacher Education (SP)
ERIC Clearinghouse on Urban Education (UD)
Institute for Development of Educational Activities, Inc. (|I|D|E|A|)
Minorities in Media (MIM)
National Association of State Textbook Administrators (NASTA)
National Clearinghouse for Bilingual Education
National Council for Accreditation of Teacher Education (NCATE)
National School Boards Association (NSBA)
Institute for the Transfer of Technology to Education (ITTE)

Education—Higher
American Association of Community Colleges (AACC)
American Association of State Colleges and Universities
Association for Continuing Higher Education (ACHE)
Association for Library and Information Science Education (ALISE)
Community College Association for Instruction and Technology (CCAIT)
Consortium of College and University Media Centers (CCUMC)
ERIC Clearinghouse for Community Colleges (JC)
ERIC Clearinghouse on Higher Education (HE)
Northwest College and University Council for the Management of Educational Technology
PBS Adult Learning Service
University Continuing Education Association (UCEA)

Equipment
Association for Childhood Education International (ACEI)
Educational Products Information Exchange (EPIE Institute)
ERIC Clearinghouse on Assessment and Evaluation (TM)
ITA
Library and Information Technology Association (LITA)
National School Supply and Equipment Association (NSSEA)
Society of Cable Telecommunications Engineers (SCTE)

ERIC
ACCESS ERIC
Adjunct ERIC Clearinghouse for Art Education (ADJ/AR)
Adjunct ERIC Clearinghouse for ESL Literacy Education (ADJ/LE)
Adjunct ERIC Clearinghouse for United States-Japan Studies (ADJ/JS)
Adjunct ERIC Clearinghouse on Clinical Schools (ADJ/CL)
Adjunct ERIC Clearinghouse on Consumer Education (ADJ/CN)
ERIC (Educational Resources Information Center)
ERIC Clearinghouse on Adult, Career, and Vocational Education (CE)
ERIC Clearinghouse on Assessment and Evaluation (TM)
ERIC Clearinghouse for Community Colleges (JC)
ERIC Clearinghouse on Counseling and Student Services (CG)
ERIC Clearinghouse on Disabilities and Gifted Education (EC)
ERIC Clearinghouse on Educational Management (EA)
ERIC Clearinghouse on Elementary and Early Childhood Education (PS)
ERIC Clearinghouse on Higher Education (HE)
ERIC Clearinghouse on Information & Technology (IR)
ERIC Clearinghouse on Languages and Linguistics (FL)
ERIC Clearinghouse on Reading, English, and Communication Skills (CS)
ERIC Clearinghouse on Rural Education and Small Schools (RC)
ERIC Clearinghouse for Science, Mathematics, and Environmental Education (SE)
ERIC Clearinghouse for Social Studies/Social Science Education (SO)
ERIC Clearinghouse on Teaching and Teacher Education (SP)
ERIC Clearinghouse on Urban Education (UD)
ERIC Document Reproduction Service (EDRS)
ERIC Processing and Reference Facility

Film and Video
(AECT) Division of Telecommunications (DOT)
(AECT) Industrial Training and Education Division (ITED)
Academy of Motion Picture Arts and Sciences (AMPAS)
Agency for Instructional Technology (AIT)
American Society of Cinematographers
Anthropology Film Center (AFC)
Association for Educational Communications and Technology (AECT)
Association of Independent Video and Filmmakers/ Foundation for Independent Video and Film (AIVF/FIVF)
Cable in the Classroom

Central Educational Network (CEN)
Children's Television International, Inc.
Close Up Foundation
Community College Satellite Network
Council on International Non-theatrical Events
(CINE)
Film Advisory Board
Film Arts Foundation (FAF)
Film/Video Arts, Inc.
Great Plains National ITV Library (GPN)
Hollywood Film Archive
International Teleconferencing Association (ITCA)
International Television Association (ITVA)
ITA
National Aeronautics and Space Administration
(NASA)
National Alliance for Media Arts and Culture
(NAMAC)
National Association of Broadcasters (NAB)
National Education Telecommunications
Organization & Education Satellite Company
(NETO/EDSAT)
National Endowment for the Humanities (NEH)
National Film Board of Canada (NFBC)
National Film Information Service (offered by
AMPAS)
National Information Center for Educational Media
(NICEM)
National ITFS Association (NIA/ITFS)
National Telemedia Council, Inc. (NTC)
The New York Festivals
Pacific Film Archive (PFA)
Public Broadcasting Service (PBS)
PBS Adult Learning Service (ALS)
PBS VIDEO
Society of Cable Telecommunications Engineers
(SCTE)

Games, Toys, Play, Simulation, Puppetry
Puppeteers of America, Inc. (POA)
Society for Computer Simulation (SCS)
USA-Toy Library Association (USA-TLA)

Health-Related Organizations
Health Science Communications Association
(HeSCA)
Lister Hill National Center for Biomedical
Communications
Medical Library Association (MLA)
National Association for Visually Handicapped
(NAVH)
Network for Continuing Medical Education
(NCME)

Information Science
Association for Library and Information Science
Education (ALISE)
ERIC Clearinghouse on Information and
Technology (IR)
Freedom of Information Center
International Information Management Congress
(IMC)

Library and Information Technology Association
(LITA)
Lister Hill National Center for Biomedical
Communications
National Commission on Libraries and Information
Science (NCLIS)

Innovation
Institute for Development of Educational Activities,
Inc. (|I|D|E|A|)
Institute for the Future (IFTF)
World Future Society (WFS)

**Instructional Technology, Design,
and Development**
(AECT) Division of Educational Media
Management (DEMM)
(AECT) Division of Instructional Development
(DID)
Agency for Instructional Technology (AIT)
Association for Educational Communications and
Technology (AECT)
Community College Association for Instruction and
Technology (CCAIT)
ERIC Clearinghouse on Information & Technology
(IR)
International Society for Performance and
Instruction (ISPI)
Professors of Instructional Design and Technology
(PIDT)
Society for Applied Learning Technology (SALT)

International Education
Adjunct ERIC Clearinghouse for US-Japan Studies
(ADJ/JS)
(AECT) International Division (INTL)
East-West Center
International Association for Learning Laboratories,
Inc. (IALL)
International Visual Literacy Association, Inc.
(IVLA)
National Clearinghouse for Bilingual Education
(NCBE)

Language
ERIC Clearinghouse on Languages and Linguistics
(FL)
ERIC Clearinghouse on Reading, English, and
Communication (CS)
International Association for Learning Laboratories,
Inc. (IALL)
National Clearinghouse for Bilingual Education
(NCBE)

Libraries—Academic, Research
American Library Association (ALA)
Association of College and Research Libraries
(ACRL)
ERIC Clearinghouse on Information & Technology
(IR)

Libraries—Public
American Library Association (ALA)
Association for Library Service to Children (ALSC)
ERIC Clearinghouse on Information & Technology
   (IR)
Library Administration and Management
   Association (LAMA)
Library and Information Technology Association
   (LITA)
Public Library Association (PLA)
Young Adult Library Services Association
   (YALSA)

Libraries and Media Centers—School
(ALA Round Table) Continuing Library Education
   Network and Exchange (CLENERT)
(AECT) Division of School Media Specialists
   (DSMS)
American Association of School Librarians (AASL)
American Library Association (ALA)
American Library Trustee Association (ALTA)
Association for Educational Communications and
   Technology (AECT)
Association for Library Collections and Technical
   Services (ALCTS)
Association for Library Service to Children (ALSC)
Catholic Library Association (CLA)
Consortium of College and University Media
   Centers
ERIC Clearinghouse on Information & Technology
   (IR)
International Association of School Librarianship
   (IASL)
Library of Congress
National Alliance for Media Arts and Culture
   (NAMAC)
National Association of Regional Media Centers
   (NARMC)
National Commission on Libraries and Information
   Science (NCLIS)
National Council of Teachers of English (NCTE),
   Commission on Media
On-Line Audiovisual Catalogers (OLAC)
Southeastern Regional Media Leadership Council
   (SRMLC)

Libraries—Special
American Library Association (ALA)
Association for Library Service to Children (ALSC)
Association of Specialized and Cooperative Library
   Agencies (ASCLA)
ERIC Clearinghouse on Information & Technology
   (IR)
Medical Library Association (MLA)
Special Libraries Association
Theater Library Association
USA Toy Library Association (USA-TLA)

Media Production
American Society of Cinematographers (ASC)
Association for Educational Communications and
   Technology (AECT)

(AECT) Media Design and Production Division
   (MDPD)
Association of Independent Video and Filmmakers/
   Foundation for Independent Video and Film
   (AIVF/FIVF)
Film Arts Foundation (FAF)
International Graphics Arts Education Association
   (IGAEA)

Museums and Archives
(AECT) Archives
Association of Systematics Collections
George Eastman House
Hollywood Film Archive
Library of Congress
Museum Computer Network (MCN)
Museum of Modern Art
National Gallery of Art (NGA)
National Public Broadcasting Archives (NPBA)
Pacific Film Archive (PFA)
Smithsonian Institution

Photography
George Eastman House
International Center of Photography (ICP)
National Press Photographers Association, Inc.
   (NPPA)
Photographic Society of America (PSA)
Society for Photographic Education (SPE)
Society of Photo Technologists (SPT)

Publishing
Graphic Arts Technical Foundation (GATF)
International Graphics Arts Education Association
   (IGAEA)
Magazine Publishers of America (MPA)
National Association of State Textbook
   Administrators (NASTA)

Radio
(AECT) Division of Telecommunications (DOT)
American Women in Radio and Television
   (AWRT)
Corporation for Public Broadcasting (CPB)
National Endowment for the Humanities (NEH)
National Federation of Community Broadcasters
   (NFCB)
National Public Broadcasting Archives (NPBA)
National Religious Broadcasters (NRB)
Western Public Radio (WPR)

Religious Education
Catholic Library Association (CLA)
National Council of the Churches of Christ in the
   USA
National Religious Broadcasters (NRB)

Research
American Educational Research Association
   (AERA)
Appalachia Educational Laboratory, Inc. (AEL)
(AECT) Research and Theory Division (RTD)

ECT Foundation
Education Development Center, Inc.
ERIC Clearinghouses
HOPE Reports
Mid-continent Regional Educational Laboratory
(McREL)
National Center for Improving Science Education
National Education Knowledge Industry
Association (NEKIA)
National Endowment for the Humanities (NEH)
National Science Foundation (NSF)
The NETWORK
North Central Regional Educational Laboratory
(NCREL)
Northwest Regional Educational Laboratory
(NWREL)
Pacific Regional Educational Laboratory (PREL)
Research for Better Schools, Inc. (RBS)
SouthEastern Regional Vision for Education
(SERVE)
Southwest Educational Development Laboratory
(SEDL)
WestEd

Special Education
American Foundation for the Blind (AFB)
Association for Experiential Education (AEE)
Association of Specialized and Cooperative Library
Agencies (ASCLA)
Council for Exceptional Children (CEC)
ERIC Clearinghouse on Adult, Career, and
Vocational Education (CE)
ERIC Clearinghouse on Disabilities and Gifted
Education (EC)
National Association for Visually Handicapped
(NAVH)
National Center to Improve Practice (NCIP)
Recording for the Blind and Dyslexic (RFB&D)

Telecommunications
(AECT) Division of Telecommunications (DOT)
Association for the Advancement of Computing in
Education (AACE)

Association of Independent Video and Filmmakers/
Foundation for Independent Video and Film
(AIVF/FIVF)
Community College Satellite Network (CCSN)
ERIC Clearinghouse on Information & Technology
(IR)
Instructional Telecommunications Council (ITC)
International Telecommunications Satellite
Organization (INTELSAT)
International Teleconferencing Association (ITCA)
Library and Information Technology Association
(LITA)
National Education Telecommunications
Organization & Education Satellite
Company (NETO/EDSAT)
Research for Better Schools, Inc. (RBS)
Teachers and Writers Collaborative (T&W)

Television
American Women in Radio and Television
(AWRT)
Central Educational Network (CEN)
Children's Television International, Inc. (CTI)
Corporation for Public Broadcasting (CPB)
International Television Association (ITVA)
National Cable Television Institute (NCTI)
National Federation of Community Broadcasters
(NFCB)
Society of Cable Telecommunications Engineers
(SCTE)

Training
(AECT) Industrial Training and Education Division
(ITED)
American Management Association (AMA)
American Society for Training and Development
(ASTD)
Association for Educational Communications and
Technology (AECT)
ERIC Clearinghouse on Adult, Career, and
Vocational Education (CE)
Federal Educational Technology Association
(FETA)
International Society for Performance Improvement
(ISPI)

ALPHABETICAL LIST

All dues are annual fees, unless stated otherwise.

*Academy of Motion Picture Arts and Sciences (AMPAS). 8949 Wilshire Blvd., Beverly Hills, CA 90211-1972. (310)247-3000. Fax (310)859-9351. Web site http://www.oscars.org. Bruce Davis, Exec. Dir. An honorary organization composed of outstanding individuals in all phases of motion pictures. Seeks to advance the arts and sciences of motion picture technology and artistry. Presents annual film awards; offers artist-in-residence programs; operates reference library and National Film Information Service. *Membership:* 6,000. *Publications: Annual Index to Motion Picture Credits*; *Academy Players Directory*.

Agency for Instructional Technology (AIT). Box A, Bloomington, IN 47402-0120. (812)339-2203. Fax (812)333-4218. E-mail ait@ait.net. Web site http://www.ait.net. Michael F. Sullivan, Exec. Dir. AIT is a nonprofit educational organization established in 1962 to develop, acquire, and distribute quality technology-based resources, providing leadership to the educational technology policy community. AIT fulfills this mission by being the largest single provider of instructional television programs and is a major player in the development of curriculum products. AIT has established a national model for contextual learning materials. AIT's strength lies in sound instructional design, early and continual involvement of classroom practitioners, formative evaluation, and creative production of video, videodisc, software, and print resources. AIT products have won many national and international awards, including the only Emmy and Peabody awards given to classroom television programs. Since 1970, 35 major curriculum packages have been developed by AIT through a process it pioneered. US state and Canadian provincial agencies have cooperatively funded and widely used these learning resources. Funding for other product development comes from state, provincial, and local departments of education; federal and private institutions, corporations, and private sponsors; and AIT's own resources. Currently, AIT offers 130 learning resource products, containing nearly 2,500 separate titles. Programming addresses pre-kindergarten through adult learners covering traditional curricular areas plus career development, early childhood, guidance, mental health, staff development, and vocational education. AIT programs account for 40 percent of the National Instructional Satellite Service (NISS) schedule, which is broadcast to K-12 classrooms across the country. AIT learning resources are used on six continents and teach nearly 34 million students in North America each year via electronic distribution and audio visual use. *Publications: TECHNOS: Quarterly for Education & Technology*, a forum for the discussion of ideas about the use of technology in education with a focus on reform ($28/yr, 4 issues). AIT is also the home of *TECHNOS Press*, publisher of *Final Exam* by Gerald W. Bracey. The Web site offers an online catalog, complete with program descriptions, ordering information, and direct links to AIT Customer Service.

*American Association of Community Colleges (AACC). One Dupont Cir. NW, Suite 410, Washington, DC 20036-1176. (202)728-0200, ext. 216. Fax (202)833-2467. Web site http://www.aacc.nche.edu. David Pierce, Pres. AACC serves the nation's 1,100 community, technical, and junior colleges through advocacy, professional development, publications, and national networking. The annual convention draws more than 2,500 middle and top-level administrators of two-year colleges. Twenty-four councils and 8 commissions address priority areas for community colleges. AACC also operates the Community College Satellite Network, providing teleconferences and other programming and services to colleges. *Membership:* 1,113 institutions, 16 international, 5 foundations, 15 corporations, 157 individuals, and 70 educational associates. *Dues:* vary by category. *Meetings:* Workforce Development Institute (WDI), Jan 27-30, 1999, San Diego. *Publications: Community College Journal* (bi-mo.); *Community College Times* (bi-weekly newspaper); *College Times*; Community College Press (books and monographs).

American Association of School Librarians (AASL). 50 E. Huron St., Chicago, IL 60611. (312)280-4386. (800)545-2433, ext. 4386. Fax (312)664-7459. E-mail aasl@ala.org. Web site http://www.ala.org/aasl. Julie A. Walker, Exec. Dir. A division of the American Library Association, AASL is interested in the general improvement and extension of school library media services for children and youth. Activities and projects of the association are divided among 55 committees and three sections. *Membership:* 8,064. *Dues:* membership in ALA (1st yr., $50; 2nd yr., $75; 3rd and subsequent yrs., $100) plus $40. Inactive, student, retired, unemployed, and reduced-salary memberships are available. *Meetings:* AASL Ninth National Conference, Nov 10–14, 1999, Birmingham, AL. *Publications: Knowledge Quest* (journal); *School Library Media Quarterly* (electronic research journal, http://www.ala.organization/aasl/SLMQ/).

American Association of State Colleges and Universities (AASCU). One Dupont Cir. NW, Suite 700, Washington, DC 20036-1192. (202)293-7070. Fax (202)296-5819. James B. Appleberry, Pres. Membership is open to regionally accredited institutions of higher education (and those in the process of securing accreditation) that offer programs leading to the degree of Bachelor, Master, or Doctor, and that are wholly or partially state-supported and state-controlled. Organized and operated exclusively for educational, scientific, and literary purposes, its particular purposes are to improve higher education within its member institutions through cooperative planning, studies, and research on common educational problems and the development of a more unified program of action among its members; and to provide other needed and worthwhile educational services to the colleges and universities it may represent. *Membership:* 393 institutions (university), 28 systems, and 10 associates. *Dues:* based on current student enrollment at institution. *Publications: MEMO: To the President; The Center Associate; Office of Federal Program Reports; Office of Federal Program Deadlines.* (Catalogs of books and other publications available upon request.)

American Educational Research Association (AERA). 1230 17th St. NW, Washington, DC 20036. (202)223-9485. Fax (202)775-1824. Email aera@gmu.edu. Web site http://www.asu.edu/aera. William J. Russell, Exec. Dir. AERA is an international professional organization with the primary goal of advancing educational research and its practical application. Its members include educators and administrators; directors of research, testing, or evaluation in federal, state, and local agencies; counselors; evaluators; graduate students; and behavioral scientists. The broad range of disciplines represented includes education, psychology, statistics, sociology, history, economics, philosophy, anthropology, and political science. AERA has over 120 Special Interest Groups including Advanced Technologies for Learning, Computer Applications in Education, Electronic Networking, Information Technology and Library Resources, Instructional Technology, and Text, Technology and Learning Strategies. *Membership:* 23,000. *Dues:* vary by category, ranging from $20 for students to $45 for voting. *Meetings:* 1999 Annual Meeting, April 19–23, Montreal. *Publications: Educational Researcher; American Educational Research Journal; Journal of Educational Statistics; Educational Evaluation and Policy Analysis; Review of Research in Education; Review of Educational Research.*

American Foundation for the Blind (AFB). 11 Penn Plaza, Suite 300, New York, NY 10001. (212)502-7600, (800)AFB-LINE (232-5463). Fax (212)502-7777. E-mail afbinfo@afb.org. Web site http://www.afb.org. Carl R. Augusto, Pres.; Liz Greco, Vice Pres. of Communications. AFB is a leading national resource for people who are blind or visually impaired, the organizations that serve them, and the general public. A nonprofit organization founded in 1921 and recognized as Helen Keller's cause in the U.S., AFB's mission is to enable people who are blind or visually impaired to achieve equality of access and opportunity that will ensure freedom of choice in their lives. AFB is headquartered in New York City with offices in Atlanta, Chicago, Dallas, and San Francisco. A governmental relations office in AFB is headquartered in New York City with offices in Atlanta, Chicago, Dallas, San Francisco, and Washington, DC. *Publications: AFB News* (free); *Journal of Visual Impairment & Blindness; AFB Press Catalog of Publications* (free).

American Library Association (ALA). 50 E. Huron St., Chicago, IL 60611. (312)944-6780. Fax (312)440-9374. Web site http://www.ala.org. William R. Gordon, Exec. Dir. The ALA is the oldest and largest national library association. Its 58,000 members represent all types of libraries: state, public, school, and academic, as well as special libraries serving persons in government, commerce, the armed services, hospitals, prisons, and other institutions. The ALA is the chief advocate of achievement and maintenance of high-quality library information services through protection of the right to read, educating librarians, improving services, and making information widely accessible. See separate entries for the following affiliated and subordinate organizations: American Association of School Librarians, American Library Trustee Association, Association for Library Collections and Technical Services, Association for Library Service to Children, Association of College and Research Libraries, Association of Specialized and Cooperative Library Agencies, Library Administration and Management Association, Library and Information Technology Association, Public Library Association, Reference and User Services Association, Young Adult Library Services Association, and Continuing Library Education Network and Exchange Round Table. *Membership:* 58,000. *Dues:* basic dues $48 first year, $95 renewing members. *Meetings:* 1999: Midwinter Meeting, Jan 22–27, Philadelphia; Annual Conference, Jun 24–Jul 1, New Orleans, LA. *Publications: American Libraries; Booklist; Choice; Book Links.*

American Library Trustee Association (ALTA). 50 E. Huron St., Chicago, IL 60611. (312)280-2161. Fax (312)280-3257. Web site http://www.ala.org. Susan Roman, Exec. Dir. A division of the American Library Association, ALTA is interested in the development of effective library service for people in all types of communities and libraries. Members, as policymakers, are concerned with organizational patterns of service, the development of competent personnel, the provision of adequate financing, the passage of suitable legislation, and the encouragement of citizen support for libraries. *Membership:* 1,710. *Dues:* $50 plus membership in ALA. *Meetings:* held in conjunction with ALA. *Publications: Trustee Voice* (q. newsletter); professional monographs and pamphlets.

American Management Association International (AMA). 1601 Broadway, New York, NY 10019-7420. (212)586-8100. Fax (212)903-8168. E-mail cust_serv@amanet.org. Web site http://www. amanet.org. Barbara M. Barrett, Pres. and CEO. Founded in 1923, AMA provides educational forums worldwide where members and their colleagues learn superior, practical business skills and explore best practices of world-class organizations through interaction with each other and expert faculty practitioners. AMA's publishing program provides tools individuals use to extend learning beyond the classroom in a process of life-long professional growth and development through education. AMA operates management centers and offices in Atlanta, Boston (Watertown), Chicago, Hamilton (NY), Kansas City (Leawood), New York, San Francisco, Saranac Lake (NY), and Washington, DC, and through AMA/International, in Brussels, Tokyo, Shanghai, Islamabad, and Buenos Aires. In addition, it has affiliated centers in Toronto, Mexico City, Sao Paulo, Taipei, Istanbul, Singapore, Jakarta, and Dubai. AMA offers conferences, seminars, and membership briefings where there is an interchange of information, ideas, and experience in a wide variety of management topics. Through its publication division, AMACOM, AMA publishes approximately 70 business-related books per year, as well as numerous surveys and management briefings. Other services offered by AMA include *FYI Video; Extension Institute* (self-study programs in both print and audio formats); *AMA Interactive Series* (self-paced learning on CD-ROM); *Operation Enterprise* (young adult program); *AMA On-Site* (videoconferences); the *Information Resource Center* (for AMA members only), a management information and library service; and six bookstores. *Membership:* over 75,000. *Dues:* corporate, $595-1645; growing company, $525-1845; indiv., $165 plus $40 per additional newsletter. *Publications* (periodicals): *Management Review* (membership); *Compensation & Benefits Review; Organizational Dynamics; HR Focus; President; Getting Results . . .;* and *The Take-Charge Assistant.*

American Montessori Society (AMS). 281 Park Ave. S, New York, NY 10010. (212)358-1250. Fax (212)358-1256. Web site http://www.amshq.org. Michael N. Eanes, Nat'l. Dir. Dedicated to promoting better education for all children through teaching strategies consistent with the Montessori system. Membership is composed of schools in the private and public sectors employing this method, as well as individuals. It serves as a resource center and clearinghouse for information and data on Montessori affiliates, trains teachers in different parts of the country, and conducts a consultation service and accreditation program for school members. *Dues:* teachers, school heads, $40; parents, $30; institutions, from $215 and up. *Meetings:* three regional and one national educational conference per year and four professional development symposia under the auspices of the AMS Teachers' Section. 39th Annual Conference, Apr 21–25, 1999, Cincinnati. *Publications: AMS Montessori LIFE* (q); *Schoolheads* (newsletter); *Montessori in Contemporary American Culture*; *Authentic American Montessori School*; *The Montessori School Management Guide*; AMS position papers.

American Society for Training and Development (ASTD). 1640 King St., Box 1443, Alexandria, VA 22313. (703)683-8100. Fax (703)683-8103. E-mail csc@astd.org. Web site http://www.astd.org. Curtis E. Plott, Pres. and CEO. Founded in 1944, ASTD is the world's premiere professional association in the field of workplace learning and performance. ASTD's membership includes more than 70,000 people in organizations from every level of the field of workplace performance in more than 100 countries. Its leadership and members work in more than 15,000 multinational corporations, small- and medium-sized businesses, government agencies, colleges, and universities. ASTD is the leading resource on workplace learning and performance issues, providing information, research, analysis, and practical information derived from its own research, the knowledge and experience of its members, its conferences and publications, and the coalitions and partnerships it has built through research and policy work. *Membership:* 70,000 National and Chapter members. *Dues:* $150. *Meetings:* International Conferences, May 22–27, 1999, Atlanta; May 20–25, 2000, Dallas. Technical Training Conferences, Sep 14–17, 1999, Minneapolis; Sep 19–22, 2000, Indianapolis. *Publications: Training & Development Magazine*; *Technical Training Magazine*; *Info-Line*; *The American Mosaic: An In-depth Report of Diversity on the Future of Diversity at Work*; *ASTD Directory of Academic Programs in T&D/HRD*; *Training and Development Handbook*; *Technical & Skills Training Handbook*. Quarterly Publications: *Performance in Practice*; *National Report on Human Resources*; *Washington Policy Report*. ASTD also has recognized professional forums, most of which produce newsletters.

*American Society of Cinematographers (ASC). 1782 N. Orange Dr., Hollywood, CA 90028. (213)969-4333. Fax (213)876-4973. Fax (213)882-6391. Victor Kemper, Pres. ASC is an educational, cultural, and professional organization. *Membership:* 336. Membership is by invitation to those who are actively engaged as directors of photography and have demonstrated outstanding ability. Classifications are Active, Active Retired, Associates, and Honorary. *Meetings:* Book Bazaar (Open House); Awards Open House; Annual ASC Awards. *Publications: American Cinematographer Video Manual*; *Light on Her Face*; and *American Cinematographers Magazine*.

American Society of Educators (ASE). 1429 Walnut St., 10th Fl., Philadelphia, PA 19102. (215)563-6005. Fax (215)587-9706. E-mail michelesok@aol.com. Web site http://www.media-methods.com. Michele Sokolof, Editorial Dir. ASE services the information needs of K–12 teachers, librarians, media specialists, curriculum directors, and administrators in evaluating the practical applications of today's multimedia and technology resources for teaching and learning purposes. *Membership:* 42,000. *Dues:* $33.50; $51.50 foreign. *Publications: Media and Methods*, bi.-mo. magazine.

American Women in Radio and Television (AWRT). 1650 Tyson Blvd., Suite 200, McLean, VA 22102-3915. (703)506-3290. Fax (703)506-3266. Terri Dickerson, Exec. Dir. Organization of professionals in the electronic media, including owners, managers, administrators, and those in creative positions in broadcasting, satellite, cable, advertising, and public relations. AWRT's objectives are to work worldwide to improve the quality of radio and television; to promote the entry, development, and advancement of women in the electronic media and allied fields; to serve as a medium of communication and idea exchange; and to become involved in community concerns. Organized in 1951. *Membership:* 40 chapters. Student memberships available. *Dues:* $125. *Publications: News and Views*; *Resource Directory*; *Careers in the Electronic Media*; *Sexual Harassment* (pamphlet).

Anthropology Film Center (AFC). 1626 Upper Canyon Rd., Santa Fe, NM 87501-6138. (505) 983-4127. E-mail ziacine@ix.netcom.com, anthrofilm@nets.com, or anthrofilm@archaeologist. com. Web site http://www.nets.com/anthrofilm. Carroll Williams, Dir. Offers the Ethnographic/ Documentary Film Program, a 30-week, full-time course in 16mm film in CD and DVD production and theory. Summer workshops are offered as well. AFC also provides consultation, research facilities, and a specialized library.

Appalachia Educational Laboratory, Inc. (AEL). PO Box 1348, Charleston, WV 25325. (304)347-0400, (800)624-9120. Fax (304)347-0487. E-mail aelinfo@ael.org. Web site http://www.ael.org. Terry L. Eidell, Exec. Dir. One of 10 Office of Educational Research and Improvement (OERI) regional educational laboratories designed to help educators and policymakers solve educational problems in their schools. Using the best available information and the experience and expertise of education professionals, AEL seeks to identify solutions to education problems, tests new approaches, furnishes research results, and provides training to teachers and administrators. AEL serves Kentucky, Tennessee, Virginia, and West Virginia.

Association for Childhood Education International (ACEI). 17904 Georgia Ave., Suite 215, Olney, MD 20832. (301)570-2111. Fax (301)570-2212. E-mail ACEIHQ@aol.com. Web site http://www.udel.edu/bateman/acei. Anne W. Bauer, Ed. and Dir. of Publications. ACEI publications reflect careful research, broad-based views, and consideration of a wide range of issues affecting children from infancy through early adolescence. Many are media-related in nature. The journal (*Childhood Education*) is essential for teachers, teachers-in-training, teacher educators, day care workers, administrators, and parents. Articles focus on child development and emphasize practical application. Regular departments include book reviews (child and adult), film reviews, pamphlets, software, research, and classroom idea-sparkers. Six issues are published yearly, including a theme issue devoted to critical concerns. *Membership:* 12,000. *Dues:* $45, professional; $26, student; $23, retired; $80, institutional. *Meeting:* 1999 Annual International Conference and Exhibition, Apr 7–11, San Antonio; 2000, Baltimore. *Publications: Childhood Education* (official journal) with *ACEI Exchange* (insert newsletter); *Journal of Research in Childhood Education*; professional division newsletters (*Focus on Infants and Toddlers, Focus on Pre-K and K, Focus on Elementary*, and *Focus on Middle School*; *Celebrating Family Literacy Through Intergenerational Programming*; *Selecting Educational Equipment for School and Home*; *Developmental Continuity Across Preschool and Primary Grades*; *Implications for Teachers*; *Developmentally Appropriate Middle Level Schools*; *Common Bonds: Antibias Teaching in a Diverse Society*; *Childhood 1892–1992*; *Infants and Toddlers with Special Needs and Their Families* (position paper); and pamphlets.

Association for Computers and the Humanities. c/o Elli Mylonas, Exec. Secretary, Box 1885-C15, Brown University, Providence, RI 02912. E-mail ach@stg.brown.edu. Web site http://www.ach.org. The Association for Computers and the Humanities is a forum for humanists who incorporate computing into their teaching and research. *Membership:* 300. *Dues:* $75. *Meetings:* Annual meetings held with the Association for Literary and Linguistic Computing. *Publication: Journal for Computers and the Humanities.*

Association for Continuing Higher Education (ACHE). Continuing Education, Trident Technical College, PO Box 118067, CE-P, Charleston, SC 29423-8067. (803)574-6658. Fax (803) 574-6470. E-mail pbarrineau@trident.tec.sc.us. Web site http://www.charleston.net/organization/ ACHE/. Wayne Whelan, Exec. Vice Pres. ACHE is an institution-based organization of colleges, universities, and individuals dedicated to the promotion of lifelong learning and excellence in continuing higher education. ACHE encourages professional networks, research, and exchange of information for its members and advocates continuing higher education as a means of enhancing and improving society. *Membership:* 1,622 individuals in 674 institutions. *Dues:* $60, professional; $240, institutional. *Meetings:* 1999 Annual Meeting, Nov 7–9, Cincinnati. 2000 Oct 14–17, Myrtle Beach, SC. *Publications: Journal of Continuing Higher Education* (3/yr.); *Five Minutes with ACHE* (newsletter, 10/yr.); *Proceedings* (annual).

Association for Educational Communications and Technology (AECT). 1025 Vermont Ave. NW, Suite 820, Washington, DC 20005. (202)347-7834. Fax (202)347-7839. Stanley Zenor, Exec. Dir. AECT is an international professional association concerned with the improvement of learning and instruction through media and technology. It serves as a central clearinghouse and communications center for its members, who include instructional technologists, library media specialists, religious educators, government media personnel, school administrators and specialists, and training media producers. AECT members also work in the armed forces, public libraries, museums, and other information agencies of many different kinds, including those related to the emerging fields of computer technology. Affiliated organizations include the Association for Media and Technology in Education in Canada (AMTEC), Community College Association for Instructional and Technology (CCAIT), Consortium of College and University Media Centers (CCUMC), Federal Educational Technology Association (FETA), Health Sciences Special Interest Group (HESIG), International Association for Learning Laboratories (IALL), International Visual Literacy Association (IVLA), Minorities in Media (MIM), National Association of Regional Media Centers (NARMC), New England Educational Media Association (NEEMA), and the Southeastern Regional Media Leadership Council (SRMLC). Each of these affiliated organizations has their own listing in the *Yearbook*. Two additional organizations, the AECT Archives and the ECT Foundation, are also related to the Association for Educational Communications and Technology and have independent listings. Divisions are listed below. *Membership:* 4,500. *Meetings:* 1999 Annual Convention and InCITE Exposition, Feb 10-14, Houston. *Publications: TechTrends* (6/yr., free with membership; $36 nonmembers); *Report to Members* (6/yr., newsletter); *Educational Technology Research and Development* (q., $40 members; $55 nonmembers); various division publications; several books; videotapes.

Association for Educational Communications and Technology (AECT) Divisions:

(AECT) Division of Educational Media Management (DEMM). 1025 Vermont Ave. NW, Suite 820, Washington, DC 20005-3516. (202)347-7834. Fax (202)347-7839. E-mail aect@aect.org. Web site http://www.aect.org/Divisions/aectdiv.html and http://teams. lacoe.edu/demm/demm.html. Jay Harriman, Pres. 1998–99 (harriman@uga.cc.uga.edu); Jay Harriman, Pres.-Elect (harriman@uga.cc.uga.edu). As leaders in the field of educational media, members of DEMM are actively involved in the design, production, and instructional applications of new and emerging multimedia technologies. DEMM members are proactive media managers who provide solutions, share information on common problems, and support the development of model media programs. *Membership:* 438. *Dues:* one division membership included in the basic AECT membership; additional division memberships $10. *Meetings:* DEMM meets in conjunction with the annual AECT National Convention. *Publication: DEMM Perspective* (newsletter, q.).

(AECT) Division of Instructional Development (DID). 1025 Vermont Ave. NW, Suite 820, Washington, DC 20005. (202)347-7834. James Klein, Pres. DID is composed of individuals from business, government, and academic settings concerned with the systematic design of instruction and the development of solutions to performance problems. Members' interests include the study, evaluation, and refinement of design processes; the creation of new models of instructional development; the invention and improvement of techniques for managing the development of instruction; the development and application of professional ID competencies; the promotion of academic programs for preparation of ID professionals; and the dissemination of research and development work in ID. *Membership:* 726. *Dues:* one division membership included in the basic AECT membership; additional division memberships $10. *Meetings:* held in conjunction with the annual AECT Convention. *Publications: DID Newsletter*; occasional papers.

(AECT) Division of Interactive Systems and Computers (DISC). 1025 Vermont Ave. NW, Suite 820, Washington, DC 20005. (202)347-7834. E-mail cwstafford@cis.purdue. edu. Web site http://www.aect.org/Divisions/disc.html. Carl Stafford, Pres. Concerned with the generation, access, organization, storage, and delivery of all forms of information used in the processes of education and training. DISC promotes the networking of its members to facilitate sharing of expertise and interests. *Membership:* 686. *Dues:* one division membership included in the basic AECT membership; additional division memberships $10. *Meetings:* held in conjunction with the annual AECT Convention. *Publication:* Newsletter; listserv at DISC-L@vm.cc.purdue.edu (to subscribe, send the message "subscribe DISC-L firstname lastname") .

(AECT) Division of Learning and Performance Environments (DLPE). 1025 Vermont Ave. NW, Suite 820, Washington, DC 20005. (202)347-7834. Web site http://dlpe.base.org. John Farquhar, Pres. (jfarquhar@psu.edu). Supports human learning and performance through the use of computer-based technology; design, development, evaluation, assessment, and implementation of learning environments and performance systems for adults. Dues: one division membership included in the basic AECT membership; additional division memberships $10. *Meetings:* held in conjunction with the annual AECT Convention.

(AECT) Division of School Media and Technology (DSMT). 1025 Vermont Ave. NW, Suite 820, Washington, DC 20005. (202)347-7834. E-mail smith@po.atlantic.county. lib.nj.us. Jim Smith, Pres. DSMS strives to improve instruction and promotes excellence in student learning in the K-12 setting by developing, implementing, and evaluating media programs and by planning and integrating technology in the classroom. *Membership:* 902. *Dues:* one division membership included in the basic AECT membership; additional division memberships $10. *Meetings:* held in conjunction with the annual AECT Convention. *Publication:* Newsletter.

(AECT) Division of Telecommunications (DOT). 1025 Vermont Ave. NW, Suite 820, Washington, DC 20005. (202)347-7834. Richard Hezel, Pres. DOT represents those members with an interest in a broad range of telecommunications as means of addressing the educational needs of students, the educational community, and the general public. *Membership:* 607. *Dues:* one division membership included in the basic AECT membership; additional division memberships $10. *Meetings:* held in conjunction with annual AECT Convention. *Publication:* Newsletter.

(AECT) Industrial Training and Education Division (ITED). 1025 Vermont Ave. NW, Suite 820, Washington, DC 20005. (202)347-7834. E-mail mlshipp@aol.com. Mary Lou Shippe, Pres. ITED is involved with designing, planning, evaluating, and managing training and performance programs, and promoting appropriate uses of educational techniques and media. *Membership:* 273. *Dues:* one division membership included in the basic AECT membership; additional division memberships $10. *Meetings:* held in conjunction with annual AECT Convention. *Publication: ITED Newsletter.* Back issues of the *Newsletter* are indexed in the ERIC database (ED 409 883).

(AECT) International Division (INTL). 1025 Vermont Ave. NW, Suite 820, Washington, DC 20005. (202)347-7834. Mei-Yan Lu, Pres. INTL encourages practice and research in educational communication and distance education for social and economic development across national and cultural lines; promotes international exchange and sharing of information, and enhances relationships among international leaders. *Membership:* 295. *Dues:* one division membership included in the basic AECT membership; additional division memberships $10. *Meetings:* held in conjunction with the annual AECT Convention. *Publication:* Newsletter.

(AECT) Media Design and Production Division (MDPD). 1025 Vermont Ave. NW, Suite 820, Washington, DC 20005. (202)347-7834. Chuck Stoddard, Pres. MDPD provides an international network which focuses on enhancing the quality and effectiveness of mediated communication, in all media formats, in educational, governmental, hospital, and corporate settings through the interaction of instructional designers, trainers, researchers, and evaluators with media designers and production team specialists who utilize state-of-the-art production skills. *Membership:* 318. *Dues:* one division membership included in the basic AECT membership; additional division memberships $10. *Meetings:* held in conjunction with annual AECT Convention. *Publication:* Newsletter.

(AECT) Research and Theory Division (RTD). 1025 Vermont Ave. NW, Suite 820, Washington, DC 20005. (202)347-7834. Dennis Hlynka, Pres. Seeks to improve the design, execution, utilization, and evaluation of educational technology research; to improve the qualifications and effectiveness of personnel engaged in educational technology research; to advise the educational practitioner as to the use of the research results; to improve research design, techniques, evaluation, and dissemination; to promote both applied and theoretical research on the systematic use of educational technology in the improvement of instruction; and to encourage the use of multiple research paradigms in examining issues related to technology in education. *Membership:* 452. *Dues:* one division membership included in the basic AECT membership; additional division memberships $10. *Meetings:* held in conjunction with annual AECT Convention. *Publication:* Newsletter.

(AECT) Systemic Change in Education Division (CHANGE). 1025 Vermont Ave. NW, Suite 820, Washington, DC 20005. (202)347-7834. Atsusi Hirumi, Pres. CHANGE advocates fundamental changes in educational settings to improve the quality of education and to enable technology to achieve its potential. *Dues:* one division membership included in the basic AECT membership; additional division memberships $10. *Meetings:* held in conjunction with the annual AECT Convention. *Publication:* Newsletter.

AECT Archives. University of Maryland at College Park, Hornbake Library, College Park, MD 20742. E-mail tc65@umail.umd.edu. Web site http://www.library.umd.edu/UMCP/NPBA/npba.html. Thomas Connors, Archivist, National Public Broadcasting Archives. (301)405-9255. Fax (301)314-2634. A collection of media, manuscripts, and related materials representing important developments in visual and audiovisual education and in instructional technology. The collection is housed as part of the National Public Broadcasting Archives. Maintained by the University of Maryland in cooperation with AECT. Open to researchers and scholars.

Association for Experiential Education (AEE). 2305 Canyon Blvd., Suite 100, Boulder, CO 80302-5651. (303)440-8844 ext. 10. Fax (303)440-9581. Web site http://www.princeton.edu/~rcurtis/aee.html. Sharon Heinlen, Exec. Dir. AEE is a nonprofit, international, professional organization with roots in adventure education, committed to the development, practice, and evaluation of experiential learning in all settings. AEE's vision is to be a leading international organization for the development and application of experiential education principles and methodologies with the intent to create a just and compassionate world by transforming education and promoting positive social change. *Membership:* more than 2,500 members in over 30 countries, including individuals and organizations with affiliations in education, recreation, outdoor adventure programming, mental health, youth service, physical education, management development training, corrections, programming for people with disabilities, and environmental education. *Dues:* $55-$95, indiv. (depending on annual income); $110-$125, family; $200-$500, organizations and corporations. *Meetings:* Annual AEE International Conference, fall. Regional Conferences held in the Northwest, Heartland, Southeast, Mid-South, Mid-Atlantic, Northeast, West, and Rocky Mountains. *Publications: Jobs Clearinghouse* (m.); *The Journal of Experiential Education* (3/yr.); *Experience and the Curriculum*; *Adventure Education*; *Adventure Therapy*; *Therapeutic Applications of Adventure Programming*; *Manual of Accreditation Standards for Adventure Programs*; *The Theory of Experiential Education, Third Edition*; *Experiential Learning in Schools and Higher Education*; *Ethical Issues in Experiential Education, Second Edition*; *The K.E.Y. (Keep Exploring Yourself) Group: An Experiential Personal Growth Group Manual*; *Book of Metaphors, Volume II*; *Women's Voices in Experiential Education*; bibliographies, directories of programs, and membership directory.

Association for Library and Information Science Education (ALISE). PO Box 7640, Arlington, VA 22207. (703)522-1899. Fax (703)243-4551. E-mail sroger7@ibm.net. Web site http://www.alise.org. Sharon J. Rogers, Exec. director Seeks to advance education for library and information science and produces annual Library and Information Science Education Statistical Report. Open to professional schools offering graduate programs in library and information science; personal memberships open to educators employed in such institutions; other memberships available to interested individuals. *Membership:* 722 individuals, 73 institutions. *Dues:* institutional, sliding scale, $325-600; $200 associate; $125 international; personal, $90 full-time; $50 part-time, $40 student, $50 retired. *Meetings:* 1999, Jan 26–29, Philadelphia; 2000, Jan 11–14, San Antonio. *Publications: Journal of Education for Library and Information Science; ALISE Directory and Handbook; Library and Information Science Education Statistical Report.*

Association for Library Collections and Technical Services (ALCTS). 50 E. Huron St., Chicago, IL 60611. (312)944-6780. Fax (312)280-3257. E-mail alcts@ala.org. Karen Muller, Exec. Dir; Janet Swan Hill, Pres., July 1998–July 1999. An affiliate of the American Library Association, ALCTS is dedicated to acquisition, identification, cataloging, classification, and preservation of library materials, the development and coordination of the country's library resources, and aspects of selection and evaluation involved in acquiring and developing library materials and resources. Sections include Acquisitions, Cataloging and Classification, Collection Management and Development, Preservation and Reformatting, and Serials. *Membership:* 5,072. *Dues:* $45 plus membership in ALA. *Meetings:* 1999 ALA Annual Conference, New Orleans, Jun 24-Jul 1; 2000, Chicago, Jul 6–13; 2001, San Francisco, Jun 14–20. 1999 ALA Midwinter Meeting, Jan 29–Feb 3, Philadelphia; 2000, Jan 14–19, San Antonio; 2001, Feb 9–14, Washington. *Publications: Library Resources & Technical Services* (q.); *ALCTS Newsletter* (6/yr.); *ALCTS Network News (AN2),* electronic newsletter issued irregularly.

Association for Library Service to Children (ALSC). 50 E. Huron St., Chicago, IL 60611. (312)280-2163. Fax (312)944-7671. E-mail alsc@ala.org. Susan Roman, Exec. Dir. A division of the American Library Association, ALSC is interested in the improvement and extension of library services for children in all types of libraries, evaluation and selection of book and nonbook library materials, and improvement of techniques of library services for children from preschool through the eighth grade or junior high school age. Committee membership open to ALSC members. *Membership:* 3,600. *Dues:* $45 plus membership in ALA. *Meetings:* annual conference and midwinter meeting with ALA. *Publications: Journal of Youth Services in Libraries* (q.); *ALSC Newsletter* (q.).

Association for the Advancement of Computing in Education (AACE). PO Box 2966, Charlottesville, VA 22902. (804)973-3987. Fax (804)978-7449. E-mail aace@virginia.edu. Web site http://www.aace.org. Gary Marks, Exec. Dir.; April Ballard, contact person. AACE is an international, educational, and professional organization dedicated to the advancement of learning and teaching at all levels with information technology. AACE publishes major journals, books, and CD-ROMs on the subject, and organizes major conferences. AACE's membership includes researchers, developers, and practitioners in schools, colleges, and universities; administrators; policy decision-makers; trainers; adult educators; and other specialists in education, industry, and the government with an interest in advancing knowledge and learning with information technology in education. *Membership:* 6,500. *Dues:* basic membership of $75 includes one journal subscription and *Educational Technology Review* subscription. *Meetings:* SITE '99 and M/SET 99, Feb 28–Mar 4, San Antonio. Ed-Media/Ed-Telecom 99, June, New Orleans. Web Net 99, Nov, Hawaii. SITE 2000, March, Phoenix. *Publications: Educational Technology Review (ED-TECH Review)* (2 or 3 times yearly); *Journal of Computers in Mathematics and Science Teaching (JCMST); Journal of Computing in Childhood Education (JCCE); Journal of Educational Multimedia and Hypermedia (JEMH); Journal of Interactive Learning Research (JILR)* (formerly *Journal of Artificial Intelligence in Education); Journal of Technology and Teacher Education (JTATE); International Journal of Educational Telecommunications (IJET).* A catalog of books and CD-ROMs is available upon request, or by visiting http://www.aace.organize/conf/pubs.

Association of American Publishers (AAP). 1718 Connecticut Avenue, NW, Washington, DC 20009. (202)232-3335. Fax (202)745-0694. Web site http://www.publishers.org. Patricia S. Schroeder, President and CEO (DC); Judith Platt, Director of Communications/Public Affairs (jplatt@publishers.org). The Association of American Publishers is the national trade association of the U.S. book publishing industry. AAP was created in 1970 through the merger of the American Book Publishers Council, a trade publishing group, and the American Textbook Publishers Institute, a group of educational publishers. AAP's approximately 200 members include most of the major commercial book publishers in the United States, as well as smaller and non-profit publishers, university presses, and scholarly societies. AAP members publish hardcover and paperback books in every field and a range of educational materials for the elementary, secondary, postsecondary, and professional markets. Members of the Association also produce computer software and electronic products and services, such as online databases and CD-ROMs. AAP's primary concerns are the protection of intellectual property rights in all media, the defense of free expression and freedom to publish at home and abroad, the management of new technologies, development of education markets and funding for instructional materials, and the development of national and global markets for its members' products.

Association of College and Research Libraries (ACRL). 50 E. Huron St., Chicago, IL 60611-2795. (312)280-3248. Fax (312)280-2520. E-mail ajenkins@ala.org. Web site http://www.ala. org/acrl.html. Althea H. Jenkins, Exec. Dir. An affiliate of the American Library Association, ACRL provides leadership for development, promotion, and improvement of academic and research library resources and services to facilitate learning, research, and the scholarly communications process. It provides access to library standards for colleges, universities, and two-year institutions, and publishes statistics on academic libraries. Committees include Academic or Research Librarian of the Year Award, Appointments, Hugh C. Atkinson Memorial Award, Budget and Finance, Colleagues, Committee on the Status of Academic Librarians, Constitution and Bylaws, Copyright, Council of Liaisons, Doctoral Dissertation Fellowship, Government Relations, Intellectual Freedom, International Relations, Samuel Lazerow Fellowhsip, Media Resources, Membership, Nominations, Orientation, Professional Development, Professional Enhancement, Publications, Racial and Ethnic Diversity, Research, K. G. Saur Award for the Best C&RL Article, Standards and Accreditation, and Statistics. The association administers 15 different awards in three categories: Achievement and Distinguished Service Awards, Research Awards/Grants, and Publications. *Membership:* over 10,000. *Dues:* $35 (in addition to ALA membership). *Meetings:* 1999 ACRL National Conference, Apr 8–12, Detroit. *Publications: College & Research Libraries* (6/yr.); *College & Research Libraries News* (11/yr.); *Rare Books and Manuscripts Librarianship* (semi-annual); *CHOICE Magazine: Current Review for Academic Libraries* (11/yr.); *CLIP Notes* (current issues are #16,17,20-26). Recent titles include: *Displays and Exhibits in College Libraries*; *Restructuring Academic Libraries*; *Documenting Cultural Diversity in the Resurgent American South*; *Choice Reviews in Women's Studies*; and *Proceedings of the 7th ACRL National Conference*. A free list of materials is available. ACRL also sponsors an open discussion listserv, ACRL-FRM@ALA.ORG.

*Association of Independent Video and Filmmakers/Foundation for Independent Video and Film (AIVF/FIVF). 304 Hudson St., 6th Floor, New York, NY 10013. (212)807-1400. Fax (212)463-8519. E-mail aivffivf@aol.com. Web site http://www.aivf.org. Ruby Lerner, Exec. Dir. AIVF/FIVF is the national trade association for independent video and filmmakers, representing their needs and goals to industry, government, and the public. Programs include screenings and seminars, insurance for members and groups, and information and referral services. Recent activities include advocacy for public funding of the arts, public access to new telecommunications systems, and monitoring censorship issues. *Dues:* $45, indiv.; $75, library; $100, nonprofit organization; $150, business/industry; $25, student. *Publications: The Independent Film and Video Monthly*; *The AIVF Guide to International Film and Video Festivals*; *The AIVF Guide to Film and Video Distributors*; *The Next Step: Distributing Independent Films and Videos*.

Association of Specialized and Cooperative Library Agencies (ASCLA). 50 E. Huron St., Chicago, IL 60611. (800)545-2433, ext. 4399. Fax (312)944-8085. E-mail ascla@ala.org. Web site http://www.ala.organization/ascla. Cathleen Bourdon, Exec. Dir. An affiliate of the American Library Association, ASCLA represents state library agencies, multitype library cooperatives, and libraries serving special clienteles to promote the development of coordinated library services with equal access to information and material for all persons. The activities and programs of the association are carried out by 21 committees, three sections, and various discussion groups. *Membership:* 1,300. *Dues:* (in addition to ALA membership) $40, personal; $50, organization; $500, state library agency. *Meetings:* 1999 Conference, Jun 24–Jul 1, New Orleans. 2000, Jul 6–13, Chicago. *Publications: Interface* (q.); *The Americans with Disabilities Act: Its Impact on Libraries*; *Deafness: An Annotated Bibliography and Guide to Basic Materials*; *Library Standards for Adult Correctional Institutions 1992*. Write for free checklist of materials.

Association of Systematics Collections (ASC). 1725 K St. NW, Suite 601, Washington, DC 20006. (202)835-9050. E-mail asc@ascoll.org. Web site http://www.ascoll.org. Fosters the care, management, and improvement of biological collections and promotes their utilization. Institutional members include free-standing museums, botanical gardens, college and university museums, and public institutions, including state biological surveys and agricultural research centers. ASC also represents affiliate societies, keeps members informed about funding and legislative issues, and provides technical consulting about collection care and taxonomy. *Membership:* 79 institutions, 25 societies, 1,200 newsletter subscribers. *Dues:* depend on the size of collections. *Publications: ASC Newsletter* (for members and nonmember subscribers, bi-mo.); *Guidelines for Institutional Policies and Planning in Natural History Collections*; *Access to Genetic Resources*; *Collections of Frozen Tissues*; *Guidelines for Institutional Database Policies*.

Cable in the Classroom. 1900 N. Beauregard St., Suite 108, Alexandria, VA 22311. (703)845-1400. Fax (703)845-1409. E-mail cicofc@aol.com. Web site http://www.ciconline.org. Megan Hookey, Managing Dir. Cable in the Classroom is the cable industry's $420 million public service initiative to enrich education. It provides free cable connections to more than 77,000 public and private K–12 schools, reaching more than 82% of all US students with commercial-free, quality educational programming. It also provides curriculum-related support materials for its programming and conducts Teacher Training and Media Literacy workshops throughout the country. *Membership:* Cable in the Classroom is a consortium of more than 8,500 local cable companies and 38 national cable programming networks. *Meetings:* Cable in the Classroom exhibits at 15 major education conferences each year. *Publications: Delivering the Future: Cable and Education Partnerships for the Information Age* (Dr. Bobbi Kamil); *Cable in the Classroom Magazine* (mo.); *Taking Charge of Your TV*; *A Guide to Critical Viewing for Parents and Children* (booklet, available on request).

Catholic Library Association (CLA). 100 North Street, Suite 224, Pittsfield, MA 01201-5109. (413)443-2CLA. Fax (413)442-2CLA. Jean R. Bostley, SSJ, Exec. Dir. Provides educational programs, services, and publications for Catholic libraries and librarians. *Membership:* approx. 1,000. *Dues:* $45, indiv.; special rates for students and retirees. *Meetings:* are held in conjunction with the National Catholic Educational Association: 1999, Apr 6–9, New Orleans. 2000, Apr 25–28, Baltimore; 2001, Apr 17–20, Milwaukee. *Publications: Catholic Library World* (q.); *Catholic Periodical and Literature Index* (q. with annual cumulations).

Central Educational Network (CEN). 1400 E. Touhy, Suite 260, Des Plaines, IL 60018-3305. (847)390-8700. Fax (847)390-9435. E-mail ceninfo@mcs.net. James A. Fellows, Pres. The Central Educational Network is a not-for-profit, public television membership organization dedicated to leading, supporting, and serving the needs and interests of community, university and state organizations that are educating and enriching their citizens through public telecommunications services. CEN's initiatives are organized through service areas that are regional, national, and international in scope, and are advised by corresponding membership councils, the Management Council, the Programming Council and the Educational Technology Council. CEN's education services provide member agencies with support for their educational outreach activities by facilitating a national instructional television screening, evaluation, acquisition and scheduling process that is a central part of the local service to elementary and secondary schools. Assistance is provided in higher education as well and emphasis is placed on advancing activities in lifelong learning through multiple technologies that support local and state educational services. *Membership:* PTV stations and educational agencies.

Children's Television International (CTI)/GLAD Productions, Inc. Planting Field Drive, South Riding, VA 20152. (800)CTI-GLAD (284-4523). Fax (703)327-6470. Ray Gladfelter, Pres. and Dir. of Customer Services. An educational organization that develops, produces, and distributes a wide variety of color television and video programming and related publications as a resource to aid the social, cultural, and intellectual development of children and young adults. Programs cover language arts, science, social studies, history, and art for home, school, and college viewing. Publications: teacher guides for instructional series; *The History Game: A Teacher's Guide*; complimentary catalog for educational videos.

Close Up Foundation. 44 Canal Center Plaza, Alexandria, VA 22314. (703)706-3300. Fax (703)706-0000. E-mail alumni@closeup.org. Web site http://www.closeup.org. Stephen A. Janger, CEO. A nonprofit, nonpartisan civic education organization promoting informed citizen participation in public policy and community service. Programs reach more than a million participants each year. Close Up brings 25,000 secondary and middle school students and teachers and older Americans each year to Washington for week-long government studies programs, and produces television programs on the C-SPAN cable network for secondary school and home audiences. Meetings are scheduled most weeks during the academic year in Washington, DC, all with a government, history, or current issues focus. *Membership:* 25,000 participants. *Publications: Current Issues*; *The Bill of Rights: A User's Guide*; *Perspectives*; *International Relations*; *The American Economy*; documentary videotapes on domestic and foreign policy issues.

Community College Association for Instruction and Technology (CCAIT). New Mexico Military Institute, 101 W. College Blvd., Roswell, NM, 88201-5173. (505)624-8382. Fax (505)624-8390. E-mail klopfer@yogi.nmmi.cc.nm.us. Jerry Klopfer, Pres. A national association of community and junior college educators interested in the discovery and dissemination of information relevant to instruction and media technology in the community environment. Facilitates member exchange of data, reports, proceedings, and other information pertinent to instructional technology and the teaching-learning process; sponsors AECT convention sessions, an annual video competition, and social activities. *Membership:* 250. *Dues:* $20. *Meetings:* 1999, AECT National Convention, Houston, Feb 10–13. *Publications:* Regular newsletter; irregular topical papers.

(AACC) Community College Satellite Network (CCSN). One Dupont Cir. NW, Suite 410, Washington, DC 20036. (202)728-0200. Fax (202)833-2467. E-mail CCSN@AACC. NCHE.EDU. Web site http://www.aacc.nche.edu. Monica W. Pilkey, Dir. An office of the American Association of Community Colleges (AACC), CCSN provides leadership and facilitates distance education, teleconferencing, and satellite training to the nation's community colleges. CCSN offers satellite training, discounted teleconferences, free program resources, and general informational assistance in telecommunications to the nation's community colleges. CCSN meets with its members at various industry trade shows and is very active in the AACC annual convention held each spring. CCSN produces a directory of community college satellite downlink and videoconference facilities. *Membership:* 150. *Dues:* $400 for AACC members; $800 for non-AACC members. *Publications: Schedule of Programming* (2/yr.; contains listings of live and taped teleconferences for training and staff development); *CCSN Fall & Spring Program Schedule* (listing of live and taped teleconferences for training, community and staff development, business and industry training, and more); *Teleconferencing at US Community Colleges* (directory of contacts for community college satellite downlink facilities and videoconference capabilities). A free catalog is available.

Computer Assisted Language Instruction Consortium (CALICO). 317 Liberal Arts Building, Southwest Texas State University, 601 University Dr., San Marcos, TX 78666. (512)245-2360. Fax (512)245-8298. E-mail execdir@calico.org. Web site http://www.calico.org. Robert Fischer, Executive Director. CALICO is devoted to the dissemination of information of the application of technology to language teaching and language learning. *Membership:* 1,000 members from US and 20 foreign countries. *Dues:* $50, indiv. *Meetings:* 1999, June, Miami University, Oxford, Ohio. *Publications: CALICO Journal* (q.); *CALICO Monograph Series.*

Computer Learning Foundation. PO Box 60007, Palo Alto, CA 94306-0007. (650)327-3347. Fax (650)327-3349. Web site http://www.ComputerLearning.org. Sally Bowman Alden, Exec. Dir. The Computer Learning Foundation is an international nonprofit educational foundation dedicated to the improvement of education and preparation of youth for the workplace through the use of technology. Foundation programs provide parents and educators with the information, resources, and assistance they need to use technology effectively with children. The Computer Learning Foundation is the official host each October of Computer Learning Month, a month-long focus on the important role technology plays in our lives and a major national grass roots educational effort. During Computer Learning Month, the Computer Learning Foundation announces new materials and projects and hosts North American annual competitions for children, adults, community groups, and schools. Thousands of dollars in technology products are awarded to winners and their schools. The Computer Learning Foundation is endorsed by and collaborates with 56 US State Departments and Canadian Ministries of Education and 26 national nonprofit organizations; however, the Foundation is funded by corporate and individual donations. *Publication: Computer Learning*; annual publication.

Computer-Using Educators, Inc. (CUE). 1210 Marina Village Parkway, Suite 100, Alameda, CA 94501. (510)814-6630. Fax (510)814-0195. E-mail cueinc@cue.org. Web site http://www.cue.org. Bob Walczak, Exec, Dir. CUE, a California nonprofit corporation, was founded in 1976 by a group of teachers interested in exploring the use of technology to improve learning in their classrooms. The organization has never lost sight of this mission. Today, CUE has an active membership of 11,000 professionals world-wide in schools, community colleges, and universities. CUE's 23 affiliates in California provide members with local year-round support through meetings, grants, events, and mini-conferences. Special Interest Groups (SIGs) support members interested in a variety of special topics. CUE's annual conferences, newsletter, advocacy, Web site, and other programs help the technology-using educator connect with other professionals. *Membership:* 11,000 individual, corporate, and institutional members. *Dues:* $30. *Meetings:* 1999 Spring CUE Conference, May 6–8, Palm Springs, CA; Fall CUE Conference, Oct. 28–30, Sacramento. 2000, May 11–13, Palm Springs; Nov 9–11, Sacramento. *Publication: CUE NewsLetter.*

Consortium of College and University Media Centers. 121 Pearson Hall-MRC, Iowa State University, Ames, IA 50011-2203. (515)294-1811. Fax (515)294-8089. E-mail donrieck@iastate.edu; ccumc@ccumc.org. Web site www.indiana.edu/~ccumc/. Don Rieck, Exec. Dir. CCUMC is a professional group of higher education media personnel whose purpose is to improve education and training through the effective use of educational media. Assists educational and training users in making films, video, and educational media more accessible. Fosters cooperative planning among university media centers. Gathers and disseminates information on improved procedures and new developments in instructional technology and media center management. *Membership:* 400. *Dues:* $160, constituent; $60, active; $160, sustaining (commercial); $25, student; $100, associate. *Meetings:* 1999, Oct 21–26, Burlington, VT; 2000, Oct 19–24, Fairborn, OH. *Publications: Leader* (newsletter to members); *University and College Media Review* (journal).

*Continuing Library Education Network and Exchange Round Table (CLENERT). 50 E. Huron St., Chicago, IL 60611. (800)545-2433. Web site http://www.ala.org. An affiliate of the American Library Association, CLENERT seeks to provide access to quality continuing education opportunities for librarians and information scientists and to create an awareness of the need for such education in helping individuals in the field to respond to societal and technological changes.

Membership: 350. *Dues:* open to all ALA members; $15, indiv.; $50, organization. *Publications: CLENExchange* (q.), available to nonmembers by subscription at $20.

Copyright Clearance Center, Inc. (CCC). 222 Rosewood Dr., Danvers, MA 01923. (978) 750-8400. Fax (978)750-4470. E-mail ihinds@copyright.com. Web site http://www.copyright.com/. Isabella Hinds, Vice President. CCC, the largest licenser of photocopy reproduction rights in the US, provides licensing systems involving the reproduction and distribution of copyrighted materials throughout the world. CCC's Academic Permissions Service enable coursepack developers to clear permissions for a broad range of works for use in the academic community. CCC's new Electronic Reserves Service assists academic institutions in clearing digital permissions for their electronic reserve programs. CCC currently manages over 1.75 million works and represents more than 9,600 publishing houses as well as hundreds of thousands of creators, directly or through their representatives. CCC provides licensing rights to thousands of academic institutions, libraries, government agencies, law firms, document suppliers, copy shops, and bookstores within the US, as well as over 9,000 corporations and subsidiaries (including 90 of the Fortune 100 companies).

Corporation for Public Broadcasting (CPB). 901 E Street, NW, Washington, DC 20004-2037. (202)879-9600. Fax (202)783-1039. E-mail info@cpb.org. Web site http://www.cpb.org. Robert T. Coonrod, Pres. and CEO. A private, nonprofit corporation created by Congress in 1967 to develop noncommercial television, radio, and online services for the American people. CPB created the Public Broadcasting Service (PBS) in 1969 and National Public Radio (NPR) in 1970. CPB distributes grants to over 1,000 local public television and radio stations that reach virtually every household in the country. The Corporation is the industry's largest single source of funds for national public television and radio program development and production. In addition to quality educational and informational programming, CPB and local public stations make important contributions in the areas of education, training, community service, and application of emerging technologies. *Publications: Annual Report; CPB Public Broadcasting Directory* ($15).

Council for Basic Education. 1319 F St. NW, Suite 900, Washington, DC 20004-1152. (202)347-4171. Email info@c-b-e.org. Web site http://www.c-b-e.org. Christopher T. Cross, Pres. Maxine P. Frost, Chair of Board of Directors. CBE's mission is to strengthen teaching and learning of the core subjects (mathematics, English, language arts, history, government, geography, the sciences, foreign languages, and the arts) in order to develop the capacity for lifelong learning and foster responsible citizenship. As an independent, critical voice for education reform, CBE champions the philosophy that all children can learn, and that the job of schools is to achieve this goal. CBE advocates this goal by publishing analytical periodicals and administering practical programs as examples to strengthen content in curriculum and teaching. CBE is completing a kit of Standards for Excellence in Education, which includes a CD-ROM, guides for teachers, parents, and principals, and a book of standards in the core subjects. *Membership*: 3,000.

Council for Exceptional Children (CEC). 1920 Association Dr., Reston, VA 20191-1589. (703)620-3660. TTY: (703)264-9446. Fax (703)264-9494. E-mail cec@cec.sped.org. Web site http://www.cec.sped.org. Nancy Safer, Exec. Dir. CEC is the largest international professional organization dedicated to improving educational outcomes for individuals with exceptionalities (students with disabilities and the gifted). CEC advocates for appropriate governmental policies, sets professional standards, provides professional development, advocates for newly and historically underserved individuals with exceptionalities, and helps professionals obtain conditions and resources necessary for effective professional practice. Services include professional development opportunities and resources, 17 divisions for specialized information, public policy advocacy and information, conferences, and standards for the preparation and certification of special educators and professional practice. CEC has expanded its professional development activities to include distance learning activities such as satellite broadcasts and internet-based study groups. The CEC annual convention features the most current educational technology as well as adaptive and assistive technology in formats ranging from full-day workshops to hands-on demonstrations. In collaboration with another agency, CEC is involved in a research project that examines teachers' use of technology to promote literacy in children with exceptionalities. *Membership:* teachers, administrators, students, parents, related support service providers. *Publications:* journals and newsletters with information on new research findings, classroom practices that work, and special education publications. (*See also* the ERIC Clearinghouse on Disabilities and Gifted Education.)

(CEC) Technology and Media Division (TAM). Council for Exceptional Children. The Technology and Media Division (TAM) of The Council for Exceptional Children (CEC) encourages the development of new applications, technologies, and media for use as daily living tools by special populations. This information is disseminated through professional meetings, training programs, and publications. TAM members receive four issues annually of the Journal of Special Education Technology containing articles on specific technology programs and applications, and five issues of the TAM newsletter, providing news of current research, developments, products, conferences, and special programs information. *Membership:* 1,700. *Dues:* $10 in addition to CEC membership.

Council on International Non-Theatrical Events (CINE). 1001 Connecticut Ave. NW, Suite 625, Washington, DC 20036. (202)785-1136. Fax (202)785-4114. Web site http://www.cine.org. Donna Tschiffely, Exec. Dir. Coordinates the selection and placement of US documentary, television, short subject, and didactic films in more than 100 overseas film festivals annually. A Golden Eagle Certificate is awarded to each professional film considered most suitable to represent the US in international competition and to winning films made by adults, amateurs, youths, and university students. Prizes and certificates won at overseas festivals are presented at an annual awards ceremony. CINE receives approximately 1300 entries annually for the competition. Deadlines for receipt of entry forms are Feb 1 and Aug 1. *Meeting:* CINE Showcase and Awards held annually in Washington, DC. *Publications: CINE Annual Yearbook of Film and Video Awards; Worldwide Directory of Film and Video Festivals and Events.*

*East-West Center. 1601 East-West Rd., Honolulu, HI 96848-1601. (808)944-7111. Fax (808)944-7376. E-mail ewcinfo@ewc.hawaii.edu. Web site http://www.ewc.hawaii.edu. Kenji Sumida, Pres. The US Congress established the East-West Center in 1960 with a mandate to foster mutual understanding and cooperation among the governments and peoples of Asia, the Pacific, and the US. Officially known as the Center for Cultural and Technical Interchange Between East and West, it is a public, nonprofit institution with an international board of governors. Principal funding for the center comes from the US government, with additional support provided by private agencies, individuals, and corporations, and more than 20 Asian and Pacific governments, private agencies, individuals, and corporations. The center, through research, education, dialog, and outreach, provides a neutral meeting ground where people with a wide range of perspectives exchange views on topics of regional concern. Some 2,000 scholars, government and business leaders, educators, journalists, and other professionals from throughout the region annually work with Center staff to address issues of contemporary significance in such areas as international economics and politics, the environment, population, energy and mineral resources, cultural studies, communications, the media, and Pacific islands development.

Educational Communications. PO Box 351419, Los Angeles, CA 90035. (310)559-9160. Fax (310)559-9160. E-mail ECNP@aol.com. Web site http://home.earthlink.net/~dragonflight/ecoprojects.htm. Nancy Pearlman, CEO. Educational Communications is dedicated to enhancing the quality of life on this planet and provides radio and television programs about the environment. Serves as a clearinghouse on ecological issues. Programming is available on 100 stations in 25 states. *Publications: Compendium Newsletter* (bi-monthly); *Directory of Environmental Organizations.*

ECT Foundation. c/o AECT, 1025 Vermont Ave. NW, Suite 820, Washington, DC 20005. Hans-Erik Wennberg, Pres. The ECT Foundation is a nonprofit organization whose purposes are charitable and educational in nature. Its operation is based on the conviction that improvement of instruction can be accomplished, in part, by the continued investigation and application of new systems for learning and by periodic assessment of current techniques for the communication of information. In addition to awarding scholarships, internships, and fellowships, the foundation develops and conducts leadership training programs for emerging professional leaders. Its operations are closely allied to AECT program goals, and the two organizations operate in close conjunction to each other.

*Education Development Center, Inc. 55 Chapel St., Newton, MA 02158-1060. (617)969-7100. Fax (617)969-5979. Web site http://www.edc.org. Janet Whitla, Pres. Seeks to improve education at all levels, in the US and abroad, through curriculum development, institutional development, and services to the school and the community. Produces videocassettes, primarily in connection with curriculum development and teacher training. *Publication: Annual Report.*

Educational Products Information Exchange (EPIE Institute). 103 W. Montauk Highway, Hampton Bays, NY 11946. (516)728-9100. Fax (516)728-9228. E-mail komoski@aurora.lionet. edu. Web site http://www.epie.org. P. Kenneth Komoski, Exec. Dir. Assesses educational materials and provides consumer information, product descriptions, and citations for virtually all educational software and curriculum-related Web sites. All of EPIE's services are available to schools and state agencies as well as parents and individuals. Online access is restricted to states with membership in the States Consortium for Improving Software Selection (SCISS). *Publications: The Educational Software Selector Database (TESS)*, available to anyone. All publication material now available on CD-ROM.

Educational Resources Information Center (ERIC). National Library of Education (NLE), Office of Educational Research and Improvement (OERI), 555 New Jersey Ave. NW, Washington, DC 20208-5720. (202)219-2289. Fax (202)219-1817. E-mail eric@inet.ed.gov. Keith Stubbs, Dir. ERIC is a federally-funded nationwide information network that provides access to the English-language education literature. The ERIC system consists of clearinghouses, adjunct clearinghouses, and system support components includings ACCESS ERIC, the ERIC Document Reproduction Service (EDRS), and the ERIC Processing and Reference Facility. ERIC actively solicits papers, conference proceedings, literature reviews, and curriculum materials from researchers, practitioners, educational associations and institutions, and federal, state, and local agencies. These materials, along with articles from nearly 800 different journals, are indexed and abstracted for entry into the ERIC database. The ERIC database (the largest education database in the world) now contains more than 850,000 records of documents and journal articles. Users can access the ERIC database online, on CD-ROM, or through print and microfiche indexes. ERIC microfiche collections, which contain the full text of most ERIC documents, are available for public use at more than 1,000 locations worldwide. Reprints of ERIC documents, on microfiche or in paper copy, can also be ordered from EDRS. Copies of journal articles can be found in library periodical collections, through interlibrary loan, or from article reprint services. A list of the ERIC Clearinghouses, together with addresses, telephone numbers, and brief domain descriptions, follows here. *Publications: Resources in Education* (U.S. Government Printing Office); *Current Index to Journals in Education* (Oryx Press).

ACCESS ERIC. Aspen Systems Corp., 2277 Research Blvd., Mailstop 7A, Rockville, MD 20850. 1-800-LET-ERIC [538-3742]. Fax (301)519-6760. E-mail acceric@inet.ed.gov. Lynn Smarte, Project Dir. ACCESS ERIC coordinates ERIC's outreach and systemwide dissemination activities, develops new ERIC publications, and provides general reference and referral services. Its publications include several reference directories designed to help the public understand and use ERIC as well as provide information about current education-related issues, research, and practice. *Publications: A Pocket Guide to ERIC*; *All About ERIC*; *The ERIC Review*; the Parent Brochure series; *Catalog of ERIC Clearinghouse Publications*; *ERIC Calendar of Education-Related Conferences*; *ERIC Directory of Education-Related Information Centers*; *ERIC User's Interchange*; *Directory of ERIC Resource Collections. Databases:* ERIC Digests Online (EDO); Education-Related Information Centers; ERIC Resource Collections; ERIC Calendar of Education-Related Conferences. (The databases are available through the Internet: http://www.aspensys.com/eric.)

ERIC Clearinghouse for Community Colleges (JC) (formerly Junior Colleges). University of California at Los Angeles (UCLA), 3051 Moore Hall, PO Box 95121, Los Angeles, CA 90024-1521. (310)825-3931, (800)832-8256. Fax (310)206-8095. E-mail ericcc@ucla.edu. Web site http://www.gseis.ucla.edu/ERIC/eric.html. Arthur M. Cohen, Dir. Topics include development, administration, and evaluation of two-year public and private community and junior colleges, technical institutes, and two-year branch university campuses; two-year college students, faculty, staff, curricula, programs, support services, libraries, and community services; linkages between two-year colleges and business, industrial, and community organizations; articulation of two-year colleges with secondary and four-year postsecondary institutions.

ERIC Clearinghouse for Social Studies/Social Science Education (SO). Indiana University, Social Studies Development Center, 2805 East 10th St., Suite 120, Bloomington, IN 47408-2698. (812)855-3838, (800)266-3815. Fax (812)855-0455. E-mail ericso@indiana. edu. Web site http://www.indiana.edu/~ssdc.eric_chess.htm. All levels of social studies and social science education; the contributions of history, geography, and other social science disciplines; applications of theory and research to social science education; education as a social science; comparative education (K–12); content and curriculum materials on social topics such as law-related education, ethnic studies, bias and discrimination, aging, and women's equity. Music and art education are also covered. Includes input from the Adjunct ERIC Clearinghouses for Law-Related Education, for U.S.–Japan Studies, and on Art Education.

> **Adjunct ERIC Clearinghouse for Art Education**. Indiana University, Social Studies Development Center, 2805 East 10th St., Suite 120, Bloomington, IN 47408-2698. (812)855-3838, (800)266-3815. Fax (812)855-0455. E-mail clarkgil@indiana.edu; zimmerm@ucs.indiana.edu. Enid Zimmerman, Director. Adjunct to the ERIC Clearinghouse on Social Studies/Social Science Education.

> **Adjunct ERIC Clearinghouse for Law-Related Education (ADJ/LR)**. Indiana University, Social Studies Development Center, 2805 East 10th St., Suite 120, Bloomington, IN 47408-2698. (812)855-3838, (800)266-3815. Fax (812)855-0455. E-mail patrick@indiana.edu, tvontz@indiana.edu. Web site http://www.indiana.edu/ ~ssdc/iplre.html. John Patrick and Robert Leming, Co-Directors. Adjunct to the ERIC Clearinghouse on Social Studies/Social Sciences Education.

> **Adjunct ERIC Clearinghouse for United States-Japan Studies (ADJ/JS)**. 2805 E. 10th St., Suite 120, Bloomington, IN 47408-2698. (812)855-3838, (800)266-3815. Fax (812)855-0455. E-mail japan@indiana.edu. Web site http://www.indiana.edu/~japan. Marcia Johnson, Assoc. Dir. Provides information on topics concerning Japan and US-Japan relations. Adjunct to the ERIC Clearinghouse for Social Studies/Social Science Education. *Publications: Guide to Teaching Materials on Japan*; *Teaching About Japan: Lessons and Resources*; *The Constitution and Individual Rights in Japan: Lessons for Middle and High School Students*; *Internationalizing the US Classroom: Japan as a Model*; *Tora no Maki II: Lessons for Teaching About Contemporary Japan*; *The Japan Digest Series* (complimentary, concise discussions of various Japan-related topics): *Fiction About Japan in the Elementary Curriculum*; *Daily Life in Japanese High Schools*; *Rice: It's More Than Food in Japan*; *Ideas for Integrating Japan into the Curriculum*; *Japanese Education*; *Japanese-US Economic Relations*; *Japan's Economy: 21st Century Challenges*; *Shinbun* (biannual project newsletter).

ERIC Clearinghouse on Adult, Career, and Vocational Education (ERIC/ACVE). The Ohio State University, Center on Education and Training for Employment, 1900 Kenny Rd., Columbus, OH 43210-1090. (614)292-4353, (800)848-4815, ext. 4-7685. Fax (614)292-1260. E-mail ericacve@postbox.acs.ohio-state.edu. Web site http://www.coe.ohio-state/cete/ ericacve/index.htm. Susan Imel, Dir. Judy Wagner, Assoc. Dir. All levels and settings of adult and continuing, career, and vocational/technical education. Adult education, from basic literacy training through professional skill upgrading. Career awareness, career decision making, career development, career change, and experience-based education. Vocational and technical education, including new subprofessional fields, industrial arts, corrections education, employment and training programs, youth employment, work experience programs, education and business partnerships, entrepreneurship, adult retraining, and vocational rehabilitation for individuals with disabilities. Includes input from the Adjunct ERIC Clearinghouse on Consumer Education.

Adjunct ERIC Clearinghouse for Consumer Education (ADJ/CN). National Institute for Consumer Education, 207 Rackham Bldg., Eastern Michigan University, Ypsilanti, MI 48197-2237. (313)487-2292. Fax (313)487-7153. E-mail nice@emuvax. emich.edu. E-mail NICE@online.emich.edu. Web site http://www.emich.edu/ public/coe/nice. Rosella Bannister, Dir. Adjunct to the ERIC Clearinghouse on Adult, Career, and Vocational Education.

ERIC Clearinghouse on Assessment and Evaluation (formerly Tests, Measurement, and Evaluation). The Catholic University of America, 210 O'Boyle Hall, Washington, DC 20064-4035. (202)319-5120, (800)464-3742. Fax (202)319-6692. E-mail eric_ae@cua.edu. Web site http://ericae.net. Lawrence M. Rudner, Dir. Tests and other measurement devices; methodology of measurement and evaluation; application of tests, measurement, or evaluation in educational projects and programs; research design and methodology in the area of assessment and evaluation; and learning theory. Includes input from the Adjunct Test Collection Clearinghouse.

ERIC Clearinghouse on Counseling and Student Services (formerly Counseling and Personnel Services). University of North Carolina at Greensboro, School of Education, 201 Ferguson Building, PO Box 26171, Greensboro, NC 27402-6171. (336)334-4114, (336) 334-4116, (800)414-9769. E-mail ericcass@uncg.edu. Web site http://www.uncg. edu/~ericcas2. Garry R. Walz, Dir. Preparation, practice, and supervision of counselors and therapists at all educational levels and in all settings; theoretical development of counseling and student services; assessment and diagnosis procedures such as testing and interviewing and the analysis and dissemination of the resultant information; outcomes analysis of counseling interventions; groups and case work; nature of pupil, student, and adult characteristics; identification and implementation of strategies which foster student learning and achievement; personnel workers and their relation to career planning, family consultations and student services activities; identification of effective strategies for enhancing parental effectiveness; and continuing preparation of counselors and therapists in the use of new technologies for professional renewal and the implications of such technologies for service provision. *Meeting:* Annual Assessment Conference. *Publications: Career Transitions in Turbulent Times; Exemplary Career Development Programs & Practices; Career Development; Counseling Employment Bound Youth; Internationalizing Career Planning; Saving the Native Son; Cultural and Diversity Issues in Counseling; Safe Schools, Safe Students;* many others. Call for catalog.

ERIC Clearinghouse on Disabilities and Gifted Education (ERIC/EC). 1920 Association Dr., Reston, VA 20191-1589. (703)264-9474, (800)328-0272. TTY: (703)264-9449. E-mail ericec@cec.sped.org. Web site http://www.cec.sped.org/ericec.htm. Bruce Ramirez, Interim Dir. ERIC EC selects and abstracts the best of the professional literature on disabilities and gifted information for inclusion into the ERIC database. Operated by The Council for Exceptional Children (see separate entry), ERIC EC responds to requests for information in special/gifted education, serves as a resource center for the general public, publishes, and disseminates information on current special/gifted education research, programs, and practices.

ERIC Clearinghouse on Educational Management (EA). University of Oregon (Dept. 5207), 1787 Agate St., Eugene, OR 97403-5207. (541)346-5043, (800)438-8841. Fax

(541)346-2334. E-mail ppiele@oregon.uoregon.edu. Philip K. Piele, Dir. The governance, leadership, management, and structure of K-12 public and private education organizations; local, state, and federal education law and policy-making; practice and theory of administration; preservice and inservice preparation of administrators; tasks and processes of administration; methods and varieties of organization and organizational change; and the social context of education organizations.

ERIC Clearinghouse on Elementary and Early Childhood Education (PS) and the **National Parent Information Network (NPIN)**. University of Illinois, Children's Research Center, 51 Gerty Dr., Champaign, IL 61820. (217)333-1386, (800)583-4135. Fax (217)333-3767. E-mail ericeece@uiuc.edu. Web site http://ericps.crc.uiuc.edu/ericeece. html. Lilian G. Katz, Dir. (l-katz@uiuc.edu). The physical, cognitive, social, educational, and cultural development of children from birth through early adolescence; prenatal factors; parents, parenting, and family relationships that impinge on education; learning theory research and practice related to the development of young children, including the preparation of teachers for this educational level; interdisciplinary curriculum and mixed-age teaching and learning; educational, social, and cultural programs and services for children; the child in the context of the family and the family in the context of society; theoretical and philosophical issues pertaining to children's development and education. Includes input from the Adjunct ERIC Clearinghouse for Child Care.

> **Adjunct ERIC Clearinghouse for Child Care (ADJ/CC)**. National Child Care Information Center, 301 Maple Ave., Suite 602, Vienna, VA 22180. (703)938-6555, (800)516-2242. Fax (800)716-2242. E-mail agoldstein@acf.dhhs.gov. Web site http://ericps.crc.uiuc.edu/nccic/nccichome.html. Anne Goldstein, Proj. Dir. Adjunct to the ERIC Clearinghouse on Elementary and Early Childhood Education.

ERIC Clearinghouse on Higher Education (HE). George Washington University, One Dupont Cir. NW, Suite 630, Washington, DC 20036-1183. (202)296-2597, (800)773-3742. Fax (202)296-8379. E-mail eric@eric-he.edu. Web site http://www.gwv.edu/~eriche. Jonathan D. Fife, Dir. Topics relating to college and university conditions, problems, programs, and students. Curricular and instructional programs, and institutional research at the college or university level. Federal programs, professional education (medicine, law, etc.), professional continuing education, collegiate computer-assisted learning and management, graduate education, university extension programs, teaching and learning, legal issues and legislation, planning, governance, finance, evaluation, interinstitutional arrangements, management of institutions of higher education, and business or industry educational programs leading to a degree. *Publications: Higher Education Leadership: Analyzing the Gender Gap; The Virtual Campus: Technology and Reform in Higher Education; Early Intervention Programs: Opening the Door to Higher Education; Enriching College with Constructive Controversy; A Culture for Academic Excellence: Implementing the Quality Principles in Higher Education; From Discipline to Development: Rethinking Student Conduct in Higher Education; Proclaiming and Sustaining Excellence: Assessment as a Faculty Role; The Application of Customer Satisfaction Principles to Universities; Saving the Other Two-Thirds: Practices and Strategies for Improving the Retention and Graduation of African American Students in Predominately White Institutions; Enrollment Management: Change for the 21st Century; Faculty Workload: States Perspectives.*

ERIC Clearinghouse on Information & Technology (IR) (formerly Information Resources). Syracuse University, 4-194 Center for Science and Technology, Syracuse, NY 13244-4100. (315)443-3640, (800)464-9107. Fax (315)443-5448. E-mail eric@ericir.syr.edu. AskERIC (question-answering service via Internet) askeric@ericir.syr.edu. Michael B. Eisenberg, Dir. Educational technology and library and information science at all levels. Instructional design, development, and evaluation within educational technology, along with the media of educational communication: computers and microcomputers, telecommunications, audio and video recordings, film and other audiovisual materials as they pertain to teaching and learning. The focus is on the operation and management of information services for education-related organizations. Includes all aspects of information technology related to education.

ERIC Clearinghouse on Languages and Linguistics (FL). Center for Applied Linguistics, 1118 22nd St. NW, Washington, DC 20037-1214. (202)429-9292, (800)276-9834. Fax (202)659-5641. E-mail eric@cal.org. Web site http://www.cal.org/ericll. Joy Peyton, Dir. Dr. Craig Packard, User Services Coordinator, contact person. Languages and language sciences. All aspects of second language instruction and learning in all commonly and uncommonly taught languages, including English as a second language. Bilingualism and bilingual education. Cultural education in the context of second language learning, including intercultural communication, study abroad, and international education exchange. All areas of linguistics, including theoretical and applied linguistics, socio-linguistics, and psycholinguistics. Includes input from the National Clearinghouse on ESL Literacy Education (NCLE).

Adjunct ERIC Clearinghouse for ESL Literacy Education (ADJ/LE). National Clearinghouse for ESL Literacy Education, Center for Applied Linguistics (CAL), 1118 22nd St. NW, Washington, DC 20037-0037. (202)429-9292, Ext. 200. Fax (202)659-5641. E-mail ncle@cal.org. Web site http://www.cal.org/ncle/. Joy Kreeft Peyton, Dir. Adjunct to the ERIC Clearinghouse on Languages and Linguistics. NCLE is the national clearinghouse focusing on the education of adults learning English as a second or additional language. NCLE collects, analyzes, synthesizes, and disseminates information on literacy education for adults and out-of-school youth. NCLE publications books (available from Delta Systems in McHenry, IL), free ERIC digests and annotated bibliographies on a wide range of topics, and *NCLE Notes*, a newsletter. *Publication: Literacy and Language Diversity in the United States* by Terrence Wiley (1996), McHenry, IL: Delta Systems.

ERIC Clearinghouse on Reading, English, and Communication (CS) (formerly Reading and Communication Skills). Indiana University, Smith Research Center, Suite 150, 2805 E. 10th St., Bloomington, IN 47408-2698. (812)855-5847, (800)759-4723. Fax (812)855-4220. E-mail ericcs@indiana.edu. Web site http://www.indiana.edu/~eric_rec. Carl B. Smith, Dir. Reading, English, and communication (verbal and nonverbal), preschool through college; research and instructional development in reading, writing, speaking, and listening; identification, diagnosis, and remediation of reading problems; speech communication (including forensics); mass communication; interpersonal and small group interaction; interpretation, rhetorical and communication theory; speech sciences; and theater. Preparation of instructional staff and related personnel. All aspects of reading behavior with emphasis on physiology, psychology, sociology, and teaching; instructional materials, curricula, tests and measurement, and methodology at all levels of reading; the role of libraries and other agencies in fostering and guiding reading; diagnostics and remedial reading services in schools and clinical settings. Preparation of reading teachers and specialists. The Web site makes available a wealth of information pertaining to the full gamut of language arts topics enumerated above.

ERIC Clearinghouse on Rural Education and Small Schools (RC). Appalachia Educational Laboratory (AEL), 1031 Quarrier St., PO Box 1348, Charleston, WV 25325-1348. (304)347-0465; (800)624-9120. Fax (304)347-0487. E-mail lanhamb@ael.org. Web page http://www.ael.org/erichp.htm. Hobart Harmon, Acting Dir. Economic, cultural, social, or other factors related to educational programs and practices for rural residents; American Indians and Alaska Natives, Mexican Americans, and migrants; educational practices and programs in all small schools; and outdoor education. Check Web site to subscribe to print newsletter, or call toll-free.

*ERIC Clearinghouse on Science, Mathematics, and Environmental Education (SE).
The Ohio State University, 1929 Kenny Road, Columbus, OH 43210-1080. (614)292-6717, (800)276-0462. Fax (614)292-0263. E-mail ericse@osu.edu. Web site http://www.ericse.org. Science, mathematics, and environmental education at all levels, and within these three broad subject areas, the following topics: development of curriculum and instruction materials; teachers and teacher education; learning theory and outcomes (including the impact of parameters such as interest level, intelligence, values, and concept development upon learning in these fields); educational programs; research and evaluative studies; media applications; computer applications.

ERIC Clearinghouse on Teaching and Teacher Education (SP) (formerly Teacher Education). American Association of Colleges for Teacher Education (AACTE), One Dupont Cir. NW, Suite 610, Washington, DC 20036-1186. (202)293-2450, (800)822-9229. Fax (202)457-8095. E-mail query@aacte.nche.edu. Web site http://www.ericsp.org. Mary E. Dilworth, Dir. School personnel at all levels. Teacher recruitment, selection, licensing, certification, training, preservice and inservice preparation, evaluation, retention, and retirement. The theory, philosophy, and practice of teaching. Curricula and general education not specifically covered by other clearinghouses. Organization, administration, finance, and legal issues relating to teacher education programs and institutions. All aspects of health, physical, recreation, and dance education. Includes input from the Adjunct ERIC Clearinghouse on Clinical Schools.

> **Adjunct ERIC Clearinghouse on Clinical Schools (ADJ/CL).** American Association of Colleges for Teacher Education, One Dupont Cir. NW, Suite 610, Washington, DC 20036-1186. (202)293-2450, (800)822-9229. Fax (202)457-8095. E-mail iabdalha@ inet.ed.gov. Web site http://www.aacte.org/menu2.html. Ismat Abdal-Haqq, Coord. Adjunct to the ERIC Clearinghouse on Teaching and Teacher Education.

ERIC Clearinghouse on Urban Education. Teachers College, Columbia University, Institute for Urban and Minority Education, Main Hall, Rm. 303, Box 40, 525 W. 120th St., New York, NY 10027-6696. (212)678-3433, (800)601-4868. Fax (212)678-4012. E-mail eric-cue@columbia.edu. Web site http://eric-web.tc.columbia.edu. Erwin Flaxman, Dir. Programs and practices in public, parochial, and private schools in urban areas and the education of particular ethnic minority children and youth in various settings; the theory and practice of educational equity; urban and minority experiences; and urban and minority social institutions and services.

ERIC Document Reproduction Service (EDRS). 7420 Fullerton Rd., Suite 110, Springfield, VA 22153-2852. (703)440-1400, (800)443-ERIC (3742). Fax (703)440-1408. E-mail service@edrs.com. Web site http://edrs.com. Peter M. Dagutis, Dir. Produces and sells microfiche, paper, and electronic copies of documents abstracted in ERIC. Electronic delivery of recent documents in ERIC available. Delivery methods include shipment of hardcopy documents and microfiche, document fax-back, and online delivery. Back collections of ERIC documents, annual subscriptions, cumulative indexes, and other ERIC-related materials are also available. ERIC documents can be ordered by toll-free phone call, fax, mail, or online through the EDRS Web site. Document ordering also available from DIALOG and OCLC. Documents available for online delivery include all Level 1 documents with the appropriate copyright release from 1993 forward (i.e., ERIC document numbers greater that ED348466).

ERIC Processing and Reference Facility. 1100 West Street, 2nd Floor, Laurel, MD 20707-3598. (301)497-4080, (800)799-ERIC (3742). Fax (301)953-0263. E-mail ericfac@inet. ed.gov. Web page http://ericfac.piccard.csc.com. Ted Brandhorst, Dir. A central editorial and computer processing agency that coordinates document processing and database building activities for ERIC; performs acquisition, lexicographic, and reference functions; and maintains systemwide quality control standards. The ERIC Facility also prepares *Resources* in Education (RIE), ERIC Processing Manual, Thesaurus of ERIC Descriptors, Identifier Authority List (IAL), ERIC Ready References, and other products.

Educational Videos and CD-ROM (originally the PCR Collection). Penn State Media Sales, 118 Wagner Building, University Park, PA 16802. Purchasing info (800)770-2111, (814)863-3102. Fax (814)865-3172. Rental information (800)826-0132. Fax (814)863-2574. Special Services Building, Penn State University, University Park, PA 16802. E-mail mediasales@cde.psu.edu. Web site http://www.cde.psu.edu/MediaSales. Sue Oram, Media Sales Coordinator. Makes available to professionals video in the behavioral sciences judged to be useful for university teaching and research. Also distributes training videos to business and industry. A catalog of the videos in the collection is available online. Special topics and individual brochures available. The online catalog now contains videos in the behavioral sciences (psychology, psychiatry, anthropology), animal behavior, sociology, teaching and learning, folklife and agriculture, business, education, biological sciences, and Pennsylvania topics. Videos and CD-ROMs may be submitted for international distribution. Stock footage available also.

Eisenhower National Clearinghouse for Mathematics and Science Education. 1929 Kenny Road, Columbus, OH 43210-1079. (800)621-5785, (614)292-7784. Fax (614)292-2066. E-mail info@enc.org. Web site http://www.enc.org. Dr. Len Simutis, Dir. The Eisenhower National Clearinghouse for Mathematics and Science Education (ENC) is located at The Ohio State University and funded by the US Department of Education's Office of Educational Research and Improvement (OERI). ENC provides K-12 teachers and other educators a central source of information on mathematics and science curriculum materials, particularly those which support education reform. Among ENC's products and services are ENC Online, which is available through a toll-free number and the Internet; 12 demonstration sites located throughout the nation; and a variety of publications, including the Guidebook of Federal Resources for K-12 Mathematics and Science, which lists federal resources in mathematics and science education. *Membership:* Users include K-12 teachers, other educators, policy makers, and parents. *Publications: ENC Update* (newsletter); *ENC Focus* (print catalog on selected topics); *ENC Online Brochure*; *Guidebook of Federal Resources for K-12 Mathematics and Science* (federal programs in mathematics and science education). ENC Online is available online (http://www.enc.org) or toll-free at (800)362-4448.

Far West Laboratory for Educational Research and Development (FWL). See listing for WestEd.

Federal Communications Commission (FCC). 1919 M St. NW, Washington, DC 20554. (202)418-0190. Web site http://www.fcc.gov. William Kennard, Chairman. The FCC regulates the telecommunication industry in the US.

Federal Educational Technology Association (FETA). FETA Membership, Sara Shick, PO Box 3412, McLean, VA 22103-3412. (703)406-3040. Fax (703)406-4318 (Clear Spring Inc.), E-mail feta@clearspringinc.com. Web site http://www.feta.org. Beth Borko, Board Chair. An affiliate of AECT, FETA is dedicated to the improvement of education and training through research, communication, and practice. It encourages and welcomes members from all government agencies, federal, state, and local; from business and industry; and from all educational institutions and organizations. FETA encourages interaction among members to improve the quality of education and training in any arena, but with specific emphasis on government-related applications. *Membership:* 150. *Dues:* $20. Meetings: meets in conjunction with AECT InCITE, concurrently with SALT's Washington meeting in August, and periodically throughout the year in Washington, DC. *Publication:* Newsletter (occasional).

Film Arts Foundation (FAF). 346 9th St., 2nd Floor, San Francisco, CA 94103. (415)552-8760. Fax (415)552-0882. E-mail filmarts@best.com. Web site http://www.filmarts.org. Gail Silva, Dir. Daven Gee, Admin. Dir. Service organization that supports and promotes independent film and video production. Services include low-cost 16mm, Super-8, S-VHS, and AVID equipment rental, resource library, group legal and health plans, monthly magazine, seminars, grants program, annual film and video festival, nonprofit sponsorship, exhibition program, and advocacy. *Membership:* 3,300 plus. *Dues:* $45. *Meetings:* Annual Festival. *Publications: Release Print*; *AEIOU (Alternative Exhibition Information of the Universe)*; *Media Catalog* (over 200 titles of independent media projects completed with FAF's nonprofit fiscal sponsorship).

*Film/Video Arts (F/VA). 817 Broadway, 2nd Floor, New York, NY 10003. (212)673-9361. Fax (212)475-3467. Frank Millspaugh, Exec. Dir. Film/Video Arts is the largest nonprofit media arts center in the New York region. Dedicated to the advancement of emerging and established media artists of diverse backgrounds, F/VA is unique in providing a fertile environment where aspiring producers can obtain training, rent equipment, and edit their projects all under one roof. Every year over 2,500 individuals participate in F/VA's programs. There are over 50 courses offered each semester, covering topics such as rudimentary technical training in 16mm filmmaking and video production, advanced editing courses in online systems, history, cultural analysis, installation art, fundraising, grant writing, and distribution. F/VA is supported by the New York State Council on the Arts, the National Endowment for the Arts, and numerous foundations and corporations, and is therefore able to offer courses and production services at the lowest possible rates. Artists who got their start at F/VA include Jim Jarmusch, Mira Nair, Leslie Harris, Kevin Smith, and Cheryl Dunye. F/VA takes pride in meeting the needs of a broad range of filmmakers, working on features, documentaries, shorts, experimental pieces, industrials, cable shows, music videos and more by offering affordable services essential to the creation of their work and development of their careers. *Membership:* $40, indiv., $70, organization.

Freedom of Information Center. 127 Neff Annex, University of Missouri, Columbia, MO 65211. (573)882-4856. Fax (573)884-4963. E-mail Kathleen_Edwards@jmail.missouri.edu. Web site http://www.missouri.edu/~foiwww. Kathleen Edwards, Manager. The Freedom of Information Center is a research library which maintains files documenting actions by governments, media, and society affecting the movement and content of information. Open 8:00 a.m. to 5:00 p.m., Monday through Friday, except holidays. Located at Missouri's School of Journalism. *Membership:* Research and referral services are available to all. *Publication: Access to Public Information: A Resource Guide to Government in Columbia and Boone County, Missouri*. Updated periodically at Web site.

George Eastman House (formerly International Museum of Photography at George Eastman House). 900 East Ave., Rochester, NY 14607. (716)271-3361. Fax (716)271-3970. Web site http://www.eastman.org. Anthony Bannon, Dir. World-renowned museum of photography and cinematography established to preserve, collect, and exhibit photographic art and technology, film materials, and related literature, and to serve as a memorial to George Eastman. Services include archives, traveling exhibitions, research library, school of film preservation, center for the conservation of photographic materials, and photographic print service. Educational programs, exhibitions, films, symposia, music events, tours, and internship stipends offered. Eastman's turn-of-the-century mansion and gardens have been restored to their original grandeur. *Dues:* $40, library; $50, family; $40, indiv.; $36, student; $30, senior citizen; $75, Contributor; $125, Sustainer; $250, Patron; $500, Benefactor; $1,000, George Eastman Society. *Membership:* 3,800. *Publications: IMAGE*; *Microfiche Index to Collections*; *Newsletter*; *Annual Report: The George Eastman House and Gardens*; *Masterpieces of Photography from the George Eastman House Collections*; and exhibition catalogs.

The George Lucas Educational Foundation. PO Box 3494, San Rafael, CA 94912. (415)662-1600. Fax (415)662-1605. E-mail edutopia@glef.org. Web site http://glef.org. Dr. Milton Chen, Exec. Dir. The Foundation promotes innovative efforts to improve education, especially those that integrate technology with teaching and learning, so all students will be prepared to learn and live in an increasingly complex world. Projects include a documentary film and resource book, a Web site, and bi-annual newsletter, all of which feature compelling education programs from around the country. The target audience is community and opinion leaders, parents, educators, media, corporate executives, and elected officials. The Foundation works to give these stakeholders useful tools to develop, make, and sustain changes in teaching and learning. The George Lucas Educational Foundation is a private operating foundation, not a grantmaking organization. *Publication: EDUTOPIA* (bi-annual newsletter).

Graphic Arts Technical Foundation (GATF). 200 Deer Run Road, Sewickley, PA 15143-2600. (412)741-6860. Fax (412)741-2311. E-mail info@gatf.org. Web site http://www.gatf.org. George Ryan, Pres. GATF is a member-supported, nonprofit, scientific, technical, and educational organization dedicated to the advancement of graphic communications industries worldwide. For 73 years GATF has developed leading-edge technologies and practices for printing, and each year the Foundation develops new products, services, and training programs to meet the evolving needs of the industry. *Membership:* 1,600 corporate members, 520 teachers, 100 students. *Dues:* $40, teachers; $30, students; corporate dues based on percentage of sales (ranges from $350-$4,000). *Meetings:* Annual GATF/PIA Joint Fall Conference. *Publications: Professional Print Buying*; *Computer-to-Plate: Automating the Printing Industry*; *Understanding Electronic Communications: Printing in the Information Age*; *On-Demand Printing: The Revolution in Digital and Customized Printing.*

Great Plains National ITV Library (GPN). PO Box 80669, Lincoln, NE 68501-0669. (402)472-2007, (800)228-4630. Fax (402)472-4076, (800)306-2330. E-mail gpn@unl.edu. Web page http://gpn.unl.edu. Lee Rockwell, Dir. Acquires, produces, promotes, and distributes educational media, videocassettes, videodiscs, and CD-ROMs. Offers more than 200 videotape (videocassette) courses and related teacher utilization materials. Available for purchase or, in some instances, lease. *Publications: GPN Educational Video Catalogs* by curriculum areas; periodic brochures.

Health Sciences Communications Association (HeSCA). One Wedgewood Dr., Suite 27, Jewett City, CT 06351-2428. (203)376-5915. Fax (203)376-6621. E-mail HeSCAOne@aol.com. Web site http://www.hesca.washington.edu. Ronald Sokolowski, Exec. Dir. An affiliate of AECT, HeSCA is a nonprofit organization dedicated to the sharing of ideas, skills, resources, and techniques to enhance communications and educational technology in the health sciences. It seeks to nurture the professional growth of its members, to serve as a professional focal point for those engaged in health sciences communications, and to convey the concerns, issues, and concepts of health sciences communications to other organizations which influence and are affected by the profession. International in scope and diverse in membership, HeSCA is supported by medical and veterinary schools, hospitals, medical associations, and businesses where media is used to create and disseminate health information. *Membership:* 150. *Dues:* $150, indiv.; $195, institutional ($150 additional institutional dues); $60, retiree; $75, student; $1,000, sustaining. All include subscriptions to the journal and newsletter. *Meetings:* Annual Meetings, May–June. *Publications: Journal of Biocommunications*; *Feedback* (newsletter); *Patient Education Sourcebook Vol. II.*

Hollywood Film Archive. 8391 Beverly Blvd., #321, Hollywood, CA 90048. (213)933-3345. D. Richard Baer, Dir. Archival organization for information about feature films produced worldwide, from the early silents to the present. *Publications:* comprehensive movie reference works for sale, including *Variety Film Reviews* (1907–1996) and the *American Film Institute Catalogs* (1893–1910, 1911–20, 1921–30, 1931–40, 1941–50, 1961–70), as well as the *Film Superlist* (1894–1939, 1940–1949, 1950–1959) volumes, which provide information both on copyrights and on motion pictures in the public domain, and *Harrison's Reports and Film Reviews* (1919–1962).

HOPE Reports, Inc. 58 Carverdale Dr., Rochester, NY 14618-4004. (716)442-1310. Fax (716)442-1725. E-mail hopereport@aol.com. Thomas W. Hope, Chairman and CEO; Mabeth S. Hope, Vice Pres. Supplies statistics, marketing information, trends, forecasts, and salary and media studies to the visual communications industries through printed reports, custom studies, consulting, and by telephone. Clients and users in the US and abroad include manufacturers, dealers, producers, and media users in business, government, health sciences, religion, education, and community agencies. *Publications: Hope Reports Presentation Media Events Calendar* (annual); *Video Post-Production*; *Media Market Trends*; *Educational Media Trends Through the 1990's*;

LCD Panels and Projectors; Overhead Projection System; Presentation Slides; Producer & Video Post Wages & Salaries; Noncommercial AV Wages & Salaries; Corporate Media Salaries; Digital Photography: Pictures of Tomorrow; Hope Reports Top 100 Contract Producers; Contract Production II; Executive Compensation; Media Production; Outsource or Insource.

Institute for Development of Educational Activities, Inc. (|I|D|E|A|). 259 Regency Ridge, Dayton, OH 45459. (937)434-6969. Fax (937)434-5203. E-mail: IDEADayton@aol.com. Web site: http://www.idea.org. Dr. Steven R. Thompson, Pres. |I|D|E|A| is an action-oriented research and development organization originating from the Charles F. Kettering Foundation. It was established in 1965 to assist the educational community in bridging the gap that separates research and innovation from actual practice in the schools. Its goal is to design and test new responses to improve education and to create arrangements that support local application. Activities include developing new and improved processes, systems, and materials; training local facilitators to use the change processes; and providing information and services about improved methods and materials. |I|D|E|A| sponsors an annual fellowship program for administrators and conducts seminars for school administrators and teachers.

Institute for the Future (IFTF). 2744 Sand Hill Rd., Menlo Park, CA 94025-7020. (650)854-6322. Fax (650)854-7850. Web site http://www.iftf.org. Robert Johansen, Pres. The cross-disciplinary professionals at IFTF have been providing global and domestic businesses and organizations with research-based forecasts and action-oriented tools for strategic decision making since 1968. IFTF is a nonprofit applied research and consulting firm dedicated to understanding technological, economic, and societal changes and their long-range domestic and global consequences. Its work falls into 4 main areas: Strategic Planning, Emerging Technologies, Health Care Horizons, and Public Sector Initiatives. IFTF works with clients to think systematically about the future, identify socioeconomic trends and evaluate their long-term implications, identify potential leading-edge markets around the world, understand the global marketplace, track the implications of emerging technologies for business and society, leverage expert judgment and data resources, offer an independent view of the big picture, and facilitate strategic planning processes.

Institute for the Transfer of Technology to Education (ITTE). See National School Boards Association.

Instructional Telecommunications Council (ITC). One Dupont Cir., NW, Suite 410, Washington, DC, 20036-1176. (202)293-3110. Fax (202)833-2467. E-mail cdalziel@aacc.nche.edu. Web site http://www.sinclair.edu/communit/itc. Christine Dalziel, contact person. ITC represents over 500 educational institutions from the US and Canada that are involved in higher educational instructional telecommunications and distance learning. ITC holds annual professional development meetings, tracks national legislation, supports research, and provides members a forum to share expertise and materials. *Membership:* 504. *Dues:* $1,500, Regional Consortia; $525, Institutional; $452, Associate; $550, Corporate; $125, Indiv. *Meetings:* 1999 Telelearning Conference. *Publications: New Connections: A Guide to Distance Education* (2nd ed); *New Connections: A College President's Guide to Distance Education; Federal Disability Law and Distance Learning; ITC News* (monthly publication/newsletter); ITC Listserv.

International Association for Language Learning Technology (IALL). IALL Business Manager, Malacester College, 1600 Grand Ave., St. Paul, MN 55105-1899. (612)696-6336. E-mail browne@macalstr.edu. Web site http://polyglot.lss.wisc.edu/IALL/. Nina Garrett, Pres. Thomas Browne, Bus. Mgr. An affiliate of AECT, IALL is a professional organization working for the improvement of second language learning through technology in learning centers and classrooms. *Members:* 700. *Dues:* $40, regular; $15, student; $40, library; $55 commercial. *Meetings:* Biennial IALL conferences treat the entire range of topics related to technology in language learning as well as management and planning. IALL also sponsors sessions at conferences of organizations with related interests, including AECT. *Publications: IALL Journal of Language Learning Technologies* (3 times annually); materials for labs, teaching, and technology.

International Association of Business Communicators (IABC). One Hallidie Plaza, Suite 600, San Francisco, CA 94102. (415)433-3400. Fax (415)362-8762. E-mail service_centre@iabc.com. Web site http://www.iabc.com. Elizabeth Allan, Pres. and CEO. IABC is the worldwide association for the communication and public relations profession. It is founded on the principle that the better an organization communicates with all its audiences, the more successful and effective it will be in meeting its objectives. IABC is dedicated to fostering communication excellence, contributing more effectively to organizations' goals worldwide, and being a model of communication effectiveness. *Membership:* 12,500 plus. *Dues:* $180 in addition to local and regional dues. *Meetings:* 1999, June 20–23, Washington, DC. 2000, June 25-28, Vancouver. *Publication: Communication World.*

International Association of School Librarianship (IASL). Box 34069, Dept. 300, Seattle, WA 98124-1069. (604)925-0266. Fax (604)925-0566. E-mail iasl@rockland.com. Web site http://www.rhi.hi.is/~anne/iasl.html. Dr. Ken Haycock, Executive Dir. Seeks to encourage development of school libraries and library programs throughout the world; to promote professional preparation and continuing education of school librarians; to achieve collaboration among school libraries of the world; to foster relationships between school librarians and other professionals connected with children and youth; and to coordinate activities, conferences, and other projects in the field of school librarianship. *Membership:* 900 plus. *Dues:* $50, personal and institution for North America, Western Europe, Japan, and Australia; $15 for all other countries. *Meetings:* 1999, Birmingham, AL, November. *Publications: IASL Newsletter* (q.); *School Libraries Worldwide* (semi-annual); *Annual Proceedings; Connections: School Library Associations and Contact People Worldwide; Sustaining the Vision: A Collection of Articles and Paper on Research in School Librarianship; School Librarianship: International Issues and Perspectives; Information Rich but Knowledge Poor? Issues for Schools and Libraries Worldwide: Selected Papers from the 26th Annual Conferences of the IASL.*

International Center of Photography (ICP). 1130 Fifth Ave., New York, NY 10128. (212)860-1777. Fax (212)360-6490. ICP Midtown, 1133 Avenue of the Americas, New York, NY 10036. (212)768-4680. Fax (212)768-4688. Web site http://www.icp.org. Willis Hartshorn, Dir.; Phyllis Levine, Dir. of Public Information. A comprehensive photographic institution whose exhibitions, publications, collections, and educational programs embrace all aspects of photography from aesthetics to technique; from the 19th century to the present; from master photographers to newly emerging talents; from photojournalism to the avant garde. Changing exhibitions, lectures, seminars, workshops, museum shops, and screening rooms make ICP a complete photographic resource. ICP offers a two-year NYU-ICP Master of Arts Degree in Studio Art with Studies in Photography and one-year certificate programs in Documentary Photography and Photojournalism and General Studies in Photography. *Membership:* 5,800. *Dues:* $50, Indiv.; $60, Double; $125, Supporting Patron; $250, Photography Circle; $500, Silver Card Patron; $1,000, Gold Card Patron; corporate memberships available. *Meetings:* ICP Infinity Awards. *Publications: Library of Photography; A Singular Elegance: The Photographs of Baron Adolph de Meyer; Talking Pictures: People Speak about the Photographs That Speak to Them; Encyclopedia of Photography: Master Photographs from PFA Collection; Man Ray in Fashion; Quarterly Program Guide; Quarterly Exhibition Schedule.*

International Copyright Information Center (INCINC). c/o Association of American Publishers, 1718 Connecticut Ave. NW, 7th Floor, Washington, DC 20009-1148. (202)232-3335. Fax (202)745-0694. E-mail CRISHER@publishers.org. Carol A. Risher, Dir. Assists developing nations in their efforts to secure permission to translate and/or reprint copyrighted works published in the United States.

International Council for Educational Media (ICEM). ICEM, Robert LeFranc, ICEM Secretariat, 29 rue d'Ulm, 25230 Oaris, Cedex 05, France. 33-1-46. Fax 33-1-46-35-78-89. Ms. Jackie Hall, General Secretariat, FUS, Grup de Fundacions, Provenca 324,3r -E08037 Barcelona, Spain; 34 3 458 30 04, fax 34 3 458 87 10. E-mail icem-cime@bcn.servicom.es. Web site http://www.cndp.fr/icem icem-cime@bcn.servicom.es and http://www.cndp.fr/icem. Richard Cornell, President and US member, University of Central Florida, Education Room 310, Orlando, FL, 32816-0992. (407)823-2053, fax (407)823-5135. E-mail cornell@pegasus.cc.ucf.edu. Web site http://pegasus. cc.ucf.edu/~cornell/icem-usa. Deputy Member from the United States: Marina McIsaac, College of Education, Box 870111, Arizona State University,Tempe, AZ 85287-0111, (602)965-4961, fax (602)965-7193. E-mail: mmcisaac@asu.edu. The objective of ICEM is to provide a channel for the international exchange of information and experience in the field of educational technology, with particular reference to preschool, primary, and secondary education, technical and vocational training, and teacher and continuing education; to encourage organizations with a professional responsibility for the design, production, promotion, distribution, and use of educational media in member countries; to promote an understanding of the concept of educational technology on the part of both educators and those involved in their training; to contribute to the pool of countries by the sponsorship of practical projects involving international cooperation and co-production; to advise manufacturers of hardware and software on the needs of an information service on developments in educational technology; to provide consultancy for the benefit of member countries; and to cooperate with other international organizations in promoting the concept of educational technology. ICEM has established official relations with UNESCO.

International Graphics Arts Education Association (IGAEA). 200 Deer Run Road, Sewickley, PA 15143-2328. (412)741-6860. Fax (412)741-2311. Web site http://www.igaea.org. 1998–99 Pres. Wanda Murphy, wmurphy184@aol.com, (704)922-8891, fax (704)922-8891. IGAEA is an association of educators in partnership with industry, dedicated to sharing theories, principles, techniques, and processes relating to graphic communications and imaging technology. Teachers network to share and improve teaching and learning opportunities in fields related to graphic arts, imaging technology, graphic design, graphic communications, journalism, photography, and other areas related to the large and rapidly changing fields in the printing, publishing, packaging, and allied industries. *Membership:* approx. 600. *Dues:* $20, regular; $12, associate (retired); $5, student; $10, library; $50-$200, sustaining membership based on number of employees. *Meetings:* 1999, Ferris State University, Big Rapids, MI, Aug 1–6. *Publications: The Communicator; Visual Communications Journal* (annual); *Research and Resources Reports.*

***International Information Management Congress (IMC)**. 1650 38th St., #205W, Boulder, CO 80301. (303)440-7085. Fax (303)440-7234. Web site http://www.iimc.org. John A. Lacy, CEO. IMC's mission is to facilitate the successful adoption of imaging, document management, and workflow technologies. IMC's primary activities include conferences, exhibitions, publications, and membership functions. *Dues:* $85, affiliate (any individual with an interest in the document-based information systems field); $200, associate (any association or society with common goals within the industry); $350-$5100, sustaining (any corporate organization with a common interest in the industry). *Meeting:* Future exhibitions planned for Dubai, UAE, and Singapore (please contact IMC for more information). *Publication: Document World Magazine* (bi-monthly).

International Society for Technology in Education (ISTE) (formerly International Council for Computers in Education [ICCE]). 1787 Agate St., Eugene, OR 97403-1923. (541)346-4414. Fax (541)346-5890. E-mail iste@oregon.uoregon.edu. Web site http://www.iste.org. David Moursund, CEO; Maia S. Howes, Exec. Sec. ISTE is the largest nonprofit professional organization dedicated to the improvement of all levels of education through the use of computer-based technology. Technology-using educators from all over the world rely on ISTE for information, inspiration, ideas, and updates on the latest electronic information systems available to the educational community. ISTE is a prominent information center and source of leadership to communicate and collaborate with educational professionals, policy makers, and other organizations worldwide. *Membership:* 12,000 individuals, 75 organizational affiliates, 25 Private Sector Council members. *Dues:* $58, indiv.; $220, all-inclusive (US); $420, Technology Leadership Membership; $1,500 - $5,000, Private Sector Council. *Meetings:* Tel-Ed and NECC. *Publications: The Update Newsletter* (7/yr.); *Learning and Leading with Technology* (formerly *The Computing Teacher*) (8/yr.); *The Journal of Research on Computing in Education* (q.); guides to instructional uses of computers at the precollege level and in teacher training, about 80 books, and a range of distance education courses that carry graduate-level credit.

International Society for Performance Improvement (ISPI). 1300 L St. NW, Suite 1250, Washington, DC 20005. (202)408-7969. Fax (202)408-7972. E-mail info@ispi.org. Web site http://www.ispi.org. Richard D. Battaglia, Exec. Dir. ISPI is an international association dedicated to increasing productivity in the workplace through the application of performance and instructional technologies. Founded in 1962, its members are located throughout the US, Canada, and 45 other countries. The society offers an awards program recognizing excellence in the field. *Membership:* 5,500. Dues: $125, active members; $40, students and retirees. *Meetings:* Annual Conference and Expo, spring; Human Performance Technology Institute (HPTI), late spring and fall. HPTI is an educational institute providing knowledge, skills, and resources necessary to make a successful transition from a training department to a human performance improvement organization. Joint conference with International Federation of Training and Development Organizations, Long Beach, CA, Mar 23–26,1999. *Publications: Performance Improvement Journal* (10/yr.); *Performance Improvement Quarterly*; *News & Notes* (newsletter, 10/yr.); *Annual Membership Directory*; *ISPI Book Program and Catalog.*

International Telecommunications Satellite Organization (INTELSAT). 3400 International Dr. NW, Washington, DC 20008. (202)944-7500. Fax (202)944-7890. Web site http://www. intelsat.int. Irving Goldstein, Dir. Gen. and CEO; Tony A. Trujillo, Dir., Corporate Communications. INTELSAT owns and operates the world's most extensive global communications satellite system. With 1996 revenues of over US $910 million, the INTELSAT system provides voice/data and video services to more than 200 countries via satellite. In addition, the Intelsat system provides educational and medical programming via satellite for selected participants around the world.

International Teleconferencing Association (ITCA). 100 Four Falls Corporate Center, Suite 105, West Conshohocken, PA 19428. (610)941-2020. Fax (610)941-2015. Fax on demand (800)891-8633. E-mail dasitca@aol.com. Web site http://www.itca.org. Henry S. Grove III, Pres.; Eileen Hering, Manager, Member Services; Rosalie DiStasio, Asst. Manager, Member Services. ITCA, an international nonprofit association, is dedicated to the growth and development of teleconferencing as a profession and an industry. ITCA provides programs and services which foster the professional development of its members, champions teleconferencing and related technologies as primary communications tools, recognizes and promotes broader applications and the development of teleconferencing and related technologies, and serves as the authoritative resource for information and research on teleconferencing and related technologies. *Membership:* ITCA represents over 1,900 teleconferencing professionals throughout the world. ITCA members use teleconferencing, manage business television and teleconferencing networks, design the technology, sell products and services, advise customers and vendors, conduct research, teach courses via teleconference, and teach about teleconferencing. They represent such diverse industry segments as health care, aerospace, government, pharmaceutical, education, insurance, finance and banking, telecommunications, and manufacturing. *Dues:* $5,000, Platinum Sustaining, $2,000, Gold Sustaining; $1,000, Sustaining; $500, Organizational; $250, Small Business; $100, Indiv.; and $30, Student. *Meetings:* annual trade show and convention, 1999, Pennsylvania Convention Center, Philadelphia, Mar 28–Apr 2. *Publications: Forum* (mo. newsletter); *Member Directory*; *Teleconferencing Success Stories.*

ITVA (International Television Association). 6311 N. O'Connor Rd., Suite 230, Irving, TX 75039. (972)869-1112. Fax (972)869-2980. E-Mail itvahq@worldnet.att.net. Web site http://www. itva.org. Fred M. Wehrli, Exec. Dir. Founded in 1968, ITVA's mission is to advance the video profession, to serve the needs and interests of its members, and to promote the growth and quality of video and related media. Association members are video, multimedia, and film professionals working in or serving the corporate, governmental, institutional, or educational markets. ITVA provides professional development opportunities through local, regional, and national workshops, video festivals, networking, and publications. ITVA welcomes anyone who is interested in professional video and who is seeking to widen horizons either through career development or networking. ITVA offers its members discounts on major medical, production, and liability insurance; hotel, car rental, and long distance telephone discounts; and a MasterCard program. The association is also a member of the Small Business Legislative Council. *Membership:* 9,000; 77 commercial member companies. *Dues:* $150, Indiv.; $425, Organizational; $1,750, Commercial Silver; $750, Commercial Bronze. *Meetings:* Annual International Conference, early summer. *Publications: ITVA News* (6/yr.); *Membership Directory* (annual); *Handbook of Treatments*; *It's a Business First . . . and a Creative Outlet Second*; *Handbook of Forms*; *Copyright Basics for Video Producers*; *How to Survive Being Laid Off*; *The Effectiveness of Video in Organizations: An Annotated Bibliography*; *Management Matters*; *A Report on the IRS Guidelines Classifying Workers in the Video Industry.*

International Visual Literacy Association, Inc. (IVLA). Gonzaga University, E. 502 Boone AD 25, Spokane, WA 99258-0001. (509)328-4220 ext. 3478, fax (509)324-5812. E-mail bclark @soe.gonzaga.edu. Richard Couch, Pres. Dr. Barbara I. Clark, Exec. Treas. IVLA provides a multidisciplinary forum for the exploration, presentation, and discussion of all aspects of visual learning, thinking, communication, and expression. It also serves as a communication link bonding professionals from many disciplines who are creating and sustaining the study of the nature of visual experiences and literacy. It promotes and evaluates research, programs, and projects intended to increase effective use of visual communication in education, business, the arts, and commerce. IVLA was founded in 1968 to promote the concept of visual literacy and is an affiliate of AECT. *Dues:* $40, regular; $20, student and retired; $45 outside US. *Meeting:* Meets in conjunction with annual AECT Convention. *Publications: Journal of Visual Literacy*; *Readings from Annual Conferences.*

ITA. 182 Nassau St., Princeton, NJ 08542-7005. (609)279-1700. Fax (609)279-1999. E-mail info@recordingmedia.org. Web site http://www.recordingmedia.org. Charles Van Horn, Exec. V.P.; Richard Bennett, Dir. Of Operations. An international association providing a forum for the exchange of management information on global trends and innovations which drive recording media technology. Members include recording media manufacturers, rights holders to video programs, recording and playback equipment manufacturers, and audio and video replicators. For more than 28 years, the Association has provided vital information and educational services throughout the magnetic and optical recording media industries. By promoting a greater awareness of marketing, merchandising, and technical developments, the association serves all areas of the entertainment, information, and delivery systems industries. *Membership:* 450 corporations. *Dues:* corporate membership dues based on sales volume. *Meetings:* 29th Annual Conference, Mar 10–14, 1999, Amelia Island, FL; REPLItech North America, Jun 7–10, 1999, San Francisco; 30th Annual Conference, Mar 15–19, 2000, La Quinta, CA. *Publications: Membership Newsletter*; *Seminar Proceedings*; *1998 International Source Directory.*

Library Administration and Management Association (LAMA). 50 E. Huron St., Chicago, IL 60611. (312)280-5038. Fax (312)280-3257. E-mail lama@ala.org. Web site http://www.ala. org/lama. Karen Muller, Exec. Dir.; Charles E. Kratz, Jr., Pres., July 1997-July 1998. Thomas L. Wilding, Pres.-Elect. An affiliate of the American Library Association, LAMA provides an organizational framework for encouraging the study of administrative theory, improving the practice of administration in libraries, and identifying and fostering administrative skills. Toward these ends, the association is responsible for all elements of general administration that are common to more than one type of library. Sections include: Buildings and Equipment Section (BES); Fundraising & Financial Development Section (FRFDS); Library Organization & Management Section (LOMS); Personnel Administration Section (PAS); Public Relation Section (PRS); Systems & Services Section (SASS); and Statistics Section (SS). *Membership:* 4,968. *Dues:* $35 (in addition to ALA membership); $15, library school students. *Meetings:* 1999 ALA Annual Conference, New Orleans, Jun 24–Jul 1. 2000, Chicago, Jul 6–13. ALA Midwinter Meeting, 1999, Philadelphia, Jan 29–Feb 3. 2000, San Antonio, Jan 14–19. *Publications: Library Administration & Management* (q); *LEADS from LAMA* (electronic newsletter, irregular).

Library and Information Technology Association (LITA). 50 E. Huron St., Chicago, IL 60611. (312)280-4270, (800)545-2433, ext. 4270. Fax (312)280-3257. E-mail lita@ala.org. Web site http://www.lita.org. Jacqueline Mundell, Exec. Dir. An affiliate of the American Library Association, LITA is concerned with library automation, the information sciences, and the design, development, and implementation of automated systems in those fields, including systems development, electronic data processing, mechanized information retrieval, operations research, standards development, telecommunications, video communications, networks and collaborative efforts, management techniques, information technology, optical technology, artificial intelligence and expert systems, and other related aspects of audiovisual activities and hardware applications. *Membership:* 5,400. *Dues:* $45 plus membership in ALA; $25, library school students; $35, first year. *Meetings:* National Forum, fall. *Publications: Information Technology and Libraries; LITA Newsletter* (electronic only; see Web site).

Library of Congress. James Madison Bldg., 101 Independence Ave. SE, Washington, DC 20540. (202)707-5000. Fax (202)707-1389. National Reference Service, (202)707-5522. Web site http://www.loc.gov. The Library of Congress is the major source of research and information for the Congress. In its role as the national library, it catalogs and classifies library materials in some 460 languages, distributes the data in both printed and electronic form, and makes its vast collections available through interlibrary loan and on-site to anyone over high school age. The Library is the largest library in the world, with more than 113 million items on 532 miles of bookshelves. The collections include more than 17 million books, 2 million recordings, 12 million photographs, 4 million maps, and 49 million manuscripts. It contains the world's largest television and film archive, acquiring materials through gift, purchase, and copyright deposit. In 1997, the materials produced by the Library in braille and recorded formats for persons who are blind or physically challenged were circulated to a readership of 780,000. The collections of the Motion Picture, Broadcasting and Recorded Sound Division include more than 770,000 moving images. The Library of Congress computer system holds a total of more than 40 million records in its databases. Its 27 million catalog records, as well as other files containing copyright and legislative information, are available over the Internet.

Lister Hill National Center for Biomedical Communications. National Library of Medicine, 8600 Rockville Pike, Bethesda, MD 20894. (301)496-4441. Fax (301)402-0118. Web site http://www.nlm.nih.gov. Alexa McCray, Ph.D., Dir. The center conducts research and development programs in three major categories: Computer and Information Science; Biomedical Image and Communications Engineering; and Educational Technology Development. Major efforts of the center include its involvement with the Unified Medical Language System (UMLS) project; research and development in the use of expert systems to embody the factual and procedural knowledge of human experts; research in the use of electronic technologies to distribute biomedical information not represented in text and in the storage and transmission of X-ray images over the Internet; and the development and demonstration of new educational technologies, including the use of microcomputer technology with videodisc-based images, for training health care professionals. A Learning Center for Interactive Technology serves as a focus for displaying new and effective applications of educational technologies to faculties and staff of health sciences, educational institutions and other visitors, and health professions educators are assisted in the use of such technologies through training, demonstrations, and consultations.

Magazine Publishers of America (MPA). 919 Third Ave., 22nd Floor, New York, NY 10022. (212)872-3700. Fax (212)888-4217. E-mail infocenter@magazine.org. Web site http://www. magazine.org. Donald D. Kummerfeld, Pres. MPA is the trade association of the consumer magazine industry. MPA promotes the greater and more effective use of magazine advertising, with ad campaigns in the trade press and in member magazines, presentations to advertisers and their ad agencies, and magazine days in cities around the US. MPA runs educational seminars, conducts surveys of its members on a variety of topics, represents the magazine industry in Washington, DC, and maintains an extensive library on magazine publishing. *Membership:* 230 publishers representing more than 1,200 magazines. *Meetings:* 1999 American Magazine Conference, Boca Resort & Country Club, Boca Raton, FL, Oct 28–31; 2000, Southampton Princess, Bermuda, Oct

22–25. *Publications: Newsletter of Consumer Marketing*; *Newsletter of Research*; *Newsletter of International Publishing*; *Magazine*; *Washington Newsletter*.

Medical Library Association (MLA). 6 N. Michigan Ave., Suite 300, Chicago, IL 60602-4805. (312)419-9094. Fax (312)419-9094. E-mail info@mlahq.org. Web site http://www.mlanet.org. Rachael K. Anderson, Pres.; Carla J. Funk, Exec. Dir., Kimberly Pierceall, Dir. of Communications. MLA is a professional organization of 5,000 individuals and institutions in the health sciences information field, dedicated to fostering medical and allied scientific libraries, promoting professional excellence and leadership of its members, and exchanging medical literature among its members. *Membership:* 5,000 individual and institutional. *Dues:* $110, regular; $25, students; $75, introductory; $65, affiliate; $2100, life. Institutional dues depend on number of periodical subscriptions. *Meeting:* 1999, Chicago, May 14–20. *Publications: MLA News* (newsletter, 10/yr.); *Bulletin of the Medical Library Association* (q.); *Dockit* series; monographs.

Mid-continent Regional Educational Laboratory (McREL). 2550 S. Parker Rd., Suite 500, Aurora, CO 80014. (303)337-0990. Fax (303)337-3005. E-mail info@mcrel.org. Web site http://www. mcrel.org. J. Timothy Waters, Exec. Dir. One of 10 Office of Educational Research and Improvement (OERI) regional educational laboratories designed to help educators and policymakers work toward excellence in education for all students. Using the best available information and the experience and expertise of professionals, McREL seeks to identify solutions to education problems, tries new approaches, furnishes research results, conducts evaluation and policy studies, and provides training to teachers and administrators. McREL serves Colorado, Kansas, Missouri, Nebraska, North Dakota, South Dakota and Wyoming. Its specialty areas are curriculum, learning, and instruction. *Publications: Changing Schools* (q. newsletter); *Noteworthy* (annual monograph on topics of current interest in education reform). Check Web site for catalog listing many other publications.

Minorities in Media (MIM). Wayne State University, College of Education, Instructional Technology, Detroit, Michigan 48202. (313)577-5139. Fax (313)577-1693. E-mail GPOWELL@CMS. CC.WAYNE.EDU. Dr. Gary C. Powell, Pres. MIM is a special interest group of AECT that responds to the challenge of preparing students-of-color for an ever-changing international marketplace and recognizes the unique educational needs of today's diverse learners. It supports the creative development of curricula, instructional strategies, and computer-based instructional materials which promote an acceptance and appreciation of racial and cultural diversity. It promotes the effective use of educational communications and technology in the learning process. MIM seeks to facilitate changes in instructional design and development, traditional pedagogy, and instructional delivery systems by responding to and meeting the significant challenge of educating diverse individuals to take their place in an ever-changing international marketplace. MIM encourages all of AECT's body of members to creatively develop curricula, instructional treatments, instructional strategies, and instructional materials which promote an acceptance and appreciation of racial and cultural diversity. Doing so will make learning for all more effective, relevant, meaningful, motivating, and enjoyable. MIM actively supports the Wes McJulien Minority Scholarship, and selects the winner. *Membership:* contact MIM president. *Dues:* $20, student; $30, non-student. *Publications:* newsletter is forthcoming online. The MIM listserv is a membership benefit.

Museum Computer Network (MCN). 8720 Georgia Ave., Suite 501, Silver Spring, MD 20910. (301)585-4413. Fax (301)495-0810. E-mail mcn@athena.mit.edu; membership office: mdevine@ asis.org. Web site http://world.std.com/nmcn/index.html. Michele Devine, Admin. Guy Herman, Pres. As a nonprofit professional association, membership in MCN provides access to professionals committed to using computer technology to achieve the cultural aims of museums. Members include novices and experts, museum professionals, and vendors and consultants, working in application areas from collections management to administrative computing. Activities include advisory services and special projects. *Dues:* $300, sponsor; $150, vendor; $150, institution; $60, indiv. *Meeting:* Annual Conference, held in the fall; educational workshops. *Publications:*

Spectra (newsletter); *CMI.* Subscription to *Spectra* is available to libraries only for $75 plus $10 surcharge for delivery.

Museum of Modern Art, Circulating Film and Video Library. 11 W. 53rd St., New York, NY 10019. (212)708-9530. Fax (212)708-9531. E-mail circfilm@moma.org. Web site http://www. moma.org. William Sloan, Libr. Provides film and video rentals and sales of over 1300 titles covering the history of film from the 1890's to the present. It also incorporates the Circulating Video Library, an important collection of work by leading video artists. The Circulating Library continues to add to its holdings of early silents, contemporary documentaries, animation, avant-garde, and independents and to make these available to viewers who otherwise would not have the opportunity to see them. The Circulating Film Library has 16mm prints available for rental, sale, and lease. A few of the 16mm titles are available on videocassette. The classic film collection is not. The video collection is available in all formats for rental and sale. *Publications:* Information on titles may be found in the free *Price List*, available from the Library. *Circulating Film and Video Catalog Vols. 1 and 2*, a major source book on film and history, is available from the Museum's Publications, Sales, and Service Dept. (For mail order, a form is included in the *Price List.*)

National Aeronautics and Space Administration (NASA). NASA Headquarters, Code FE, Washington, DC 20546. (202)358-1110. Fax (202)358-3048. E-mail malcom.phelps@hq.nasa. gov. Web site http://www.nasa.gov. Dr. Malcom V. Phelps, Asst. Dir.; Frank C. Owens, Dir., Education Division. From elementary through postgraduate school, NASA's educational programs are designed to capture students' interests in science, mathematics, and technology at an early age; to channel more students into science, engineering, and technology career paths; and to enhance the knowledge, skills, and experiences of teachers and university faculty. NASA's educational programs include NASA Spacelink (an electronic information system); videoconferences (60-minute interactive staff development videoconferences to be delivered to schools via satellite); and NASA Television (informational and educational television programming). Additional information is available from the Education Division at NASA Headquarters and counterpart offices at the nine NASA field centers. Over 200,000 educators make copies of Teacher Resource Center Network materials each year, and thousands of teachers participate in interactive video teleconferencing, use Spacelink, and watch NASA Television. Additional information may be obtained from Spacelink (spacelink.msfc.nasa.gov or http://spacelink.msfc.nasa.gov).

National Alliance for Media Arts and Culture (NAMAC). 346 9th St., San Francisco, CA 94103. (415)431-1391. Fax (415)431-1392. E-mail namac@namac.org. Web site http://www. namac.org. Helen DeMichel, National Dir. NAMAC is a nonprofit organization dedicated to increasing public understanding of and support for the field of media arts in the US. Members include media centers, cable access centers, universities, and media artists, as well as other individuals and organizations providing services for production, education, exhibition, distribution, and preservation of video, film, audio, and intermedia. NAMAC's information services are available to the general public, arts and non-arts organizations, businesses, corporations, foundations, government agencies, schools, and universities. *Membership:* 200 organizations, 150 individuals. *Dues:* $50-$250, institutional (depending on annual budget); $50, indiv. *Publications: Media Arts Information Network*; *The National Media Education Directory.*

National Association for the Education of Young Children (NAEYC). 1509 16th St. NW, Washington, DC 20036-1426. (202)232-8777, (800)424-2460. Fax (202)328-1846. E-mail naeyc@naeyc.org. Web site http://www.naeyc.org. Marilyn M. Smith, Exec. Dir.; Pat Spahr, contact person. Dedicated to improving the quality of care and education provided to young children (birth–8 years). *Membership:* over 100,000. *Dues:* $25. *Meeting:* 1999 Annual Conference, Nov 10–13, New Orleans. *Publications: Young Children* (journal); more than 60 books, posters, videos, and brochures.

National Association for Visually Handicapped (NAVH). 22 W. 21st St., 6th Floor, New York, NY 10010. (212)889-3141. Fax (212)727-2931. E-mail staff@navh.org. Web site http://www.navn. org. Lorraine H. Marchi, Founder/Exec. Dir.; Eva Cohen, Asst. to Exec. Dir., 3201 Balboa St., San

Francisco, CA 94121. (415)221-3201. Serves the partially sighted (not totally blind). Offers informational literature for the layperson and the professional, most in large print. Maintains a loan library of large-print books. Provides counseling and guidance for the visually impaired and their families and the professionals and paraprofessionals who work with them. *Membership:* 12,000. *Dues:* Full membership $40 for indiv.; free for those unable to afford membership. *Publications:* Newsletters for adults (*Seeing Clearly*) and for children (*In Focus*) are published at irregular intervals and distributed free throughout the English-speaking world. *NAVH Update* (quarterly); *Visual Aids and Informational Material Catalog*; *Large Print Loan Library*; informational pamphlets on topics ranging from Diseases of the Macula to knitting and crochet instructions.

National Association of Regional Media Centers (NARMC). NARMC, Education Service Center, Region 20, 1314 Hines Ave., San Antonio, TX 78208. (210)270-9256. Fax (210)224-3130. E-mail jtaylor@tenet.edu. Web site http://esu3.k12.ne.us/prof/narmc. Larry Vice, Pres.; James H. Taylor, Treasurer. An affiliate of AECT, NARMC is committed to promoting leadership among its membership through networking, advocacy, and support activities that will enhance the equitable access to media, technology, and information services to educational communities. The purpose of NARMC is to foster the exchange of ideas and information among educational communications specialists whose responsibilities relate to the administration of regional media centers and large district media centers. *Membership:* 285 regional centers (institutions), 70 corporations. *Dues:* $55, institutions; $250, corporations. *Meetings:* held annually with AECT/Incite. Regional meetings are held throughout the US annually. *Publications:* Membership newsletter is 'ETIN. NARMC Press was established in 1996 to provide members with publications related to the field of media and technology. These publications are available for purchase through this publication outlet. Publications are solicited and submitted from the NARMC membership. Current publications include *An Anthology of Internet Acceptable Use Policies* and *Basic MAC/Windows Internet*. In addition, there is the *Annual Membership Report* and the *Biannual Survey Report of Regional Media Centers*.

*National Association of State Textbook Administrators (NASTA). E-mail president@nasta.org. Web site http://www.nasta.org. William Lohman, Pres. NASTA's purposes are (1) to foster a spirit of mutual helpfulness in adoption, purchase, and distribution of instructional materials; (2) to arrange for study and review of textbook specifications; (3) to authorize special surveys, tests, and studies; and (4) to initiate action leading to better quality instructional materials. Services provided include a working knowledge of text construction, monitoring lowest prices, sharing adoption information, identifying trouble spots, and discussions in the industry. The members of NASTA meet to discuss the textbook adoption process and to improve the quality of the instructional materials used in the elementary, middle, and high schools. NASTA is not affiliated with any parent organization and has no permanent address. *Membership:* textbook administrators from each of the 23 states that adopt textbooks at the state level. *Dues:* $25, indiv. *Meetings:* conducted with the American Association of Publishers and the Book Manufacturers' Institute.

The National Cable Television Institute (NCTI). 801 W. Mineral Ave., Littleton CO 80120. (303)797-9393. Fax (303)797-9394. Email info@ncti.com. Web site http://www.ncti.com. Doug Nickelson, President; Ed Cook, Director of Corporate Services. The National Cable Television Institute is the largest independent provider of broadband technology training in the world. More than 120,000 students have graduated from these courses since 1968. NCTI partners with companies by providing self-paced study manuals to be complemented by company hands-on experiences. NCTI administers lessons and final examinations and issues the Certificate of Graduation, which is recognized throughout the industry as a symbol of competence and technical achievement.

The National Center for Improving Science Education. 2000 L St. NW, Suite 616, Washington, DC 20036. (202)467-0652. Fax (202)467-0659. E-mail info@ncise.org. Web site www.wested.org. Senta A. Raizen, Dir. A division of WestEd (see separate listing) that works to promote changes in state and local policies and practices in science curriculum, teaching, and assessment through research and development, evaluation, technical assistance, and dissemination.

Publications: Science and Technology Education for the Elementary Years: Frameworks for Curriculum and Instruction; Developing and Supporting Teachers for Elementary School Science Education; Assessment in Elementary School Science Education; Getting Started in Science: A Blueprint Elementary School Science Education; Elementary School Science for the 90s; Building Scientific Literacy: Blueprint for the Middle Years; Science and Technology Education for the Middle Years: Frameworks for Curriculum and Instruction; Assessment in Science Education: The Middle Years; Developing and Supporting Teachers for Science Education in the Middle Years; The High Stakes of High School Science; Future of Science in Elementary Schools: Educating Prospective Teachers; Technology Education in the Classroom: Understanding the Designed World; What College-Bound Students Abroad Are Expected to Know About Biology (with AFT); *Examining the Examinations: A Comparison of Science and Mathematics Examinations for College-Bound Students in Seven Countries. Bold Ventures series: Vol. 1:Patterns of US Innovations in Science and Mathematics Education; Vol. 2: Case Studies of US Innovations in Science Education; Vol. 3: Case Studies of US Innovations in Mathematics.* A publications catalog and project summaries are available on request.

National Center to Improve Practice (NCIP). Education Development Center, Inc., 55 Chapel St., Newton, MA 02158-1060. (617)969-7100 ext. 2387. TTY (617)969-4529. Fax (617)969-3440. E-mail ncip@edc.org. Web site http://www.edc.org/FSC/NCIP. Judith Zorfass, Project Dir.; Lucy Lorin, information. NCIP, a project funded by the US Department of Education's Office for Special Education Programs (OSEP), promotes the effective use of technology to enhance educational outcomes for students (preschool to grade 12) with sensory, cognitive, physical, social, and emotional disabilities. NCIP's award-winning Web site offers users online discussions (topical discussions and special events) about technology and students with disabilities, an expansive library of resources (text, pictures, and video clips), online workshops, "guided tours" of exemplary classrooms, "spotlights" on new technology, and links to more than 100 sites dealing with technology and/or students with disabilities. NCIP also produces a series of videos, illustrating how students with disabilities use a range of assistive and instructional technologies to improve their learning. *Dues:* membership and dues are not required. *Meetings:* NCIP presents sessions at various educational conferences around the country. *Publications:* Video Profile Series: *Multimedia and More: Help for Students with Learning Disabilities; Jeff with Expression: Writing in the Word Prediction Software; "Write" Tools for Angie: Technology for Students Who Are Visually Impaired; Telling Tales in ASL and English: Reading, Writing and Videotapes; Welcome to My Preschool: Communicating with Technology.* Excellent for use in trainings, workshops, and courses, videos may be purchased individually or as a set of five by calling (800)793-5076. A new video to be released this year focuses on standards, curriculum, and assessment in science.

National Clearinghouse for Bilingual Education (NCBE). The George Washington University, 1118 22nd St. NW, Washington, DC 20037. (202)467-0867. Fax (800)531-9347, (202)467-4283. E-mail askncbe@ncbe.gwu.edu. Web site http://www.ncbe.gwu.edu. Joel Gomez, Dir. NCBE is funded by the US Department of Education's Office of Bilingual Education and Minority Languages Affairs (OBEMLA) to collect, analyze, synthesize, and disseminate information relating to the education of linguistically and culturally diverse students in the US. NCBE is operated by The George Washington University Graduate School of Education and Human Development, Center for the Study of Language and Education in Washington, DC. Online services include the NCBE Web site containing an online library of over 500 cover-to-cover documents, resources for teachers and administrators, and library of links to related Internet sites; an email-based, weekly news bulletin, *Newsline*; an electronic discussion group, *NCBE Roundtable*; and an e-mail-based question answering service, *AskNCBE. Publications:* short monographs, syntheses, and a quarterly newsletter (*CrossCurrents).* Request a publications catalog for prices. The catalog and some publications are available at no cost from the NCBE Web site.

National Commission on Libraries and Information Science (NCLIS). 1110 Vermont Ave. NW, Suite 820, Washington, DC 20005-3522. (202)606-9200. Fax (202)606-9203. E-mail jw_nclis @inet.ed.gov. Web site http://www.nclis.gov. Jane Williams, Acting Exec. Dir. A permanent independent agency of the US government charged with advising the executive and legislative branches on national library and information policies and plans. The commission reports directly to the White House and the Congress on the implementation of national policy; conducts studies, surveys, and analyses of the nation's library and information needs; appraises the inadequacies of current resources and services; promotes research and development activities; conducts hearings and issues publications as appropriate; and develops overall plans for meeting national library and information needs and for the coordination of activities at the federal, state, and local levels. The Commission provides general policy advice to the Institute of Museum and Library Services (IMLS) director relating to library services included in the Library Services and Technology Act (LSTA). *Membership:* 16 commissioners (14 appointed by the president and confirmed by the Senate, the Librarian of Congress, and the Director of the IMLS). *Publication:* Annual Report.

National Communication Association (NCA) (formerly Speech Communication Association). 5105 Backlick Rd., Bldg. E, Annandale, VA 22003. (703)750-0533. Fax (703)914-9471. Web page http://www.natcom.org. James L. Gaudino, Exec. Dir. A voluntary society organized to promote study, criticism, research, teaching, and application of principles of communication, particularly of speech communication. *Membership:* 7,000. *Meetings:* 1999 Annual Meeting, Nov 4–7, Chicago. *Publications: Spectra Newsletter* (mo.); *Quarterly Journal of Speech; Communication Monographs; Communication Education; Critical Studies in Mass Communication; Journal of Applied Communication Research; Text and Performance Quarterly; Speech Communication Teacher; Index to Journals in Communication Studies through 1995; National Communication Directory of NCA and the Regional Speech Communication Organizations* (CSSA, ECA, SSCA, WSCA). For additional publications, request brochure.

National Council for Accreditation of Teacher Education (NCATE). 2010 Massachusetts Ave. NW, Suite 500, Washington, DC 20036. (202)466-7496. Fax (202)296-6620. E-mail ncate@ncate.org. Web site http://www.ncate.org. Arthur E. Wise, Pres. NCATE is a consortium of professional organizations that establishes standards of quality and accredits professional education units in schools, colleges, and departments of education, and is interested in the self-regulation and improvement of standards in the field of teacher education. *Membership:* 500 colleges and universities, 30 educational organizations. *Publications: Standards, Procedures and Policies for the Accreditation of Professional Education Units; Teacher Education: A Guide to NCATE-Accredited Colleges and Universities; Quality Teaching* (newsletter, 2/yr.).

National Council of Teachers of English (NCTE), Commission on Media. 1111 W. Kenyon Rd., Urbana, IL 61801-1096. (217)328-3870. Fax (217)328-0977. Lawrence B. Fuller, Commission Dir. The functions of the Commission are to study emerging technologies and their integration into English and language arts curricula and teacher education programs; to identify the effects of such technologies on teachers, students, and educational settings, with attention to people of color, challenged, and other students who are not well served in current programs; to explore means of disseminating information about such technologies to the NCTE membership; to serve as liaison between NCTE and other groups interested in computer-based education in English and language arts; and to liaison with the NCTE Commission on Media and other Council groups concerned with instructional technology.

National Council of the Churches of Christ in the USA. Communication Commission, 475 Riverside Dr., New York, NY 10115. (212)870-2574. Fax (212)870-2030. Web site http://www. ncccusa.org. Randy Naylor, Dir. Ecumenical arena for cooperative work of Protestant and Orthodox denominations and agencies in broadcasting, film, cable, and print media. Offers advocacy to government and industry structures on media services. Services provided include liaison to network television and radio programming; film sales and rentals; distribution of information about syndicated religious programming; syndication of some programming; cable television and emerging technologies information services; news and information regarding work of the National Council of Churches, related denominations, and agencies. Works closely with other faith groups in the Interfaith Broadcasting Commission. Online communication via Ecunet/NCCLink. *Membership:* 34 denominations. *Publication: EcuLink.*

National Education Knowledge Industry Association (NEKIA) (formerly Council for Educational Development and Research). 1200 19th St. NW, Suite 300, Washington, DC 20036. (202)429-5101. Fax (202)785-3849. Web site http://www.nekia.org. C. Todd Jones, Pres. The National Education Knowledge Industry Association (NEKIA) is the only national trade association for organizations dedicated to educational research and development. The mission of NEKIA is to serve the nation's common schools by making cost-effective education innovation and expertise available to all communities. Members of NEKIA include the nations' foremost research and development institutions devoted to using research-based products and services to enhance the quality of education for the common good. NEKIA serves as a national voice for its members, making sure knowledge from research, development, and practical experience is part of the national discussion on education. NEKIA also ensures that educational research and development institutions are able to maintain neutrality and objectivity in reporting findings, and ensures a field-based, decentralized system of setting priorities. *Membership*: 15. *Publications: Checking Up on Early Childhood Care and Education*; *What We Know About Reading Teaching and Learning*; *Plugging In: Choosing and Using Educational Technology*; *Probe: Designing School Facilities for Learning*; *Education Productivity*; *Technology Infrastructure in Schools.*

National Education Telecommunications Organization & EDSAT Institute (NETO/EDSAT). 1899 L Street NW, Suite 600, Washington, DC 20036. (202)293-4211. Fax (202)293-4210. E-mail neto-edsat@mindspring.com. Web site http://www.netoedsat.org. Shelly Weinstein, Pres. and CEO. NETO/EDSAT is a nonprofit organization bringing together US and non-US users and providers of telecommunications to deliver education, instruction, health care, and training in classrooms, colleges, workplaces, health centers, and other distance education centers. NETO/EDSAT facilitates and collaborates with key stakeholders in the education and telecommunications fields. Programs and services include research and education, outreach, seminars and conferences, and newsletters. The NETO/EDSAT mission is to help create an integrated multitechnology infrastructure, a dedicated satellite that links space and existing secondary access roads (telephone and cable) over which teaching and education resources are delivered and shared in a user friendly format with students, teachers, workers, and individuals. NETO/EDSAT seeks to create a modern-day "learning place" for rural, urban, migrant, suburban, disadvantaged, and at-risk students which provides equal and affordable access to and utilization of educational resources. *Membership:* Members includes over 60 US and non-US school districts, colleges, universities, state agencies, public and private educational consortia, libraries, and other distance education providers. *Publications: NETO/EDSAT "UPDATE"* (newsletter, q.); *Analysis of a Proposal for an Education Satellite, EDSAT Institute, 1991*; and *Global Summit on Distance Education Final Report,* Oct, 1996; *International Report of the NETO/EDSAT Working Group on the Education and Health Care Requirements for Global/Regional Dedicated Networks,* June, 1998.

National Endowment for the Humanities (NEH). Division of Public Programs, Media Program, 1100 Pennsylvania Ave. NW, Room 426, Washington, DC 20506. (202)606-8269. E-mail info@neh.gov. Web site http://www.neh.gov. Fax (202)606-8557. Jim Vore, Manage of Media/Special Projects. The NEH is an independent federal grant-making agency that supports research, educational, and public programs grounded in the disciplines of the humanities. The Media Program supports film and radio programs in the humanities for public audiences, including children and adults. *Publications: Overview of Endowment Programs*; *Humanities Projects in Media* (for application forms and guidelines).

National Federation of Community Broadcasters (NFCB). Ft. Mason Center, Bldg. D, San Francisco, CA 94123. (415)771-1160. E-mail nfcb@aol.com. Web site http://www.nfcb.org. Lynn Chadwick, Pres. NFCB represents non-commercial, community-based radio stations in public policy development at the national level and provides a wide range of practical services, including technical assistance. *Membership:* 200. *Dues:* range from $150 to $2500 for participant and associate members. *Meetings:* 1999, San Francisco. *Publications: Legal Handbook*; *Audio Craft*; *Community Radio News.*

National Film Board of Canada (NFBC). 350 Fifth Ave., Suite 4820, New York, NY 10118. (212)629-8890. Fax (212)629-8502. E-mail gsem78a@prodigy.com. John Sirabella, US Marketing Mgr./Nontheatrical Rep. Established in 1939, the NFBC's main objective is to produce and distribute high-quality audiovisual materials for educational, cultural, and social purposes.

National Film Information Service (offered by the Margaret Herrick Library of the Academy of Motion Picture Arts and Sciences). Center for Motion Picture Study, 333 So. La Cienega Blvd., Beverly Hills, CA 90211. (310)247-3000. The purpose of this service is to provide information on film. The service is fee-based and all inquiries must be accompanied by a #10 self-addressed stamped envelope. NFIS does not reply to e-mail queries.

National Gallery of Art (NGA). Department of Education Resources: Art Information and Extension Programs, Washington, DC 20565. (202)842-6273. Fax (202)842-6935. Web site http://www.hga.gov. Ruth R. Perlin, Head. This department of NGA is responsible for the production and distribution of educational audiovisual programs, including interactive technologies. Materials available (all loaned free to schools, community organizations, and individuals) range from films, videocassettes, and color slide programs to videodiscs. A free catalog of programs is available upon request. Two videodiscs on the gallery's collection are available for long-term loan. *Publication: Extension Programs Catalogue.*

National Information Center for Educational Media (NICEM). PO Box 8640, Albuquerque, NM 87198-8640. (505)265-3591, (800)926-8328. Fax (505)256-1080. E-mail nicem@nicem.com. Web page http://www.nicem.com. Roy Morgan, Exec. Dir.; Marjorie M. K. Hlava, Pres., Access Innovations, Inc. The National Information Center for Educational Media maintains an international database of information about educational non-print materials for all age levels and subject areas in all media types. NICEM editors collect, catalog, and index information about media which is provided by producers and distributors. This information is entered into an electronic masterfile. Anyone who is looking for information about educational media materials can search the database by a wide variety of criteria to locate existing and archival materials. Producer and distributor information in each record then leads the searcher to the source of the educational media materials needed. NICEM makes the information from the database available in several forms and through several vendors. CD-ROM editions are available from NICEM, SilverPlatter, and BiblioFile. Online access to the database is available through NICEM, EBSCO, SilverPlatter, The Library Corporation, Dialog, and the Human Resources Information Network. Print versions are available from Plexus Publishing. NICEM also conducts custom searches and prepares custom catalogs. NICEM is used by college and university media centers, public school libraries and media centers, public libraries, corporate training centers, students, media producers and distributors, and researchers. *Membership:* NICEM is a nonmembership organization. There is no charge for submitting information to be entered into the database. Corporate member of AECT, AIME, NARMC, CCUMC. *Publications: International Directory of Educational Audiovisuals; A-V Online on SilverPlatter; NICEM A-V MARC by BiblioFile; Film & Video Finder; Index to A-V Producers & Distributors.*

National ITFS Association (NIA). 2330 Swan Blvd., Milwaukee, WI 53226. (414)229-5470. Fax (414)229-4777. Web site http://www.itfs.org. Theodore Steinke, Chair, Bd. of Dirs.; Don MacCullough, Exec. Sec. Established in 1978, NIA/ITFS is a nonprofit, professional organization of Instructional Television Fixed Service (ITFS) licensees, applicants, and others interested in ITFS broadcasting. The goals of the association are to gather and exchange information about ITFS, to gather data on utilization of ITFS, and to act as a conduit for those seeking ITFS information or assistance. The NIA represents ITFS interests to the FCC, technical consultants, and equipment manufacturers. The association provides its members with a quarterly newsletter and an FCC regulation update as well as information on excess capacity leasing and license and application data. *Meetings:* with AECT and InCITE. *Publications: National ITFS Association Newsletter* (q.); FCC regulation update.

National PTA. 330 N. Wabash, Suite 2100, Chicago, IL 60611. (312)670-6782. Fax (312)670-6783. Web site http://www.pta.com. Lois Jean White, Pres.; Patty Yoxall, Public Relations Dir. Advocates for the education, health, safety, and well-being of children and teens. Provides parenting education and leadership training to PTA volunteers. The National PTA continues to be very active in presenting Family and Television Critical TV Viewing workshops across the country in cooperation with the National Cable Television Association. The workshops teach parents and educators how to evaluate programming so they can make informed decisions about what to allow their children to see. The National PTA in 1997 convinced the television industry to add content information to the TV rating system. *Membership:* 6.8 million. *Dues:* vary by local unit. *Meeting:* national convention, held annually in June in different regions of the country, is open to PTA members; convention information available on the Web site. *Publications: Our Children* (magazine); *What's Happening in Washington* (legislative newsletters). In addition, information can be downloaded from the Web site. Catalog available.

National Press Photographers Association, Inc. (NPPA). 3200 Croasdaile Dr., Suite 306, Durham, NC 27705. (919)383-7246. Fax (919)383-7261. E-mail 72640.21@compuserve.com. Ellen LoCurto, CAE, Exec. Dir. An organization of professional news photographers who participate in and promote photojournalism in publications and through television and film. Sponsors workshops, seminars, and contests; maintains an audiovisual library of subjects of media interest. *Membership:* 11,000. *Dues:* $75, domestic; $105, international; $40, student. *Meetings:* Annual Convention and Education Days, summer. An extensive array of other conferences, seminars, and workshops are held throughout the year. *Publications: News Photographer* (magazine, mo.); *The Best of Photojournalism PJ022* (annual book).

National Public Broadcasting Archives (NPBA). Hornbake Library, University of Maryland, College Park, MD 20742. (301)405-9255. Fax (301)314-2634. E-mail tc65@umail.umd.edu. Web site http://www.library.umd.edu/UMCP/NPBA/npba.html. Thomas Connors, Archivist. NPBA brings together the archival record of the major entities of noncommercial broadcasting in the US. NPBA's collections include the archives of the Corporation for Public Broadcasting (CPB), the Public Broadcasting Service (PBS), and National Public Radio (NPR). Other organizations represented include the Midwest Program for Airborne Television Instruction (MPATI), the Public Service Satellite Consortium (PSSC), America's Public Television Stations (APTS), Children's Television Workshop (CTW), and the Joint Council for Educational Telecommunications (JCET). NPBA also makes available the personal papers of many individuals who have made significant contributions to public broadcasting, and its reference library contains basic studies of the broadcasting industry, rare pamphlets, and journals on relevant topics, plus up-to-date clippings from the PBS press clipping service. NPBA also collects and maintains a selected audio and video program record of public broadcasting's national production and support centers and of local stations. Oral history tapes and transcripts from the NPR Oral History Project are also available at the archives. The archives are open to the public from 9 am to 5 pm, Monday through Friday. Research in NPBA collections should be arranged by prior appointment. For further information, call (301)405-9988.

National Religious Broadcasters (NRB). 7839 Ashton Ave., Manassas, VA 20109. (703)330-7000. Fax (703)330-7100. E-mail ssmith@nrb.organization. Web site http://www.nrb.org. E. Brandt Gustavson, Pres. NRB essentially has two goals: (1) to ensure that religious broadcasters have access to the radio and television airwaves, and (2) to encourage broadcasters to observe a high standard of excellence in their programming and station management for the clear presentation of the gospel. Holds national and regional conventions. *Membership:* 1,000 organizational stations, program producers, agencies, and individuals. *Dues:* based on income. Meetings: 55th Annual NRB Convention and Exhibition, Jan 31–Feb 3, 1998, Washington, DC. *Publications: Religious Broadcasting Magazine* (mo.); *Annual Directory of Religious Media*; *Religious Broadcasting Resources Library Brochure*; *Religious Broadcasting Cassette Catalog*.

National School Boards Association (NSBA) Institute for the Transfer of Technology to Education (ITTE). 1680 Duke St., Alexandria, VA 22314. (800)838-6722. Fax (703)683-7590. E-mail itte@nsba.org. Web site http://www.nsba.org/itte. Cheryl S. Williams, Dir. ITTE was created to help advance the wise uses of technology in public education. ITTE renders several services to state school boards associations, sponsors conferences, publishes, and engages in special projects. The Technology Leadership Network, the membership component of ITTE, is designed to engage school districts nationwide in a dialogue about technology in education. This dialogue is carried out via newsletters, meetings, special reports, projects, and on-line communications. The experience of the Network is shared more broadly through the state associations' communications with all school districts. *Membership:* Over 400 school districts in 44 states, Canada, and the UK. *Dues:* based upon the school district's student enrollment. *Meetings:* 1999: Technology & Learning Conference, Nov 10–12, Dallas. 2000: Nov 15–17, Denver. *Publications: Investing in School Technology: Strategies to Meet the Funding Challenge/School Leader's Version*; *Technology for Students with Disabilities: A Decision Maker's Resource Guide*; *Leadership and Technology: What School Board Members Need to Know*; *Plans and Policies for Technology in Education: A Compendium*; *Telecommunications and Education: Surfing and the Art of Change*; *Multimedia and Learning: A School Leader's Guide*; *Electronic School* (q.).

National School Supply and Equipment Association (NSSEA). 8300 Colesville Rd., Suite 250, Silver Spring, MD 20910. (301)495-0240. Fax (301)495-3330. E-mail nssea@aol.com. Web site http://www.nssea.org. Tim Holt, Pres. A service organization of more than 1,600 manufacturers, distributors, retailers, and independent manufacturers' representatives of school supplies, equipment, and instructional materials. Seeks to maintain open communications between manufacturers and dealers in the school market, and to encourage the development of new ideas and products for educational progress. *Meetings:* 1999, Ed Expo '99, Atlanta, Mar 11–13; The School Equipment Show, Denver, Feb 18–20; 83rd Annual Fall Show, Orlando, Nov 4–7. *Publications: Tidings*; *Annual Membership Directory*.

National Science Foundation (NSF). 4201 Wilson Blvd., Arlington, VA 22230. (703)306-1070. Mary Hanson, Chief, Media Relations and Public Affairs. Linda Boutchyard, Contact Person, lboutchy@nsf.gov. NSF is an independent federal agency responsible for fundamental research in all fields of science and engineering, with an annual budget of about $3 billion. NSF funds reach all 50 states, through grants to more than 2,000 universities and institutions nationwide. NSF receives more than 50,000 requests for funding annually, including at least 30,000 new proposals. Applicants should refer to the NSF Guide to Programs. Scientific material and media reviews are available to help the public learn about NSF-supported programs. NSF news releases and tipsheets are available electronically via *NSFnews*. To subscribe, send an e-mail message to listmanager @nsf.gov; in the body of the message, type "subscribe nsfnews" and then type your name. Also see NSF news products at http://www.nsf.gov:80/od/lpa/start.htm, http://www.eurekalert.org/, and http://www.ari.net/newswise. In addition, NSF has developed a Web site that offers information about NSF directorates, offices, programs, and publications at http://nsf.gov.

National Telemedia Council Inc. (NTC). 120 E. Wilson St., Madison, WI 53703. (608)257-7712. Fax (608)257-7714. E-mail NTelemedia@aol.com. Web site http://danenet.wicip. org/NTC. Rev. Stephen Umhoefer, Interim Pres.; Marieli Rowe, Exec. Dir. The NTC is a national nonprofit professional organization dedicated to promoting media literacy, or critical media viewing skills. This is done primarily through work with teachers, parents, and caregivers. NTC activities include publishing *Telemedium: The Journal of Media Literacy*, the Teacher Idea Exchange (T.I.E.), the Jessie McCanse Award for individual contribution to media literacy, assistance to media literacy educators and professionals. *Dues:* $30, basic; $50, contributing; $100, patron. *Publications: Telemedium*; *The Journal of Media Literacy* (newsletter, q.).

Native American Public Telecommunications (NAPT). 1800 North 33rd St., PO Box 83111, Lincoln, NE 68501-3111. (402)472-3522. Fax (402)472-8675. Web site http://indian.monterey. edu/napt. Frank Blythe, Exec. Dir. The mission of NAPT is to inform, educate, and encourage the awareness of tribal histories, cultures, languages, opportunities, and aspirations through the fullest participation of America Indians and Alaska Natives in creating and employing all forms and educational and public telecommunications programs and services, thereby supporting tribal sovereignty. *Dues:* range from $20 (Turtle) to $1,000 (Eagle). *Publication: The Vision Maker* (newsletter).

*Network for Continuing Medical Education (NCME). One Harmon Plaza, 7th Floor, Secaucus, NJ 07094. (201)867-3550. Produces and distributes videocassettes to hospitals for physicians' continuing education. Programs are developed for physicians in the practice of General Medicine, Anesthesiology, Emergency Medicine, Gastroenterology, and Surgery. Physicians who view all the programs can earn up to 25 hours of Category 1 (AMA) credit and up to 10 hours of Prescribed (AAFP) credit each year. *Membership:* More than 1,000 hospitals provide NCME programs to their physicians. *Dues:* subscription fees: VHS-$2,160/yr. Sixty-minute videocassettes are distributed to hospital subscribers every eighteen days.

The NETWORK, Inc. 136 Fenno Drive, Rowley, MA 01969. (978)948-7764. Fax (978)948-7836. E-mail davidc@network.org. David Crandall, contact person. A nonprofit research and service organization providing training, research and evaluation, technical assistance, and materials for a fee to schools, educational organizations, and private sector firms with educational interests. The NETWORK has been helping professionals manage and learn about change since 1969. A Facilitator's Institute is held at least annually for trainers and staff developers who use the simulations. *Publications: An Action Guide for School Improvement*; *Making Change for School Improvement: A Simulation Game*; *Systems Thinking/Systems Changing: A Simulation Game*; *People, Policies, and Practices: Examining the Chain of School Improvement*; *Systemic Thinking: Solving Complex Problems*; *Benchmarking: A Guide for Educators*.

New England Educational Media Association (NEEMA). c/o Jean Keilly, 58 South Mammoth Road, Manchester, NH 03109. (603)622-9626. Fax (603)424-6229. An affiliate of AECT, NEEMA is a regional professional association dedicated to the improvement of instruction through the effective utilization of school library media services, media, and technology applications. For over 75 years, it has represented school library media professionals through activities and networking efforts to develop and polish the leadership skills, professional representation, and informational awareness of the membership. The Board of Directors consists of Departments of Education as well as professional leaders of the region. An annual conference program and a Leadership Program are offered in conjunction with the various regional state association conferences.

The New York Festivals (formerly the International Film and TV Festival of New York). 780 King St., Chappaqua, NY 10514. (914)238-4481. Fax (914)236-5040. E-mail: info@nyfests.com. Web site http://www.nyfests.com. Bilha Goldberg, Vice Pres. The New York Festivals sponsors the International Non-Broadcast Awards, which are annual competitive festivals for industrial and educational film and video productions, filmstrips and slide programs, multi-image business theater and interactive multimedia presentations, and television programs. Entry fees begin at $125. First entry deadline is Aug 4 for US entrants and Sept 16 for overseas entrants. The Non-Broadcast competition honors a wide variety of categories including Education Media. As one of the largest competitions in the world, achieving finalist status is a notable credit to any company's awards roster. Winners are announced each year at a gala awards show in New York City and published on the World Wide Web.

North Central Regional Educational Laboratory (NCREL). 1900 Spring Rd., Suite 300, Oak Brook, IL 60523-1480. (630)571-4700, (800)356-2735. Fax (630)571-4716. E-mail info@ncrel.org. Web site http://www.ncrel.org/. Jan Bakker, Resource Center Dir. NCREL's work is guided by a focus on comprehensive and systemic school restructuring that is research-based and learner-centered. One of 10 Office of Educational Research and Improvement (OERI) regional educational laboratories, NCREL disseminates information about effective programs, develops educational products, holds conferences, provides technical assistance, and conducts research and evaluation. A special focus is on technology and learning. In addition to conventional print publications, NCREL uses computer networks, videoconferencing via satellite, and video and audio formats to reach its diverse audiences. NCREL's Web site includes the acclaimed *Pathways to School Improvement*. NCREL operates the Midwest Consortium for Mathematics and Science Education which works to advance systemic change in mathematics and science education. Persons living in Illinois, Indiana, Iowa, Michigan, Minnesota, Ohio, and Wisconsin are encouraged to call NCREL Resource Center with any education-related questions. *Meetings:* the annual Leadership Academy, a leadership development program for practicing and aspiring school leaders, supports leaders in undertaking and implementing effective schoolwide improvement and reform. NCREL also hosts the North Central Regional Technology in Education Consortium which helps states and local educational agencies successfully integrate advanced technologies into K–12 classrooms, library media centers, and other educational settings. *Publications: R&D Watch* (q.). A catalog of print, video, and other media products is available by calling the main number.

Northwest College and University Council for the Management of Educational Technology (NW/MET). c/o WITS, Willamette University, 900 State St., Salem, OR 97301. (503)370-6650. Fax (503)375-5456. E-mail mmorandi@willamette.edu. Listserv NW-MET@willamette.edu. John Root, Pres.; Marti Morandi, Membership Chair. NW/MET is the first regional group representing institutions of higher education in Alberta, Alaska, British Columbia, Idaho, Montana, Oregon, Saskatchewan, and Washington to receive affiliate status in AECT. Membership is restricted to media managers with campus-wide responsibilities for educational technology services in the membership region. Corresponding membership is available to those who work outside the membership region. Current issues under consideration include managing emerging technologies, reorganization, copyright, and management/administration issues. Organizational goals include identifying the unique status problems of media managers in higher education. *Membership:* approx. 85. *Dues:* $35. *Meetings:* an annual conference and business meeting are held each year, rotating through the region. *Publications:* two annual newsletters and *NW/MET Journal*.

Northwest Regional Educational Laboratory (NWREL). 101 SW Main St., Suite 500, Portland, OR 97204. (503)275-9500. Fax (503)275-0448. E-mail info@nwrel.org. Web site http://www.nwrel.org. Dr. Ethel Simon-McWilliams, Exec. Dir. One of 10 Office of Educational Research and Improvement (OERI) regional educational laboratories, NWREL works with schools and communities to improve educational outcomes for children, youth, and adults. NWREL provides leadership, expertise, and services based on the results of research and development. The specialty area of NWREL is school change processes. It serves Alaska, Idaho, Oregon, Montana, and Washington. *Membership:* 817. *Dues:* none. *Publication: Northwest Report* (newsletter).

On-line Audiovisual Catalogers (OLAC). Formed as an outgrowth of the ALA conference, OLAC seeks to permit members to exchange ideas and information, and to interact with other agencies that influence audiovisual cataloging practices. *Membership:* 700. *Dues:* available for single or multiple years; $10-$27, indiv.; $16-$45, institution. Slight increase expected in 1999. *Meetings:* biannual. *Publication: OLAC Newsletter*.

Online Computer Library Center, Inc.(OCLC). 6565 Frantz Rd., Dublin, OH 43017-3395. (614)764-6000. Fax (614)764-6096. E-mail oclc@oclc.org. Web site http://www.oclc.org. K. Wayne Smith, Pres. and CEO. Nita Dean, Mgr., Public Relations. A nonprofit membership organization that engages in computer library service and research and makes available computer-based processes, products, and services for libraries, other educational organizations, and library users. From its facility in Dublin, Ohio, OCLC operates an international computer network that libraries use to catalog books, order custom-printed catalog cards and machine-readable records for local catalogs, arrange interlibrary loans, and maintain location information on library materials. OCLC also provides online reference products and services for the electronic delivery of information. More than 25,000 libraries contribute to and/or use information in WorldCat (the OCLC Online Union Catalog). *Publications: OCLC Newsletter* (6/yr.); *OCLC Reference News* (4/yr.); *Annual Report*.

Pacific Film Archive (PFA). University of California, Berkeley Art Museum, 2625 Durant Ave., Berkeley, CA 94720-2250. (510)642-1437 (library); (510)642-1412 (general). Fax (510) 642-4889. E-mail pfalibrary@uclink.berkeley.edu. Web site http://www.bampfa.berkeley.edu. Edith Kramer, Dir. and Curator of Film; Nancy Goldman, Head, PFA Library and Film Study Center. Sponsors the exhibition, study, and preservation of classic, international, documentary, animated, and avant-garde films. Provides on-site research screenings of films in its collection of over 7,000 titles. Provides access to its collections of books, periodicals, stills, and posters (all materials are noncirculating). Offers BAM/PFA members and University of California, Berkeley affiliates reference and research services to locate film and video distributors, credits, stock footage, etc. Library hours are 1pm–5pm Mon–Thurs. *Membership:* through parent organization, the Berkeley Art Museum. *Dues:* $40 indiv. and nonprofit departments of institutions. *Publication: BAM/PFA Calendar* (6/yr.).

Pacific Resources for Education and Learning (PREL). 828 Fort Street Mall Suite 500, Honolulu, HI 96813-4321. (808)533-6000. Fax (808)533-7599. E-mail askprel@prel.hawaii.edu. Web site http://prel.hawaii.edu. John W. Kofel, Exec. Dir. One of ten regional educational laboratories designed to help educators and policymakers solve educational problems in their schools. Using the best available information and the expertise of professionals, PREL furnishes research results, provides training to teachers and administrators, and helps to implement new approaches in education. The PREL Star program, funded by a US Department of Education Star Schools Grant, utilizes telecommunications technology to provide distance learning opportunities to the Pacific region. PREL serves American Samoa, Commonwealth of the Northern Mariana Islands, Federated States of Micronesia, Guam, Hawaii, Republic of the Marshall Islands, and Republic of Palau.

Photographic Society of America (PSA). 3000 United Founders Blvd., Suite 103, Oklahoma City, OK 73112. (405)843-1437. Fax (405)843-1438. E-mail 74521,2414@compuserve.com. Web site http://www.psa-photo.org. Jacque Noel, Operations Mgr. A nonprofit organization for the development of the arts and sciences of photography and for the furtherance of public appreciation of photographic skills. Its members, largely advanced amateurs, consist of individuals, camera clubs, and other photographic organizations. Divisions include electronic imaging, color slide, video motion picture, nature, photojournalism, travel, pictorial print, stereo, and techniques. Sponsors national, regional, and local meetings, clinics, and contests. *Membership:* 7,000. *Dues:* $40, North America; $45 elsewhere. *Meetings:* 1999 International Conference of Photography, Aug 30–Sep 4, Toronto, Delta Meadowvale Hotel. *Publication: PSA Journal.*

Professors of Instructional Design and Technology (PIDT). Instructional Technology Dept., 220 War Memorial Hall, Virginia Tech, Blacksburg, VA 24061-0341. (540)231-5587. Fax (540)231-9075. E-mail moorem@VT.EDU. Web site http://www.conted.VT.edu/pidt/pidt.html. Dr. Mike Moore, contact person. An informal organization designed to encourage and facilitate the exchange of information among members of the instructional design and technology academic and corporate communities. Also serves to promote excellence in academic programs in instructional design and technology and to encourage research and inquiry that will benefit the field while providing leadership in the public and private sectors in its application and practice. *Membership:* 300 faculty employed in higher education institutions whose primary responsibilities are teaching and research in this area, their corporate counterparts, and other persons interested in the goals and activities of the PIDT. *Dues:* none. *Meetings:* Annual Conference; see Web site for information and registration.

*Public Broadcasting Service (PBS). 1320 Braddock Pl., Alexandria, VA 22314. Web site http://www.pbs.org. Ervin S. Duggan, CEO and Pres. National distributor of public television programming, obtaining all programs from member stations, American independent producers, or foreign sources. PBS also offers educational services for teachers, students, and parents including the National Program Service, PBS Online, and Teacher Resource Service. PBS services include program acquisition, distribution, and scheduling; development and fundraising support; and engineering and technical development. Subsidiaries of PBS include PBS Adult Learning Service, and PBS Video, which are described below. PBS is owned and operated by local public television organizations through annual membership fees, and governed by a board of directors elected by PBS members for three-year terms. *Membership:* 172 organizations operating 349 stations.

PBS Adult Learning Service (ALS). 1320 Braddock Pl., Alexandria, VA 22314-1698. (800)257-2578. Fax (703)739-8471. E-mail als@pbs.org. Web site http://www.pbs.org/als/college. Will Philipp, Senior Dir. The mission of ALS is to help colleges, universities, and public television stations increase learning opportunities for distance learners; enrich classroom instruction; update faculty; train administrators, management, and staff; and provide other educational services for local communities. A pioneer in the widespread use of video and print packages incorporated into curricula and offered for credit by local colleges, ALS began broadcasting telecourses in 1981. Since that time, over 3 million students have earned college credit through telecourses offered in partnership with more than two-thirds of the nation's colleges and universities. In 1988, ALS established the Adult Learning Satellite Service (ALSS) to provide colleges, universities, and other organizations with a broad range of educational programming via direct satellite. Since 1994, ALS has facilitated the capability for colleges nationwide to offer full two-year degrees at a distance through the popular Going the Distance® project. Over 170 colleges are currently participating in 37 states. In 1998, ALS launched the first teleWEBcourse^{SM}, *Internet Literacy*, an online credit offering available through the PBS Website. *Membership:* 700-plus colleges, universities, hospitals, and government agencies are now ALSS Associates. Organizations that are not Associates can still acquire ALS programming, but at higher fees. *Dues:* $1,500; multisite and consortia rates are available. *Publications: ALSS Programming Line-Up* (catalog of available programming, 3/yr.); *The Agenda* (news magazine about issues of interest to distance learning and adult learning administrators); *Changing the Face of Higher Education* (an overview of ALS services); *Teaching Telecourses: Opportunities and Options; Ideas for Increasing Telecourse Enrollment; Going the Distance® Handbook* (case studies for offering distance learning degrees).

PBS VIDEO. 1320 Braddock Pl., Alexandria, VA 22314. (703)739-5380; (800)344-3337. Fax (703)739-5269. Jon Cecil, Dir., PBS VIDEO Marketing. Markets and distributes PBS television programs for sale on videocassette or videodisc to colleges, public libraries, schools, governments, and other organizations and institutions. *Publications: PBS VIDEO Resource Catalog; PBS VIDEO Catalogs of New and Popular Videos* (6/yr.).

Public Library Association (PLA). 50 E. Huron St., Chicago, IL 60611. (312)280-5PLA. Fax (312)280-5029. E-mail pla@ala.org. Greta Southard, Exec. Dir. An affiliate of the American Library Association, PLA is concerned with the development, effectiveness, and financial support of public libraries. It speaks for the profession and seeks to enrich the professional competence and opportunities of public librarians. Sections include Adult Lifelong Learning, Community Information, Metropolitan Libraries, Public Library Systems, Small and Medium-sized Libraries, Public Policy for Public Libraries, Planning, Measurement and Evaluation, and Marketing of Public Library Services. *Membership:* 8,500. *Dues:* $50, open to all ALA members. *Meetings:* 1999 PLA Spring Symposium, Mar 25–28; 2000 PLA National Conference, Mar 28–Apr 1. "Public Libraries: Vital, Valuable, Virtual." *Publication: Public Libraries* (bi-mo.). Two PLA Committees of particular interest to the Educational Technology field are listed below.

Audiovisual Committee (of the Public Library Association). 50 E.Huron St., Chicago, IL 60611. (312)280-5752. James E. Massey, Chair. Promotes use of audiovisual materials in public libraries.

Technology in Public Libraries Committee (of the Public Library Association). 50 E. Huron St., Chicago, IL 60611. (312)280-5752. William Ptacek, Chair. Collects and disseminates information on technology applications in public libraries.

*Puppeteers of America, Inc. (POA). #5 Cricklewood Path, Pasadena, CA 91107-1002. (818)797-5748. Gayle Schluter, Membership Officer. Web site http://www.puppeteers.org. Formed in 1937, POA holds festivals for puppetry across the country, sponsors local guilds, presents awards, sponsors innovative puppetry works, provides consulting, and provides materials through the Audio-Visual Library. *Members:* over 2,000. *Dues:* $40, regular; $50, couple; $20, junior; $60, family; $30, journal subscription. *Meetings:* National Festival, Aug 1-7, 1999, Seattle. *Publication: The Puppetry Journal* (q).

Recording for the Blind and Dyslexic (RFB&D). 20 Roszel Road, Princeton, NJ 08540. Main phone (609)452-0606. Customer Service (800)221-4792. Fax (609)987-8116. E-mail information@rfbd.org. Web site http://www.rfbd.org. Ritchie Geisel, President. RFB&D is a national nonprofit organization that provides educational and professional books in accessible format to people with visual impairments, learning disabilities, or other physical disabilities that prevent them from reading normal printed material. This includes students from kindergarten to graduate school and people who no longer attend school but who use educational books to pursue careers or personal interests. RFB&D's 75,000-volume collection of audio titles is the largest educational resource of its kind in the world. RFB&D provides a wide range of library services as well as "E-Text" books on computer disk, including dictionaries, computer manuals, and other reference books. For an additional fee, a custom recording service is also available, to make other publications accessible. Potential individual members must complete an application form, which contains a "disability verification" section. *Membership:* 39,139 individuals, 275 institutions. *Dues:* for qualified individuals, $50 registration, $25 annual. Institutional Memberships also available (contact Customer Service).

Recording Industry Association of America, Inc. (RIAA). 1330 Connecticut Ave. NW #300, Washington DC, 20036; (202)775-0101. Fax (202)775-7253. Website http://www.riaa.com/. Hilary Rosen Pres. and CEO. Founded in 1952, RIAA's mission is to promote the mutual interests of recording companies, as well as the betterment of the industry overall through successful government relations (both federal and state), intellectual property protection, and international activities. RIAA represents the recording industry, whose members create and/or distribute approximately 90 percent of all legitimate sound recordings produced and sold in the US. RIAA is the official certification agency for gold, platinum, and multi-platinum record awards. *Membership:* over 250 recording companies. *Publications: Annual Report; Fact Book.*

Reference and User Services Association (RUSA). 50 E. Huron St., Chicago, IL 60611. (800)545-2433, ext. 4398. Fax (312)944-8085. Cathleen Bourdon, Exec. Dir. A division of the American Library Association, RUSA is responsible for stimulating and supporting in every type of library the delivery of reference information services to all groups and of general library services and materials to adults. *Membership:* 5,500. *Dues:* $45 plus membership in ALA. *Publications: RUSQ* (q.); *RUSA Update.*

*Research for Better Schools, Inc. (RBS). 444 North Third St., Philadelphia, PA 19123-4107. (215)574-9300. Fax (215)574-0133. Website http://www.rbs.org/. John Connolly, Exec. Dir. RBS is a private, nonprofit corporation which currently operates the Mid-Atlantic Eisenhower Consortium for Mathematics and Science Education, and the Mid-Atlantic Telecommunications Alliance. In its 30 years of service to the education community, RBS has also offered educational technology, development, evaluation, technical assistance, and training services with client funding. RBS also operates an educational publications division.

Smithsonian Institution. 1000 Jefferson Drive SW, Washington, DC 20560. (202)357-2700. Fax (202)786-2515. Web site http://www.si.edu. I. Michael Heyman, Sec. An independent trust instrumentality of the US that conducts scientific, cultural, and scholarly research; administers the national collections; and performs other educational public service functions, all supported by Congress, trusts, gifts, and grants. Includes 16 museums, including the National Museum of Natural History, the National Museum of American History, the National Air and Space Museum, and the National Zoological Park. Museums are free and open daily except December 25. The Smithsonian Institution Traveling Exhibition Service (SITES) organizes exhibitions on art, history, and science and circulates them across the country and abroad. *Membership:* Smithsonian Associates. *Dues:* $24-$45. *Publications: Smithsonian; Air & Space/Smithsonian; The Torch* (staff newsletter, mo.); *Research Reports* (semi-technical, q.); Smithsonian Institution Press Publications, 470 L'Enfant Plaza, Suite 7100, Washington, DC 20560.

Society for Applied Learning Technology (SALT). 50 Culpeper St., Warrenton, VA 20186. (540)347-0055. Fax (540)349-3169. E-mail info@lti.org. Web site http://www.salt.org. Raymond G. Fox, Pres. The society is a nonprofit, professional membership organization that was founded in 1972. Membership in the society is oriented to professionals whose work requires knowledge and communication in the field of instructional technology. The society provides members a means to enhance their knowledge and job performance by participation in society-sponsored meetings, subscription to society-sponsored publications, association with other professionals at conferences sponsored by the society, and membership in special interest groups and special society-sponsored initiatives. In addition, the society offers member discounts on society-sponsored journals, conferences, and publications. *Membership:* 1,000. *Dues:* $45.*Meetings:* Orlando Multimedia '99, Kissimmee, FL; Interactive Multimedia '99, Arlington, VA. *Publications: Journal of Educational Technology Systems; Journal of Instruction Delivery Systems; Journal of Interactive Instructional Development; Journal of Medical Education Technologies.* Send for list of books.

Society for Computer Simulation (SCS). PO Box 17900, San Diego, CA 92177-7900. (619)277-3888. Fax (619)277-3930. E-mail info@scs.org. Web site http://www.scs.org. Bill Gallagher, Exec. Dir. Founded in 1952, SCS is a professional-level technical society devoted to the art and science of modeling and simulation. Its purpose is to advance the understanding, appreciation, and use of all types of computer models for studying the behavior of actual or hypothesized systems of all kinds and to sponsor standards. Additional office in Ghent, Belgium. *Membership:* 1,900. *Dues:* $75 (includes journal subscription). *Meetings:* local, regional, and national technical meetings and conferences, such as the Western Simulation Multiconference Jan 17–21, 1999, San Francisco; Summer and Winter Computer Simulation Conferences, Applied Simulation Technologies Conference, Apr 12–15, 1999, San Diego; and National Educational Computing Conference (NECC). *Publications: Simulation* (mo.); *Simulation* series (q.); *Transactions of SCS* (q.).

Society for Photographic Education (SPE). PO Box 2811, Daytona Beach, FL 32120-2811. (904)255-8131, ext. 3944. Fax (904)255-3044. E-mail SocPhotoEd@aol.com or SPENews@aol. com. Web site http://www.spenational.org. James J. Murphy, Exec. Dir. An association of college and university teachers of photography, museum photographic curators, writers, and publishers. Promotes discourse in photography education, culture, and art. *Membership:* 1,700. *Dues:* $55. *Meetings:* 1999, Mar 11–14, Tucson. 2000, Mar 16–19, Cleveland. *Publication: Exposure* (newsletter).

Society of Cable Telecommunications Engineers (SCTE). 140 Philips Rd., Exton, PA 19341-1319. (610)363-6888. Fax (610)363-5898. E-mail info@scte.org. Web site http://www.scte.org. William W. Riker, Pres. SCTE is dedicated to the technical training and further education of members. A nonprofit membership organization for persons engaged in engineering, construction, installation, technical direction, management, or administration of cable television and broadband communications technologies. Also eligible for membership are students in communications, educators, government and regulatory agency employees, and affiliated trade associations. SCTE provides technical training and certification, and is an American National Standards Institute (ANSI)-approved Standards Development Organization for the cable telecommunications industry. *Membership:* 15,500 US and International. *Dues:* $40. *Meetings:* 1999, Conference on Emerging Technologies, Feb 3–5, Dallas; Cable-Tec Expo, May 25–27, Orlando (hardware exhibits and engineering conference). 2000 Cable-Tec Expo, June 26–29, Las Vegas. *Publications: The Interval*; technical documents, training materials, and videotapes (some available in Spanish).

Society of Photo Technologists (SPT). 11112 S. Spotted Rd., Cheney, WA 99004. (888)662-7678 or (509)624-9621. Fax (509)323-4811 or (509)624-5320. E-mail spt@usa.net. An organization of photographic equipment repair technicians, which improves and maintains communications between manufacturers and independent repair technicians. *Membership:* 1,000. *Dues:* $80-$360. *Publications: SPT Journal; SPT Parts and Services Directory; SPT Newsletter; SPT Manuals—Training and Manufacturer's Tours.*

Southeastern Regional Media Leadership Council (SRMLC). Dr. Vykuntapathi Thota, Director, Virginia State University, PO Box 9198, Petersburg, VA 23806. (804)524-5937. Fax (804)524-5757. An affiliate of AECT, the purpose of the SRMLC is to strengthen the role of the individual state AECT affiliates within the Southeastern region; to seek positive change in the nature and status of instructional technology as it exists within the Southeast; to provide opportunities for the training and development of leadership for both the region and the individual affiliates; and to provide opportunities for the exchange of information and experience among those who attend the annual conference.

SouthEastern Regional Vision for Education (SERVE). SERVE Tallahassee Office, 1203 Governor's Square Blvd., Suite 400, Tallahassee, FL 32301. (800)352-6001, (904)671-6000. Fax (904)671-6020. E-mail bfry@SERVE.org. Mr. Don Holznagel, Exec. Dir. Betty Fry, Contact Person. SERVE is a regional educational research and development laboratory funded by the US Department of Education to help educators, policymakers, and communities improve schools so that all students achieve their full potential. The laboratory offers the following services: field-based models and strategies for comprehensive school improvement; publications on hot topics in education, successful implementation efforts, applied research projects and policy issues; database searches and information search training; a regional bulletin board service that provides educators electronic communication and Internet access; information and assistance for state and local policy development; and services to support the coordination and improvement of assistance for young children and their families. The Eisenhower Mathematics and Science Consortium at SERVE promotes improvement of education in these targeted areas by coordinating regional resources, disseminating exemplary instructional materials, and offering technical assistance for implementation of effective teaching methods and assessment tools. *Meetings:* for dates and topics of conferences and workshops, contact Betty Fry, (800)352-6001. *Publications: Reengineering High Schools for Student Success; Schools for the 21st Century: New Roles for Teachers and Principals* (rev. ed.); *Designing Teacher Evaluation Systems That Promote Professional Growth; Learning by Serving: 2,000 Ideas for Service-Learning Projects; Sharing Success: Promising Service-Learning Programs; Future Plans* (videotape, discussion guide, and pamphlet); *Future Plans Planning Guides.*

Southwest Educational Development Laboratory (SEDL). 211 East Seventh St., Austin, TX 78701. (512)476-6861. Fax (512)476-2286. E-mail info@sedl.org. Web site http://www.sedl.org/. Dr. Wesley A. Hoover, President and CEO; Dr. Joyce Pollard, Dir., Institutional Communications & Policy Services. One of 10 Office of Educational Research and Improvement (OERI) regional educational laboratories designed to help educators and policymakers solve educational problems in their schools. Using the best available information and the experience and expertise of professionals, SEDL seeks to identify solutions to education problems, tries new approaches, furnishes research results, and provides training to teachers and administrators. SEDL serves Arkansas, Louisiana, New Mexico, Oklahoma, and Texas. *Publications: SEDLETTER* for free general distribution and a range of topic-specific publications related to educational change, education policy, mathematics, language arts, science, and disability research.

Special Libraries Association. 1700 Eighteenth St., NW, Washington, DC, 20009-2514. (202)234-4700. Fax (202)265-9317. Email sla@sla.org. Web site http://www.sla.org. Dr. David R. Bender, Exec. Dir. The Special Libraries Association is an international association representing the interests of nearly 15,000 information professionals in 60 countries. Special Librarians are information and resource experts who collect, analyze, evaluate, package, and disseminate information to facilitate accurate decision-making in corporate, academic, and government settings.

The association offers myriad programs and services designed to help its members serve their customers more effectively and succeed in an increasingly challenging environment of information management and technology. These services include career and employment services, and professional development opportunities. *Membership:* 14,500. *Dues*: $105, indiv.; $25, student. *Meetings:* 1999, Jan 21–23, San Francisco; Jun 5–10, Minneapolis. 2000, Jan 20–22, St. Louis; Jun 10–15, Philadelphia; Oct 16–19, Brighton, UK. *Publications: Information Outlook* (monthly glossy magazine that accepts advertising). Special Libraries Association also has an active book publishing program.

Teachers and Writers Collaborative (T&W). 5 Union Square W., New York, NY 10003-3306. (212)691-6590. Toll-free (888)266-5789. Fax (212)675-0171. E-mail info@twc.org. Web site http://www.twc.org. Nancy Larson Shapiro, Dir. Sends writers and other artists into New York public schools to work with teachers and students on writing and art projects. Hosts seminars for creative work from across the US and beyond. Recent projects include the creation of WriteNet, a series of on-line forums and information for people interested in teaching creative writing. Also, in conjunction with NBC TV, T&W set up a series of residencies around the country focused on teaching creative writing using "classic" literature. See Web site for updated schedule of events. *Membership:* over 1,000; for people interested in the teaching of writing. *Dues:* $35, basic personal membership. *Publications: Teachers & Writers* (magazine, 5/yr); *The Story in History*; *The T&W Handbook of Poetic Forms*; *Personal Fiction Writing*; *Luna, Luna, Creative Writing from Spanish and Latino Literature*; *The Nearness of You: Students and Teachers Writing On-Line.* Request free publications catalog for list of titles.

Theatre Library Association (TLA). 149 W. 45th St., New York, NY 10036. (212)944-3895. Fax (212)944-4139. Web site http://www.brown.edu/Facilities/University_Library/beyond/TLA/TLA.html. Maryann Chach, Exec. Sec. Seeks to further the interests of collecting, preserving, and using theater, cinema, and performing arts materials in libraries, museums, and private collections. *Membership:* 500. *Dues:* $30, indiv.; $30, institutional; $20, students and retirees. *Publication: Performing Arts Resources* (membership annual, Vol. 20, Denishawn Collections).

USA Toy Library Association (USA-TLA). 2530 Crawford Ave., Suite 111, Evanston, IL 60201. (847)864-3330. Fax (847)864-3331. E-mail foliog@aol.com. Judith Q. Iacuzzi, Exec. Dir. The mission of the USA-TLA is to provide a networking system answering to all those interested in play and play materials to provide a national resource to toy libraries, family centers, resource and referrals, public libraries, schools, institutions serving families of special need, and other groups and individuals involved with children; to support and expand the number of toy libraries; and to advocate for children and the importance of their play in healthy development. Individuals can find closest toy libraries by sending an e-mail or written inquiry in a self-addressed stamped envelope. *Membership:* 60 institutions, 150 individuals. *Dues:* $165, comprehensive; $55, basic; $15, student. *Meetings:* national meetings in the spring and fall. *Publications: Child's Play* (q. newsletter); *How to Start and Operate a Toy Library*; *Play Is a Child's Work* (videotapes), other books on quality toys and play.

University Continuing Education Association (UCEA). One Dupont Cir. NW, Suite 615, Washington, DC 20036. (202)659-3130. Fax (202)785-0374. Web site http://www.nucea.edu. Sue Maes, Pres. 1998-99; Kay J. Kohl, Exec. Dir.; Susan Goewey, Dir. of Pubs.; Edward Gehres, Dir. of Govt. Relations & Public Affairs, Joelle Brink, Director of Information Services. UCEA is an association of public and private higher education institutions concerned with making continuing education available to all population segments and to promoting excellence in continuing higher education. Many institutional members offer university and college courses via electronic instruction. *Membership:* 425 institutions, 2,000 professionals. *Dues:* vary according to membership category. *Meetings:* UCEA has an annual national conference and several professional development seminars throughout the year. *Publications:* monthly newsletter; quarterly; occasional papers; scholarly journal, *Continuing Higher Education Review*; *Independent Study Catalog*. With Peterson's, *The Guide to Distance Learning*; *Guide to Certificate Programs at American*

Colleges and Universities; UCEA-ACE/Oryx Continuing Higher Education book series; *Lifelong Learning Trends* (a statistical factbook on continuing higher education); organizational issues series; membership directory.

WestEd. 730 Harrison St., San Francisco, CA 94107-1242. (415)565-3000. Fax (415)565-3012. E-mail tross@wested.org. Web site http://www.WestEd.org. Glen Harvey, CEO. WestEd is a nonprofit research, development, and service agency dedicated to improving education and other opportunities for children, youth, and adults. Drawing on the best from research and practice, WestEd works with practitioners and policymakers to address critical issues in education and other related areas, including early childhood intervention; curriculum, instruction and assessment; the use of technology; career and technical preparation; teacher and administrator professional development; science and mathematics education; and safe schools and communities. WestEd was created in 1995 to unite and enhance the capacity of Far West Laboratory and Southwest Regional Laboratory, two of the nation's original education laboratories. In addition to its work across the nation, WestEd serves as the regional education laboratory for Arizona, California, Nevada, and Utah. *Publication:* catalog is available.

Western Public Radio (WPR). Ft. Mason Center, Bldg. D, San Francisco, CA 94123. (415)771-1160. Fax (415)771-4343. E-mail WPR SF@aol.com. Karolyn van Putten, President/CEO; Lynn Chadwick, Vice President/COO. WPR provides analog and digital audio production training, public radio program proposal consultation, and studio facilities for rent.

World Future Society (WFS). 7910 Woodmont Ave., Suite 450, Bethesda, MD 20814. (301)656-8274, fax (301)951-0394. E-mail wfsinfo@wfs.org. Web site http://www.wfs.org/wfs. Edward Cornish, Pres. Organization of individuals interested in the study of future trends and possibilities. Its purpose is to provide information on trends and scenarios so that individuals and organizations can better plan their future. *Membership*: 30,000. *Dues*: $35, general; $95, professional; call Society for details on all membership levels and benefits. *Meeting*: 1999: Ninth General Assembly, July 18–22, Washington. 2000: Annual Conference, July 23–25, Houston. *Publications*: *The Futurist: A Journal of Forecasts, Trends and Ideas About the Future*; *Futures Research Quarterly*; *Future Survey*. The society's bookstore offers audio- and videotapes, books, and other items.

Young Adult Library Services Association (YALSA). 50 E. Huron St., Chicago, IL 60611. (312)280-4390. Fax (312)664-7459. E-mail yalsa@ala.org. Web site http://www.ala.organization/yalsa. Julie A. Walker, Exec. Dir.; Linda Waddle, Deputy Exec. Dir.; Michael Cart, Pres. An affiliate of the American Library Association, YALSA seeks to advocate, promote, and strengthen service to young adults as part of the continuum of total library services, and assumes responsibility within the ALA to evaluate and select books and nonbook media, and to interpret and make recommendations regarding their use with young adults. Committees include Best Books for Young Adults, Popular Paperbacks, Recommended Books for the Reluctant Young Adult Reader, Media Selection and Usage, Publishers' Liaison, and Selected Films for Young Adults. *Membership:* 2,223. *Dues:* $40 (in addition to ALA membership); $15, students. *Publications: Journal of Youth Services in Libraries* (q.); *VOICES Newsletter* (available only to members).

Canada

This section includes information on nine Canadian organizations whose principal interests lie in the general fields of educational media, instructional technology, and library and information science.

*ACCESS NETWORK. 3720 - 76 Ave., Edmonton, AB T6B 2N9, Canada. (403)440-7777. Fax (403)440-8899. E-mail promo@ccinet.ab.ca. Dr. Ronald Keast, Pres.; John Verburgt, Creative Services Manager. The ACCESS Network (Alberta Educational Communications Corporation) was purchased by Learning and Skills Television of Alberta in 1995. The newly privatized network works with Alberta's educators to provide all Albertans with a progressive and diverse television-based educational and training resource to support their learning and skills development needs using cost-effective methods and innovative techniques, and to introduce a new private sector model for financing and efficient operation of educational television in the province.

Association for Media and Technology in Education in Canada (AMTEC). 3-1750 The Queensway, Suite 1318, Etobicoke, ON M9C 5H5, Canada. (604)323-5627. Fax (604)323-5577. E-mail maepp@langara.bc.ca. Web site http://www.canosun.bc.ca/~amtec/. Dr. Richard Schwier, Pres.; Dr. Katy Campbell, Pres. Elect; Mary Anne Epp, Sec./Treas. AMTEC is Canada's national association for educational media and technology professionals. The organization provides national leadership through annual conferences, publications, workshops, media festivals, and awards. It responds to media and technology issues at the international, national, provincial, and local levels, and maintains linkages with other organizations with similar interests. *Membership:* AMTEC members represent all sectors of the educational media and technology fields. *Dues:* $101.65, Canadian regular; $53.50, student and retiree. *Meeting:* Annual Conferences take place in late May or early June. 1999, Ottawa; 2000, Vancouver. *Publications: Canadian Journal of Educational Communication* (q.); *Media News* (3/yr.); *Membership Directory* (with membership).

*Canadian Broadcasting Corporation (CBC)/Société Radio-Canada (SRC). PO Box 500, Station A, Toronto, Ontario, Canada. Web site http://www.cbc.ca. The CBC is a publicly owned corporation established in 1936 by an Act of the Canadian Parliament to provide a national broadcasting service in Canada in the two official languages. CBC services include English and French television networks; English and French AM Mono and FM Stereo radio networks virtually free of commercial advertising; CBC North, which serves Canada's North by providing radio and television programs in English, French, and eight native languages; Newsworld and its French counterpart, Le Réseau de l'information (RDI), 24-hour national satellites to cable English-language and French-language news and information service respectively, both funded entirely by cable subscription and commercial advertising revenues; and Radio Canada International, a shortwave radio service that broadcasts in seven languages and is managed by CBC and financed by External Affairs. The CBC is financed mainly by public funds voted annually by Parliament.

Canadian Education Association/Association canadienne d'éducation (CEA). 252 Bloor St. W., Suite 8-200, Toronto, ON M5S 1V5, Canada. (416)924-7721. Fax (416)924-3188. E-mail acea@hookup.net. Web site http://www.acea.ca. Penny Milton, Exec. Dir.; Suzanne Tanguay, Director of Publications. The Canadian equivalent of the US National Education Association, CEA has one central objective: to promote the improvement of education. It is the only national, bilingual organization whose function is to inform, assist, and bring together all sectors of the educational community. *Membership:* all 12 provincial and territorial departments of education, the federal government, 400 individuals, 120 organizations, 100 school boards. *Dues:* $90, indiv.; $280, organization; 10 cents per pupil, school boards. *Meetings:* Annual CEA Convention. *Publications: CEA Handbook; Education Canada* (q.); *CEA Newsletter* (8/yr.); *Education in Canada: An Overview; Class Size, Academic Achievement and Public Policy; Disruptive Behaviour in Today's Classroom; Financing Canadian Education; Secondary Schools in Canada: The National Report of the Exemplary Schools Project; Making Sense of the Canadian Charter of Rights and Freedom: A Handbook for Administrators and Teachers; The School Calendar*.

Canadian Library Association. 200 Elgin St., Suite 602, Ottawa, ON K2P IL5, Canada. (613)232-9625. Fax (613)563-9895. E-mail ai075@freenet.carleton.ca. Web site http://www.cla. amlibs.ca. Vicki Whitmell, Exec. Dir. The mission of the Canadian Library Association is to provide leadership in the promotion, development, and support of library and information services in Canada for the benefit of Association members, the profession, and Canadian society. In the spirit of this mission, CLA aims to engage the active, creative participation of library staff, trustees, and governing bodies in the development and management of high quality Canadian library service; to assert and support the right of all Canadians to the freedom to read and to free universal access to a wide variety of library materials and services; to promote librarianship and to enlighten all levels of government as to the significant role that libraries play in educating and socializing the Canadian people; and to link libraries, librarians, trustees, and others across the country for the purpose of providing a unified nationwide voice in matters of critical concern. *Membership:* 2,300 individuals, 700 institutions, 100 Associates and Trustees. *Dues:* $50-$300. *Meetings:* 1999 Annual Conference, Jun 18–22, Toronto; 2000, Edmonton, June. *Publication: Feliciter* (membership magazine, 10/yr.).

Canadian Museums Association/Association des musées canadiens (CMA/AMC). 280 Metcalfe St., Suite 400, Ottawa, ON K2P 1R7, Canada. (613)567-0099. Fax (613)233-5438. E-mail info@museums.ca. Web site http://www.museums.ca. John G. McAvity, Exec. Dir. The Canadian Museums Association is a nonprofit corporation and registered charity dedicated to advancing public museums and museum works in Canada, promoting the welfare and better administration of museums, and fostering a continuing improvement in the qualifications and practices of museum professionals. *Membership:* 2,000. *Meeting:* CMA Annual Conference, summer. *Publications: Museogramme* (bi-mo. newsletter); *Muse* (q. journal, Canada's only national, bilingual, scholarly magazine devoted to museums, it contains museum-based photography, feature articles, commentary, and practical information); *The Official Directory of Canadian Museums and Related Institutions* (1997-99 edition) lists all museums in Canada plus information on government departments, agencies, and provincial and regional museum associations.

Canadian Publishers' Council (CPC). 250 Merton St., Suite 203, Toronto, ON M4S 1B1 Canada. (416)322-7011. Fax (416)322-6999. Web site http://www.pubcouncil.ca. Jacqueline Hushion, Exec. Dir. CPC members publish and distribute an extensive list of Canadian and imported learning materials in a complete range of formats from traditional textbook and ancillary materials to CDs and interactive video. The primary markets for CPC members are schools, universities and colleges, bookstores, and libraries. CPC also provides exhibits throughout the year and works through a number of subcommittees and groups within the organization to promote effective book publishing. CPC was founded in 1910. *Membership:* 27 companies, educational institutions, or government agencies that publish books as an important facet of their work.

National Film Board of Canada (NFBC). 350 Fifth Ave., Suite 4820, New York, NY 10118. (212)629-8890. Fax (212)629-8502. E-mail gsem78a@prodigy.com. John Sirabella, US Marketing Mgr./Nontheatrical Rep. Established in 1939, the NFBC's main objective is to produce and distribute high-quality audiovisual materials for educational, cultural, and social purposes.

Ontario Film Association, Inc. (also known as the Association for the Advancement of Visual Media/L'association pour l'avancement des médias visuels). 3-1750 The Queensway, Suite 1341, Etobicoke, ON M9C 5H5, Canada. (416)761-6056. Fax (905)820-7397. Margaret Nix., Exec. Dir. A volunteer organization of buyers and users of media whose objectives are to promote the sharing of ideas and information about media, to showcase media, to publish *Visual Média/Medias Visuels*, to do advocacy, and to present workshops. *Membership:* 122. *Dues:* $120, regular and commercial; $180, extended. *Meeting:* OFA Media Showcase, spring. *Publication: Visual Media/ Médias Visuels* (5/yr.).

Part Six
Graduate Programs

Introduction

This directory describes graduate programs in Instructional Technology, Educational Media and Communications, School Library Media, and closely allied programs in the United States. This year's list includes four new programs. One institution indicated that its program had been discontinued, and has been deleted from the listings. Master's, Specialist, and doctoral degrees are combined into one unified list.

Information in this section can be considered current as of early 1998 for most programs. In the majority of cases, department chairs or their representatives responded to a questionnaire mailed or e-mailed to them during November of 1997. Programs for which we received no updated information are indicated by an asterisk (*).

Entries provide as much of the following information as furnished by respondents: (1) name and address of the institution; (2) chairperson or other individual in charge of the program; (3) types of degrees offered and specializations, emphases, or tracks, including information on careers for which candidates are prepared; (4) special features of the degree program; (5) admission requirements; (6) degree requirements; (7) number of full-time and part-time faculty; (8) number of full-time and part-time students; (9) types of financial assistance available; and (10) the number of degrees awarded by type in 1997. All grade-point averages (GPAs), test scores, and degree requirements are minimums unless stated otherwise. The Graduate Record Examination, Miller Analogies Test, National Teacher's Examination, and other standardized tests are referred to by their acronyms. The Test of English as a Foreign Language (TOEFL) appears in many of the *Admission Requirements*, and in most cases this test is required only for international students. Although some entries explicitly state application fees, most do not. Prospective students should assume that most institutions require a completed application, transcripts of all previous collegiate work, and a non-refundable application fee.

Directors of advanced professional programs for instructional technology or media specialists should find this degree program information useful as a means of comparing their own offerings and requirements with those of institutions offering comparable programs. This listing, along with the Classified List, should also assist individuals in locating institutions that best suit their interests and requirements. In addition, a comparison of degree programs across several years may help scholars with historical interests trace trends and issues in the field over time.

Additional information on the programs listed, including admission procedure instructions, may be obtained by contacting individual program coordinators. General or graduate catalogs and specific program information usually are furnished for a minimal charge. In addition, most graduate programs now have e-mail contact addresses and Web sites which provide a wealth of descriptive information.

We are greatly indebted to those individuals who responded to our requests for information. Although the editors expended considerable effort to ensure currency and completeness of the listings, there may be institutions within the United States that now have programs of which we are unaware. Readers are encouraged to furnish new information to the publisher who, in turn, will contact the program for inclusion in the next edition of *EMTY*.

Institutions in this section are listed alphabetically by state.

CLASSIFIED LIST

Computer Applications
California State University-San Bernardino [M.A.]
State University of New York at Stony Brook [Master's: Technological Systems Management/Educational Computing]
University of Iowa [M.A.]
Valdosta State University [M.Ed. in IT/ Technology Applications]

Computer Education
Appalachian State University [M.A.: Educational Media and Technology/Computers]
Arizona State University, Department of Educational Media and Computers [M.A., Ph.D.: Educational Media and Computers]
Arkansas Tech University [Master's]
Buffalo State College [M.S.: Education/Educational Computing]
California State University-Dominguez Hills [M.A., Certificate: Computer-Based Education]
California State University-Los Angeles [M.A. in Education/Computer Education]
California State University-San Bernardino [Advanced Certificate Program: Educational Computing]
Central Connecticut State University [M.S.: Educational Technology/Computer Technologies]
Concordia University [M.A.: Computer Science Education]
East Carolina University [M.A.: Education/IT Computers]
Eastern Washington University [M.Ed.: Computer Education]
Fairfield University [M.A.: Media/Educational Technology with Computers in Education]
Florida Institute of Technology [Master's, Ph.D.: Computer Education]
Fontbonne College [M.S.]
George Mason University [M.Ed.: Special Education Technology, Computer Science Educator]
Iowa State University [M.S., M.Ed., Ph.D.: Curriculum and IT/Instructional Computing]
Jacksonville University [Master's: Computer Education]
Kansas State University [M.S. in Secondary Education/Educational Computing; Ed.D., Ph.D.: Curriculum and Instruction/ Educational Computing]
Kent State University [M.A., M.Ed.: Instructional Computing]
Minot State University [M.Ed., M.S.: Math and Computer Science]
New York Institute of Technology [Specialist Certificate: Computers in Education]
North Carolina State University [M.S., M.Ed.: IT-Computers]

Northern Illinois University [M.S.Ed., Ed.D.: IT/Educational Computing]
Northwest Missouri State University [M.S.: School Computer Studies; M.S.Ed.: Educational Uses of Computers]
Nova Southeastern University [M.S., Ed.S.: Computer Science Education]
Ohio University [M.Ed.: Computer Education and Technology]
Pace University [M.S.E.: Curriculum and Instruction/Computers]
San Diego State University [Master's in Educational Technology/Computers in Education]
San Francisco State University [Master's: Instructional Computing]
State University College of Arts and Sciences at Potsdam [M.S.Ed.: IT and Media Management/Educational Computing]
State University of New York at Stony Brook [Master's: Technological Systems Management/Educational Computing]
Syracuse University [M.S., Ed.D., Ph.D., Advanced Certificate: Media Production]
Texas A&M University-Commerce [Master's: Learning Technology and Information Systems/Educational Micro Computing]
Texas Tech University [M.Ed.: IT/Educational Computing]
University of Georgia [M.Ed., Ed.S.: Computer-Based Education]
University of Illinois at Urbana-Champaign [M.A., M.S., Ed.M.: Educational Computing; Ph.D.: Education Psychology/Educational Computing]
University of North Texas [M.S.: Computer Education and Instructional Systems]
The University of Oklahoma [Master's: Computer Applications]
University of Toledo [Master's, Ed.S., D.Ed.: Instructional Computing]
University of Washington [Master's, Ed.D., Ph.D.]
Virginia Polytechnic Institute and State University [M.A., Ed.D., Ph.D.: IT]
Wright State University [M.Ed.: Computer Education; M.A.: Computer Education]

Distance Education
Fairfield University [M.A.: Media/Educational Technology with Satellite Communications]
Iowa State University [M.S., M.Ed., Ph.D.: Curriculum and IT]
New York Institute of Technology [Specialist Certificate]
Nova Southeastern University [M.S., Ed.D.: IT]
Texas A&M University [Ph.D.: EDCI]
Texas Tech University [M.Ed.: IT]

University of Northern Colorado [Ph.D.: Educational Technology]
Western Illinois University [Master's]

Educational Leadership
Auburn University [Ed.D.]
Barry University [Ph.D.: Educational Technology Leadership]
George Washington University [M.A.: Education and Human Development/Educational Technology Leadership]
United States International University [Master's, Ed.D.: Technology Leadership for Learning]
University of Colorado at Denver [Ph.D.: Educational Leadership and Innovation/ Curriculum, Learning, and Technology]
Valdosta State University [M.Ed., Ed.S.: IT/ Technology Leadership]

Human Performance
Boise State University [M.S.: IT and Performance Technology]
Governors State University [M.A.: Communication with Human Performance and Technology]
University of Southern California [Ed.D.: Human Performance Technology]
University of Toledo [Master's, Ed.S., Ed.D.: Human Resources Development]

Information Studies
Drexel University [M.S., M.S.I.S.]
Emporia State University [Ph.D.: Library and Information Management]
Rutgers [M.L.S.: Information Retrieval; Ph.D.: Communication (Information Systems)]
Simmons College [M.S.: Information Science/ Systems]
Southern Connecticut State University [Sixth Year Professional Diploma: Library-Information Studies/IT]
St. Cloud State University [Master's, Ed.S.: Information Technologies]
Texas A&M-Commerce [Master's: Learning Technology and Information Systems/ Library and Information Science]
University of Alabama [Ph.D.]
University of Arizona [M.A.: Information Resources and Library Science]
University of Central Arkansas [M.S.: Information Science/Media Information Studies]
University of Maryland [Doctorate: Library and Information Services]
University of Missouri-Columbia [Ph.D.: Information and Learning Technologies]
The University of Oklahoma [Dual Master's: Educational Technology and Library and Information Systems]
The University of Rhode Island [M.L.I.S.]
University of Washington [Master's, Ed.D., Ph.D.]
Western Oregon State College [MS: Information Technology]

Innovation
Pennsylvania State University [M.Ed., M.S., Ed.D., Ph.D.: Instructional Systems/Emerging Technologies]
University of Colorado at Denver [Ph.D.: Educational Leadership and Innovation]
Walden University [M.S., Ph.D.: Educational Change and Technology Innovation]

Instructional Design and Development
Auburn University [M.Ed., M.S.]
Bloomsburg University [M.S.: IT]
Brigham Young University [M.S., Ph.D.]
Clarion University of Pennsylvania [M.S.: Communication/Training and Development]
Fairfield University [Certificate of Advanced Studies: Media/Educational Technology: Instructional Development]
George Mason University [M.Ed.: IT/Instructional Design and Development]
Governors State University [M.A.: Communication with Human Performance and Training/ Instructional Design]
Indiana University [Ph.D., Ed.D.: Instructional Analysis, Design, and Development]
Iowa State University [M.S., M.Ed., Ph.D.: Curriculum and IT/Instruction Design]
Ithaca College [M.S.: Corporate Communications]
Lehigh University [Master's]
Michigan State University [M.A.: Educational Technology and Instructional Design]
North Carolina Central University [M.S.: Instructional Development/Design]
Northern Illinois University [M.S.Ed., Ed.D.: IT/Instructional Design]
Pennsylvania State University [M.Ed., M.S., D.Ed., Ph.D.: Instructional Systems/Systems Design]
Purdue University [Master's, Specialist, Ph.D.: Instructional Development]
San Francisco State University [Master's/Training and Designing Development]
Southern Illinois University at Carbondale [M.S.: Education/Instructional Design]
State University of New York at Albany [M.Ed., Ph.D.: Curriculum and Instruction/ Instructional Design and Technology]
State University of New York at Stony Brook [Master's: Technological Systems Management/Educational Computing]
Syracuse University [M.S., Ed.D., Ph.D., Advanced Certificate: Instructional Design; Educational Evaluation; Instructional Development]
Towson State University [M.S.: Instructional Development]
University of Cincinnati [M.A., Ed.D.: Curriculum and Instruction/Instructional Design and Technology]
University of Colorado at Denver [Master's, Ph.D.: Instructional Design]

University of Illinois at Urbana-Champaign [M.A.,
M.S., Ed.M..; Ph.D. in Educational
Psychology/Instructional Design]
University of Iowa [M.A., Ph.D.: Training and
Human Resources Development]
University of Massachusetts-Boston [M.Ed.]
University of Northern Colorado [Ph.D. in Educa-
tional Technology/Instructional Develop-
ment and Design]
The University of Oklahoma [Master's]
University of Toledo [Master's, Specialist,
Doctorate: Instructional Development]
University of Washington [Master's, Ed.D., Ph.D.]
Utah State University [M.S., Ed.S.: Instructional
Development]
Virginia Polytechnic Institute and State University
[Master's, Ed.D., Ph.D.: IT]

Instructional Technology [IT]
Appalachian State University [M.A.: Educational
Media and Technology]
Arizona State University, Learning and IT Dept.
[M.Ed., Ph.D.]
Azusa Pacific University [M.Ed.]
Barry University [M.S., Ed.S.: Educational
Technology]
Bloomsburg University [M.S.: IT]
Boise State University [M.S.]
Boston University [Ed.M., Certificate of Advanced
Graduate Study: Educational Media & Tech-
nology; Ed.D.: Curriculum and Teaching/
Educational Media and Technology]
California State University-Los Angeles [M.A.:
Education/IT]
California State University-San Bernardino
[Advanced Certificate in Educational
Technology]
Central Connecticut State University [M.S.:
Educational Technology]
Clarke College [M.A.: Technology and Education]
East Carolina University [M.A.: Education/IT
Computers]
East Tennessee State [M.Ed.]
Eastern Michigan University [M.A.: Educational
Psychology/Educational Technology]
Edgewood College [M.A.: Education/IT]
Fairfield University [M.A., Certificate of Advanced
Study: Media/Educational Technology]
Fitchburg State College [M.S.: Communications
Media/IT]
Florida Institute of Technology [Master's, Ph.D.]
George Mason University [M.Ed., Ph.D.]
George Washington University [M.A.: Education
and Human Development/Educational
Technology Leadership]
Georgia Southern University [M.Ed., Ed.S.: IT;
Ed.D.: Curriculum Studies/IT]
Georgia State University [M.S., Ph.D.]
Harvard University [M.Ed.: Technology in
Education]
Indiana State University [Master's, Ed.S.]
Indiana University [M.S., Ed.S., Ed.D., Ph.D.]

Iowa State University [M.S., M.Ed., Ph.D.:
Curriculum and IT]
Jacksonville University [Master's: Educational
Technology and Integrated Learning]
Johns Hopkins University [M.S. in Educational
Technology for Educators]
Kent State University [M.Ed., M.A; Ph.D.:
Educational Psychology/IT]
Lehigh University [Master's; Ed.D.: Educational
Technology]
Lesley College [M.Ed., Certificate of Advanced
Graduate Study: Technology Education;
Ph.D.: Education/Technology Education]
Mankato State University [M.S.: Educational
Technology]
Michigan State University [M.A.: Educational
Technology]
Montclair State College [certification]
New York Institute of Technology [Master's]
New York University [M.A., Certificate of Ad-
vanced Study in Education, Ed.D., Ph.D.]
North Carolina Central University [M.A.:
Educational Technology]
North Carolina State University [M.Ed., M.S.:
IT—Computers; Ph.D.: Curriculum and
Instruction/IT]
Northern Illinois University [M.S.Ed., Ed.D.]
Nova Southeastern University [Ed.S., M.S.: Educa-
tional Technology; M.S., Ed.D.: IT]
Ohio University [M.Ed.: Computer Education and
Technology]
Purdue University [Master's, Specialist, Ph.D.:
Educational Technology]
Radford University [M.S.: Education/Educational
Media/Technology]
Rosemont College [M.Ed.: Technology in Educa-
tion; Certificate in Professional Study in
Technology in Education]
San Diego State University [Master's: Educational
Technology]
Southern Connecticut State University [M.S.]
Southern Illinois University at Carbondale [M.S.:
Education; Ph.D.: Education/IT]
State University College of Arts and Sciences at
Potsdam [M.S.: Education/IT]
State University of New York at Albany [M.Ed.,
Ph.D.: Curriculum and Instruction/Instruc-
tional Theory, Design, and Technology]
State University of West Georgia [M.Ed., Ed.S.]
Texas A&M-Commerce [Master's: Learning Tech-
nology and Information Systems/Educational
Media and Technology]
Texas A&M University [M.Ed.: Educational Tech-
nology; Ph.D.: EDCI/Educational Technol-
ogy; Ph.D.: Educational Psychology
Foundations/Learning and Technology]
Texas Tech University [M.Ed.; Ed.D.]
United States International University [Ed.D.:
Technology and Learning]
University of Central Florida [M.A.: IT/Instruc-
tional Systems, IT/Educational Media;
Doctorate: Curriculum and Instruction/IT]

University of Cincinnati [M.A., Ed.D.: Curriculum and Instruction/Instructional Design and Technology]

University of Colorado at Denver [Master's, Ph.D.: Learning Technologies]

University of Connecticut [Master's, Ph.D.: Educational Technology]

University of Georgia [M.Ed., Ed.S., Ph.D.]

University of Hawaii-Manoa [M.Ed.: Educational Technology]

University of Louisville [M.Ed.: Occupational Education/IT]

University of Maryland [Ph.D.: Library Science and Educational Technology/Instructional Communication]

University of Massachusetts-Lowell [M.Ed., Ed.D., Certificate of Advanced Graduate Study: Educational Technology]

University of Michigan [Master's, Ph.D.: IT]

University of Missouri-Columbia [Master's, Ed.S., Ph.D.]

University of Nebraska at Kearney [M.S.]

University of Nevada [M.S., Ph.D.]

University of Northern Colorado [M.A., Ph.D.: Educational Technology]

University of Northern Iowa [M.A.: Educational Technology]

The University of Oklahoma [Master's: Educational Technology Generalist; Educational Technology; Teaching with Technology; dual Master's: Educational Technology and Library and Information Systems; Doctorate: Instructional Psychology and Technology]

University of South Alabama [M.S., Ph.D.]

University of South Carolina [Master's]

University of Southern California [M.A., Ed.D., Ph.D.]

University of Tennessee-Knoxville [M.S.: Education, Ed.S., Ed.D., Ph.D.]

The University of Texas [Master's, Ph.D.]

University of Toledo [Master's, Specialist, Doctorate]

University of Virginia [M.Ed., Ed.S., Ed.D., Ph.D.]

University of Washington [Master's, Ed.D., Ph.D.]

University of Wisconsin-Madison [M.S., Ph.D.]

Utah State University [M.S., Ed.S., Ph.D.]

Virginia Polytechnic Institute and State University [M.A., Ed.D., Ph.D.: IT]

Virginia State University [M.S., M.Ed.: Educational Technology]

Wayne State University [Master's, Ed.D., Ph.D., Ed.S.]

Webster University [Master's]

Western Illinois University [Master's]

Western Washington University [M.Ed.: IT in Adult Education; Elementary Education; IT in Secondary Education]

Wright State University [Specialist: Curriculum and Instruction/Educational Technology; Higher Education/Educational Technology]

Integration

Bloomsburg University [M.S.: IT]

George Mason University [M.Ed.: IT/Integration of Technology in Schools]

Jacksonville University [Master's: Educational Technology and Integrated Learning]

University of Northern Colorado [Ph.D.: Educational Technology/Technology Integration]

Management

Bloomsburg University [M.S.: IT]

Central Connecticut State University [M.S.: Educational Technology/Media Management]

Drexel University [M.S., M.S.I.S.]

Emporia State University [Ph.D.: Library and Information Management]

Fairfield University [Certificate of Advanced Studies: Media/Educational Technology with Media Management]

Fitchburg State College [M.S.: Communications Media/Management]

Indiana University [Ed.D., Ph.D.: Implementation and Management]

Minot State University [M.S.: Management]

Northern Illinois University [M.S.Ed., Ed.D.: IT/Media Administration]

Rutgers [M.L.S.: Management and Policy Issues]

Simmons College [M.L.S.: History (Archives Management); Doctor of Arts: Administration; Media Management]

State University College of Arts and Science [M.S.: Education/IT and Media Management]

State University of New York at Stony Brook [Master's: Technological Systems Management]

Syracuse University [M.S., Ed.D., Ph.D., Advanced Certificate]

University of Tennessee-Knoxville [Certification: Instructional Media Supervisor]

Virginia Polytechnic Institute and State University [M.A., Ed.D., Ph.D.: IT]

Wright State University [M.Ed.: Media Supervisor; Computer Coordinator]

Media

Appalachian State University [M.A.: Educational Media and Technology/Media Management]

Arizona State University, Department of Educational Media and Computers [M.A., Ph.D.: Educational Media and Computers]

Boston University [Ed.M.., Certificate of Advanced Graduate Study: Educational Media and Technology; Ed.D.: Curriculum and Teaching/Educational Media and Technology]

Central Connecticut State University [M.S.: Educational Technology/Materials Production]

Fitchburg State College [M.S.: Communications Media]

Indiana State University [Ph.D.: Curriculum and Instruction/Media Technology]

Indiana University [Ed.D., Ph.D.: Instructional Development and Production]
Jacksonville State University [M.S.: Education/ Instructional Media]
Montclair State College [Certification]
Radford University [M.S.: Education/Educational Media/Technology]
Simmons College [Master's: Media Management]
St. Cloud State University [Master's, Ed.S.: Educational Media]
State University College of Arts and Science at Potsdam [M.S.: Education/IT and Media Management]
Syracuse University [M.S., Ed.D., Ph.D., Advanced Certificate: Media Production]
Texas A&M-Commerce [Master's: Learning Technology and Information Systems/Educational Media and Technology]
University of Central Florida [M.Ed.: IT/ Educational Media]
University of Iowa [M.A.: Media Design and Production]
University of Nebraska at Kearney [M.S., Ed.S.: Educational Media]
University of Nebraska-Omaha [M.S.: Education/ Educational Media; M.A.: Education/ Educational Media]
University of South Alabama [M.A., Ed.S.]
University of Tennessee-Knoxville [Ph.D.: Instructional Media and Technology; Ed.D.: Curriculum and Instruction/Instructional Media and Technology]
University of Virginia [M.Ed., Ed.S., Ed.D., Ph.D.: Media Production]
Virginia Polytechnic Institute and State University [M.A., Ed.D., Ph.D.: IT]
Wright State University [M.Ed.: Educational Media; Media Supervision; M.A.: Educational Media]

Multimedia
Bloomsburg University [M.S.: IT]
Brigham Young University [M.S.: Multimedia Production]
Fairfield University [M.A.: Media/Educational Technology with Multimedia]
Ithaca College [M.S.: Corporate Communications]
Jacksonville University [Master's: Educational Technology and Integration Learning]
Johns Hopkins University [Graduate Certificate]
Lehigh University [Master's]
New York Institute of Technology [Specialist Certificate]
San Francisco State University [Master's: Instructional Multimedia Design]
State University of New York at Stony Brook [Master's: Technological Systems Management/Educational Computing]
Syracuse University [M.S., Ed.D., Ph.D., Advanced Certificate: Media Production]
Texas A&M University [M.Ed.: Educational Technology]

University of Northern Colorado [Ph.D.: Educational Technology/Interactive Technology]
University of Virginia [M.Ed., Ed.S., Ed.D., Ph.D.: Interactive Multimedia]
University of Washington [Master's, Ed.D., Ph.D.]
Utah State University [M.S., Ed.S.]
Wayne State University [Master's: Interactive Technologies]
Western Illinois University [Master's: Interactive Technologies]

Research
Brigham Young University [M.S., Ph.D.: Research and Evaluation]
Drexel University [M.S., M.S.I.S.]
Iowa State University [Ph.D.: Educational/ Technology Research]
Syracuse University [M.S., Ed.D., Ph.D., Advanced Certificate: Educational Research and Theory]
University of Washington [Master's, Ed.D., Ph.D.]

School Library Media
Alabama State University [Master's, Ed.S., Ph.D.]
Arkansas Tech University [Master's]
Auburn University [M.ED., Ed.S.]
Bloomsburg University [M.S.]
Boston University [Massachusetts certification]
Bridgewater State College [M.Ed.]
Central Connecticut State University [M.S.: Educational Technology/Librarianship]
Chicago State University [Master's]
East Carolina University [M.L.S., Certificate of Advanced Study]
East Tennessee State [M.Ed.: Instructional Media]
Emporia State University [Ph.D.: Library and Information Management; M.L.S.; School Library certification]
Kent State University
Louisiana State University [M.L.I.S., C.L.I.S. (post-Master's Certificate), Louisiana School Library certification]
Mankato State University [M.S.]
Northern Illinois University [M.S.Ed. Instructional Technology with Illinois state certification]
Nova Southeastern University [Ed.S, M.S.: Educational Media]
Radford University [M.S.: Education/Educational Media; licensure]
Rutgers [M.L.S., Ed.S.]
Simmons College [M.L.S.: Education]
Southern Illinois University at Edwardsville [M.S. in Education: Library/Media]
Southwestern Oklahoma State University [M.Ed.: Library/Media Education]
St. Cloud State University [Master's, Ed.S.]
St. John's University [M.L.S.]
State University of West Georgia [M.Ed., Ed.S.: Media]
Towson State University [M.S.]
University of Alabama [Master's, Ed.S.]
University of Central Arkansas [M.S.]

University of Georgia [M.Ed., Ed.S]
University of Maryland [M.L.S.]
University of Montana [Master's, Ed.S.]
University of North Carolina [M.S.]
University of Northern Colorado [M.A.: Educational Media]
University of South Florida [Master's]
University of Toledo
University of Wisconsin-La Crosse [M.S.: Professional Development/Initial Instructional Library Specialist; Instructional Library Media Specialist]
Utah State University [M.S., Ed.S.]
Valdosta State University [M.Ed., Ed.S.: Instructional Technology/Library/Media]
Webster University
Western Maryland College [M.S.]
William Paterson College [M.Ed., Ed.S., Associate]

Special Education
George Mason University [M.Ed.: IT/Assistive/Special Education Technology; M.Ed.: Special Education Technology; Ph.D.: Special Education Technology]
Johns Hopkins University [M.S. in Special Education/Technology in Special Education]
Minot State University [M.S.: Early Childhood Special Education; Severe Multiple Handicaps; Communication Disorders]
Western Washington University [M.Ed.: IT in Special Education]

Systems
Bloomsburg University [M.S.: IT]
Drexel University [M.S., M.S.I.S.]
Florida State University [M.S., Ed.S., Ph.D.: Instructional Systems]
Pennsylvania State University [M.Ed., M.S., D.Ed.., Ph.D.: Instructional Systems]
Simmons College [Master's: Information Science/Systems]
Southern Illinois University at Edwardsville [M.S.: Education/Instructional Systems Design]
State University of New York at Stony Brook [Master's: Technological Systems Management]
Texas A&M University-Commerce [Master's: Learning Technology and Information Systems]
University of Central Florida [M.A.: IT/Instructional Systems]
University of Maryland, Baltimore County [Master's: School Instructional Systems]

University of North Texas [M.S.: Computer Education and Instructional Systems]
The University of Oklahoma [Dual Master's: Educational Technology and Library and Information Systems]

Technology Design
Governors State University [M.A.: Design Logistics]
Kansas State University [Ed.D., Ph.D.: Curriculum and Instruction/Educational Computing, Design, and Telecommunications]
United States International University [Master's, Ed.D.: Designing Technology for Learning]
University of Colorado at Denver [Master's, Ph.D.: Design of Learning Technologies]

Telecommunications
Appalachian State University [M.A.: Educational Media and Technology/Telecommunications]
Johns Hopkins University [Graduate Certificate]
Kansas State University [Ed.D., Ph.D.: Curriculum and Instruction/Educational Computing, Design, and Telecommunications]
Western Illinois University [Masters: Telecommunications]

Training
Clarion University of Pennsylvania [M.S.: Communication/Training and Development]
Pennsylvania State University [M.Ed., M.S., D.Ed.., Ph.D.: Instructional Systems/Corporate Training]
St. Cloud State University [Master's, Ed.S.: Human Resources Development/Training]
Syracuse University [M.S., Ed.D., Ph.D., Advanced Certificate]
University of Maryland, Baltimore County [Master's: Training in Business and Industry]
University of Northern Iowa [M.A.: Communications and Training Technology]
Wayne State University [Master's: Business and Human Services Training]

Video Production
California State University-San Bernardino [M.A.]
Fairfield University [Certificate of Advanced Study: Media/Educational Technology with TV Production]

ALABAMA

Alabama State University. P.O. Box 271, Montgomery, AL 36101-0271. (334)229-4462. Fax (334)229-4961. Web site http://www.alasu.edu. Dr. Deborah Little, Coord., Instructional Technology and Media. *Specializations:* School media specialist preparation (K-12) only; Master's and Specialist degrees. *Admission Requirements:* Master's: undergraduate degree with teacher certification, two years classroom experience. Specialist: Master's degree in library/media education. *Degree Requirements:* Master's: 33 semester hours with 300 clock-hour internship. Specialist: 33 semester hours in 600-level courses. *Faculty:* 3 full-time, 2 part-time. *Students:* Master's, 27 part-time; Specialist, 6 part-time. *Financial Assistance:* assistantships, student loans, scholarships. *Degrees Awarded 1997:* Master's, 9; Specialist, 1.

Auburn University. Educational Foundations, Leadership, and Technology, 4036 Haley Center, Auburn, AL 36849-5221. (334)844-4291. Fax (334)844-5785. E-mail bannosh@mail.auburn.edu. Susan H. Bannon, Coord., Educational Media and Technology. *Specializations:* M.Ed. (non-thesis) and Ed.S. for Library Media certification; M.Ed. (non-thesis) or M.S. (with thesis) for instructional design specialists who want to work in business, industry, and the military. Ed.D. in Educational Leadership with emphasis on curriculum and new instructional technologies. *Features:* All programs emphasize interactive technologies and computers. *Admission Requirements:* all programs: recent GRE test scores, 3 letters of recommendation, Bachelor's degree from accredited institution, teacher certification (for library media program only). *Degree Requirements:* Library Media Master's: 52 qtr. hours. Instructional Design: 48 qtr. hours. Specialist: 48 qtr. hours. Ed.D.: 120 qtr. hours beyond B.S. degree. *Faculty:* 4 full-time, 3 part-time. *Students:* 3 full-time, 18 part-time. *Financial Assistance:* graduate assistantships.

Jacksonville State University. Instructional Media Division, Jacksonville, AL 36265. (256)782-5011. E-mail mmerrill@jsucc.jsu.edu. Martha Merrill, Coord., Dept. of Educational Resources. *Specializations:* M.S. in Education with emphasis on Library Media. *Admission Requirements:* Bachelor's degree in Education. *Degree Requirements:* 36-39 semester hours including 24 in library media. *Faculty:* 2 full-time. *Students:* 20 full- and part-time. *Degrees Awarded 1997:* approx. 10.

University of Alabama. School of Library and Information Studies, Box 870252, Tuscaloosa, AL 35487-0252. (205)348-4610. Fax (205)348-3746. E-mail GCOLEMAN@UA1VM.UA.EDU. Web site http://www.slism.slis.ua.edu. J. Gordon Coleman, Jr., Chair. Marion Paris, Ph.D. contact person. *Specializations:* M.L.I.S., Ed.S., and Ph.D. degrees in a varied program including school, public, academic, and special libraries. Ph.D. specializations in Historical Studies, Information Studies, Management, and Youth Studies; considerable flexibility in creating individual programs of study. *Admission Requirements:* M.L.I.S., Ed.S.: 3.0 GPA; 50 MAT or 1500 GRE. Doctoral: 3.0 GPA; 60 MAT or 1650 GRE. *Degree Requirements:* Master's: 36 semester hours. Specialist: 33 semester hours. Doctoral: 48 semester hours plus 24 hours dissertation research. *Faculty:* 10 full-time. *Students:* Master's, 55 full-time, 20 part-time; Specialist, 2 full-time; doctoral, 6 full-time, 6 part-time. *Financial Assistance:* assistantships, grants, student loans, scholarships, work assistance, campus work. *Degrees Awarded 1997:* Master's, 69; Ph.D., 1.

University of South Alabama. Department of Behavioral Studies and Educational Technology, College of Education, University Commons 3100, Mobile, AL 36688. (334)380-2861. Fax (334)380-2758. John Lane, Department Chair; Gayle Davidson-Shivers, Program Dir. *Specializations:* M.A. and Ed.S. in Educational Media, M.S. in Instructional Technology, Ph.D. in Instructional Technology. *Features:* The program emphasizes an extensive training sequence in the instructional systems design process, as well as multimedia-based training. *Admissions Requirements:* Master's: undergraduate degree in appropriate academic field; admission to Graduate

School; 40 MAT or 800 GRE (any two areas). Ph.D.: Master's degree, transcripts, three recommendations, goal statement, GRE score. *Degree Requirements:* Master's: 3.0 GPA, 61 quarter hours. Ph.D.: 120 quarter hours, dissertation. *Faculty:* 20 full-time in department. *Students:* Master's, 30; Ph.D., 65. *Financial Assistance:* 10 graduate assistantships. *Degrees Awarded 1997:* 10.

ARIZONA

Arizona State University, Dept. of Learning and Instructional Technology. Box 870611, Tempe, AZ 85287-0611. (602)965-3384. Fax (602)965-0300. Web site http://seamonkey.ed.asu. edu/~gail/programs/lnt.htm. James D. Klein, Prof. (james.klein@asu.edu); Nancy Archer, Admissions Secretary (icnla@asuvm.inre.asu.edu). *Specializations*: M.Ed. and Ph.D. with focus on the design, development, and evaluation of learning systems. *Features*: research and publication prior to candidacy. *Admission Requirements*: M.Ed.: 3.0 undergraduate GPA, 500 GRE (verbal) or 50 MAT, 550 TOEFL. Ph.D.: 3.2 undergraduate GPA, 1200 GRE (V+Q), 600 TOEFL. *Degree Requirements*: M.Ed.: 30 semester hours, internship, comprehensive exam. Ph.D.: 84 semester hours beyond Bachelor's degree, comprehensive exam, research/publication, dissertation. *Faculty*: 6 full-time. *Students*: M.Ed., 15 full-time, 20 part-time; Ph.D., 10 full-time, 10 part-time. *Financial Assistance*: assistantships, tuition waivers, and student loans for qualified applicants. *Degrees Awarded 1997:* M.Ed., 11; Ph.D., 2.

Arizona State University, Dept. of Educational Media and Computers. Box 870111, Tempe, AZ 85287-0111. (602)965-7192. Fax (602)965-7193. E-mail bitter@asu.edu. Dr. Gary G. Bitter, Coord. *Specializations:* M.A. and Ph.D. in Educational Media and Computers. *Features:* A three semester-hour course in Instructional Media Design is offered via CD-ROM or World Wide Web. *Admission Requirements:* M.A.: Bachelor's degree, 550 TOEFL, 500 GRE, 45 MAT. *Degree Requirements:* M.A.: 36 semester hours (24 hours in educational media and computers, 9 hours education, 3 hours outside education); internship; comprehensive exam; practicum; thesis not required. Ph.D.: 93 semester hours (24 hours in educational media and computers, 57 hours in education, 12 hours outside education); thesis; internship; practicum. *Faculty:* 5 full-time, 1 part-time. *Financial Assistance:* assistantships, grants, student loans, scholarships.

University of Arizona. School of Information Resources and Library Science, 1515 E. First St., Tucson, AZ 85719. (520)621-3565. Fax (520)621-3279. E-mail sirls@u.arizona.edu. Web site http://www.sir.arizona.edu. C.D. Hurt, Professor and Dir. *Specializations:* M.A. and Ph.D. in Library Science. The School of Information Resources and Library Science offers courses focusing on the study of information and its impact as a social phenomenon. The School offers a M.A. degree with a major in Information Resources and Library Science, which is heavily weighted in technology and emphasizes theoretical constructs. Competence and adaptability in managing information and in utilizing advancing technologies are key aims of the curriculum. The program is fully accredited by the American Library Association. The School offers course work that leads toward the Ph.D. degree with a major in Library Science. *Features:* The School offers a virtual education program via the Internet. Between two and three courses are offered per semester. *Admission Requirements:* very competitive for both degrees. Minimum criteria include: undergraduate GPA of 3.0 or better; competitive GRE scores; two letters of recommendation reflecting the writer's opinion of the applicant's potential as a graduate student; a resume of work and educational experience; written statement of intent. The School receives a large number of applications and accepts the best qualified students. Admission to the doctoral program may require a personal interview and a faculty member must indicate willingness to work with the student. *Degree Requirements:* M.A.: a minimum of 36 units of graduate credit. Students may elect the thesis option replacing 6 units of course work. Ph.D.: at least 48 hours of course work in the major, a substantial number of hours in a minor subject supporting the major, dissertation. The University has a 12-unit residency requirement which may be completed in the summer or in a regular semester. More detailed descriptions of the program are available at the School's Web site. *Faculty:* 5 full-time. *Students:* 303 total; M.A.: 51 full-time; Ph.D.: 8 full-time. *Degrees Awarded 1997:* M.A.: 75.

ARKANSAS

Arkansas Tech University. Russellville, AR 72801-2222. (501)968-0434. Fax (501)964-0811. E-mail SECZ@atuvm.atu.edu, czimmer@cswnet.com. Web site http://www.atu.edu, http://www. angelfire.com/ar/librarymedia. Connie Zimmer, Asst. Professor of Secondary Education, Coord. *Specializations:* Master's degrees in Education in Instructional Technology with specializations in library media education, computer education, general program of study, and training education. NCATE accredited institution. *Admission Requirements:* GRE, 2.5 undergraduate GPA, Bachelor's degree. *Degree Requirements:* 36 semester hours, B average in major hours, action research project. *Faculty:* 1 full-time, 5 part-time. *Students:* 22 full-time, 57 part-time. *Financial Assistance:* graduate assistantships, grants, student loans. *Degrees Awarded 1997:* 50.

University of Central Arkansas. Educational Media/Library Science, Campus Box 4918, Conway, AR 72035. (501)450-5463. Fax (501)450-5680. E-mail selvinr@mail.uca.edu. Web site http://www.coe.uca.edu/aboutaat.htm. Selvin W. Royal, Prof., Chair, Applied Academic Technologies. *Specializations:* M.S. in Educational Media/Library Science and Information Science. Tracks: School Library Media, Public Information Agencies, Media Information Studies. *Admission Requirements:* transcripts, GRE scores, 2 letters of recommendation, personal interview, written rationale for entering the profession. *Degree Requirements:* 36 semester hours, optional thesis, practicum (for School Library Media), professional research paper. *Faculty:* 5 full-time, 2 part-time. *Students:* 6 full-time, 42 part-time. *Financial Assistance:* 3 to 4 graduate assistantships each year. *Degrees Awarded 1997:* 28.

CALIFORNIA

Azusa Pacific University. 901 E. Alosta, Azusa, CA, 91702. (626)815-5376, fax (626)815-5416. E-mail arnold@apu.edu. Brian Arnold, contact person. *Specializations:* M.Ed. with emphasis in Technology. *Admission Requirements:* undergraduate degree from accredited institution, 3.0 GPA, ownership of a designated laptop computer and software. *Faculty:* 2 full-time, 16 part-time. *Students:* 180 part-time. *Financial assistance:* student loans. *Degrees Awarded 1997:* 20.

California State University-Dominguez Hills. 1000 E. Victoria St., Carson, CA 90747. (310)243-3524. Fax (310)243-3518. E-mail pdesberg@dhvx20.csudh.edu. Web site http://www. csudh.soe.edu. Peter Desberg, Prof., Coord., Computer-Based Education Program. *Specializations*: M.A. and Certificate in Computer-Based Education. *Admission Requirements*: 2.75 GPA. *Degree Requirements*: M.A.: 30 semester hours including project. Certificate: 15 hours. *Faculty*: 2 full-time, 2 part-time. *Students*: 50 full-time, 40 part-time. *Degrees Awarded 1997*: M.A., 20.

California State University-Los Angeles. Division of Educational Foundations and Interdivisional Studies, Charter School of Education, 5151 State University Drive, Los Angeles, CA 90032. (213)343-4330. Fax (213)343-5336. E-mail blee@calstatela.edu. Web site http://web. calstatela.edu/academic/found/efis/index.html. Dr. Simeon P. Slovacek, Division Chairperson. *Specializations:* M.A. degree in Education, option in Instructional Technology or Computer Education. *Degree Requirements:* 2.75 GPA in last 90 qtr. units, 45 qtr. units, comprehensive written exam or thesis or project. Must also pass Writing Proficiency Examination (WPE), a California State University-Los Angeles requirement. *Faculty:* 7 full-time. *Degrees Awarded 1997:* 16.

*California State University-San Bernardino. 5500 University Parkway, San Bernardino, CA 92407. (909)880-5600, (909)880-5610. Fax (909)880-7010. E-mail monaghan@wiley.csusb.edu. Web site http://soe.csusb.edu/soe/programs/eyec. Dr. Jim Monaghan, Program Coord. *Specializations:* M.A. with two emphases: Video Production and Computer Applications. These emphases allow students to choose courses related to the design and creation of video products or courses involving lab and network operation of advanced microcomputer applications. The program does not require teaching credential certification. Advanced certificate programs in Educational Computing and Educational Technology are available. *Admission Requirements:* Bachelor's degree, appropriate work experience, 3.0 GPA, completion of introductory computer course and expository writing course. *Degree Requirements:* 48 units including a Master's project (33 units completed in residence); 3.0 GPA; grades of "C" or better in all courses. *Faculty:* 5 full-time, 1 part-time. *Students:* 106. *Financial Assistance:* Contact Office of Graduate Studies. *Degrees Awarded 1996:* 12.

San Diego State University. Educational Technology, San Diego, CA 92182-1182. (619)594-6718. Fax (619)594-6376. E-mail patrick.harrison@sdsu.edu. Web site http://edweb.sdsu.edu. Dr. Patrick Harrison, Prof., Chair. *Specialization:* Master's degree in Educational Technology with specializations in Computers in Education, Workforce Education, and Lifelong Learning. The Educational Technology Department participates in a College of Education joint doctoral program with The Claremont Graduate School. *Degree Requirements:* 36 semester hours (including 6 prerequisite hours), 950 GRE (verbal + quantitative). *Faculty:* 8 full-time, 5 part-time. *Students:* 120. *Financial Assistance:* graduate assistantships. *Degrees Awarded 1996:* Master's, 40.

San Francisco State University. College of Education, Department of Instructional Technology, 1600 Holloway Ave., San Francisco, CA 94132. (415)338-1509. Fax (415)338-0510. E-mail michaels@sfsu.edu. Dr. Eugene Michaels, Chair; Mimi Kasner, Office Coord. *Specializations:* Master's degree with emphasis on Instructional Multimedia Design, Training and Designing Development, and Instructional Computing. The school also offers an 18-unit Graduate Certificate in Training Systems Development, which can be incorporated into the Master's degree. *Features:* This program emphasizes the instructional systems approach, cognitivist principles of learning design, practical design experience, and project-based courses. *Admission Requirements:* Bachelor's degree, appropriate work experience, 2.5 GPA, interview with the department chair. *Degree Requirements:* 30 semester hours, field study project, or thesis. *Faculty:* 1 full-time, 16 part-time. *Students:* 250-300. *Financial Assistance:* Contact Office of Financial Aid. *Degrees Awarded 1998:* 50.

*United States International University. School of Education, 10455 Pomerado Rd., San Diego, CA 92131-1799. (619)635-4715. Fax (619)635-4714. E-mail feifer@sanac.usiu.edu. Richard Feifer, contact person. *Specializations:* Master's in Designing Technology for Learning, Planning Technology for Learning, and Technology Leadership for Learning. Ed.D. in Technology and Learning offers three specializations: Designing Technology for Learning, Planning Technology for Learning, and Technology Leadership for Learning. *Features:* interactive multimedia, cognitive approach to integrating technology and learning. *Admission Requirements:* Master's: English proficiency, interview, 3.0 GPA with 1900 GRE or 2.0 GPA with satisfactory MAT score. *Degree Requirements:* Ed.D.: 88 graduate qtr. units, dissertation. *Faculty:* 2 full-time, 4 part-time. *Students:* Master's, 32 full-time, 12 part-time; doctoral, 6 full-time, 1 part-time. *Financial Assistance:* internships, graduate assistantships, grants, student loans, scholarships. *Degrees Awarded 1996:* Master's, 40; Ed.D., 2.

University of Southern California. 702C W.P.H., School of Education, Los Angeles, CA 90089-0031. (213)740-3288. Fax (213)740-3889. Instructional Technology, Dept. of Educational Psychology and Technology. E-mail kazlausk@mizar.usc.edu. Web site http://www.usc.edu/department/itp/; also http://www.usc.edu/department/education/sed.index.htm. Dr. Richard Clark, Prof., Doctoral programs; Dr. Edward J. Kazlauskas, Prof., Program Chair, Master's programs in Instructional Technology. *Specializations:* M.A., Ed.D., Ph.D. to prepare individuals to teach instructional technology; manage educational media and training programs in business, industry, research and development organizations, schools, and higher educational institutions; perform research in instructional technology and media; and deal with computer-driven technology. A new Ed.D. program in Human Performance Technology was implemented in 1996 with satellite programs in Silicon Valley and Orange County. *Features:* special emphasis upon instructional design, systems analysis, and computer-based training. *Admission Requirements:* Bachelor's degree, 1000 GRE. *Degree Requirements:* M.A.: 28 semester hours, thesis optional. Doctoral: 67 units, 20 of which can be transferred from a previous Master's degree. Requirements for degree completion vary according to type of degree and individual interest. Ph.D. requires an outside field in addition to course work in instructional technology and education, more methodology and statistics work, and coursework in an outside field. *Faculty:* 5 full-time, 1 part-time. *Students:* M.A., 5 full-time, 15 part-time; doctoral, 50 full-time, 15 part-time. *Financial Assistance:* part-time, instructional technology-related work available in the Los Angeles area and on campus.

COLORADO

University of Colorado at Denver. School of Education, Campus Box 106, P.O. Box 173364, Denver CO 80217-3364. (303)556-6022. Fax (303)556-4479. E-mail brent.wilson@cudenver.edu. Web site http://www.cudenver.edu/public/education/ilt/ILThome.html. Brent Wilson, Program Chair, Information and Learning Technologies, Division of Technology and Special Services. *Specializations*: M.A.; Ph.D. in Educational Leadership and Innovation with emphasis in Curriculum, Learning, and Technology. *Features*: design and use of learning technologies; instructional design. Ph.D. students complete 10 semester hours of doctoral labs (small groups collaborating with faculty on difficult problems of practice). Throughout the program, students complete a product portfolio of research, design, teaching, and applied projects. The program is cross-disciplinary, drawing on expertise in technology, adult learning, systemic change, research methods, reflective practice, and cultural studies. *Admission Requirements*: M.A. and Ph.D.: satisfactory GPA, GRE, writing sample, letters of recommendation, transcripts. *Degree Requirements*: M.A.: 36 semester hours including 19 hours of core course work and portfolio; practicum and additional requirements for state certification in library media; internship required for careers in corporate settings. Ph.D.: 40 semester hours of coursework and labs, plus 30 dissertation hours; portfolio; dissertation. *Faculty*: 5 full-time, 3 part-time. Students: M.A., 25 full-time, 120 part-time; Ph.D., 6 full-time, 20 part-time. *Financial Assistance*: assistantships, internships. *Degrees Awarded 1997*: M.A., 30; Ph.D., 6.

University of Northern Colorado. Division of Educational Psychology, Statistics, and Technology, College of Education, Greeley, CO 80639. (970)351-2368. Fax (970)351-1622. E-mail bauer@edtech.unco.edu. Web site http://www.edtech.unco.edu/COE/EDTECH/EDTECH.html. Jeffrey Bauer, Assoc. Prof., Chair, Educational Technology. *Specializations:* M.A. in Educational Technology; M.A. in Educational Media; Ph.D. in Educational Technology with emphases in Distance Education, Instructional Development/Design, Interactive Technology, and Technology Integration. *Features:* Graduates are prepared for careers as instructional technologists, course designers, trainers, instructional developers, media specialists, and human resource managers. *Admission Requirements:* M.A.: Bachelor's degree, 3.0 undergraduate GPA, 1500 GRE. Ph.D.: 3.2 GPA, three letters of recommendation, congruency between applicant's statement of career goals and program goals, 1650 GRE, interview with faculty. *Faculty:* 5 full-time, 2 part-time. *Students:* M.A., 5 full-time, 60 part-time; Ph.D., 12 full-time, 22 part-time. *Financial Assistance:* assistantships, grants, student loans, scholarships. *Degrees Awarded 1997:* M.A., 25; Ph.D., 5.

CONNECTICUT

Central Connecticut State University. 1615 Stanley St., New Britain, CT 06050. (860)832-2130. Fax (860)832-2109. E-mail abedf@ccsu.ctstateu.edu. Web site http://www.ccsu.edu. Farough Abed, Coord., Educational Technology Program. *Specializations:* M.S. in Educational Technology. Curriculum emphases include instructional technology, instructional design, message design, and computer technologies. *Features:* The program supports the Center for Innovation in Teaching and Technology to link students with client-based projects. *Admission Requirements:* Bachelor's degree, 2.7 undergraduate GPA. *Degree Requirements:* 33 semester hours, optional thesis or Master's final project (3 credits). *Faculty:* 2 full-time, 4 part-time. *Students:* 45. *Financial Assistance:* graduate assistant position. *Degrees Awarded 1997:* 14.

Fairfield University. N. Benson Road, Fairfield, CT 06430. (203)254-4000. Fax (203)254-4087. E-mail imhefzallah@fair1.fairfield.edu. Dr. Ibrahim M. Hefzallah, Prof., Dir., Media/Educational Technology Program; Dr. John Schurdak, Assoc. Prof., Dir., Computers in Education Program.

Specializations: M.A. in Media/Educational Technology. A Certificate of Advanced Studies in Media/Educational Technology is available, which includes instructional development, television production, and media management; customized course of study also available. *Features:* emphasis on theory, practice, and new instructional developments in computers in education, multimedia, and satellite communications. *Admission Requirements:* Bachelor's degree from accredited institution with 2.67 GPA. *Degree Requirements:* 33 credits. *Faculty:* 2 full-time, 6 part-time. *Students:* 4 full-time, 60 part-time. *Financial Assistance:* assistantships, student loans. *Degrees Awarded 1997:* 13.

Southern Connecticut State University. Department of Library Science and Instructional Technology, 501 Crescent St., New Haven, CT 06515. (203)392-5781. Fax (203)392-5780. E-mail libscienceit@scsu.ctstateu.edu. Web site http://scsu.ctstateu.edu. Nancy Disbrow, Chair. *Specializations:* M.S. in Instructional Technology; Sixth-Year Professional Diploma Library-Information Studies (student may select area of specialization in Instructional Technology). *Degree Requirements:* for Instructional Technology only, 36 semester hours. For sixth-year degree: 30 credit hours with 6 credit hours of core requirements, 9-15 credit hours in specialization. *Faculty:* 1 full-time. *Students:* 3 full-time and 38 part-time in M.S./IT program. *Financial Assistance:* graduate assistantship (salary $1,800 per semester; assistants pay tuition and a general university fee sufficient to defray cost of student accident insurance). *Degrees Awarded 1997:* M.S., 2.

University of Connecticut. U-64, Storrs, CT 06269-2064. (860)486-0181. Fax (860)486-0180. E-mail sbrown@UConnvm.UConn.edu, or myoung@UConnvm.UConn.edu. Web site http://www.ucc.uconn.edu/~wwwepsy. Scott W. Brown, Chair; Michael Young, contact person. *Specializations:* M.A. and Ph.D. degrees with an emphasis in Educational Technology as a specialization within the Program of Cognition and Instruction, in the Department of Educational Psychology. *Features:* The emphasis in Educational Technology is a unique program at UConn. It is co-sponsored by the Department of Educational Psychology in the School of Education and the Psychology Department in the College of Liberal Arts and Sciences. The emphasis in Educational Technology within the Cognition and Instruction Program seeks to provide students with knowledge of theory and applications regarding the use of advanced technology to enhance learning and thinking. This program provides suggested courses and opportunities for internships and independent study experiences that are directed toward an understanding of both the effects of technology on cognition and instruction, and the enhancement of thinking and learning with technology. Facilities include the UCEML computer lab featuring Mac and IBM networks upgraded for 1998 and a multimedia development center. The School of Education also features a multimedia classroom and auditorium. Faculty research interests include interactive videodisc for anchored instruction and situated learning, telecommunications for cognitive apprenticeship, technology-mediated interactivity for generative learning, and in cooperation with the National Research Center for Gifted and Talented, research on the use of technology to enhance cooperative learning and the development of gifted performance in all students. *Admission Requirements:* admission to the graduate school at UConn, GRE scores (or other evidence of success at the graduate level). Previous experience in a related area of technology, education, or training is a plus. *Faculty:* The program in Cognition and Instruction has 7 full-time faculty; 3 full-time faculty administer the emphasis in Educational Technology. *Students:* M.A. 4, Ph.D., 16. *Financial Assistance:* graduate assistantships, research fellowships, teaching assistantships, and federal and minority scholarships are available competitively. *Degrees Awarded 1997:* Ph.D., 3.

DISTRICT OF COLUMBIA

*George Washington University. School of Education and Human Development, Washington, DC 20052. (202)994-1701. Fax (202)994-2145. Web site http://www.gwu.edu/~etl. Dr. William Lynch, Educational Technology Leadership Program. Program is offered through Jones Education Company (JEC). Contact student advisors at (800)777-MIND. *Specialization:* M.A. in Education and Human Development with a major in Educational Technology Leadership. *Features:* 36-hour degree program available via cable television, satellite, Internet, and/or videotape to students across North America and in other locations. The degree is awarded by George Washington University (GWU). Students may work directly with JEC or GWU to enroll. Student advisors at JEC handle inquiries about the program, send out enrollment forms and applications, process book orders, and set up students on an electronic listserv or Web forum. *Admission Requirements:* application fee, transcripts, GRE or MAT scores (50th percentile), two letters of recommendation from academic professionals, computer access, undergraduate degree with 2.75 GPA. *Degree Requirements:* 36 credit hours (including 24 required hours). Required courses include computer application management, media and technology application, software implementation and design, public education policy, and quantitative research methods. *Faculty:* Courses are taught by GWU faculty. *Financial Assistance:* For information, contact the Office of Student Financial Assistance, GWU. Some cable systems that carry JEC offer local scholarships.

FLORIDA

Barry University. Department of Educational Computing and Technology, School of Education, 11300 N.E. Second Ave., Miami Shores, FL 33161. (305)899-3608. Fax (305)899-3718. E-mail jlevine@bu4090.barry.edu. Joel S. Levine, Dir. *Specializations:* M.S. and Ed.S. in Educational Technology, Ph.D. degree in Educational Technology Leadership. *Features:* Majority of the courses (30/36) in M.S. and Ed.S. programs are in the field of Educational Technology. *Admission Requirements:* GRE scores, letters of recommendation, GPA, interview, achievements. *Degree Requirements:* M.S. or Ed. S.: 36 semester credit hours. Ph.D.: 54 credits beyond the Master's including dissertation credits. *Faculty:* 7 full-time, 10 part-time. *Students:* M.S., 8 full-time, 181 part-time; Ed.S., 5 full-time, 44 part-time; Ph.D., 3 full-time, 15 part-time. *Financial Assistance:* assistantships, student loans. *Degrees Awarded 1997:* M.S., 37; Ed.S., 6; Ph.D., 2.

Florida Institute of Technology. Science Education Department, 150 University Blvd., Melbourne, FL 32901-6988. (407)674-8126. Fax (407)674-7598. E-mail fronk@fit.edu. Dr. Robert Fronk, Dept. Head. Web site http://www.fit.edu/AcadRes/sci-ed/degree.html#comp-tech-ed. *Specializations*: Master's degree options in Computer Education and Instructional Technology; Ph.D. degree options in Computer Education and Instructional Technology. *Admission Requirements:* 3.0 GPA for regular admission; 2.75 for provisional admission. *Degree Requirements:* Master's: 33 semester hours (15 in computer or and technology education, 9 in education, 9 electives); practicum; no thesis or internship required. Ph.D.: 48 semester hours (12 in computer and technology education, 12 in education, 24 dissertation and research). *Faculty*: 5 full-time. *Students:* 11 full-time, 10 part-time. *Financial Assistance:* graduate student assistantships (full tuition plus stipend) available. *Degrees Awarded 1997:* Master's, 7; Ph.D., 3.

Florida State University. Instructional Systems Program, Department of Educational Research, College of Education, 305 Stone Bldg., Tallahassee, FL 32306. (904)644-4592. Fax (904)644-8776. Web site http://www.fsu.edu/~edres. *Specializations:* M.S., Ed.S, Ph.D. in Instructional Systems with specializations for persons planning to work in academia, business, industry, government, or military. *Features:* Core courses include systems and materials development, development of multimedia, project management, psychological foundations, current trends in instructional design, and research and statistics. Internships are recommended. *Admission Requirements:* M.S.: 3.2 GPA in last two years of undergraduate program, 1000 GRE (verbal plus quantitative), 550 TOEFL (for international applicants). Ph.D.: 1100 GRE (V+Q), 3.5 GPA in last two years; international students, 550 TOEFL. *Degree Requirements:* M.S.: 36 semester hours, 2-4 hour internship, written comprehensive exam. *Faculty:* 5 full-time, 5 part-time. *Students:* M.S., 55; Ph.D., 50. *Financial Assistance:* some graduate research assistantships on faculty grants and contracts, university fellowships. *Degrees Awarded 1997:* M.S., 38; Ph.D., 14 (approximate).

Jacksonville University. Division of Education, 2800 University Boulevard North, Jacksonville, FL 32211. (904)745-7132. Fax (904)745-7159. E-mail mjanz@mail.ju.edu. Dr. Margaret Janz, Interim Dir., School of Education, or Dr. June Main, Coordinator of MAT in Integrated Learning with Educational Technology (jmain@junix.ju.edu). *Specializations:* The Master's in Educational Technology and Integrated Learning is an innovative program designed to guide certified teachers in the use and application of educational technologies in the classroom. It is based on emerging views of how we learn, of our growing understanding of multiple intelligences, and of the many ways to incorporate technology in teaching and learning. Activity-based classes emphasize instructional design for a multimedia environment to reach all students. M.A.T. degrees in Computer Education and in Integrated Learning with Educational Technology. *Features:* The M.A.T. in Computer Education is for teachers who are already certified in an area of education, for those who wish to be certified in Computer Education, kindergarten through community college level. *Degree Requirements:* M.A.T. in Computer Education and in Integrated Learning with Educational Technology: 36 semester hours, including 9-12 hours in core education graduate courses and the rest in computer education with comprehensive exam in last semester of program. Master's in Educational Technology and Integrated Learning: 36 semester hours, including 9 in core graduate education courses, 6 in integrated learning, and the rest in educational technology. Comprehensive exam is to develop a practical group of multimedia applications. *Financial Assistance:* student loans and discounts to graduate education students. *Students:* Computer Education, 8; Integrated Learning with Educational Technology, 20. *Degrees Awarded 1996-97:* Computer Education, 12; Integrated Learning with Educational Technology, 24.

Nova Southeastern University. Fischler Center for the Advancement of Education, 3301 College Ave., Fort Lauderdale, FL 33314. (954)475-7440. (800)986-3223, ext. 7440. Fax (954)476-4764. E-mail gtep@fcae.nova.edu; pet@fcae.nova.edu. Web site http://www.fcae.nova.edu. Dr. Abbey Manburg, Dir., programs in Instructional Technology and Distance Education (ITDE); Deo Nellis, Dir., Graduate Teacher Education Program. *Specializations:* Ed.S. and M.S. programs for teachers in Educational Technology, Educational Media, and Computer Science Education; M.S. and Ed.D. program in Instructional Technology and Distance Education (ITDE). *Features:* ITDE is delivered online via Internet to students worldwide, who also spend a few extended weekends on campus. *Admission Requirements:* B.A. or B.S. for M.S. and Ed.S. programs plus field experience. *Degree Requirements:* M.S.: 36 semester hours including practicum (1 to 1.5 years). Ed.S.: 62 semester hours including practicum (2 years). *Faculty:* 9 full-time, 40 part-time. *Students:* 100. *Financial Assistance:* student loans.

University of Central Florida. College of Education, ED Room 318, UCF, Orlando, FL 32816-1250. (407)823-2153. Fax (407)823-5622. Web sites http://pegasus.cc.ucf.edu/~edmedia and http://pegasus.cc.ucf.edu/~edtech. Richard Cornell, Instructional Systems (cornell@pegasus. cc.ucf.edu); Judy Lee, Educational Media (jlee@pegasus.cc.ucf.edu); Glenda Gunter, Educational Technology (ggunter@pegasus.cc.ucf.edu). *Specializations:* M.A. in Instructional Technology/ Instructional Systems; M.Ed. in Instructional Technology/Educational Media; M.A. in Instructional Technology/Educational Technology. A doctorate in Curriculum and Instruction with an emphasis on Instructional Technology is offered. *Admission Requirements:* interviews for Educational Media and Educational Technology programs. *Degree Requirements:* M.A. in Instructional Technology/Instructional Systems, 39-42 semester hours; M.Ed. in Instructional Technology/ Educational Media, 39-45 semester hours; M.A. in Instructional Technology/Educational Technology, 36-45 semester hours. Practicum required in all three programs; thesis, research project, or substitute additional course work. *Students:* Instructional Systems, 70; Educational Media, 35; Educational Technology, 50. Full-time, 120; part-time, 35. *Faculty:* 4 full-time, 6 part-time. *Financial Assistance:* competitive graduate assistantships in department and college, numerous paid internships, limited number of doctoral fellowships. *Degrees Awarded 1997:* 40.

University of South Florida. Instructional Technology Program, Secondary Education Department, College of Education. 4202 Fowler Ave. East, EDU 208B, Tampa, FL 33620. (813)974-1632 (M.Ed.); (813)974-1629 (doctoral). Fax (813)974-3837. E-mail breit@tempest. coedu.usf.edu (M.Ed.), jwhite@typhoon.coedu.usf.edu (doctoral). Web site http://www.coedu.usf. edu/institute_tech. Dr. Frank Breit, master's program, Dr. James A. White, doctoral program. *Specialization:* M.Ed. in Curriculum and Instruction with emphasis in Instructional Technology; Ph.D. in Curriculum and Instruction with emphasis in Instructional Technology. *Features:* Student gain practical experience in the Florida Center for Instructional Technology (FCIT), which provides services to the Department of Education and other grants and contracts, and the Virtual

Instructional Team for the Advancement of Learning (VITAL), which provides USF faculty with course development services. The College of Education is one of the largest in the U.S. in terms of enrollment and facilities. As of Fall 1997, a new, technically state-of-the-art building was put into service. *Admission Requirements:* M.Ed.: 3.0 undergraduate GPA, at least half of undergraduate degree earned from accredited institution, and 800 GRE (V+Q), or 2.5 undergraduate GPA in last half of undergraduate degree from accredited institution and 1000 GRE, or a prior graduate degree from an accredited institution and 800 GRE. Applicants must also have a minimum of two years of relevant educational or professional experience as judged by the program faculty. Ph.D.: contact Dr. White for full details; include 3.0 undergraduate GPA in last half of coursework or 3.5 GPA at master's level and 1000 GRE, a master's degree from an accredited institution, three letters of recommendation, and favorable recommendations from program faculty. *Degree Requirements:* M.Ed.: 36-38 semester hours, comprehensive exam. Ph.D.: 77-79 hours, two research tools, two semesters of residency, qualifying examination, and dissertation. *Faculty:* 3 full-time, 2 part-time. *Students:* M.Ed.: 100 full-time, 100 part-time (approx.); Ph.D.: 2 full-time, 14 part-time. *Financial Assistance:* assistantships, grants, loans, scholarships, and fellowships. *Degrees Awarded 1997:* M.Ed., 40, Ph.D., 2.

GEORGIA

Georgia Southern University. College of Education, Statesboro, GA 30460-8131. (912)681-5307. Fax (912)681-5093. Kenneth F. Clark, Assoc. Prof., Dept. of Leadership, Technology, and Human Development. *Specialization:* M.Ed. The school also offers a six-year specialist degree program (Ed.S.), and an Instructional Technology strand is available in the Ed.D. program in Curriculum Studies. *Features:* strong emphasis on technology. *Degree Requirements:* 36 semester hours, including a varying number of hours of media for individual students. *Financial Assistance:* See graduate catalog for general financial aid information. *Faculty:* 4 full-time.

Georgia State University. Middle-Secondary Education and Instructional Technology, University Plaza, Atlanta, GA 30303. (404)651-2510. Fax (404)651-2546. E-mail swharmon@gsu.edu. Web site http://www.gsu.edu/~wwwmst. Dr. Stephen W. Harmon, contact person. *Specializations:* M.S., Ed.S., and Ph.D. in Instructional Technology or Library Media. *Features:* focus on research and practical application of instructional technology in educational and corporate settings. *Admission Requirements:* M.S.: Bachelor's degree, 2.5 undergraduate GPA, 44 MAT or 800 GRE, 550 TOEFL. Ed.S.: Master's degree, teaching certificate, 3.25 graduate GPA, 48 MAT or 900 GRE. Ph.D.: Master's degree, 3.30 graduate GPA, 53 MAT or 500 verbal plus 500 quantitative GRE or 500 analytical GRE. *Degree Requirements:* M.S.: 36 sem. hours, internship, portfolio, comprehensive examination. Ed.S.: 30 sem. hours, internship, scholarly project. Ph.D.: 66 sem. hours, internship, dissertation. *Faculty:* 6 full-time, 3 part-time. *Students:* 200 M.S., 30 Ph.D. *Financial Assistance:* assistantships, grants, student loans. *Degrees Awarded 1997:* Ph.D., 5; M.S., 30.

State University of West Georgia (formerly West Georgia College). Department of Research, Media, and Technology, 137 Education Annex, Carrollton, GA 30118. (770)836-6558. Fax (770)836-6729. E-mail bmckenzi@westga.edu. Web site http://www.westga.edu/soe/rmt. Dr. Barbara K. McKenzie, Assoc. Prof., Chair. *Specializations:* M.Ed. with specializations in Media and Instructional Technology and add-on certification for students with Master's degrees in other disciplines. The school also offers an Ed.S. program in Media with two options, Media Specialist or Instructional Technology. The program strongly emphasizes technology in the schools. *Admission Requirements:* M.Ed.: 800 GRE, 44 MAT, 550 NTE Core, 2.5 undergraduate GPA. Ed.S.: 900 GRE, 48 MAT, or 575 NTE and 3.25 graduate GPA. *Degree Requirements:* minimum of 60 qtr. hours. *Faculty:* 4 full-time in Media/Technology and 3 in Research; 2 part-time in Media/Technology. *Students:* 6 full-time, 110 part-time. *Financial Assistance:* three graduate assistantships and three graduate research assistantships for the department. *Degrees Awarded 1997:* M.Ed., 15; Ed.S., 15.

University of Georgia. Department of Instructional Technology, College of Education, 604 Aderhold Hall, Athens, GA 30602-7144. (706)542-3810. Fax (706)542-4032. E-mail kgustafs@coe.uga.edu. Web site http://itech1.coe.uga.edu. Kent L. Gustafson, Prof. and Chair. *Specializations:* M.Ed. and Ed.S. in Instructional Technology; Ph.D. for leadership positions as specialists in instructional design and development and college faculty. The program offers advanced study for individuals with previous preparation in instructional media and technology, as well as a preparation for personnel in other professional fields requiring a specialty in instructional systems or instructional technology. Representative career fields for graduates include designing new courses; tutorial programs; and instructional materials in the military, industry, medical professional schools, allied health agencies, teacher education, staff development, state and local school systems, higher education, research, and in instructional products development. *Features:* minor areas of study available in a variety of other departments. Personalized programs are planned around a common core of courses and include practica, internships, or clinical experiences. Research activities include special assignments, applied projects, and task forces, as well as thesis and dissertation studies. *Admission Requirements:* all degrees: application to graduate school, satisfactory GRE score, other criteria as outlined in Graduate School Bulletin. *Degree Requirements:* M.Ed.: 36 semester hours with 3.0 GPA, portfolio with oral exam. Ed.S.: 30 semester hours with 3.0 GPA and portfolio exam. Ph.D.: three full years of study beyond the Master's degree, two consecutive semesters full-time residency, comprehensive exam with oral defense, internship, dissertation with oral defense. *Faculty:* 10 full-time, 2 part-time. *Students:* M.Ed and Ed.S., 20 full-time, 60 part-time; Ph.D., 25 full-time, 10 part-time. *Financial Assistance:* graduate assistantships available. *Degrees Awarded 1997:* M.Ed. and Ed.S., 16; Ph.D., 2.

Valdosta State University. College of Education, 1500 N. Patterson St., Valdosta, GA 31698. (912)333-5927. Fax (912)333-7167. E-mail cprice@valdosta.edu. Catherine B. Price, Prof., Head, Dept. of Instructional Technology. *Specializations:* M.Ed. in Instructional Technology with three tracks: Library/Media, Technology Leadership, or Technology Applications; Ed.S. in Instructional Technology; Ed.D. in Curriculum and Instruction. *Features:* The program has a strong emphasis on technology in M.Ed., Ed.S., and Ed.D.; strong emphasis on applied research in Ed.S and Ed.D. *Admission Requirements:* M.Ed.: 2.5 GPA, 750 GRE. Ed.S.: Master's in Instructional Technology or related area, 3.0 GPA, 850 GRE. Ed.D.: Master's degree, 3 years of experience, 3.50 GPA, 1000 GRE. *Degree Requirements:* M.Ed.: 33 semester hours. Ed.S.: 27 semester hours. *Faculty:* 6 full-time, 3 part-time. *Students:* 15 full-time, 90 part-time. *Financial Assistance:* graduate assistantships, student loans, scholarships. *Degrees Awarded 1997:* M.Ed., 16; Ed.S. and Ed.D., 0 (new programs).

HAWAII

University of Hawaii-Manoa. Educational Technology Department, 1776 University Ave., Honolulu, HI 96822. (808)956-7671. Fax (808)956-3905. E-mail ETDEPT-L@uhunixuhcc. hawaii.edu. Web site http://www2.hawaii.edu/edtech. Geoffrey Z. Kucera, Prof., Chair, Educational Technology Dept. *Specialization:* M.Ed. in Educational Technology. *Degree Requirements:* 39 semester hours (all in educational technology, including 3 in practicum, 3 in internship), thesis and non-thesis available. *Faculty:* 5 full-time, 3 part-time. *Students:* 3 full-time, 43 parttime. *Financial Assistance:* Consideration given to meritorious second-year students for tuition waivers and scholarship applications. *Degrees Awarded July 1996 through June 1997:* 9.

IDAHO

Boise State University. IPT, 1910 University Drive, Boise, ID 83725. (208)385-4457, (800)824-7017 ext. 4457. Fax (208)342-7203. E-mail bsu-ipt@micron.net. Web site http://www.cot.idbsu.edu/~ipt. Dr. David Cox, IPT Program Dir.; Jo Ann Fenner, IPT Program Developer and distance program contact person. *Specialization:* M.S. in Instructional & Performance Technology available in a traditional campus setting or via computer conferencing to students located anywhere on the North American continent. The program is fully accredited by the Northwest Association of Schools and

Colleges and is the recipient of an NUCEA award for Outstanding Credit Program offered by distance education methods. *Features:* Leading experts in learning styles, evaluation, and leadership principles serve as adjunct faculty in the program via computer and modem from their various remote locations. *Admission Requirements:* undergraduate degree with 3.0 GPA, one-to-two page essay describing why you want to pursue this program and how it will contribute to your personal and professional development, and a resume of personal qualifications and work experience. *Degree Requirements:* 36 semester hours in instructional and performance technology and related course work; project or thesis available for on-campus program and an oral comprehensive exam required for distance program (included in 36 credit hours). *Faculty:* 3 full-time, 7 part-time. *Students:* 140 part-time. *Financial Assistance:* DANTES funding for some military personnel, low-interest loans to eligible students, graduate assistantships for on-campus enrollees. *Degrees Awarded 1997:* 12.

ILLINOIS

Chicago State University. Department of Library Science and Communications Media, Chicago, IL 60628. (312)995-2278, (312)995-2503. Fax (312)995-2473. Janice Bolt, Prof., Chair, Dept. of Library Science and Communications Media. *Specialization:* Master's degree in School Media. Program has been approved by NCATE: AECT/AASL through accreditation of University College of Education; State of Illinois Entitlement Program. *Admission Requirements:* teacher's certification or Bachelor's in Education; any B.A. or B.S. *Degree Requirements:* 36 semester hours; thesis optional. *Faculty:* 2 full-time, 5 part-time. *Students:* 88 part-time. *Financial Assistance:* assistantships, grants, student loans. *Degrees Awarded 1997:* 15.

Concordia University. 7400 Augusta St., River Forest, IL 60305-1499. (708)209-3088. Fax (708)209-3176. E-mail boosmb@crf.cuis.edu. Web site http://www.curf.edu. Dr. Manfred Boos, Chair, Mathematics/Computer Science Education Dept. *Specialization:* M.A. in Computer Science Education. *Admission Requirements:* 2.85 GPA (2.25 to 2.85 for provisional status); Bachelor's degree from regionally accredited institution; two letters of recommendation. *Degree Requirements:* 33 semester hours of course work. *Faculty:* 7 full-time, 5 part-time. *Students:* 1 full-time, 13 part-time. *Financial Assistance:* a number of graduate assistantships, Stafford student loans, Supplement Loan for Students. *Degrees Awarded 1997:* 3.

Governors State University. College of Arts and Sciences, University Park, IL 60466. (708)534-4082. Fax (708)534-7895. E-mail: m-stelni@govst.edu. Michael Stelnicki, Prof., Human Performance and Training. *Specializations:* M.A. in Communication with HP&T major. *Features:* emphasizes 3 professional areas: Instructional Design, Performance Analysis, and Design Logistics. *Admission Requirements:* undergraduate degree in any field. *Degree Requirements:* 36 credit hours (trimester), all in instructional and performance technology; internship or advanced field project required. Metropolitan Chicago area based. *Faculty:* 2 full-time. *Students:* 38 part-time. *Degrees Awarded 1997:* 10.

Northern Illinois University. Leadership and Educational Policy Studies Department, College of Education, DeKalb, IL 60115-2896. (815)753-0464. Fax (815)753-9371. E-mail LSTOTT@ NIU.EDU. Web site http://coe.cedu.niu.edu. Dr. Peggy Bailey, Chair, Instructional Technology. *Specializations*: M.S.Ed. in Instructional Technology with concentrations in Instructional Design, Distance Education, Educational Computing, and Media Administration; Ed.D. in Instructional Technology, emphasizing instructional design and development, computer education, media administration, and preparation for careers in business, industry, and higher education. In addition, Illinois state certification in school library media is offered in conjunction with either degree or alone. *Features:* considerable flexibility in course selection, including advanced seminars, numerous practicum and internship opportunities, individual study, and research. Program is highly individualized. More than 60 courses offered by several departments or faculties, including communications, radio/television/film, art, journalism, educational psychology, computer science, and research and evaluation. Facilities include well-equipped computer labs. Students are encouraged to create individualized Web pages. Master's program started in 1968, doctorate in 1970. *Admission Requirements:* M.S.: 2.75 undergraduate GPA, GRE verbal and quantitative scores, two references. Ed.D.: 3.5 M.S. GPA, GRE verbal and quantitative scores (waiver possible), writing sample, three references. *Degree Requirements:* M.S.: 39 hours, including 30 in instructional technology; no thesis. Ed.D.: 63 hours beyond Master's, including 15 hours for dissertation. *Faculty:* 8 full-time, 12 part-time. *Students:* M.S., 135 part-time; Ed.D., 115 part-time. *Financial Assistance:* assistantships available at times in various departments, scholarships, minority assistance. *Degrees Awarded 1997:* M.S., 26; Ed.D., 6.

Southern Illinois University at Carbondale. Department of Curriculum and Instruction, Carbondale, IL 62901-4610. (618)536-2441. Fax (618)453-4244. E-mail sashrock@siu.edu. Web site http://www.siu.edu/~currinst/index.html. Sharon Shrock, Coord., Instructional Technology/ Development. *Specializations*: M.S. in Education with specializations in Instructional Development and Instructional Technology; Ph.D. in Education including specialization in Instructional Technology. *Features*: All specializations are oriented to multiple education settings. The ID program emphasizes nonschool (primarily corporate) learning environments. *Admission Requirements*: M.S.: Bachelor's degree, 2.7 undergraduate GPA, transcripts. Ph.D.: Master's degree, 3.25 GPA, MAT or GRE scores, letters of recommendation, transcripts, writing sample. *Degree Requirements:* M.S., 32 credit hours with thesis; 36 credit hours without thesis; Ph.D., 40 credit hours beyond the master's degree in courses, 24 credit hours for the dissertation. *Faculty:* 5 full-time, 2 part-time. *Students*: M.S., 35 full-time, 45 part-time; Ph.D., 8 full-time, 19 part-time. *Financial Assistance*: some graduate assistantships and scholarships available to qualified students. *Degrees Awarded 1997*: Master's, 16; Ph.D., 4.

Southern Illinois University at Edwardsville. Instructional Technology Program, School of Education, Edwardsville, IL 62026-1125. (618)692-3277. Fax (618)692-3359. E-mail cnelson@siue.edu. Web site http://www.siue.edu. Dr. Charles E. Nelson, Dir., Dept. of Educational Leadership. *Specialization:* M.S. in Education with concentrations in (1) Instructional Design and (2) Teaching, Learning, and Technology. *Features:* evening classes only. *Degree Requirements:* 36 semester hours; thesis optional. *Faculty:* 6 part-time. *Students:* 125. *Degrees Awarded 1997:* 30.

University of Illinois at Urbana-Champaign. Department of Educational Psychology, 210 Education Bldg., 1310 S. 6th St., Champaign, IL 61820. (217)333-2245. Fax (217)244-7620. E-mail c-west@uiuc.edu. Charles K. West, Prof., Div. of Learning and Instruction, Dept. of Educational Psychology. *Specializations:* M.A., M.S., and Ed.M. with emphasis in Instructional Design and Educational Computing. Ph.D. in Educational Psychology with emphasis in Instructional Design and Educational Computing. *Features:* Ph.D. program is individually tailored and strongly research-oriented with emphasis on applications of cognitive science to instruction. *Admission Requirements*: excellent academic record, high GRE scores, and strong letters of recommendation. *Degree Requirements:* 8 units for Ed.M., 6 units and thesis for M.A. or M.S. Ph.D.: 8 units coursework, approx. 4 units of research methods courses, minimum 8 hours of written qualifying exams, 8 units Thesis credits. *Faculty:* 8 full-time, 5 part-time. *Students:* 31 full-time, 7 part-time. *Financial Assistance:* scholarships, research assistantships, and teaching assistantships available; fellowships for very highly academically talented; some tuition waivers. *Degrees Awarded 1997:* Ph.D., 5.

Western Illinois University. Instructional Technology and Telecommunications, 37 Harrabin Hall, Macomb, IL 61455. (309)298-1952. Fax (309)298-2978. E-mail mh-hassan@wiu.edu. Web site http://www.wiu.edu/users/miitt. M.H. Hassan, Chair. *Specialization:* Master's degree. *Features:* new program approved by Illinois Board of Higher Education in January 1996 with emphasis in Instructional Technology, Telecommunications, Interactive Technologies, and Distance Education. Selected courses delivered via satellite TV and compressed video. *Admission Requirements:* Bachelor's degree. *Degree Requirements:* 32 semester hours, thesis or practicum; or 35 semester hours with portfolio. *Faculty:* 7 full-time. *Students:* 30 full-time, 115 part-time. *Financial Assistance:* graduate and research assistantships, internships, residence hall assistants, veterans' benefits, loans, and part-time employment.

INDIANA

Indiana State University. Dept. of Curriculum, Instruction, and Media Technology, Terre Haute, IN 47809. (812)237-2937. Fax (812)237-4348. E-mail efthomp@befac.indstate.edu. Dr. James E. Thompson, Program Coord. *Specializations:* Master's degree in Instructional Technology with education focus or with non-education focus; Specialist Degree program in Instructional Technology; Ph.D. in Curriculum, Instruction with specialization in Media Technology. *Degree Requirements:* Master's: 32 semester hours, including 18 in media; thesis optional; Ed.S.: 60 semester hours beyond bachelor's degree; Ph.D., approximately 100 hours beyond bachelor's degree. *Faculty:* 5 full-time. *Students:* 17 full-time, 13 part-time. *Financial Assistance:* 7 assistantships. *Degrees Awarded 1997:* Master's, 2; Ph.D., 1.

*Indiana University. School of Education, W. W. Wright Education Bldg., Rm. 2276, 201 N. Rose Ave., Bloomington, IN 47405-1006. (812)856-8451 (information), (812)856-8239 (admissions). Fax (812)856-8239. Thomas Schwen, Chair, Dept. of Instructional Systems Technology. *Specializations:* M.S. and Ed.S. degrees designed for individuals seeking to be practitioners in the field of Instructional Technology. Offers Ph.D. and Ed.D. degrees with four program focus areas: Foundations; Instructional Analysis, Design, and Development; Instructional Development and Production; and Implementation and Management. *Features:* requires computer skills as a prerequisite and makes technology utilization an integral part of the curriculum; eliminates separation of various media formats; and establishes a series of courses of increasing complexity integrating production and development. The latest in technical capabilities have been incorporated in the new Center for Excellence in Education, including teaching, photographic, computer, and science laboratories, a 14-station multimedia laboratory, and television studios. *Admission Requirements:* M.S.: Bachelor's degree from an accredited institution, 1350 GRE (3 tests required), 2.65 undergraduate GPA. Ed.D and Ph.D.: 1550 GRE (3 tests required), 3.5 graduate GPA. *Degree Requirements:* M.S.: 40 credit hours (including 16 credits in required courses); colloquia; an instructional product or Master's thesis; and 12 credits in outside electives. Ed.D.: 60 hours in addition to previous Master's degree, thesis. Ph.D.: 90 hours, thesis. *Faculty:* 6 full-time, 5 part-time. *Financial Assistance:* assistantships, scholarships. *Degrees Awarded 1996:* M.S., 59; Ed.S., 1; Ed.D., 1; Ph.D., 5.

Purdue University. School of Education, Department of Curriculum and Instruction, W. Lafayette, IN 47907-1442. (765)494-5669. Fax (765)496-1622. E-mail lehman@purdue.edu. Web site http://www.soe.purdue.edu. Dr. James D. Lehman, Prof. of Educational Technology. *Specializations:* Master's degree, Educational Specialist, and Ph.D. in Educational Technology. Master's program started in 1982, Specialist and Ph.D. in 1985. *Admission Requirements:* Master's and Ed.S.: 3.0 GPA, three letters of recommendation, statement of personal goals. Ph.D.: 3.0 GPA, three letters of recommendation, statement of personal goals, 1000 GRE (V+Q). *Degree Requirements:* Master's: 33 semester hours (15 in educational technology, 9 in education, 12 unspecified); thesis optional. Specialist: 60-65 semester hours (15-18 in educational technology, 30-35 in education); thesis, internship, practicum. Ph.D.: 90 semester hours (15-18 in educational technology, 42-45 in education); thesis, internship, practicum. *Faculty:* 6 full-time. *Students:* M.S., 49; Ed.S, 1; Ph.D., 54. *Financial Assistance:* assistantships and fellowships. *Degrees Awarded 1997:* Master's, 16; Ph.D., 13.

IOWA

Clarke College. Graduate Studies, 1550 Clarke Drive, Dubuque, IA 52001. (319)588-6331. Fax (319)588-6789. E-mail RADAMS@KELLER.CLARKE.EDU. Web site http://www.clarke.edu. Robert Adams, Clarke College, (319)588-6416. *Specializations:* M.A. in Technology and Education. *Admission Requirements:* 2.5 GPA, GRE (verbal + quantitative) or MAT, $25 application fee, two letters of recommendation. *Degree Requirements:* 25 semester hours in computer courses, 12 hours in education. *Faculty:* 1 full-time, 1-2 part-time. *Students:* 20 part-time. *Financial Assistance:* scholarships, student loans. *Degrees Awarded 1997:* 8.

Iowa State University. College of Education, Ames, IA 50011. (515)294-6840. Fax (515)294-9284. E-mail mrs@iastate.edu. Michael Simonson, Prof. and Coord., Curriculum and Instruction Technology (including Media and Computers). *Specializations:* M.S., M.Ed., and Ph.D. in Curriculum and Instructional Technology with specializations in Instructional Computing, Instructional Design, and Distance Education; Ph.D. in Education with emphasis in Instructional Computing, Instructional Design, and Technology Research. Participates in Iowa Distance Education Alliance, Iowa Star Schools Project. *Features:* practicum experiences related to professional objectives, supervised study and research projects tied to long-term studies within the program, development and implementation of new techniques, teaching strategies, and operational procedures in instructional resources centers and computer labs. *Admission Requirements:* M.S. and M.Ed.: three letters, top half of undergraduate class, autobiography. Ph.D.: three letters, top half of undergraduate class, autobiography, GRE scores. *Degree Requirements:* Master's: 30 semester hours, thesis, no internship or practicum. Ph.D.: 78 semester hours, thesis, no internship or practicum. *Faculty:* 4 full-time, 6 part-time. *Students:* Master's, 40 full-time, 40 part-time; Ph.D., 30 full-time, 20 part-time. *Financial Assistance:* 10 assistantships. *Degrees Awarded 1997:* Master's, 10; Ph.D., 7.

University of Iowa. Division of Psychological and Quantitative Foundations, College of Education, Iowa City, IA 52242. (319)335-5519. Fax (319)335-5386. Web site http://www.uiowa. edu/~coe2/facstaff/salessi.htm. Stephen Alessi, 361 Lindquist Center, Iowa City, IA 52242. *Specializations:* M.A. and Ph.D. with specializations in Training and Human Resources Development, Computer Applications, and Media Design and Production (MA only). *Features:* flexibility in planning to fit individual needs, backgrounds, and career goals. The program is interdisciplinary, involving courses within divisions of the College of Education, as well as in the schools of Business, Library Science, Radio and Television, Linguistics, and Psychology. *Admission Requirements:* MA: 2.8 undergraduate GPA, 500 GRE (V+Q), personal letter of interest. Ph.D.: Master's degree, 1000 GRE (V+Q), 3.2 GPA on all previous graduate work for regular admission. Conditional admission may be granted. Teaching or relevant experience may be helpful. *Degree Requirements:* MA: 35 semester hours, 3.0 GPA, final project or thesis, comprehensive exam. Ph.D.: 90 semester hours, comprehensive exams, dissertation. *Faculty:* 4 full-time, 3 part-time. *Financial Assistance:* assistantships, grants, student loans, and scholarships.

University of Northern Iowa. Educational Technology Program, Cedar Falls, IA 50614-0606. (319)273-3250. Fax (319)273-5886. E-mail SmaldinoS@UNI.edu. Web site www.uni.edu/edtech. Sharon E. Smaldino, contact person. *Specialization:* M.A. in Educational Technology, M.A. in Communications and Training Technology. *Admission Requirements:* Bachelor's degree, 3.0 undergraduate GPA, 500 TOEFL. *Degree Requirements:* 38 semester credits, optional thesis worth 6 credits or alternative research paper of project, comprehensive exam. *Faculty:* 3 full-time, 6 part-time. *Students:* 120. *Financial Assistance:* assistantships, grants, student loans, scholarships, student employment. *Degrees Awarded 1997:* 20.

KANSAS

Emporia State University. School of Library and Information Management, 1200 Commercial, P.O. Box 4025, Emporia, KS 66801. (316)341-5203. Fax (316)341-5233. E-mail vowellfa@esumail. emporia.edu. Web site http://www.emporia.edu/slim/slim.htm. Faye N. Vowell, Dean. *Specializations:* Master's of Library Science (ALA accredited program); School Library Certification program, which includes 27 hours of the M.L.S. program; Ph.D. in Library and Information Management. *Features:* The M.L.S. program is also available in Colorado, Oregon, Utah, and Nebraska. Internet courses are under development. *Admission Requirements:* selective admissions process for M.L.S. and Ph.D. based on a combination of admission criteria, including (but not limited to) GRE or TOEFL score, personal interview, GPA, statement of goals and references. Request admission packet for specific criteria. *Degree Requirements:* M.L.S.: 42 semester hours, comprehensive exam. Ph.D.: total of 83-97 semester hours depending on the number of hours received for an M.L.S. *Faculty:* 12 full-time, 35 part-time. *Students:* M.L.S., 64 full-time, 305 part-time; Ph.D., 23 part-time. *Financial Assistance:* assistantships, grants, student loans, scholarships. *Degrees Awarded 1997:* 156.

Kansas State University. Educational Computing, Design, and Telecommunications, 363 Bluemont Hall, Manhattan, KS 66506. (913)532-7686. Fax (913)532-7304. E-mail dmcgrath@coe. educ.ksu.edu. Web site http://www2.educ.ksu.edu/Faculty/McGrathD/ECDT/ECDTProg..htm. Dr. Diane McGrath, contact person. *Specializations:* M.S. in Secondary Education with an emphasis in Educational Computing, Design, and Telecommunications; Ph.D. and Ed.D. in Curriculum & Instruction with an emphasis in Educational Computing, Design, and Telecommunications. Master's program started in 1982; doctoral in 1987. *Admissions Requirements:* M.S.: B average in undergraduate work, one programming language, 590 TOEFL. Ed.D. and Ph.D.: B average in undergraduate and graduate work, one programming language, GRE or MAT, three letters of recommendation, experience or course in educational computing. *Degree Requirements:* M.S.: 30 semester hours (minimum of 12 in Educational Computing); thesis, internship, or practicum not required, but all three are possible. Ed.D.: 94 semester hours (minimum of 18 hours in Educational Computing or related area approved by committee, 16 hours dissertation research, 12 hours internship); thesis. Ph.D.: 90 semester hours (minimum of 21 hours in Educational Computing, Design, and Telecommunications or related area approved by committee, 30 hours for dissertation research); thesis; internship or practicum not required but available. *Faculty:* 2 full-time, 1 part-time. *Students:* M.S., 10 full-time, 27 part-time; doctoral, 16 full-time, 14 part-time. *Financial Assistance:* currently four assistantships directly associated with the program; other assistantships sometimes available in other departments depending on skills and funds available. *Degrees Awarded 1997:* M.S., 7.

KENTUCKY

University of Louisville. School of Education, Louisville, KY 40292. (502)852-0609. Fax (502)852-1417. E-mail crrude01@ulkyvm.louisville.edu. Web site http://www.louisville.edu/edu. Carolyn Rude-Parkins, Dir., Education Resource & Technology Center. *Specialization:* M.Ed. in Early Childhood, Middle School, Secondary Education, Training and Development with Instructional Technology focus. *Features:* technology courses appropriate for business or school audiences. Program is based on ISTE standards as well as ASTD standards. *Admission Requirements:* 2.75 GPA, 800 GRE, 2 letters of recommendation, application fee. *Degree Requirements:* 30 semester hours, thesis optional. *Faculty:* 2 full-time, 3 part-time. *Students:* 4 full-time, 30 part-time. *Financial Assistance:* graduate assistantships. *Degrees Awarded 1997:* 10.

LOUISIANA

Louisiana State University. School of Library and Information Science, Baton Rouge, LA 70803. (504)388-3158. Fax (504)388-4581, Web site http://adam.slis.lsu.edu. Bert R. Boyce, Dean, Prof., School of Library and Information Science. *Specializations:* M.L.I.S., C.L.I.S. (post-Master's certificate), Louisiana School Library Certification. An advanced certificate program is available. *Degree Requirements:* M.L.I.S.: 37 hours, comprehensive exam, one semester full-time residence, completion of degree program in five years. *Faculty:* 10 full-time. *Students:* 84 full-time, 86 part-time. *Financial Assistance:* A large number of graduate assistantships are available to qualified students. *Degrees Awarded 1997:* 91.

MARYLAND

The Johns Hopkins University. Graduate Division of Education, Technology for Educators Program, Columbia Gateway Park, 6740 Alexander Bell Drive, Columbia, MD 21046. (410)309-9537. Fax (410)290-0467. Web site http://www.jhu.edu. Dr. Jacqueline A. Nunn, Department Chair; Dr. Linda Tsantis, Program Coordinator (tsantis@jhu.edu). *Specialization:* The Department of Technology for Education offers programs leading to the M.S. degree in Education, the M.S. in Special Education, and three specialized advanced Graduate Certificates: Technology for Multimedia and Internet-Based Instruction; Teaching with Technology for School to Career Transition; and Assistive Technology for Communication and Social Interaction. *Features:* focuses on training educators to become decision makers and leaders in the use of technology, with competencies in the design, development, and application of emerging technologies for teaching and learning. Incorporates basic elements that take into account the needs of adult learners, the constantly changing nature of technology, and the need for schools and universities to work together for schoolwide change. The Center for Technology in Education is a partnership project linking research and teaching of the University with the leadership and policy direction of the Maryland State Department of Education. The Center is directed by Dr. Nunn (2500 E. Northern Parkway, Baltimore, MD 21214-1113, 254-8466, jnunn@jhuniz.hcf.jhu.edu). *Admission Requirements:* Bachelor's degree with strong background in teaching, curriculum and instruction, special education, or a related service field. *Degree Requirements:* M.S. in Education, Technology for Educators: 36 semester hours (including 9 credits technical courses, 18 credits instructional courses, 9 credits research and school improvement courses). M.S. in Special Education, Technology in Special Education: 36 semester hours (including 9 credits technical courses, 15 credits instructional courses, 12 credits research and school improvement courses). *Faculty:* 2 full-time, 30 part-time. *Students:* 201 part-time. *Financial Assistance:* grants, student loans, scholarships. *Degrees Awarded 1997:* 38.

Towson University. College of Education, Hawkins Hall, Rm. 206, Towson, MD 21204. (410)830-2194. Fax (410)830-2733. E-mail rosecransg@toe.towson.edu. Web site http://www.towson.edu/~coe/istc.html. Dr. Gary W. Rosecrans, Assoc. Prof., General Education Dept. *Specializations:* M.S. degrees in Instructional Development and School Library Media. *Admission Requirements:* Bachelor's degree from accredited institution with 3.0 GPA. (Conditional admission requires 2.5 GPA.) Instructional Development program requires media utilization course as prerequisite. School Media program requires teacher certification or completion of specified course work in education. *Degree Requirements:* 36 graduate semester hours without thesis; 33 hours with thesis. *Faculty:* 7 full-time, 4 adjunct. *Students:* 150. *Financial Assistance:* graduate assistantships, work assistance, scholarships. *Degrees Awarded 1997:* 18.

University of Maryland. College of Library and Information Services, 4105 Hornbake Library Bldg., South Wing, College Park, MD 20742-4345. (301)405-2038. Fax (301)314-9145. Ann Prentice, Dean and Program Chair. *Specializations:* Master's of Library Science, including specialization in School Library Media; doctorate in Library and Information Services; Ph.D. in Library Science and Educational Technology/Instructional Communication. *Features:* program is broadly conceived and interdisciplinary in nature, using the resources of the entire campus. The student and the advisor design a program of study and research to fit the student's background, interests, and professional objectives. Students prepare for careers in teaching and research in information science and librarianship and elect concentrations including Educational Technology and Instructional Communication. *Admission Requirements:* doctoral: Bachelor's degree (the majority of doctoral students enter with Master's degrees in Library Science, Educational Technology, or other relevant disciplines), GRE general tests, three letters of recommendation, statement of purpose. Interviews required when feasible for doctoral applicants. *Degree Requirements:* M.L.S.: 36 semester hours; thesis optional. *Faculty:* 15 full-time, 8 part-time. *Students:* Master's, 106 full-time, 149 part-time; doctoral, 5 full-time, 11 part-time. *Financial Assistance:* assistantships, grants, student loans, scholarships.

University of Maryland, Baltimore County (UMBC). Department of Education, 1000 Hilltop Circle, Baltimore, MD 21250. (410)455-2310. Fax (410)455-3986. Email gist@umbc.edu. Web site http://www.research.umbc.edu/~eholly/ceduc/isd. Dr. William R. Johnson, Dir., Graduate Programs in Education. *Specializations:* M.A. degrees in School Instructional Systems, Post-Baccalaureate Teacher Certification, Training in Business and Industry. *Admissions Requirements:* 3.0 undergraduate GPA, GRE scores. *Degree Requirements:* 36 semester hours (including 18 in systems development for each program); internship. *Faculty:* 18 full-time, 25 part-time. *Students:* 59 full-time, 254 part-time. *Financial Assistance:* assistantships, scholarships. *Degrees Awarded 1997:* 68.

Western Maryland College. Department of Education, Main St., Westminster, MD 21157. (410)857-2507. Fax (410)857-2515. E-mail rkerby@wmdc.edu. Dr. Ramona N. Kerby, Coord., School Library Media Program, Dept. of Education. *Specializations*: M.S. in School Library Media. *Degree Requirements*: 33 credit hours (including 19 in media and 6 in education), comprehensive exam. *Faculty*: 1 full-time, 7 part-time. *Students*: 140, most part-time.

MASSACHUSETTS

Boston University. School of Education, 605 Commonwealth Ave., Boston, MA 02215-1605. (617)353-3181. Fax (617)353-3924. E-mail whittier@bu.edu. Web site http://web.bu.edu/EDUCATION. David B. Whittier, Asst. Professor and Coord., Program in Educational Media and Technology. *Specializations*: Ed.M., CAGS (Certificate of Advanced Graduate Study) in Educational Media and Technology; Ed.D. in Curriculum and Teaching, Specializing in Educational Media and Technology; preparation for Massachusetts public school certificates as Library Media Specialist and Instructional Technologist. *Features:* The Master's Program prepares graduates for professional careers as educators, instructional designers, developers of educational materials, and managers of the human and technology-based resources necessary to support education and training with technology. Graduates are employed in settings such as K-12 schools, higher education, industry, medicine, government, and publishing. Students come to the program from many different backgrounds and with a wide range of professional goals. The doctoral program sets the study of Educational Media & Technology within the context of education and educational research in general, and curriculum and teaching in particular. In addition to advanced work in the field of Educational Media and Technology, students examine and conduct research and study the history of educational thought and practice relating to teaching and learning. Graduates make careers in education as professors and researchers, technology directors and managers, and as developers of technology-based materials and systems. Graduates also make careers in medicine, government, business, and industry as instructional designers, program developers, project managers, and training directors. Graduates who work in both educational and non-educational organizations are often responsible for managing the human and technological resources required to create learning experiences that include the development and delivery of technology-based materials and distance education.: *Admission Requirements*: Ed.M.: good recommendations, solid graduate test scores, 2.7 undergraduate GPA, GRE or MAT must be completed within past five years. CAGs: Ed.M., good recommendations, solid graduate test scores, 2.7 undergraduate GPA, GRE or MAT must be completed within past five years. Ed.D.: 3 letters of recommendation, 50 MAT or GRE scores, transcripts, writing samples, statement of goals and qualifications, analytical essay, 2.7 GPA. *Degree Requirements:* Ed.M.: 36 credit hours (including 22 hours from required core curriculum, 14 from electives). CAGs: 32 credits beyond Ed.M., one of which must be a curriculum and teaching course and a mini-comprehensive exam. Ed.D.: 60 credit hours of courses in Educational Media and Technology, curriculum and teaching, and educational thought and practice with comprehensive exams; course work and apprenticeship in research; 60 credit hours; dissertation. *Faculty*: 1 full-time, 1 half-time, 10 part-time. *Students*: 2 full-time, 12 part-time. *Financial Assistance*: U.S. Government sponsored work study, assistantships, grants, student loans, scholarships. *Degrees Awarded 1997*: Ed.M., 11; Ed.D., 1.

Bridgewater State College. Library Media Program, Hart Hall, Rm. 219, Bridgewater, MA 02325. (508)697-1320. Fax (508)697-1771. E-mail fzilonis@bridgew.edu. Web site http://www.bridgew.edu. Mary Frances Zilonis, Coord., Library Media Program. *Specialization:* M.Ed. in Library Media Studies. *Features:* This program heavily emphasizes teaching and technology. *Degree Requirements:* 39 semester hours; comprehensive exam. *Faculty:* 2 full-time, 6 part-time. *Students:* 58 in degree program, 30 non-degree. *Financial Assistance:* graduate assistantships, graduate internships. *Degrees Awarded 1997:* 5.

Fitchburg State College. Division of Graduate and Continuing Education, 160 Pearl St., Fitchburg, MA 01420. (978)665-3181. Fax (978)665-3658. E-mail dgce@fsc.edu. Web site http://www.fsc.edu. Dr. Elena Kyle, Chair. *Specialization:* M.S. in Communications Media with specializations in

Management, Technical and Professional Writing, Instructional Technology, and Library Media. *Features:* Collaborating with professionals working in the field both for organizations and as independent producers, Fitchburg offers a unique M.S. program. The objective of the Master of Science in Communications/Media Degree Programs is to develop in candidates the knowledge and skills for the effective implementation of communication within business, industry, government, not-for-profit agencies, health services, and education. *Admission Requirements:* MAT or GRE scores, official transcript(s) of a baccalaureate degree, two or more years of experience in communications or media, department interview and portfolio presentation, three letters of recommendation. *Degree Requirements:* 36 semester credit hours. *Faculty:* 1 full-time, 7 part-time. *Students:* 84 part-time. *Financial Assistance:* assistantships, student loans, scholarships. *Degrees Awarded 1997:* 42.

Harvard University. Appian Way, Cambridge, MA 02138. (617)495-3541. Fax (617)495-3626. E-mail Admit@hugse2.harvard.edu. Web site http://GSEWeb.harvard.edu/TIEHome.html. David Perkins, Interim Dir. of Technology in Education Program. *Specialization:* M.Ed. in Technology in Education; an advanced certificate program is available. *Admission Requirements:* Bachelor's degree, MAT or GRE scores, 600 TOEFL, 3 recommendations. Students interested in print information about the TIE Program should e-mail a request to the address above. *Degree Requirements:* 32 semester credits. *Faculty:* 1 full-time, 9 part-time. *Students:* approx. 50: 39 full-time, 11 part-time. *Financial Assistance:* within the school's policy. *Degrees Awarded 1997:* 50.

Lesley College. 29 Everett St., Cambridge, MA 02138-2790. (617)349-8419. Fax (617)349-8169. E-mail nroberts@mail.lesley.edu. Web site http://www.lesley.edu. Dr. Nancy Roberts, Prof. of Education. *Specializations:* M.Ed. in Technology Education; C.A.G.S. (Certificate of Advanced Graduate Study) in Technology Education; Ph.D. in Education with a Technology Education major. *Features:* M.Ed. program is offered off-campus at 45 sites in 16 states; contact Professional Outreach Associates [(800)843-4808] for information. The degree is also offered completely online. Contact Maureen Yoder, myoder@mail.lesley.edu, or (617)348-8421 for information. *Degree Requirements:* M.Ed.: 33 semester hours in technology, integrative final project in lieu of thesis, no internship or practicum. C.A.G.S.: 36 semester hours. Ph.D. requirements available on request. *Faculty:* 9 full-time, 122 part-time on the Master's and C.A.G.S. levels. *Students:* 1,200 part-time. *Degrees Awarded 1997:* 575.

Simmons College. Graduate School of Library and Information Science, 300 The Fenway, Boston, MA 02115-5898. (617)521-2800. Fax (617)521-3192. E-mail jbaughman@simmons.edu. Web site http://www.simmons.edu/gslis. Dr. James C. Baughman, Prof. *Specializations:* M.S. Dual degrees: M.L.S./M.A. in Education (for School Library Media Specialists); M.L.S./M.A. in History (Archives Management Program). A Doctor of Arts in Administration is also offered. *Features:* The program prepares individuals for a variety of careers, media technology emphasis being only one. There are special programs for School Library Media Specialist and Archives Management with strengths in Information Science/Systems, Media Management. *Admission Requirements:* B.A. or B.S. degree with 3.0 GPA, statement, three letters of reference. *Degree Requirements:* 36 semester hours. *Faculty:* 14 full-time. *Students:* 75 full-time, 415 part-time. *Financial Assistance:* assistantships, grants, student loans, scholarships. *Degrees Awarded 1997:* Master's, 185.

University of Massachusetts-Boston. Graduate College of Education, 100 Morrissey Blvd., Boston, MA 02125. (617)287-5980. Fax (617)287-7664. E-mail babcock@umbsky.cc.umb.edu. Web site http://www.umb.edu. Donald D. Babcock, Graduate Program Dir. *Specialization:* M.Ed. in Instructional Design. *Admission Requirements:* MAT or previous Master's degree, goal statement, three letters of recommendation, resume, interview. *Degree Requirements:* 36 semester hours, thesis or project. *Faculty:* 1 full-time, 9 part-time. *Students:* 8 full-time, 102 part-time. *Financial Assistance:* graduate assistantships providing tuition plus stipend. *Degrees Awarded 1997:* 24.

University of Massachusetts-Lowell. College of Education, One University Ave., Lowell, MA 01854-2881. (508)934-4621. Fax (508)934-3005. E-mail John_Lebaron@uml.edu. Web site http://www.uml.edu/College/Education. John LeBaron, Faculty Chair. *Specializations:* M.Ed and Ed.D. Educational Technology may be pursued in the context of any degree program area. The Certificate of Advanced Graduate Study (CAGS), equivalent to 30 credits beyond a M.Ed., is also offered. *Admission Requirements:* Bachelor's degree in cognate area, GRE or MAT scores, statement of purpose, three recommendations. *Degree Requirements:* M.Ed.: 30 credits beyond Bachelor's. Ed.D.: 60 credits beyond Master's. *Faculty:* 1 full-time for technology courses. *Students:* 454. *Financial Assistance:* assistantships, student loans, limited scholarships. *Degrees Awarded 1997:* M.Ed., 120; Ed.D., 14; CAGS, 5.

MICHIGAN

Eastern Michigan University. 234 Boone Hall, Ypsilanti, MI 48197. (734)487-3260. Fax (734)484-6471. Anne Bednar, Prof., Coord., Dept. of Teacher Education. *Specialization:* M.A. in Educational Psychology with concentration in Educational Technology. *Admission Requirements:* Bachelor's degree, 2.75 undergraduate GPA or MAT score, 500 TOEFL. *Degree Requirements:* 30 semester hours, optional thesis worth 6 credits. *Faculty:* 3 full-time. *Students:* 15. *Financial Assistance:* graduate assistantship. *Degrees Awarded 1997:* 12.

Michigan State University. College of Education, 431 Erickson, East Lansing, MI 48824. (517)355-6684. Fax (517)353-6393. E-mail yelons@pilot.msu.edu. Dr. Stephen Yelon. *Specialization:* M.A. in Educational Technology and Instructional Design. *Admission Requirements:* Bachelor's degree, 800 TOEFL, recommendations, goal statement. *Degree Requirements:* 30 semester hours, certification exam, field experience. *Faculty:* 5 full-time. *Students:* approx. 45. *Financial Assistance:* some assistantships for highly qualified students. *Degrees Awarded 1997:* approx. 12.

University of Michigan. Department of Educational Studies, 610 East University, Ann Arbor MI 48109-1259. (313)763-4668. Fax (313)763-4663. E-mail carl.berger@umich.edu. Web site http://www.soe.umich.edu. Carl F. Berger, Chair. *Specializations:* M.Ed.; Ph.D. in Instructional Technology with concentrations in Science, Math, or Literacy. *Features:* Programs are individually designed. *Admission Requirements:* GRE, B.A. for M.Ed., Master's for Ph.D. *Degree Requirements:* M.Ed.: 30 hours beyond B.A. Ph.D.: 60 hours beyond B.A. or 30 hours beyond Master's plus comprehensive exams and dissertation. *Faculty:* 3 full-time, 6 part-time. *Students:* 35 full-time, 7 part-time. *Financial Assistance:* assistantships, grants, student loans, scholarships, internships. *Degrees Awarded 1997:* M.Ed., 15; Ph.D., 3.

Wayne State University. Wayne State University. 381 Education, Detroit, MI 48202. (313) 577-1728. Fax (313)577-1693. Web site http://www.coe.wayne.edu/InstructionalTechnology. E-mail rrichey@coe.wayne.edu. Rita C. Richey, Prof., Program Coord., Instructional Technology Programs, Div. of Administrative and Organizational Studies, College of Education. *Specializations*: M.Ed. degrees in Performance Improvement and Training, K-12 Educational Technology, and Interactive Technologies. Ed.D. and Ph.D. programs to prepare individuals for leadership in business, industry, health care, and the K-12 school setting as instructional design and development specialists; media or learning resources managers or consultants; specialists in instructional video; and computer-assisted instruction and multimedia specialists. The school also offers a six-year specialist degree program in Instructional Technology. *Features*: Guided experiences in instructional design and development activities in business and industry are available. *Admission Requirements*: Ph.D.: Master's degree, 3.5 GPA, GRE, MAT, strong professional recommendations, interview. *Degree Requirements*: M.Ed.: 36 semester hours, including required project; internship recommended. *Faculty:* 4.5 full-time, 5 part-time. *Students*: M.Ed., 400; doctoral, 125, most part-time. *Financial Assistance*: student loans, scholarships, and paid internships. *Degrees Awarded 1996–1997:* M.Ed., 47; doctoral, 9.

MINNESOTA

Mankato State University. MSU Box 20, P.O. Box 8400, Mankato, MN 56001-8400. (507)389-1965. Fax (507)389-5751. E-mail pengelly@mankato.msus.edu. Web site http://lme. mankato.msus.edu. Kenneth C. Pengelly, Assoc. Prof., Dept. of Library Media Education. *Specialization:* M.S. in Educational Technology with three tracks. *Admission Requirements:* Bachelor's degree, 3.0 undergraduate GPA. *Degree Requirements:* 51 qtr. credits, comprehensive exam. *Faculty:* 4 full-time. *Degrees Awarded 1997:* 12.

St. Cloud State University. College of Education, St. Cloud, MN 56301-4498. (612)255-2022. Fax (612)255-4778. E-mail jberling@tigger.stcloud.msus.edu. John G. Berling, Prof., Dir., Center for Information Media. *Specializations:* Master's degrees in Information Technologies, Educational Media, and Human Resources Development/Training. A Specialist degree is also offered. *Admission Requirements:* acceptance to Graduate School, written preliminary examination, interview. *Degree Requirements:* Master's: 51 qtr. hours with thesis; 54 qtr. hours, Plan B; 57 qtr. hours, portfolio; 200-hour practicum is required for media generalist licensure. Course work applies to Educational Media Master's program. *Faculty:* 7 full-time. *Students:* 15 full-time, 150 part-time. *Financial Assistance:* assistantships, scholarships. *Degrees Awarded 1997:* Master's, 12.

Walden University. 155 5th Avenue South, Minneapolis, MN 55401. (800)444-6795. E-mail www@waldenu.edu or info@waldenu.edu. Web sites http://www.waldenu.edu; http://www.waldenu.edu/ecti/ecti.html. Dr. Gwen Hillesheim, Chair. *Specializations:* M.S. in Educational Change and Technology Innovation. Ph.D. in Education in Learning and Teaching with specialization in Educational Technology. In 1998 a specialization in Distance Learning will be added. In addition, there is a generalist Ph.D. in Education in which students may choose and design their own areas of specialization. *Features:* delivered primarily on-line. *Admission Requirements:* accredited Bachelor's. Ph.D.: accredited Master's, goal statement, letters of recommendation. *Degree Requirements:* Master's: 45 credit curriculum, 2 brief residencies, Master's project. *Faculty:* 18 part-time. *Students:* 50 full-time, 53 part-time in Master's program. *Financial Assistance:* student loans, 3 fellowships with annual review. *Degrees Awarded 1997:* 4 (program instituted in 1996).

MISSOURI

Fontbonne College. 6800 Wydown Blvd., St. Louis, MO 63105. (314)889-1497. Fax (314)889-1451. E-mail mabkemei@fontbonne.edu. Dr. Mary K. Abkemeier, Chair. *Specialization:* M.S. in Computer Education. *Features:* small classes and course work immediately applicable to the classroom. *Admission Requirements:* 2.5 undergraduate GPA, 3 letters of recommendation. *Degree Requirements:* 33 semester hours, 3.0 GPA. *Faculty:* 2 full-time, 12 part-time. *Students:* 1 full-time, 110 part-time. *Financial Assistance:* grants. *Degrees Awarded 1997:* 29.

Northwest Missouri State University. Department of Computer Science/Information Systems, 800 University Ave., Maryville, MO 64468. (660)562-1600. E-mail pheeler@acad.nwmissouri.edu. Web site http://www.nwmissouri.edu/~csis. Dr. Phillip Heeler, Chairperson. *Specializations:* M.S. in School Computer Studies; M.S.Ed. in Educational Uses of Computers. *Features:* These degrees are designed for computer educators at the elementary, middle school, high school, and junior college level. *Admission Requirements:* 3.0 undergraduate GPA, 700 GRE (V+Q). *Degree Requirements:* 32 semester hours of graduate courses in computer science and/or educational computing courses. *Faculty:* 12 full-time, 4 part-time. *Students:* 5 full-time, 20 part-time. *Financial Assistance:* assistantships, grants, student loans, and scholarships. *Degrees Awarded 1997:* 8.

University of Missouri-Columbia. College of Education, 217 Townsend Hall, Columbia, MO 65211. (573)882-4546. Fax (573)884-4944. Jim Laffey, Assoc. Prof. (cilaffey@showme.missouri.edu). Gail Fitzgerald, Assoc. Prof. (spedfitz@showme.missouri.edu), Information Science and

Learning Technologies Program, School of Information Science & Learning Technologies. *Specializations*: Master's degree program prepares professionals to design, develop, and implement technology in educational settings. Ph.D. in Information Science & Learning Technologies prepares professionals to understand and influence learning, information organization and retrieval, and performance in diverse learning environments, especially through the design, development, and use of interactive technologies. An Education Specialist degree program is also available. *Features*: Master's program is competency-based. Graduates leave with the ability to plan, implement, and evaluate educational technology innovations, and to design, develop, and evaluate technology-based learning and performance support products. Ph.D. program includes a major in Information Science and Learning Technologies with two support areas (e.g., Educational Psychology and Computer Science), research tools, and R&D apprenticeship experiences. In addition to the competency-based objectives of the Master's program, doctoral graduates will be able to conduct systematic research which contributes to the knowledge base of learning, information organization and retrieval, performance, and technology. *Admission Requirements*: Master's: Bachelor's degree, MAT score. Ph.D.: 3.2 graduate GPA, 1500 GRE, letter of recommendation, statement of purpose. *Faculty*: Master's, 8 full-time, 10 part-time; Ph.D., 13 full-time, 18 part-time, plus selected faculty in related fields. *Students*: Master's, 20 full-time, 10 part-time; Ph.D., 20 full-time, 12 part-time. *Financial Assistance*: Master's: assistantships, grants, student loans, scholarships. Ph.D.: graduate assistantships with tuition waivers; numerous academic scholarships ranging from $200 to $18,000. *Degrees Awarded 1997*: Master's, 8; Ph.D., 6.

Webster University. Instructional Technology, St. Louis, MO 63119. (314)968-7490. Fax (314)968-7118. E-mail steinmpe@websteruniv.edu. Web site http://www.websteruniv.edu. Paul Steinmann, Assoc. Dean and Dir., Graduate Studies and Instructional Technology. *Specialization:* Master's degree (M.A.T.); State Certification in Media Technology is a program option. *Admission Requirements:* Bachelor's degree with 2.5 GPA. *Degree Requirements:* 33 semester hours (including 24 in media); internship required. *Faculty:* 5. *Students:* 7 full-time, 28 part-time. *Financial Assistance:* partial scholarships, minority scholarships, government loans, and limited state aid. *Degrees Awarded 1997:* 6.

MONTANA

University of Montana. School of Education, Missoula, MT 59812. (406)243-5785. Fax (406)243-4908. E-mail cjlott@selway.umt.edu. Dr. Carolyn Lott, Assoc. Prof. of Library/Media. *Specializations:* M.Ed. and Specialist degrees; K-12 School Library Media specialization with School Library Media Certification endorsement. *Admission Requirements:* (both degrees): letters of recommendation, 2.5 GPA. *Degree Requirements:* M.Ed.: 37 semester credit hours (18 overlap with library media endorsement). Specialist: 28 semester hours (18 overlap). *Faculty:* 2 full-time. *Students:* 5 full-time, 20 part-time. *Financial Assistance:* assistantships; contact the University of Montana Financial Aid Office. *Degrees Awarded 1997:* 14.

NEBRASKA

University of Nebraska at Kearney. Kearney, NE 68849-1260. (308)865-8833. Fax (308)865-8097. E-mail fredrickson@platte.unk.edu. Dr. Scott Fredrickson, Dir. of Instructional Technology. Web site http://www.unk.edu/departments/pte. *Specializations:* M.S. in Instructional Technology, M.S. in Educational Media, Specialist in Educational Media. *Admission Requirements:* M.S. and Specialist: GRE, acceptance into graduate school, approval of Instructional Technology Committee. *Degree Requirements:* M.S.: 36 credit hours, Master's comprehensive exam or field study. Specialist: 39 credit hours, field study. *Faculty:* 5 full-time, 10 part-time. *Students:* 62 full-time. *Financial Assistance:* assistantships, grants, student loans. *Degrees Awarded 1997:* M.S., 12; Ed.S., 0.

University of Nebraska-Omaha. Department of Teacher Education, College of Education, Kayser Hall 208D, Omaha, NE 68182. (402)554-2211. Fax (402)554-3491. E-mail hasel@cwis. unomaha.edu. Verne Haselwood, Prof., Educational Media Program in Teacher Education. *Specializations:* M.S. in Education, M.A. in Education, both with Educational Media concentration. *Degree Requirements:* 36 semester hours (including 24 in media), practicum; thesis optional. *Faculty:* 2 full-time, 4 part-time. *Students:* 10 full-time, 62 part-time. *Financial Assistance:* Contact Financial Aid Office. *Degrees awarded 1997:* 45.

NEVADA

University of Nevada. Counseling and Educational Psychology Dept., College of Education, Reno, NV 89557. (702)784-6327. Fax (702)784-1990. E-mail ljohnson@unr.edu. Web site http://www.unr.edu/unr/colleges/educ/cep/cepindex.html. Dr. LaMont Johnson, Program Coord., Information Technology in Education. Marlowe Smaby, Dept. Chair. *Specializations:* M.S. and Ph.D. *Admission Requirements:* Bachelor's degree, 2.75 undergraduate GPA, 750 GRE (V+Q). *Degree Requirements:* 36 semester credits, optional thesis worth 6 credits, comprehensive exam. *Faculty:* 2 full-time, 1 part-time. *Students:* M.S., 15; Ph.D., 10. *Degrees Awarded 1997:* M.S., 4; Ph.D., 1.

NEW JERSEY

Montclair State University. Department of Reading and Educational Media, Upper Montclair, NJ 07043. (973)655-7040. Fax (973)655-5310. Web site http://www.monclair.edu. Robert R. Ruezinsky, Dir. of Academic Technology. *Specializations:* No degree program exists. Two certification programs, A.M.S. and E.M.S, exist on the graduate level. *Certification Requirements:* 18-21 semester hours of media and technology are required for the A.M.S. program and 30-33 hours for the E.M.S. program. *Faculty:* 7 part-time. *Students:* 32 part-time.

Rutgers-The State University of New Jersey. Ph.D. Program in Communication, Information, and Library Studies, The Graduate School, New Brunswick, NJ 08901-1071. (732)932-7447. Fax (732)932-6916. Lea P. Stewart, Prof., Dir., Master's Program, Dept. of Library and Information Studies, School of Communication, Information and Library Studies. (732)932-9717. Fax (732)932-2644. Dr. David Carr, Chair. *Specializations:* M.L.S. degree with specializations in Information Retrieval, Technical and Automated Services, Reference, School Media Services, Youth Services, Management and Policy Issues, and Generalist Studies. Ph.D. programs in Communication; Information Systems, Structures, and Users; Information and Communication Policy and Technology; and Library and Information Services. The school also offers a six-year specialist certificate program. *Features:* Ph.D. Program provides doctoral-level course work for students seeking theoretical and research skills for scholarly and professional leadership in the information and communication fields. A course on multimedia structure, organization, access, and production is offered. *Admission Requirements:* Ph.D.: Master's degree in Information Studies, Communication, Library Science, or related field; 3.0 undergraduate GPA; GRE scores; TOEFL (for applicants whose native language is not English). *Degree Requirements:* M.L.S.: 36 semester hours, in which the hours for media vary for individual students; practicum of 150 hours. *Faculty:* M.L.S., 15 full-time, 12 adjunct; Ph.D., 43. *Students:* M.L.S., 97 full-time, 199 part-time; Ph.D., 104. *Financial Assistance:* M.L.S.: scholarships, fellowships, and graduate assistantships. Ph.D.: assistantships. *Degrees Awarded 1997:* Master's, 169; Ph.D., 4.

William Paterson University. College of Education, 300 Pompton Rd., Wayne, NJ 07470. (973)720-2140. Fax (973)720-2585. Web site http://pwcweb.wilpaterson.edu/wpcpages/library/ default.htp. Dr. Amy G. Job, Librarian, Assoc. Prof., Coord., Program in Library/Media, Curriculum and Instruction Dept. *Specializations:* M.Ed. for Educational Media Specialist, Associate Media Specialist, Ed.S. *Admission Requirements:* M.Ed.: certificate, 2.75 GPA, MAT or GRE scores, 1 year teaching experience. Ed.S.: certificate, 2.75 GPA. *Degree Requirements:* M.Ed.: 33 semester hours, including research projects and practicum. Ed.S.: 18 sem. hours. *Faculty:* 6

full-time, 2 part-time. *Students:* 30 part-time. *Financial Assistance:* limited. *Degrees Awarded 1997:* M.Ed., 4; Ed.S., 2.

NEW YORK

Buffalo State College. 1300 Elmwood Ave., Buffalo, NY 14222-1095. (716)878-4923. Fax (716)878-6677. E-mail nowakoaj@buffalostate.edu. Dr. Anthony J. Nowakowski, Program Coord. *Specializations:* M.S. in Education in Educational Computing. *Admission Requirements:* Bachelor's degree from accredited institution, 3.0 GPA in last 60 hours, 3 letters of recommendation. *Degree Requirements:* 33 semester hours (15 hours in computers, 12-15 hours in education, 3-6 electives); thesis or project. *Faculty:* 6 part-time. *Students:* 9 full-time, 74 part-time. *Degrees Awarded 1997:* 19.

Fordham University. Rose Hill Campus, 441 E. Fordham Rd., Bronx, NY 10458. (718)817-4860. Fax (718)817-4868. E-mail pcom@murray.fordham.edu. Web site http://www.fordham.edu. Robin Andersen, Department Chair; James Capo, Director of Graduate Studies. *Specializations:* M.A. in Public Communications. *Features:* internship or thesis option; full-time students can complete program in twelve months. *Admission Requirements:* 3.0 undergraduate GPA. *Degree Requirements:* 10 courses plus internship or thesis. *Faculty:* 8 full-time, 2 part-time. *Students:* 8 full-time, 22 part-time. *Financial Assistance:* assistantships, student loans, scholarships. *Degrees Awarded 1997:* 12.

Ithaca College. School of Communications, Ithaca, NY 14850. (607)274-1025. Fax (607)274-1664. E-mail Herndon@Ithaca.edu. Web site http://www.ithaca.edu/rhp/corpcomm/corpcomm1. Sandra L. Herndon, Prof., Chair, Graduate Corporate Communications; Roy H. Park, School of Communications. *Specialization:* M.S. in Corporate Communications. Students in this program find employment in such areas as instructional design, multimedia, public relations and marketing, and employee communication. The program can be tailored to individual career goals. *Admission Requirements:* 3.0 GPA, TOEFL 550 (where applicable). *Degree Requirements:* 36 semester hours, seminar. *Faculty:* 8 full-time. *Students:* approx. 25 full-time, 15 part-time. *Financial Assistance:* graduate assistantships, Park Graduate Fellowships. *Degrees Awarded 1997:* 18.

New York Institute of Technology. Dept. of Instructional Technology, Tower House, Old Westbury, NY 11568. (516)686-7777. Fax (516)686-7655. E-mail dplumer460@aol.com. Web site http://www.nyit.edu. Davenport Plumer, Chair, Depts. of Instructional Technology and Elementary Education. *Specializations:* M.S. in Instructional Technology; M.S. in Elementary Education; Specialist Certificates in Computers in Education, Distance Learning, and Multimedia (not degrees, but are earned after the first 18 credits of the Master's degree). *Features:* computer integration in virtually all courses; online courses; evening, weekend, and summer courses. *Admission Requirements:* Bachelor's degree from accredited college with 2.85 cumulative average. *Degree Requirements:* 36 credits with 3.0 GPA for M.S., 18 credits with 3.0 GPA for certificates. *Faculty:* 11 full-time, 42 part-time. *Students:* 112 full-time, 720 part-time. *Financial Assistance:* graduate assistantships, institutional and alumni scholarships, student loans. *Degrees Awarded 1997:* M.S., 42; Specialist, 37.

New York University. Educational Communication and Technology Program, School of Education, 239 Greene St., Suite 300, New York, NY 10003. (212)998-5520. Fax (212)995-4041. Web site http://www.nyu.edu. Francine Shuchat Shaw, Assoc. Prof., Dir.; Donald T. Payne, Assoc. Prof., Doctoral Advisor. *Specializations:* M.A., Ed.D., and Ph.D. in Education for the preparation of individuals to perform as instructional media designers, developers, producers, and researchers in education, business and industry, health and medicine, community services, government, museums, and other cultural institutions; and to teach in educational communications and instructional technology programs in higher education, including instructional television, microcomputers, multimedia, and telecommunications. The school also offers a post-M.A. 30-point Certificate of Advanced Study in Education. *Features:* emphasizes theoretical foundations, especially a cognitive perspective of learning and instruction, and their implications for designing media-based learning environments. All efforts focus on multimedia, instructional television, and telecommunications; participation in special research and production projects and field internships. *Admission Requirements:* M.A.: 3.0 undergraduate GPA, responses to essay questions, interview related to academic and professional goals. Ph.D.: 3.0 GPA, 1000 GRE, responses to essay questions, interview related to academic or professional preparation and career goals. For international students, 600 TOEFL and TWE. *Degree Requirements:* M.A.: 36 semester hours including specialization, elective courses, thesis, English Essay Examination. Ph.D.: 57 semester hours including specialization, foundations, research, content seminar, and elective course work; candidacy papers; dissertation; English Essay Examination. *Faculty:* 2 full-time, 10 part-time. *Students:* M.A.: 40 full-time, 35 part-time. Ph.D.: 14 full-time, 20 part-time. *Financial Assistance:* graduate and research assistantships, student loans, scholarships, and work assistance programs. *Degrees Awarded 1997:* M.A., 12; Ph.D., 2.

Pace University. Westchester Dept, School of Education, Bedford Road, Pleasantville, NY 10570. (914)773-3829, (914)773-3979. Fax (914)773-3521. Web site http://www.pace.edu. E-mail keyes@pacevm.dac.pace.edu. Dr. Carol Keyes, Chair. *Specialization:* M.S.E. in Curriculum and Instruction with a concentration in Computers. Computer courses are related to evaluating program packages, instructional applications of computer technology in educational software, and the Internet, multimedia in the classroom, and cognitive processing with computers. *Admission Requirements:* GPA 3.0, interview. *Degree Requirements:* 33-34 semester hours (15 in computers, 18 in educational administration). *Faculty:* 8 full-time, 50 part-time. *Students:* 60-70 part-time. *Financial Assistance:* assistantships, scholarships.

St. John's University. Division of Library and Information Science, 8000 Utopia Parkway, Jamaica, NY 11439. (718)990-6200. Fax (718)990-2071. E-mail libis@stjohns.edu. Web site http://www.stjohns.edu/gsas/dlis. James Benson, Dir. *Specializations:* M.L.S. with specialization in School Media. The school also offers a 24-credit Advanced Certificate program. *Admission Requirements:* 3.0 GPA, 2 letters of reference, statement of professional goals. *Degree Requirements:* 36 semester hours, comprehensive exam, practicum. *Faculty:* 7 full-time, 12 part-time. *Students:* 19 full-time, 78 part-time. *Financial Assistance:* 8 assistantships. *Degrees Awarded 1997:* Master's, 48.

State University College of Arts and Science at Potsdam. School of Education, 116 Satterlee Hall, Potsdam, NY 13676. (315)267-2535. Fax (315)267-4895. E-mail mlynarhc@potsdam.edu, Dr. Charles Mlynarczyk, Chair, education Department. *Specializations*: M.S. in Education in Instructional Technology and Media Management with concentrations in General K-12, Educational Communications Specialist, and Training and Development. *Degree Requirements*: 33 semester hours, including internship or practicum; culminating project required. *Faculty*: 3 full-time, 2 part-time. *Students:* 35 full-time, 105 part-time. *Financial Assistance*: student loans, student assistantships. *Degrees Awarded 1997*: 38.

State University of New York at Albany. School of Education, 1400 Washington Ave., Albany, NY 12222. (518)442-5032. Fax (518)442-5008. E-mail swan@cnsunix.albany.edu. Karen Swan (ED114A), contact person. *Specialization:* M.Ed. and Ph.D. in Curriculum and Instruction with specializations in Instructional Theory, Design, and Technology. *Admission Requirements:* Bachelor's degree, GPA close to 3.0; transcript, three letters of recommendation. Students desiring New York State permanent teaching certification should possess preliminary certification. *Degree Requirements:* M.Ed.: 30 semester hours with 15-18 credits in specialization. Ph.D.: 78 semester hours, internship, portfolio certification, thesis. *Faculty:* 13 full-time, 7 part-time. *Students:* 100 full-time, 350 part-time. *Financial Assistance:* fellowships, assistantships, grant, student loans, minority fellowships. *Degrees Awarded 1997:* M.Ed., 165; Ph.D., 7.

State University of New York at Stony Brook. Technology & Society, College of Engineering & Applied Sciences, SUNY at Stony Brook, Stony Brook, NY 11794-2250. (516)632-8763. (516)632-7809. E-mail dferguson@dts.tns.sunysb.edu. Web site: http://www.ceas.sunysb.edu/DTS.

Prof. David L. Ferguson, Contact Person. *Specializations:* Master's Degree in Technological Systems Management with concentration in Educational Computing. *Features:* emphasis on courseware design, multimedia and modeling, applications, and problem-solving. *Admission Requirements:* bachelor's degree in engineering, natural sciences, social sciences, mathematics, or closely related area; 3.0 undergraduate GPA, experience with computer applications or computer applications or use of computers in teaching. *Degree Requirements:* 30 semester credits, including two general technology core courses, 5 required educational computing courses, and 3 eligible electives. *Faculty:* 5 full-time, 3 part-time. *Students:* 10 full-time, 15 part-time. *Financial Assistance:* assistantships, grants, student loans. *Degrees Awarded 1997:* 5.

Syracuse University. Instructional Design, Development, and Evaluation Program, School of Education, 330 Huntington Hall, Syracuse, NY 13244-2340. (315)443-3703. Fax (315)443-5732. E-mail lltucker@sued.syr.edu. Web site http://www.idde.syr.edu. Philip L. Doughty, Prof., Chair. *Specializations:* M.S., Ed.D., and Ph.D. degree programs for Instructional Design of programs and materials, Educational Evaluation, Human Issues in Instructional Development, Media Production (including computers and multimedia), and Educational Research and Theory (learning theory, application of theory, and educational media research). Graduates are prepared to serve as curriculum developers, instructional developers, program and product evaluators, researchers, resource center administrators, communications coordinators, trainers in human resource development, and higher education instructors. The school also offers an advanced certificate program. *Features:* field work and internships, special topics and special issues seminar, student- and faculty-initiated minicourses, seminars and guest lecturers, faculty-student formulation of department policies, and multiple international perspectives. *Admission Requirements:* M.S.: undergraduate transcripts, recommendations, personal statement, interview recommended; TOEFL for international applicants; GRE recommended. Doctoral: relevant Master's degree from accredited institution, GRE (3 tests required) scores, recommendations, personal statement, TOEFL for international applicants; interview recommended. *Faculty:* 2 full-time, 4 part-time. *Degree Requirements:* M.S.: 36 semester hours, comprehensive exam and portfolio required. *Students:* M.S., 18 full-time, 22 part-time; doctoral, 25 full-time, 30 part-time. *Financial Assistance:* fellowships, scholarships, and graduate assistantships entailing either research or administrative duties in instructional technology. *Degrees Awarded 1997:* M.S., 21; doctorate, 6.

NORTH CAROLINA

Appalachian State University. Department of Leadership and Educational Studies, Boone, NC 28608. (704)262-2243. Fax (704)262-2128. E-mail Webbbh@appstate.edu. Web site http://www. ced.appstate.edu/ltl.html. John H. Tashner, Prof., Coord. *Specialization:* M.A. in Educational Media and Technology with three areas of concentration: Computers, Telecommunications, and Media Production. *Features:* IMPACT NC (business, university, and public school) partnership offers unusual opportunities. *Degree Requirements:* 36 semester hours (including 15 in Computer Education), internship; thesis optional. *Faculty:* 2 full-time, 1 part-time. *Students:* 10 full-time, 60 part-time. *Financial Assistance:* assistantships, grants, student loans. *Degrees Awarded 1997:* 15.

East Carolina University. Department of Library Studies and Educational Technology, Greenville, NC 27858-4353. (919)328-6621. Fax (919)328-4368. E-mail kesterd@mail.ecu.edu. Web site eastnet.educ.ecu.edu/schofed/lset. Dr. Diane D. Kester, Assoc. Prof., Chair. *Specializations:* Master of Library Science; Certificate of Advanced Study (Library Science); Master of Arts in Education (Instructional Technology Computers). *Features:* M.L.S. graduates are eligible for North Carolina School Media Coord. certification; C.A.S. graduates are eligible for North Carolina School Media Supervisor certification; M.A.Ed. graduates are eligible for North Carolina Instructional Technology-Computers certification. *Admission Requirements:* Master's: Bachelor's degree; C.A.S.: M.L.S. or equivalent degree. *Degree Requirements:* M.L.S.: 38 semester hours; M.A.Ed.: 36 semester hours; C.A.S.: 30 semester hours. *Faculty:* 9 full-time. *Students:* 7 full-time, 150 part-time. *Financial Assistance:* assistantships. *Degrees Awarded 1997:* M.L.S., 21; M.A.Ed., 19; C.A.S., 3.

North Carolina Central University. School of Education, 1801 Fayetteville St., Durham, NC 27707. (919)560-6692. Fax (919)560-5279. Dr. James N. Colt, Assoc. Prof., Coordinator., Graduate Program in Educational Technology. *Specialization:* M.A. with special emphasis on Instructional Development/Design. *Features:* Graduates are prepared to implement and utilize a variety of technologies applicable to many professional ventures, including institutions of higher education (college resource centers), business, industry, and professional schools such as medicine, law, dentistry, and nursing. *Admission Requirements:* undergraduate degree with at least 6 hours in education, GRE. *Degree Requirements*: 33 semester hours (including thesis). *Faculty*: 2 full-time, 1 part-time. *Students*: 25 full-time, 30 part-time. *Financial Assistance*: assistantships, grants, student loans. *Degrees Awarded 1997*: 7.

North Carolina State University. Department of Curriculum and Instruction, P.O. Box 7801, Raleigh, NC 27695-7801. (919)515-1779. Fax (919)515-6978. E-mail esvasu@unity.ncsu.edu. Dr. Ellen Vasu, Assoc. Prof. *Specializations:* M.Ed. and M.S. in Instructional Technology-Computers (program track within one Master's in Curriculum and Instruction). Ph.D. in Curriculum and Instruction with focus on Instructional Technology as well as other areas. *Admission Requirements:* Master's: undergraduate degree from an accredited institution, 3.0 GPA in major or in latest graduate degree program; transcripts; GRE or MAT scores; 3 references; goal statement, interview (see http://www2.ncsu.edu/ncsu/cep/ci/it/mitmain.html). Ph.D.: undergraduate degree from accredited institution, 3.0 GPA in major or latest graduate program; transcripts; recent GRE scores, writing sample, interview, three references, vita, goal statement (see http://www2.acs.ncsu.edu/grad/admision.htm). *Degree Requirements:* Master's: 36 semester hours, practicum, thesis optional; Ph.D.: 60 hours beyond Master's (minimum 33 in Curriculum and Instruction core, 27 in Research); other information available upon request. *Faculty:* 2 full-time. *Students:* Master's, 32 part-time; Ph.D., 6 part-time. *Degrees Awarded 1997:* Master's, 1; Ph.D., 2.

University of North Carolina. School of Information and Library Science (CB#3360), Chapel Hill, NC 27599. (919)962-8062, 962-8366. Fax (919)962-8071. E-mail daniel@ils.unc.edu. Web site http://www.ils.unc.edu. Evelyn H. Daniel, Prof., Coord., School Media Program. *Specialization:* Master of Science Degree in Library Science (M.S.L.S.) with specialization in school library media work. *Features:* rigorous academic program plus teaching practicum requirement; excellent placement record. *Admission Requirements:* competitive admission based on all three GRE components, undergraduate GPA, letters of recommendation, and student statement of career interest. *Degree Requirements:* 48 semester hours, comprehensive exam, Master's paper. *Faculty:* 18 full-time, 10 part-time. *Students:* 30 full-time, 20 part-time. *Financial Assistance:* grants, assistantships, student loans. *Degrees Awarded 1997* (School Media Certification): 30.

NORTH DAKOTA

Minot State University. 500 University Ave. W., Minot, ND 58707. (701)858-3250. Fax (701)839-6933. Dr. Jack L. Rasmussen, Dean of the Graduate School. *Specializations:* M.S. in Elementary Education (including work in educational computing); M.S. in Special Education with Specialization in Severe Multiple-Handicaps, Early Childhood Special Education, Education of the Deaf, and Learning Disabilities; M.S. in Communication Disorders, Specializations in Audiology and Speech Language Pathology. *Features:* All programs include involvement in computer applications appropriate to the area of study, including assistive technologies for persons with disabilities. Computer laboratories are available for student use in the library and various departments. Some courses are offered through the Interactive Video Network, which connects all universities in North Dakota. All programs have a rural focus and are designed to offer a multitude of practical experiences. *Admission Requirements:* $25 fee, three letters of recommendation, 300-word autobiography, transcripts, GRE in Communication Disorders or GMAT for M.S. in Management. *Degree Requirements:* 30 semester hours (hours in computers, education, and outside education vary according to program); written comprehensive exams; oral exams; thesis or project. *Faculty:* 10 full-time. *Students:* 61 full-time, 63 part-time. *Financial Assistance:* loans, assistantships, scholarships. *Degrees Awarded 1997:* M.S.: Elementary Education, 15; S.P.Ed., Severe

Multiple Handicaps, 4; S.P.Ed. Early Childhood Special Education, 4; Communication Disorders, 35; S.P.Ed. Learning Disabilities, 13.

OHIO

*Kent State University. 405 White Hall, Kent, OH 44242. (330)672-2294. Fax (330)672-2512. E-mail tchandler@emerald.edu.kent.edu. Web site http://amethyst.educ.kent./edu/itec. Dr. Theodore Chandler, Coord., Instructional Technology Program. *Specializations:* M.Ed. or M.A. in Instructional Technology, Instructional Computing, and Library/Media Specialist; Ph.D. in Educational Psychology with emphasis in Instructional Technology. *Features:* Programs are planned individually to prepare students for careers in elementary, secondary, or higher education, business, industry, government agencies, or health facilities. Students may take advantage of independent research, individual study, practica, and internships. *Admission Requirements:* Master's: Bachelor's degree with 2.75 undergraduate GPA. *Degree Requirements:* Master's: 34 semester hours; thesis required for M.A. *Faculty:* 5 full-time, 7 part-time. *Students:* 39. *Financial Assistance:* 6 graduate assistantships, John Mitchell and Marie McMahan Awards, 4 teaching fellowships. *Degrees Awarded 1996:* Master's, 14.

Ohio University. School of Curriculum and Instruction, 248 McCracken Hall, Athens, OH 45701-2979. (740)593-9826. Fax (740)593-0177. Sandra Turner, Chair. *Specialization:* M.Ed. in Computer Education and Technology. Ph.D. in Curriculum and Instruction with emphasis in Technology also available; call for details. *Admission Requirements:* Bachelor's degree, 2.5 undergraduate GPA, 35 MAT, 420 GRE (verbal), 400 GRE (quantitative), 550 TOEFL, three letters of recommendation. *Degree Requirements:* 54 qtr. credits, optional thesis worth 2-10 credits or alternative seminar and paper. Students may earn two graduate degrees simultaneously in education and in any other field. *Faculty:* 2 full-time, 1 part-time. *Students:* M.Ed., 60. *Financial Assistance:* assistantships. *Degrees to Be Awarded 1998:* 25.

*University of Cincinnati. College of Education, 401 Teachers College, ML002, Cincinnati, OH 45221-0002. (513)556-3577. Fax (513)556-2483. Web site http://uc.edu. Randall Nichols and Janet Bohren, Div. of Teacher Education. *Specialization:* M.A. or Ed.D. in Curriculum and Instruction with an emphasis on Instructional Design and Technology; Educational Technology degree programs for current professional, technical, critical, and personal knowledge. *Admission Requirements:* Bachelor's degree from accredited institution, 2.8 undergraduate GPA; conditional admission for candidates not meeting first two criteria possible. *Degree Requirements:* 54 qtr. hours, written exam, thesis or research project. *Faculty:* 3 full-time. *Students:* 20 full-time. *Financial Assistance:* scholarships, assistantships, grants. *Degrees Awarded 1996:* M.A., 12.

University of Toledo. Area of Education, 2801 West Bancroft, Toledo, OH 43606. (419)530-6176. Fax (419)530-7719. E-mail APATTER@UTNET.UTOLEDO.EDU. Web site http://carver.carver.utoledo. Dr. Lester J. Elsie, Dir. *Specializations:* Master's (M.Ed. and M.S.Ed.), Ed.S., doctorate (Ed.D., Ph.D.) degrees in Instructional Development, Library/Media Education, Instructional Computing, and Human Resources Development. *Admission Requirements:* Master's: 3.0 undergraduate GPA, GRE, recommendations; Ed.S.: Master's Degree, GRE, recommendations; doctorate: Master's degree, GRE, TOEFL, recommendations, entrance writing sample, and interview. *Degree Requirements:* Master's: 36 semester hours, Master's project; Ed.S.: 32 semester hours, internship; doctorate: 84 semester hours, dissertation. *Faculty:* 5 full-time, 1 part-time. *Students:* Master's, 10 full-time, 72 part-time; Ed.S., 2 full-time, 21 part-time; doctoral, 9 full-time, 56 part-time. *Financial Assistance:* assistantships, student loans, scholarships, work assistance program. *Degrees Awarded 1997:* Master's, 26; Ed.S., 3; doctoral, 3.

Wright State University. College of Education and Human Services, Dept. of Educational Leadership, 244 Millett Hall, Dayton, OH 45435. (513)873-2509 or (513)873-2182. Fax (513)873-4485. E-mail bmathies@desire.wright.edu or bonniekwsu@aol.com. Web site http:// www.ed.wright.edu. Dr. Bonnie K. Mathies, Asst. Dean, Communication and Technology. *Specializations:* M.Ed. in

Educational Media or Computer Education, or for Media Supervisor or Computer Coord.; M.A. in Educational Media or Computer Education; Specialist degree in Curriculum and Instruction with a focus on Educational Technology; Specialist degree in Higher Education with a focus on Educational Technology. *Admission Requirements:* completed application with nonrefundable application fee, Bachelor's degree from accredited institution, official transcripts, 2.7 overall GPA for regular status (conditional acceptance possible), statement of purpose, satisfactory scores on MAT or GRE. *Degree Requirements:* M.Ed. requires a comprehensive exam that includes a portfolio with videotaped presentation to the faculty. M.A. requires a 9-hour thesis. *Faculty:* 2 full-time, 12 part-time, including other university full-time faculty and staff. *Students:* approx. 5 full-time, approx. 70 part-time. *Financial Assistance:* 3 graduate assistantships in the College's Educational Resource Center; limited number of small graduate scholarships. *Degrees Awarded 1997:* 12.

OKLAHOMA

Southwestern Oklahoma State University. School of Education, 100 Campus Drive, Weatherford, OK 73096. (405)774-3140. Fax (405)774-7043. E-mail mossg@swosu.edu. Web site http://www.swosu.edu. Gregory Moss, Asst. Prof., Chair, Dept of School Service Programs. *Specialization:* M.Ed. in Library/Media Education. *Admission Requirements:* 2.5 GPA, GRE or GMAT scores, letter of recommendation, GPA x 150 + GRE = 1100. *Degree Requirements:* 32 semester hours (including 24 in library media). *Faculty:* 1 full-time, 4 part-time. *Students:* 17 part-time. *Degrees Awarded 1997:* 11.

*The University of Oklahoma. Instructional Psychology and Technology, Department of Educational Psychology, 321 Collings Hall, Norman, OK 73019. (405)325-2882. Fax (405)325-6655. E-mail psmith@ou.edu. Web site http://www.uoknor.edu/education/iptwww. Dr. Patricia L. Smith, Chair. *Specializations:* Master's degree with emphases in Educational Technology Generalist, Educational Technology, Computer Application, Instructional Design, Teaching with Technology; Dual Master's Educational Technology and Library and Information Systems. Doctoral degree in Instructional Psychology and Technology. *Features:* strong interweaving of principles of instructional psychology with design and development of Instructional Technology. Application of IP&T in K-12, vocational education, higher education, business and industry, and governmental agencies. *Admission Requirements:* Master's: acceptance by IPT program and Graduate College based on minimum 3.00 GPA for last 60 hours of undergraduate work or last 12 hours of graduate work; written statement that indicates goals and interests compatible with program goals. Doctoral: 3.0 in last 60 hours undergraduate, 3.25 GPA, GRE scores, written statement of background and goals. *Degree Requirements:* Master's: approx. 39 hours course work (specific number of hours dependent upon Emphasis) with 3.0 GPA; successful completion of thesis or comprehensive exam. Doctorate: see program description from institution or http://www.ou.education.iptwww. *Faculty:* 10 full-time. *Students:* Master's, 10 full-time, 200 part-time; doctoral, 10 full-time, 50 part-time. *Financial Assistance:* assistantships, grants, student loans, scholarships. *Degrees Awarded 1997:* Master's, 35; doctoral, 4.

OREGON

*Western Oregon State College. 345 N. Monmouth Ave., Monmouth, OR 97361. (503)838-8471. Fax (503)838-8228. E-mail engler@fsa.wosc.osshe.edu. Dr. Randall Engle, Chair. *Specialization:* M.S. in Information Technology. *Features:* offers advanced courses in library management, instructional development, multimedia, and computer technology. Additional course offerings in distance delivery of instruction and computer-interactive video instruction. *Admission Requirements:* 3.0 GPA, GRE or MAT. *Degree Requirements:* 45 qtr. hours; thesis optional. *Faculty:* 3 full-time, 6 part-time. *Students:* 6 full-time, 131 part-time. *Financial Assistance:* assistantships, grants, student loans, scholarship, work assistance. *Degrees Awarded 1997:* 12.

PENNSYLVANIA

Bloomsburg University. Institute for Interactive Technologies, 1210 McCormick Bldg., Blooms-burg, PA 17815. (717)389-4506. Fax (717)389-4943. E-mail tphillip@bloomu.edu. Web site http://iit.bloomu.edu. Dr. Timothy L. Phillips, contact person. *Specialization:* M.S. in Instructional Technology with emphasis on preparing for careers as interactive media specialists. The program is closely associated with the Institute for Interactive Technologies. *Features:* instructional design, authoring languages and systems, media integration, managing multimedia projects. *Admission Requirements:* Bachelor's degree. *Degree Requirements:* 33 semester credits (27 credits + 6 credit thesis, or 30 credits + three credit internship). *Faculty:* 4 full-time. *Students:* 53 full-time, 50 part-time. *Financial Assistance:* assistantships, grants, student loans. *Degrees Awarded 1997:* 50.

Clarion University of Pennsylvania. Becker Hall, Clarion, PA 16214. (814)226-2245. Fax (814)226-2186. Carmen S. Felicetti, Chair, Dept. of Communications. *Specialization:* M.S. in Communication with specialization in Training and Development. The curriculum is process and application oriented with basic courses in television and computer applications, Internet, Web, and HTML authoring. Major projects are team and client oriented with an emphasis on multimedia presentations. *Admission Requirements:* Bachelor's degree; 2.75 undergraduate GPA, MAT score. *Degree Requirements:* 36 semester credits (including 27 specific to Training and Development) with 3.0 GPA, optional thesis worth 6 credits. *Faculty:* 9 full-time. *Financial Assistance:* ten 1/4 time or five 20-hour graduate assistantships. *Degrees awarded 1997:* 5.

Drexel University. College of Information Science and Technology, Philadelphia, PA 19104. (215)895-2474. Fax (215)895-2494. Richard H. Lytle, Prof. and Dean. Web site http://www.cis.drexel.edu. *Specializations:* M.S. in Library and Information Science; M.S.I.S. in Information Systems. *Admission Requirements:* GRE scores; applicants with a minimum 3.2 GPA in last half of undergraduate credits may be eligible for admission without GRE scores. *Degree Requirements:* 60 credits. *Faculty:* 16 full-time, 47 adjunct. *Students:* M.S., 29 full-time, 174 part-time; M.S.I.S., 23 full-time, 275 part-time. *Degrees Awarded 1997:* M.S., 69; M.S.I.S, 57.

Lehigh University. College of Education, Bethlehem, PA 18015. (610)758-3231. Fax (610)758-6223. E-mail WMC0@LEHIGH.EDU. Web site http://www.lehigh.edu. Francis Harvey, Coord., Educational Technology Program. *Specializations:* M.S. degree with emphasis on design and development of interactive multimedia (both stand-alone and on the Web) for teaching and learning; Ed.D. in Educational Technology. *Admission Requirements:* M.S.: competitive; 2.75 undergraduate GPA or 3.0 graduate GPA, GRE recommended, transcripts, at least 2 letters of recommendation, statement of personal and professional goals, application fee. Ed.D.: 3.5 graduate GPA, GRE required. Deadlines are Jul 15 for fall admission, Dec 1 for spring admission, Apr 30 for summer admission. *Degree Requirements:* M.S.: 33 semester hours (including 8 in media); thesis option. Ed.D.: 48 hours past the Master's plus dissertation. *Faculty:* 3 full-time, 2 part-time. *Students:* M.S., 13 full-time, 34 part-time; Ed.D., 6 full-time, 32 part-time. *Financial Assistance:* university graduate and research assistantships, graduate student support as participants in R&D projects, employment opportunities in local businesses and schools doing design and development. *Degrees Awarded 1997:* M.S., 16; Ed.D., 3.

Pennsylvania State University. 314 Keller Bldg., University Park, PA 16802. (814)865-0473. Fax (814)865-0128. E-mail bgrabowski@psu.edu. B. Grabowski, Prof. in Charge. *Specializations:* M.Ed., M.S., D.Ed, and Ph.D. in Instructional Systems. Current teaching emphases are on Corporate Training, Interactive Learning Technologies, and Educational Systems Design. Research interests include multimedia, visual learning, educational reform, emerging technologies, and constructivist learning. *Features:* A common thread throughout all programs is that candidates have basic competencies in the understanding of human learning; instructional design, development, and evaluation; and research procedures. Practical experience is available in mediated independent learning, research, instructional development, computer-based education, and dissemination projects. *Admission Requirements:* D.Ed., Ph.D.: GRE, TOEFL, transcript, three letters of recommendation, writing sample, vita or resume, and letter of application detailing rationale for interest in the degree. *Degree Requirements:* M.Ed.: 33 semester hours; M.S.: 36 hours, including either a thesis or project paper; doctoral: candidacy exam, courses, residency, comprehensives, dissertation. *Faculty:* 10 full-time, 4 affiliate. *Students:* Master's, approx. 160; doctoral, 25 full-time, 20 part-time. *Financial Assistance:* assistantships, graduate fellowships, student aid loans, internships; assistantships on grants, contracts, and projects. *Degrees Awarded 1997:* master's, 9; doctoral, 10.

Rosemont College. Graduate Studies in Education, 1400 Montgomery Ave., Rosemont, PA 19010-1699. (610)526-2982; (800)531-9431 outside 610 area code. Fax (610)526-2964. E-mail roscolgrad@rosemont.edu. Web site http://techined.rosemont.edu/CSTE/info.html. Dr. Richard Donagher, Dir. *Specializations:* M.Ed. in Technology in Education, Certificate in Professional Study in Technology in Education. *Admission Requirements:* GRE or MAT scores. *Degree Requirements:* Completion of 12 units (36 credits) and comprehensive exam. *Faculty:* 7 full-time, 10 part-time. *Students:* 110 full- and part-time. *Financial Assistance:* graduate student grants, assistantships, Federal Stafford Loan Program. *Degrees Awarded 1997:* 13.

RHODE ISLAND

The University of Rhode Island. Graduate School of Library and Information Studies, Rodman Hall, Kingston, RI 02881-0815. (401)874-2947. Fax (401)874-4964. Web site http://www.uri.edu/artsci/lsc. W. Michael Novener, Assoc. Prof. and Dir. *Specializations:* M.L.I.S. degree with specialties in Archives, Law, Health Sciences, Rare Books, and Youth Services Librarianship. *Degree Requirements:* 42 semester-credit program offered in Rhode Island and regionally in Boston and Amherst, MA, and Durham, NH. *Faculty:* 7 full-time, 24 part-time. *Students:* 48 full-time, 196 part-time. *Financial Assistance:* graduate assistantships, some scholarship aid, student loans. *Degrees Awarded 1997:* 73.

SOUTH CAROLINA

University of South Carolina. Educational Psychology Department, Columbia, SC 29208. (803)777-6609. Dr. Margaret Gredler, Prof., Chair. *Specialization*: Master's degree. *Degree Requirements*: 33 semester hours, including instructional theory, computer design, and integrated media. *Faculty*: 3. *Students*: 10.

TENNESSEE

East Tennessee State University. College of Education, Dept. of Curriculum and Instruction., Box 70684, Johnson City, TN 37614-0684. (423)439-4186. Fax (423)439-8362. *Specializations:* M.Ed. in Instructional Media (Library), M.Ed. in Instructional Technology. *Admission Requirements:* Bachelor's degree from accredited institution, transcripts, personal essay; in some cases, GRE and/or interview. *Degree Requirements:* 39 semester hours, including 18 hours in instructional technology. *Faculty:* 2 full-time, 4 part-time. *Students:* 9 full-time, 40 part-time. *Financial Assistance:* scholarships, assistantships, aid for disabled. *Degrees Awarded 1997:* 12.

*University of Tennessee-Knoxville. College of Education, Education in the Sciences, Mathematics, Research, and Technology Unit, 319 Claxton Addition, Knoxville, TN 37996-3400. (423)974-4222 or (423)974-3103. Dr. Al Grant, Coord., Instructional Media and Technology Program. *Specializations:* M.S. in Ed., Ed.S., and Ed.D. under Education in Sciences, Mathematics, Research, and Technology; Ed.D. in Curriculum and Instruction, concentration in Instructional Media and Technology; Ph.D. under the College of Education, concentration in Instructional Media and Technology. *Features:* course work in media management, advanced software production, utilization, research, theory, psychology, instructional computing, television, and instructional development. Course work will also meet the requirements for state certification as

Instructional Materials Supervisor in the public schools of Tennessee. *Admission Requirements:* Send for Graduate Catalog, The University of Tennessee. *Degree Requirements:* M.S.: 33 semester hours; thesis optional. *Faculty:* 1 full-time, with additional assistance from Curriculum and Instruction and university faculty. *Students:* M.S., 4 part-time; Ed.S., 2 part-time.

TEXAS

Texas A&M University. Educational Technology Program, Dept. of Curriculum & Instruction, College of Education, College Station, TX 77843. (409)845-7276. Fax (409)845-9663. E-mail zellner@tamu.edu. Web site http://educ.coe.tamu.edu/~edtc/edtc/prog/edtcintro.html. Ronald D. Zellner, Assoc. Prof., Coord. *Specializations*: M.Ed. in Educational Technology; EDCI Ph.D. program with specializations in Educational Technology and in Distance Education; Ph.D. in Educational Psychology Foundations: Learning & Technology. The purpose of the Educational Technology Program is to prepare educators with the competencies required to improve the quality and effectiveness of instructional programs at all levels. A major emphasis is placed on multimedia instructional materials development and techniques for effective distance education and communication. Teacher preparation with a focus on field-based instruction and school to university collaboration is also a major component. The program goal is to prepare graduates with a wide range of skills to work as professionals and leaders in a variety of settings, including education, business, industry, and the military. *Features*: Program facilities include laboratories for teaching, resource development, and production. Computer, video, and multimedia development are supported in a number of facilities. The college and university also maintain facilities for distance education materials development and fully equipped classrooms for course delivery to nearby collaborative school districts and sites throughout the state. *Admission Requirements*: M.Ed.: Bachelor's degree, 800 GRE, 550 TOEFL; Ph.D.: 3.0 GPA, 800 GRE. *Degree Requirements*: M.Ed.: 39 semester credits, oral exam; Ph.D.: course work varies with student goals. *Faculty*: 4 full-time. *Students*: M.Ed., 25 full-time, 15 part-time; Ph.D., 2 full-time, 6 part-time. *Financial Assistance*: several graduate and teaching assistantships. *Degrees Awarded 1997*: M.Ed., 18.

Texas A&M University-Commerce. Department of Secondary and Higher Education, East Texas Station, Commerce, TX 75429-3011. (903)886-5607. Fax (903)886-5603. E-mail bob_mundayb@tamu-commerce.edu. Dr. Robert Munday, Prof., Head. *Specialization:* M.S. or M.Ed. degree in Learning Technology and Information Systems with emphases on Educational Computing, Educational Media and Technology, and Library and Information Science. *Admission Requirements:* 700 GRE (combined). *Degree Requirements:* 36 hours (Educational Computing): 30 hours in Educational Technology. M.S. (Educational Media and Technology): 21 hours in Educational Technology. M.S. (Library and Information Science): 15 hours in Library/Information Science, 12 hours in Educational Technology. *Faculty:* 3 full-time, 5 part-time. *Students:* 30 full-time, 150 part-time. *Financial Assistance:* graduate assistantships in teaching and research, scholarships, federal aid program.

Texas Tech University. College of Education, Box 41071, TTU, Lubbock, TX 79409. (806)742-1997, ext. 299. Fax (806)742-2179. Web site http://www.educ.ttu.edu. Dr. Robert Price, Dir., Instructional Technology. *Specializations:* M.Ed. in Instructional Technology (Educational Computing and Distance Education emphasis); Ed.D. in Instructional Technology. *Features:* Program is NCATE accredited and follows ISTE and AECT guidelines. *Admission Requirements:* M.Ed.: 850 GRE, 3.0 GPA on last 30 hours of undergraduate program; Ed.D.: 1050 GRE, 3.0 GPA on last 30 hours. *Degree Requirements:* M.Ed.: 39 hours (24 hours in educational technology, 15 hours in education or outside education); practicum. Ed.D.: 87 hours (45 hours in educational technology, 18 hours in education, 15 hours in resource area or minor); practicum. *Faculty:* 5 full-time. *Students:* M.Ed., 5 full-time, 25 part-time; Ed.D., 10 full-time, 10 part-time. *Financial Assistance:* teaching and research assistantships available ($8,500 for 9 months); small scholarships. *Degrees Awarded 1997:* Ed.D., 5; M.Ed., 6.

University of North Texas. College of Education, Box 311337, Denton, TX 76203-1337. (817)565-2057. Fax (817)565-2185. Web site http://www.cecs.unt.edu. Dr. Terry Holcomb, Program Coord., Computer Education and Cognitive Systems. Dr. Jon Young, Chair, Dept. of Technology and Cognition. *Specializations:* M.S. in Computer Education and Instructional Systems. *Admission Requirements:* 1000 GRE (400 verbal and 400 quantitative minimums). *Degree Requirements:* 36 semester hours (including 27 in Instructional Technology and Computer Education), comprehensive exam. *Faculty:* 7 full-time, 1 part-time. *Students:* 85, approx. half full-time. *Degrees Awarded 1997:* 30.

The University of Texas. College of Education, Austin, TX 78712. (512)471-5211. Fax (512)471-4607. Web site http://www.edb.utexas./coe/depts/ci/c&i.html. Paul Resta, Professor, Department of Curriculum and Instruction, College of Education, The University of Texas, Austin, Texas 78753. E-mail resta@mail.utexas.edu. *Specializations*: Master's degree (MA and MEd). Ph.D. program emphasizes research, design, and development of instructional systems and communications technology. *Features*: The program is interdisciplinary in nature, although certain competencies are required of all students. Programs of study and dissertation research are based on individual needs and career goals. Learning resources include a model Learning Technology Center, computer labs and classrooms, a television studio, and interactive multimedia lab. Many courses are offered cooperatively by other departments, including Radio-TV Film, Computer Science, and Educational Psychology. *Admission Requirements*: both degrees: 3.5 GPA, 1150 GRE. *Degree Requirements*: Master's: 30-36 semester hours depending on selection of program (21 in Instructional Technology plus research course); thesis option. A 6-hour minor is required outside the department. Ph.D.: written comprehensive and specialization exam with oral defense, dissertation with oral defense. *Faculty:* 3 full-time, 4 part-time. *Students*: approx. 45 master's, 55 doctoral. *Financial Assistance*: Assistantships may be available to develop instructional materials, teach undergraduate computer tools, and assist with research projects. There are also some paid internships. *Degrees Awarded 1997*: master's, 13; doctorate, 9.

UTAH

Brigham Young University. Department of Instructional Psychology and Technology, 201 MCKB, BYU, Provo, UT 84602. (801)378-5097. Fax (801)378-8672. E-mail paul_merrill@byu. edu. Web site http://www.byu.edu/acd1/ed/InSci/InSci.html. Paul F. Merrill, Prof., Chair. *Specializations:* M.S. degrees in Instructional Design, Research and Evaluation, and Multimedia Production. Ph.D. degrees in Instructional Design, and Research and Evaluation. *Features:* Course offerings include principles of learning, instructional design, assessing learning outcomes, evaluation in education, empirical inquiry in education, project management, quantitative reasoning, microcomputer materials production, multimedia production, naturalistic inquiry, and more. Students participate in internships and projects related to development, evaluation, measurement, and research. *Admission Requirements:* both degrees: transcript, 3 letters of recommendation, letter of intent, GRE scores. Apply by Feb 1. Students agree to live by the BYU Honor Code as a condition for admission. *Degree Requirements:* Master's: 38 semester hours, including prerequisite (3 hours), core courses (14 hours), specialization (12 hours), internship (3 hours), thesis or project (6 hours) with oral defense. Ph.D.: 94 semester hours beyond the Bachelor's degree, including: prerequisite and skill requirements (21 hours), core course (16 hours), specialization (18 hours), internship (12 hours), projects (9 hours), and dissertation (18 hours). The dissertation must be orally defended. Also, at least two consecutive 6-hour semesters must be completed in residence. *Faculty:* 9 full-time, 2 half-time. *Students:* master's, 25 full-time, 2 part-time; Ph.D., 47 full-time, 3 part-time. *Financial Assistance:* internships, tuition scholarships, loans, and travel to present papers. *Degrees Awarded 1997:* master's, 7; Ph.D., 3.

Utah State University. Department of Instructional Technology, College of Education, Logan, UT 84322-2830. (435)797-2694. Fax (435)797-2693. E-mail dsmellie@cc.usu.edu. Web site http://www.coe.usu:edu/it. Dr. Don C. Smellie, Prof., Chair. *Specializations:* M.S. and Ed.S. with concentrations in the areas of Instructional Development, Multimedia, Educational Technology, and Information Technology/School Library Media Administration. Ph.D. in Instructional Technology is offered for individuals seeking to become professionally involved in instructional development in corporate education, public schools, community colleges, and universities. Teaching and research in higher education is another career avenue for graduates of the program. *Features:* M.S. and Ed.S. programs in Information Technology/School Library Media Administration and Educational Technology are also delivered via an electronic distance education system. The doctoral program is built on a strong Master's and Specialist's program in Instructional Technology. All doctoral students complete a core with the remainder of the course selection individualized, based upon career goals. *Admission Requirements:* M.S. and Ed.S.: 3.0 GPA, a verbal and quantitative score at the 40th percentile on the GRE or 43 MAT, three written recommendations. Ph.D.: Master's degree in Instructional Technology, 3.0 GPA, verbal and quantitative score at the 40th percentile on the GRE, three written recommendations. *Degree Requirements:* M.S.: 39 sem. hours; thesis or project option. Ed.S.: 30 sem. hours if M.S. is in the field, 40 hours if not. Ph.D.: 62 total hours, dissertation, 3-sem. residency, and comprehensive examination. *Faculty:* 9 full-time, 7 part-time. *Students:* M.S., 70 full-time, 85 part-time; Ed.S., 6 full-time, 9 part-time; Ph.D., 15 full-time, 14 part-time. *Financial Assistance:* approx. 18 to 26 assistantships (apply by April 1). *Degrees Awarded 1997:* M.S., 42; Ed.S., 3; Ph.D., 3.

VIRGINIA

George Mason University. Center for Interactive Educational Technology, Mail Stop 4B3, 4400 University Dr., Fairfax, VA 22030-4444. (703)993-2051. Fax (703)993-2013. E-mail mbehrman@wpgate.gmu.edu. Web site http://gse.gmu.edu/depart/instred.htm. Dr. Michael Behrmann, Coord. of Instructional Technology Academic Programs. *Specializations:* M.Ed. in Curriculum and Instruction with tracks in Instructional Design and Development, Integration of Technology in Schools, and Assistive/Special Education Technology; M.Ed. in Special Education; Ph.D. with specialization in Instructional Technology or Special Education Technology. *Features:* Master's program started in 1983 and doctoral in 1984. Integration of Technology in Schools is a cohort program in which students are admitted in the Spring semester only. All other tracks admit throughout the year. *Admission Requirements:* teaching or training experience, introductory programming course or equivalent; introductory course in educational technology or equivalent. *Degree Requirements:* M.Ed. in Curriculum and Instruction: 36 hours; practicum, internship, or project. M.Ed. in Special Education: 36-42 hours. Ph.D.: 56-62 hours beyond Master's degree for either specialization. *Faculty:* 6 full-time, 5 part-time. *Students:* M.Ed. in Curriculum and Instruction: 5 full-time, 125 part-time. M.Ed. in Special Education: 10 full-time, 8 part-time. Ph.D.: 19 part-time. *Financial Assistance:* Assistantships and tuition waivers available for full-time graduate students. *Degrees Awarded 1997:* M.Ed. in Curriculum and Instruction, 17; M.Ed. in Special Education Technology, 6.

Radford University. Educational Studies Department, College of Education and Human Development, P.O. Box 6959, Radford, VA 24142. (540)831-5302. Fax (540)831-6053. E-mail ljwilson @runet.edu. Web site http://www.radford.edu. Dr. Linda J. Wilson. *Specialization:* M.S. in Education with Educational Media/Technology emphasis. *Features:* School Library Media Specialist licensure. *Admission Requirements:* Bachelor's degree, 2.7 undergraduate GPA. *Degree Requirements:* 36 semester hours, practicum; thesis optional. *Faculty:* 2 full-time, 3 part-time. *Students:* 2 full-time, 23 part-time. *Financial Assistance:* assistantships, grants, student loans, scholarships. *Degrees Awarded 1997:* 4.

University of Virginia. Department of Leadership, Foundations, and Policy, Curry School of Education, Ruffner Hall, Charlottesville, VA 22903. (804)924-7471. Fax (804)924-0747. E-mail jbbunch@virginia.edu. Web site http://curry.edschool.virginia.edu/curry/dept/edlf/instrtech. John B. Bunch, Assoc. Prof., Coord., Instructional Technology Program, Dept. of Leadership, Foundations and Policy Studies. *Specializations:* M.Ed., Ed.S., Ed.D., and Ph.D. degrees with focal areas in Media Production, Interactive Multimedia, and K-12 Educational Technologies. *Admission Requirements:* undergraduate degree from accredited institution in any field, undergraduate GPA

3.0, 1000 GRE (V+Q), 600 TOEFL. Admission application deadline is March 1st of each year for the fall semester for both Master's and doctoral degrees. *Degree Requirements:* M.Ed.: 36 semester hours, comprehensive examination. Ed.S.: 60 semester hours beyond undergraduate degree. Ed.D.: 54 semester hours, dissertation, at least one conference presentation or juried publication, comprehensive examination, residency; Ph.D.: same as Ed.S. with the addition of 18 semester hours. For specific degree requirements, see Web site, write to the address above, or refer to the UVA *Graduate Record. Faculty:* 4 full-time, 1 part-time. *Students:* M.Ed., 24; Ed.D, 3; Ph.D., 15. *Financial Assistance:* some graduate assistantships and scholarships are available on a competitive basis. *Degrees Awarded 1996:* master's, 4; doctorate, 2.

Virginia Polytechnic Institute and State University (Virginia Tech). College of Human Resources and Education, 220 War Memorial Hall, Blacksburg, VA 24061-0341. (540)231-5587. Fax (540)231-9075. Web site http://www.chre.vt.edu/Admin/IT. E-mail moorem@vt.edu. David M. (Mike) Moore, Program Area Leader, Instructional Systems Development, Dept. of Teaching and Learning. *Specializations*: M.A., Ed.D., and Ph.D. in Instructional Technology. Preparation for education, higher education, faculty development, business, and industry. *Features*: Areas of emphasis are Instructional Design, Educational Computing, Evaluation, and Media Management and Development. Facilities include two computer labs (70 IBM and Macintosh computers), plus interactive video, speech synthesis, telecommunication labs, distance education classroom, and computer graphics production areas. *Admission Requirements*: Ed.D. and Ph.D.: 3.3 GPA from Master's degree, GRE scores, interview, three letters of recommendation, transcripts. MA.: 3.0 GPA Undergraduate. *Degree Requirements*: Ph.D.: 96 hrs above B.S., 2 year residency, 12 hrs. research classes, 30 hrs. dissertation; Ed.D.: 90 hrs. above B.S., 1 year residency, 12 hrs. research classes; MA.: 30 hrs. above B.S. *Faculty*: 8 full-time, 5 part-time. *Students*: 35 full-time and 10 part-time at the doctoral level. 10 full-time and 15 part-time at the master's level. *Financial Assistance*: 10 assistantships, limited tuition scholarships. *Degrees Awarded 1997*: doctoral, 3; master's, 2.

Virginia State University. School of Liberal Arts & Education, Petersburg, VA 23806. (804)524-6886. Vykuntapathi Thota, Chair, Dept. of Education. *Specializations:* M.S., M.Ed. in Educational Technology. *Features:* Video Conferencing Center and PLATO Laboratory, internship in ABC and NBC channels. *Degree Requirements:* 30 semester hours plus thesis for M.S.; 33 semester hours plus project for M.Ed.; comprehensive exam. *Faculty:* 1 full-time, 2 part-time. *Students:* 8 full-time, 50 part-time. *Financial Assistance:* scholarships through the School of Graduate Studies.

WASHINGTON

Eastern Washington University. Department of Computer Science, Cheney, WA 99004-2431. (509)359-7093. Fax (509)359-2215. E-mail LKieffer@ewu.edu. Dr. Linda M. Kieffer, Assoc. Prof. of Computer Science. *Specializations:* M.Ed. in Computer and Technology Supported Education; M.S. in Computer Education (Interdisciplinary). Master's program started in 1983. *Admission Requirements:* 3.0 GPA for last 90 qtr. credits. *Degree Requirements:* M.S.: 52 qtr. hours (30 hours in computers, 15 hours outside education; the hours do not total to 52 because of freedom to choose where Methods of Research is taken, where 12 credits of supporting courses are taken, and where additional electives are taken); research project with formal report. M.Ed.: 52 qtr. hours (28 hours in computer education, 16 hours in education, 8 hours outside education). *Features:* Many projects involve the use of high-level authoring systems to develop educational products, technology driven curriculum, and Web projects. *Faculty:* 3 full-time. *Students:* approx. 35. *Financial Assistance:* some research and teaching fellowships. *Degrees Awarded 1997:* 3.

University of Washington. College of Education, 115 Miller Hall, Box 353600 Seattle, WA 98195-3600. (206)543-1847. Fax (206)543-8439. E-mail stkerr@u.washington.edu. Web site http://www.educ.washington.edu/COE/c-and-i/c_and_i_med_ed_tech.htm. Stephen T. Kerr, Prof. of Education. *Specializations:* M.Ed., Ed.D., and Ph.D. for individuals in business, industry, education, public schools, and organizations concerned with education or communication (broadly defined). *Features:* emphasis on instructional design as a process of making decisions about the shape of instruction; additional focus on research and development in such areas as message design (especially graphics and diagrams); electronic information systems; interactive instruction via videodisc, multimedia, and computers. *Admission Requirements:* M.Ed.: goal statement (2-3pp.), writing sample, 1000 GRE (verbal plus quantitative), undergraduate GPA indicating potential to successfully accomplish graduate work. Doctoral: GRE scores, letters of reference, transcripts, personal statement, Master's degree or equivalent in field appropriate to the specialization with 3.5 GPA, two years of successful professional experience and/or experience related to program goals. *Degree Requirements:* M.Ed.: 45 qtr. hours (including 24 in media); thesis or project optional. Ed.D.: see www.educ.washington.edu/COE/admissions/DoctorOf EducationProgram.htm. Ph.D.: see www.educ.washington.edu/COE/admissions/DoctorOfPhilosophy Degree.htm. *Faculty:* 2 full-time, 3 part-time. *Students:* 12 full-time, 32 part-time; 26 M.Ed., 18 doctoral. *Financial Assistance:* assistantships awarded competitively and on basis of program needs; other assistantships available depending on grant activity in any given year. *Degrees Awarded 1997:* M.Ed., 10; doctorate, 4.

Western Washington University. Woodring College of Education, Instructional Technology, MS 9087, Bellingham, WA 98225-9087. (360)650-3387. Fax (360)650-6526. E-mail lblack@wce. wwu.edu. Web site http://www.wce.wwu.edu/depts/IT. Dr. Les Blackwell, Prof., Program Chair. *Specializations:* M.Ed. with emphasis in Instructional Technology in Adult Education, Special Education, Elementary Education, and Secondary Education. *Admission Requirements:* 3.0 GPA in last 45 qtr. credit hours, GRE or MAT scores, 3 letters of recommendation, and, in some cases, 3 years of teaching experience. *Degree Requirements:* 48-52 qtr. hours (24-28 hours in instructional technology; 24 hours in education-related courses, thesis required; internship and practicum possible). *Faculty:* 5 full-time, 8 part-time. *Students:* 5 full-time, 13 part-time. *Financial Assistance:* assistantships, student loans, scholarships. *Master's Degrees Awarded 1997:* 5.

WISCONSIN

Edgewood College. Department of Education, 855 Woodrow St., Madison, WI 53711-1997. (608)257-4861, ext. 2293. Fax (608)259-6727. E-mail schmied@edgewood.edu. Web site http://www.edgewood.edu. Dr. Joseph E. Schmiedicke, Chair, Dept. of Education. *Specializations:* M.A. in Education with emphasis on Instructional Technology. Master's program started in 1987. *Features:* classes conducted in laboratory setting with emphasis on applications and software. *Admission Requirements:* 2.75 GPA. *Degree Requirements:* 36 semester hours. *Faculty:* 2 full-time, 3 part-time. *Students:* 5 full-time, 135 part-time. *Financial Assistance:* grants, student loans. *Degrees Awarded 1997:* 12.

University of Wisconsin-La Crosse. Educational Media Program, Rm. 235C, Morris Hall, La Crosse, WI 54601. (608)785-8121. Fax (608)785-8128. E-mail viner@mail.uwlax.edu. Dr. Russell Phillips, Dir. *Specializations:* M.S. in Professional Development with specializations in Initial Instructional Library Specialist, License 901; Instructional Library Media Specialist, License 902 (39 credits). *Degree Requirements:* 30 semester hours, including 15 in media; no thesis. *Faculty:* 2 full-time, 4 part-time. *Students:* 21. *Financial Assistance:* guaranteed student loans, graduate assistantships.

University of Wisconsin-Madison. Dept. of Curriculum and Instruction, School of Education, 225 N. Mills St., Madison, WI 53706. (608)263-4672. Fax (608)263-9992. E-mail adevaney @facstaff.wisc.edu. Ann De Vaney, Prof. *Specializations:* M.S. degree and State Instructional Technology License; Ph.D. programs to prepare college and university faculty. *Features:* The program is coordinated with media operations of the university. Traditional instructional technology courses are processed through a social, cultural, and historical frame of reference. Current curriculum emphasizes communication and cognitive theories, critical cultural studies, and theories of textual analysis and instructional development. Course offered in the evening. *Admission Requirements:* Master's and Ph.D.: previous experience in Instructional Technology preferred, previous teaching experience, 3.0 GPA on last 60 undergraduate credits, acceptable scores on GRE, 3.0 GPA on all graduate work. *Degree Requirements:* M.S.: 24 credits plus thesis and exam; Ph.D.: 3 years of residency beyond the Bachelor's (Master's degree counts for one year; one year must be full-time), major, minor, and research requirements, preliminary exam, dissertation, and oral exam. *Faculty:* 3 full-time, 1 part-time. *Students:* M.S., 33; Ph.D., 21. Most master's candidates are part-time; half of Ph.D. students are full-time. *Financial Assistance:* several stipends of approx. $1000 per month for 20 hours of work per week; other media jobs are also available. *Degrees Awarded 1997:* M.S., 16; Ph.D., 3.

Part Seven
Mediagraphy
Print and Nonprint Resources

Introduction

CONTENTS

This resource lists media-related journals, books, ERIC documents, journal articles, and nonprint media resources of interest to practitioners, researchers, students, and others concerned with educational technology and educational media. The primary goal of this section is to list current publications in the field. The majority of materials cited here were published in 1997 or early 1998. Media-related journals include those listed in past issues of *EMTY* and new entries in the field.

It is not the intention of the authors for this chapter to serve as a specific resource location tool, although it may be used for that purpose in the absence of database access. Rather, readers may peruse the categories of interest in this chapter to gain an idea of recent developments within the field. For archival purposes, this chapter serves as a snapshot of the field in 1997. Readers must bear in mind that technological developments occur well in advance of publication, and should take that fact into consideration when judging the timeliness of resources listed in this chapter.

SELECTION

Items were selected for the Mediagraphy in several ways. The ERIC (Educational Resources Information Center) database was the source for most ERIC document and journal article citations. Others were reviewed directly by the editors. Items were chosen for this list when they met one or more of the following criteria: reputable publisher; broad circulation; coverage by indexing services; peer review; and filled a gap in the literature. The editors chose items on subjects that seem to reflect the Instructional Technology field as it is today. Due to the increasing tendency for media producers to package their products in more that one format and for single titles to contain mixed media, titles are no longer separated by media type. The editors make no claims as to the comprehensiveness of this list. It is, instead, intended to be representative.

OBTAINING RESOURCES

Media-Related Periodicals and Books. Publisher, price, and ordering/subscription address are listed wherever available.

ERIC Documents. ERIC documents can be read and often copied from their microfiche form at any library holding an ERIC microfiche collection. The identification number beginning with ED (for example, ED 332 677) locates the document in the collection. Copies of most ERIC documents can also be ordered from the ERIC Document Reproduction Service. Prices charged depend upon format chosen (microfiche or paper copy), length of the document, and method of shipping. Online orders, fax orders, and expedited delivery are available.

To find the closest library with an ERIC microfiche collection, contact:

ACCESS ERIC
1600 Research Blvd.
Rockville, MD 20850-3172
1-800-LET-ERIC (538-3742)
E-mail: acceric@inet.ed.gov

To order ERIC documents, contact:

ERIC Document Reproduction Service (EDRS)
7420 Fullerton Rd., Suite 110
Springfield, VA 22153-2852
Voice: 1-800-443-ERIC (443-3742), 703-440-1400
Fax: 703-440-1408
E-mail: service@edrs.com.

Journal Articles. Photocopies of journal articles can be obtained in one of the following ways: 1) from a library subscribing to the title; 2) through interlibrary loan; 3) through the purchase of a back issue from the journal publisher; or 4) from an article reprint service such as UMI.

UMI Information Store
500 Sansome St., Suite 400
San Francisco, CA 94111
1-800-248-0360 (toll-free in U.S. and Canada)
415-433-5500 (outside U.S. and Canada)
E-mail: orders@infostore.com

Journal articles can also be obtained through the Institute for Scientific Information (ISI).

ISI Document Solution
P.O. Box 7649
Philadelphia, PA 19104-3389
215-386-4399
Fax: 215-222-0840 or 215-386-4343
E-mail: ids@isinet.com

ARRANGEMENT

Mediagraphy entries are classified according to major subject emphasis under the following headings:

- Artificial Intelligence, Robotics, and Electronic Performance Support Systems
- Computer-Assisted Instruction
- Distance Education
- Educational Research
- Educational Technology
- Information Science and Technology
- Innovation
- Instructional Design and Development
- Interactive Multimedia
- Libraries and Media Centers
- Media Technologies
- Professional Development
- Simulation, Gaming, and Virtual Reality
- Special Education and Disabilities
- Telecommunications and Networking

Mediagraphy

ARTIFICIAL INTELLIGENCE, ROBOTICS, AND ELECTRONIC PERFORMANCE SUPPORT SYSTEMS

Bastiaens, T. J., & others. (1997). **Electronic performance support for telephone operators**. [ED 406 569]. Describes an evaluation of an EPSS for telephone operators.

du Boulay, B., & Mizoguchi, R. (1997). **Artificial intelligence in education**. [Book, 702pp., $108]. IOS Press, van Diemenstraat 94, 1013 CN Amsterdam, market@iospress.nl. Contains papers on topics that explore knowledge and media in learning systems, including computer-supported collaboration, student modeling, and distributed intelligent tutoring.

International Journal of Robotics Research. MIT Press, Journals, 55 Hayward St., Cambridge, MA 02142. [Bi-mo., $82 indiv. (foreign $140), $230 inst. (foreign $252), $50 students and retired (foreign $72)]. Interdisciplinary approach to the study of robotics for researchers, scientists, and students.

Journal of Artificial Intelligence in Education. Association for Advancement of Computing in Education, Box 2966, Charlottesville, VA 22902-2966. [Q., $65 indiv. (foreign $75), $103 inst. ($113 foreign)]. International journal publishes articles on how intelligent computer technologies can be used in education to enhance learning and teaching. Reports on research and developments, integration, and applications of artificial intelligence in education.

Knowledge-Based Systems. Elsevier Science Inc., P.O. Box 882, Madison Square Station, New York, NY 10159-0882. [Q., $641]. Interdisciplinary applications-oriented journal on fifth-generation computing, expert systems, and knowledge-based methods in system design.

Minds and Machines. Kluwer Academic Publishers, Box 358, Accord Station, Hingham, MA 02018-0358. [Q., $333.50, American inst.]. Discusses issues concerning machines and mentality, artificial intelligence, epistemology, simulation, and modeling.

COMPUTER-ASSISTED INSTRUCTION

Abramovich, S., & Nabors, W. (1997). Spreadsheets as generators of new meanings in middle school algebra. **Computers in the Schools, 13** (1-2), 13-25. Describes how using spreadsheets helped seventh-grade algebra students develop problem-solving skills. Topics include the functional dualism of the spreadsheet as a text, uniting enactive and numeric modeling of word problems, new meanings and reciprocal learning, learning through problem "posing," higher levels of thinking, and decreasing intellectual risk and increasing dialogic exchange in a computerized classroom.

Apple Library Users Group Newsletter. Library Users Group, Infinite Way, MS3042A, Cupertino, CA 95014. [4/yr., free]. For people interested in using Apple and Macintosh computers in libraries and information centers.

Berge, Z. (1997). Characteristics of online teaching in post-secondary, formal education. **Educational Technology, 37** (3), 35, 38-47. Reports on a survey of 42 post-secondary teachers about online instructional methods and strategies. The results are discussed in terms of Yelon's instructional principles: meaningfulness, prerequisites, open communication, organized essential ideas, learning aids, novelty, modeling, active appropriate practice, pleasant conditions and consequences, and consistency. Suggests areas for further research in computer-mediated, online teaching.

Bull, S. (1997). Promoting effective learning strategy use in computer assisted language learning (CALL). **Computer Assisted Language Learning, 10** (1), 3-39. Presents research on second language learning strategies, including both those with a general application and those relating to computer assisted language learning (CALL). Findings reveal that the issue of learning strategies looms as an important topic and that a detailed consideration of them in CALL is feasible.

BYTE. Box 550, Hightstown, NJ 08520-9886. [Mo., $29.95 US, $34.95 Canada and Mexico, $50 elsewhere]. Current articles on microcomputers provide technical information as well as information on applications and products for business and professional users.

CALICO Journal. Computer Assisted Language and Instruction Consortium, 014 Language Center, Box 90264, Duke University, Durham, NC 27708-0267. [Q., $35 indiv., $65 inst., $125 corps.]. Provides information on the applications of technology in teaching and learning languages.

Cates, W. M., & Goodling, S. C. (1997). The relative effectiveness of learning options in multimedia computer-based fifth-grade spelling instruction. **Educational Technology Research and Development, 45** (2), 27-46. A study of 38 fifth-grade students investigated the effectiveness of two interactive multimedia instructional spelling programs, one offering behaviorist-visual learning options and the other offering cognitivist-phonological learning options. Both groups showed increased spelling ability, though neither program outperformed the other, suggesting computer-based spelling instruction can be an effective instructional tool.

Christmann, E., & others. (1997). Progressive comparison of the effects of computer-assisted instruction on the academic achievement of secondary students. **Journal of Research on Computing in Education, 29** (4), 325-27. Describes a study that used meta-analysis to compare the academic achievement during a 12-year period of secondary students who were instructed through traditional methods, traditional methods supplemented with computer-assisted instruction (CAI), or CAI alone. Results were compared with earlier research and indicate that the effect of CAI on academic achievement has declined.

Cognition and Technology Group at Vanderbilt University. (1997). **The Jasper Project: Lessons in curriculum, instruction, and professional development**. [Book, 200pp., $19.95]. Learning, Inc., 10 Industrial Ave., Mahwah, NY 07430. Describes the Jasper Project from a developmental perspective; summarizes the Jasper episodes and addresses issues of curriculum integration.

Computer Book Review. 735 Ekekela Pl., Honolulu, HI 96817. [6/yr., $30]. Provides critical reviews of books on computers and computer-related subjects.

Computers and Composition. Ablex Publishing Corp., 55 Old Post Rd., No. 2, P.O. Box 5297, Greenwich, CT 06831-0504, (203)661-7602, fax (203)661-0792. [3/yr., $40 indiv., $79.50 inst.]. International journal for teachers of writing focuses on the use of computers in writing instruction and related research and dialogue.

Computers and Education. Elsevier Science, 660 White Plains Rd., Tarrytown, NY 10591-5153. [8/yr., $945]. Presents technical papers covering a broad range of subjects for users of analog, digital, and hybrid computers in all aspects of higher education.

Computers and the Humanities. Kluwer Academic Publishers Group, P.O. Box 358, Accord Station, Hingham, MA 02018-0358. [Bi-mo., $310.50 US inst.]. Contains papers on computer-aided studies, applications, automation, and computer-assisted instruction.

Computers in Human Behavior. Pergamon Press, 660 White Plains Rd., Tarrytown, NY 10591-5153. [Q., $638]. Addresses the psychological impact of computer use on individuals, groups, and society.

Computers in the Schools. Haworth Press, 10 Alice St., Binghamton, NY 13904-1580, (800)HAWORTH, fax (800)895-0582, getinfo@haworth.com, http://www.haworth.com. [Q., $40 indiv., $85 inst., $250 libr.]. Features articles that combine theory and practical applications of small computers in schools for educators and school administrators.

Dr. Dobb's Journal. Miller Freeman Inc., 600 Harrison St., San Francisco, CA 94107. [Mo., $34.95 US, $45 Mexico and Canada, $70 elsewhere]. Articles on the latest in operating systems, programming languages, algorithms, hardware design and architecture, data structures, and tele-communications; in-depth hardware and software reviews.

Education Technology News. Business Publishers, Inc., 951 Pershing Dr., Silver Spring, MD 20910-4464. [Bi-w., $286]. For teachers and those interested in educational uses of computers in the classroom. Features articles on applications and educational software.

Electronic Learning. Scholastic Inc., 555 Broadway, New York, NY 10012, (212)505-4900. [6/yr., $23.95, single copy, $4]. Features articles on applications and advances of technology in education for K-12 and college educators and administrators.

Hack, L., & Smey, S. (1997). A survey of Internet use by teachers in three urban Connecticut schools. **School Library Media Quarterly, 25** (3), 151-55. This study focused on two elementary schools and a high school in urban Connecticut to determine the number of teachers who had Internet access at home, and their proficiency and frequency of Internet use; levels of Internet access in the schools; integration of Internet into the curriculum; and possible future Internet use.

Holsbrink-Engels, G. A., & Geralien, A. (1997). Computer-based role-playing for interpersonal skills training. **Simulation & Gaming, 28** (2), 164-80. Examines design and evaluation of computer-based role-playing. University students (n=41) were divided into two groups to use instructional programs with and without computer-based role-playing. Findings indicated that computer-based role-playing enhanced interpersonal skills development by employing a conversational model, offering opportunities for reflection, performing protagonist roles, and capturing individual contribution and learning.

Home Office Computing. Box 51344, Boulder, CO 80321-1344. [Mo., $19.97, foreign $27.97]. For professionals who use computers and conduct business at home.

InfoWorld. InfoWorld Publishing, 155 Bovet Rd., Suite 800, San Mateo, CA 94402. [W., $145]. News and reviews of PC hardware, software, peripherals, and networking.

Ivers, K. S., & Barron, A. E. (1997). Training for telecommunications: Examining the effects of video- and computer-based instruction on preservice teachers' achievement, near-transfer performance, and perception of instruction. **Journal of Computing in Teacher Education, 13** (3), 23-29. Discusses the results of two different delivery methods (video and computer-based instruction) for teaching preservice educators how to use an electronic mail system. Analysis of student questionnaires and achievement found significant differences between the methods on students' perceptions of instruction and near-transfer performance (favoring the computer-based instruction group).

Johnson, D. (1997). The effect of computer-assisted instruction on the vocabulary knowledge of college freshmen. **Research and Teaching in Developmental Education, 13** (2), 31-44. Presents a study of outcomes of three methods of vocabulary instruction (i.e., the use of contextual cues, the use of definitions, and a mixed approach) when supplemented by computer-assisted instruction (CAI) using a mixed approach. Reports that CAI was effective with contextual only, definition only, and mixed approaches.

Johnson, J. M., ed. (1997). **1997 educational software preview guide**. [Book, 128pp., $14.95]. ISTE, University of Oregon, 1787 Agate St., Eugene, OR 97403-1923, (800)336-5191, cust_svc@ccmail.uoregon.edu. Designed for educators seeking software for preview, this guide lists more than 700 titles of favorably reviewed software for K-12 classroom use.

Journal of Computer Assisted Learning. Blackwell Scientific Publications, Journal Subscription Dept., Marstan Book Services, Box 87, Oxford OX2 0DT, England. [Q., $307 inst.]. Articles and research on the use of computer-assisted learning.

Journal of Educational Computing Research. Baywood Publishing Co., 26 Austin Ave., P.O. Box 337, Amityville, NY 11701. [8/yr. (2 vols., 4 each), $95 indiv. (per vol.), $195 inst. (per vol.)]. Presents original research papers, critical analyses, reports on research in progress, design and development studies, article reviews, and grant award listings.

Journal of Research on Computing in Education. ISTE, University of Oregon, 1787 Agate St., Eugene, OR 97403-1923, (800)336-5191, cust_svc@ccmail.uoregon.edu. [Q., $78 nonmembers, $32.10 Canada, $88 intl., $98 intl. air]. Contains articles reporting on the latest research findings related to classroom and administrative uses of technology, including system and project evaluations.

Kutnick, P. (1997). Computer-based problem-solving: The effects of group composition and social skills on a cognitive, joint action task. **Educational Research, 39** (2), 135-47. Children ages 9-10 (n=30) were given social skills training and their scores on computer tasks were compared with 30 controls. Males scored highest on the pre- and post-test. Females in mixed-sex groups scored better than females in girls-only groups. Girls who received social skills training had the highest rate of improvement.

Lamb, A. (1997). **The magic carpet ride—Integrating technology into the K-12 classroom**. [Book, 207pp., $23.95]. ISTE, University of Oregon, 1787 Agate St., Eugene, OR 97403-1923, (800)336-5191, cust_svc@ccmail.uoregon.edu. Addresses educational software selection, integrating learning resources, developing multimedia projects, and using HyperStudio.

Land, M., & Turner, S. (1997). **Tools for schools: Applications software for the classroom**. 2nd ed. [Book, 320pp.]. Wadsworth Publishing Co., 10 Davis Dr., Belmont, CA 94002-3098. One-semester text that illustrates computer applications as teaching tools.

Learning and Leading with Technology: Serving Teachers in the Classroom. ISTE, University of Oregon, 1787 Agate St., Eugene, OR 97403-1923, (800)336-5191, cust_svc@ccmail. uoregon.edu. [8/yr., $65 nonmembers, Canada $79.55, intl. $75, intl. air $95]. Focuses on the use of technology, coordination, and leadership; written by educators for educators. Appropriate for classroom teachers, lab teachers, technology coordinators, and teacher educators.

Levy, M. (1997). Theory-driven computer assisted language learning (CALL) and the development process. **Computer Assisted Language Learning, 10** (1), 41-56. Reflects upon the nature of theory-driven computer assisted second language learning (CALL), particularly as it relates to the courseware development process. The study examines the implications for theory-driven CALL as well as the concept of "fit" between the theoretical framework or pedagogy and the computer's capabilities. The study addresses real conditions and derives principles meaningful to CALL authors.

Lu, C. R., & others. (1997). The effect of a microcomputer-based biology study center on learning in high school biology students. **American Biology Teacher, 59** (5), 270-78. Describes a computer-assisted instruction (CAI) package covering biology concepts for an entire school year and evaluates the effect of this CAI on learning. Findings indicate positive effects of CAI on achievement and attitude.

MacWorld. MacWorld Communications, Box 54529, Boulder, CO 80322-4529. [Mo., $30]. Describes hardware, software, tutorials, and applications for users of the Macintosh microcomputer.

Microcomputer Abstracts. Information Today, 143 Old Marlton Pike, Medford, NJ 08055, (800)300-9868. [4/yr., $199 US, $208 Canada/Mexico, $214 elsewhere]. Abstracts literature on the use of microcomputers in business, education, and the home, covering over 175 publications.

Moore, J. W., & Mitchem, C. E. (1997). Outcomes assessment of computer-assisted behavioral objectives for accounting graduates. **Journal of Education for Business, 72** (4), 201-4. Presents behavioral objectives for accounting students and an outcomes assessment plan with five steps: 1) identification and definition of student competencies; 2) selection of valid instruments; 3) integration of assessment and instruction; 4) determination of levels of assessment; and 5) attribution of improvements to the program.

PC Magazine: The Independent Guide to IBM-Standard Personal Computing. Ziff-Davis Publishing Co., Box 54093, Boulder, CO 80322. [Bi-w., $49.97]. Comparative reviews of computer hardware and general business software programs.

PC Week. Ziff-Davis Publishing Co., 10 Presidents Landing, Medford, MA 02155-5146. [W., $195 US, Canada and Mexico $250, free to qualified personnel]. Provides current information on the IBM PC, including hardware, software, industry news, business strategies, and reviews of hardware and software.

PC World. PC World Communications, Inc., Box 55029, Boulder, CO 80322-5029. [Mo., $29.90 US, $53.39 Canada, $49.90 Mexico, $75.90 elsewhere]. Presents articles on applications and columns containing news, systems information, product announcements, and hardware updates.

Rogan, J. M. (1997). Online mentoring: Reflections and suggestions. **Journal of Computing in Teacher Education, 13** (3), 5-13. Reports a study of "Reach for the Sky," a telecommunications project offering rural teachers access to the Internet and online courses. Teachers received Internet training, then became mentors for other teachers enrolled in online courses. Interviews and analysis of E-mail messages highlighted lessons learned about mentoring and online education.

Sandberg, J., & Barnard, Y. (1997). Deep learning is difficult. **Instructional Science, 25** (1), 15-36. Explanations for poor learning include inadequate subject matter, students, and approach, but this article argues that the information processing needed for deep learning is hampered when students cannot spontaneously engage in cognitive activities fostering such learning. Describes three studies in which high school students learned about the tides with computer tutors.

Simonson, M. R., & Thompson, A. (1997). **Educational computing foundations**. 3rd ed. [Book, 512pp.]. Merrill/Prentice Hall, 445 Hutchinson Ave., Columbus, OH 43235-5677. Provides fundamental principles of classroom computer use. The third edition adds sections addressing the Web, hypermedia, and statistical software.

Social Science Computer Review. Sage Publications Inc., 2455 Teller Rd., Thousand Oaks, CA 91320. [Q., $160 inst.]. Features include software reviews, new product announcements, and tutorials for beginners.

Software Digest (formerly Software Digest Ratings Report). National Software Testing Laboratories Inc., Plymouth Corporate Center, Box 1000, Plymouth Meeting, PA 19462. [Mo., $450]. For IBM personal computer users. Each issue reports the ratings for one category of IBM PC software, based on multiple-user tests.

Software Magazine. Sentry Publishing Co., Inc., 1 Research Dr., Suite 400B, Westborough, MA 01581-3907. [Mo., $65 US, $75 Canada, $125 elsewhere, free to qualified personnel]. Provides information on software and industry developments for business and professional users, and announces new software packages.

Waddick, J. (1997). Physical considerations in the development of a computer learning environment. **British Journal of Educational Technology, 28** (1), 69-71. A group of 20 students studied chemistry with the same lecturer in three different physical environments: 1) computers on lab benches, 2) computers around the walls, and 3) computers in cluster groups of four. Students preferred the cluster groups, suggesting that physical features of learning environments should be considered in learning with computers.

Yu, F. Y. (1996-1997). Competition or noncompetition: Its impact on interpersonal relationships in a computer-assisted learning environment. **Journal of Educational Technology Systems, 25** (1), 13-24. Describes a study of fifth-grade students in Taiwan that explored the differential effects of intergroup competition on intragroup cooperation and interpersonal relationships within groups in a computer-assisted instruction (CAI) environment. Statistically significant differences were found between the two treatment conditions (with and without competition) in student perceptions toward dyads.

DISTANCE EDUCATION

American Journal of Distance Education. American Center for the Study of Distance Education, Pennsylvania State University, 110 Rackley Building, University Park, PA 16802-3202, http://www.cde.psu.edu/ACSDE/ [3/yr., $35 indiv. ($41 Canada and Mexico, $50 elsewhere), $65 inst. (Canada and Mexico $71, $80 elsewhere)]. Created to disseminate information and act as a forum for criticism and debate about research in and practice of distance education in the Americas. Focuses on the role of print, electronic, and telecommunications media and multimedia systems in the delivery of education and training in universities and colleges, business and industry, the military, and in the public schools.

Biner, P., & Dean, R. S. (1997). Profiling the successful tele-education student. **Distance Education Report, 1** (2), 1, 3. Results of a personality assessment questionnaire revealed three basic personality characteristics that are predictive of student achievement in telecourses: 1) high performers were the most self-sufficient; 2) the least compulsive students earned the highest grades in their courses; and 3) telecourse students who performed at the highest levels tend to be highly expedient in their daily lives.

Biner, P. M., Welsh, K. D., Barone, N. M., Summers, M., & Dean, R. S. (1997). The impact of remote-site group size on student satisfaction and relative performance in interactive telecourses. **American Journal of Distance Education, 11** (1), 23-33. Reports that remote group size predicted satisfaction with all aspects of a distance course.

Brown, S. (1997). **Open and distance learning: Case studies from education, industry and commerce**. [Book, 224pp., $57.50]. Cassell/Stylus, P.O. Box 605, Herndon, VA 20172-0605, (800)232-0223, fax (703)661-1510, styluspub@aol.com. Discusses the blending of distance learning strategies with more traditional instructional methods. Topics include support issues, cost-effectiveness comparisons, and problems.

Buchanan, J., & MacIntosh, J. (1997). Trust: A process and an outcome in an audio-teleconferencing learning environment. **Canadian Journal of University Continuing Education, 23** (1), 49-60. Nursing students taking courses via audio-teleconferencing (n=24) gave their perspectives on factors facilitating trust in a distance education environment. Students trusted teachers who believed in their ability to develop and who provided experiences that enabled students to control their own learning.

Burgess, W. E. (1997). **The Oryx guide to distance learning**. 2nd ed. [Book, 528pp., $98.50]. Oryx Press, 4041 North Central Ave., Suite 700, Phoenix, AZ 85012-3397, (800)279-6799, fax (800)279-4663. Directory of more than 4,000 electronic and other media-assisted, for-credit courses at 430 accredited post-secondary institutions. Includes course descriptions and subject, institution, and delivery method indexes.

Crowe, D., & Zand, H. (1997). Novices entering mathematics: The impact of new technology. **Computers & Education, 28** (1), 43-54. Reports the results of a case study at the Open University (Great Britain), which shows that the learning environment for distance education students of mathematics can be substantially improved by the use of electronic communication between students or teachers. Future plans are also discussed.

Cyrs, T. E., ed. (1997). **Teaching and learning at a distance: What it takes to effectively design, deliver, and evaluate programs**. New Directions for Teaching and Learning. [Serial, $22 each issue]. Jossey-Bass, Inc., 350 Sansome St., San Francisco, CA 94104, (888)378-2537, fax (800)605-2665. Discusses effective distance learning in conjunction with adult learning principles; details features of delivery alternatives.

Dickinson, K. (1997). Distance learning on the Internet: Testing students using Web forms and the computer gateway interface. **TechTrends, 42** (2), 43-46. Introduces technical issues for supporting distance learning via the Internet, including delivery mechanisms, CGI, Web-based tests, and authoring tools.

Distance Education. University College of Southern Queensland Publications, Darling Heights, Toowoomba, Queensland 4350, Australia. [Semi-ann., $67]. Papers on the history, politics, and administration of distance education.

Distance Education Report. Magna Publications, Inc., 2718 Dryden Dr., Madison, WI 53704. [Mo., $299]. Digests periodical, Internet, and conference information into monthly reports.

Easterday, N. (1997). Distance education and two-year colleges. **Community College Journal of Research and Practice, 21** (1), 23-36. Presents results from a study of the status of distance education in community colleges. Discusses the design, support, and administration of telecourses; staffing and teacher training practices; course offerings; and existing assessment and evaluation studies. Addresses criticisms of distance education and cites research results on its effectiveness.

Ehrhard, B. J., & Schroeder, B. L. (1997). Videoconferencing: What is it and how is it being used? **TechTrends, 42** (3), 32-34. Defines videoconferencing, and describes the technology along with its current applications and implementation obstacles.

Freeman, R. (1997). **Managing open systems**. [Book, 192pp., $29.95]. Cassell/Stylus, P.O. Box 605, Herndon, VA 20172-0605, (800)232-0223, fax (703)661-1510, styluspub@aol.com. Presents the information needed to enable decisions regarding open learning systems, learners' needs, and management issues.

Harris, J. (1998). **Virtual architecture: Designing and directing curriculum-based telecomputing**. [Book, 180pp., $19.95]. ISTE, 480 Charnelton St., Eugene, OR 97401-2626, (800)336-5191, fax (541)302-3887. Asserts that integrating computer-mediated technology into the classroom is worthwhile as long as it helps accomplish innovative and sound educational goals. Presents an adaptable framework for enacting such a program.

Hipp, H. (1997). Women studying at a distance: What do they need to succeed? **Open Learning, 12** (2), 41-49. Presents the results of a survey and interviews with women enrolled at the University of South Australia. Highlights issues that should be considered to ensure the success of women distance education students: confidence and finding a voice; overcoming isolation; and connected learning, in which members of a student group nurture each others' ideas.

Hoadley, Maidment, E. (1997). From "story" to art: The acquisition of academic writing skills in an open-learning context. **Language and Education, 11** (1), 55-68. Examines the acquisition of academic writing skills by adult students studying by distance learning in the United Kingdom. Results indicate that the text-based nature of distance learning affects both the ways in which students acquire writing skills and the development of their identity as academic writers. Differences in the learning process were also found between arts and humanities students and social science students.

Hobbs, V., & Christianson, J. S. (1997). **Educational opportunity through two-way interactive television**. [Book, 300pp., $49.95]. Technomic Publishing Co., Inc., Lancaster, PA. Reviews use of two-way interactive television as a distance learning technology in rural community development settings.

Journal of Distance Education. Canadian Association for Distance Education, Secretariat, One Stewart St., Suite 205, Ottawa, ON K1N 6H7, Canada. (Text in English and French). [2/yr., $40, add $5 outside Canada]. Aims to promote and encourage scholarly work of empirical and theoretical nature relating to distance education in Canada and throughout the world.

Marland, P. (1997). **Towards more effective open and distance teaching**. [Book, 192pp., $27.50]. Cassell/Stylus, P.O. Box 605, Herndon, VA 20172-0605, (800)232-0223, fax (703)661-1510, styluspub@aol.com. Relates experiential and teaching perspectives for distance educators, with supporting case studies.

McCulloch, K. H. (1997). Participatory evaluation in distance learning. **Open Learning, 12** (1), 24-30. Analyzes the evaluation of student feedback to a tutor in the Open University (Great Britain). Discusses tutor effectiveness in supporting individual students; group tutorials; self-help and mutual support by students; formative feedback on written assignments; participatory evaluation; and power relations, including "pseudoempowerment."

McHenry, L., & Bozik, M. (1997). From a distance: Student voices from the interactive video classroom. **TechTrends, 42** (6), 20-24. Examines community college students enrolled in an interactive video class, exploring their reactions thematically.

Miller, G. (1997). Agricultural education at a distance: Attitudes and perceptions of secondary teachers. **Journal of Agricultural Education, 38** (1), 54-60. Responses from 102 of 140 Iowa secondary agriculture teachers revealed attitudes toward the interactive communications network (ICN), a two-way fiber-optic telecommunications system. Teachers were concerned about such obstacles as scheduling ICN use and managing laboratory and supervised agricultural experience activities. They were undecided about ICN's usefulness as a teaching tool.

Miller, G. (1997). Studying agriculture through videotape: Learner strategies and cognitive styles. **Journal of Agricultural Education, 38** (1), 21-28. Agriculture students (n=157) taking videotaped courses were asked about their learning strategies and cognitive styles. They liked the convenience of videos, studied independently, and rarely consulted instructors. Field-dependent and -independent learners used similar strategies. Most used a consistent approach to the task of learning from videotape.

Miller, G., & Carr, A. (1997). Information and training needs of agricultural faculty related to distance education. **Journal of Applied Communications, 81** (1), 1-9. Survey responses from 158 agricultural faculty and deans found they were most interested in distance education applications to credit courses and placed greater emphasis on planning and teaching behavior topics than on learning and learner-related topics. Designing instruction for nonformal groups received low ratings, as did technical (hardware, software, site facilitation) issues.

Moskal, P., Martin, B., & Foshee, N. (1997). Educational technology and distance education in central Florida: An assessment of capabilities. **American Journal of Distance Education, 11** (1), 6-22. Relates the results of a regional assessment of influencing factors as perceived by instructors, variations of experience due to differing delivery systems, and instructor expertise with instructional design principles.

Murphy, K. L., Cathcart, S., & Kodali, S. (1997). Integrating distance education technologies in a graduate course. **TechTrends, 42** (1), 24-28. Details the course development process for distance education graduate classes, including planning, technology, pedagogy, and obstacles.

Oliver, R., & McLoughlin, C. (1997). Interactions in audiographics teaching and learning environments. **American Journal of Distance Education, 11** (1), 34-54. Audiographics is a low-cost delivery system for distance learning using a telecommunications link between computers and an audioconferencing medium. A study of the interactions between teachers and 10- to 12-year-old students in western Australia indicated that, although audiographics can support interactions of many forms, teachers used a limited range of interactions for classroom management and content delivery.

Open Learning. Pitman Professional, Subscriptions Dept., P.O. Box 77, Harlow, Essex CM19 5BQ, England. [3/yr., £68 UK, £73 Europe, $78 elsewhere]. Academic, scholarly publication on aspects of open and distance learning anywhere in the world. Includes issues for debate and research notes.

Open Praxis. International Council for Distance Education, National Extension College, 18 Brooklands Ave., Cambridge CB2 2HN, England. [2/yr., $70 indiv., $55 libr.]. Reports on activities and programs of the ICDE.

Prosst, K., & others. (1997). Effects of gender on perceptions of preferences for telematic learning environments. **Journal of Research on Computing in Education, 29** (4), 370-84. Describes a study that investigated gender differences in perceptions of and preferences for telematic learning environments based on questionnaires completed by open and distance learning university students. Significant gender differences were found, but none of the variables explained differences in students' perceptions and preferences.

Rogan, J. M. (1997). Online mentoring: Reflections and suggestions. **Journal of Computing in Teacher Education, 13** (3), 5-13. Reports a study of "Reach for the Sky," a telecommunications project offering rural teachers access to the Internet and online courses. Teachers received Internet training, then became mentors for other teachers enrolled in online courses. Interviews and analysis of E-mail messages highlighted lessons learned about mentoring and online education.

Rumble, G. (1997). **The costs and economics of open and distance learning**. [Book, 224pp., $35]. Cassell/Stylus, P.O. Box 605, Herndon, VA 20172-0605, (800)232-0223, fax (703)661-1510, styluspub@aol.com. Lists costs associated with distance learning, explains significance of each one, and offers guidelines for planning open learning systems.

Schlosser, C., & Anderson, M. (1997). **Distance education: A review of the literature**. 2nd ed. [Book, 64pp., $15]. AECT, 1025 Vermont Ave. NW, Suite 820, Washington, DC 20005-3547. Provides brief but comprehensive literature review. Defines distance education, discusses major theories, summarizes history and current issues.

Schrum, L., with Luetkehans, L. (1997). **A primer on distance education considerations for decision makers**. [Book, approx. 100pp., $7.95]. AECT, 1025 Vermont Ave., NW, Suite 820, Washington, DC 20005-3547. Provides an introduction to the field of distance education; describes concepts, vocabulary, current status, and issues involved in the understanding of this current field.

Stevenson, J., & McKavanagh, C. (1997). The role of cognitive structures in the transfer of first-aid knowledge acquired in distance education. **Australian and New Zealand Journal of Vocational Education Research, 5** (1), 131-57. Participants learning first aid at a distance through printed self-paced materials attempted tasks involving near and far transfer. They performed well on near transfer tasks but the controlled cognitive processing involved in far transfer caused recurrence of errors that had been corrected earlier.

Struempler, B., & others. (1997). Using distance education to teach the new food label to extension educators. **Journal of Extension, 35** (2). Satellite training about the new national food labeling system was provided to 97 Alabama extension agents and 67 program assistants. The program, which consisted of a 30-minute video and 25-minute question/answer call-in, proved an effective means of distance education.

Tiene, D. (1997). Student perspectives on distance learning with interactive television. **TechTrends, 42** (1), 41-47. A survey of 52 high school students taking advanced placement courses in psychology, French, Spanish, German, and Latin via interactive television revealed that 90 percent agreed that the learning experience was different from a regular classroom; 77 percent agreed that a fax machine sped up the exchange of materials; and 61 percent agreed that technical difficulties interfered with the course.

Westbrook, T. S. (1997). Changes in students' attitudes toward graduate business instruction via interactive television. **American Journal of Distance Education, 11** (1), 55-69. Examines interaction, satisfaction, and perceptions of technological interference. Findings suggest that attitudes change significantly over the course of a term and that a significant amount of variation is due to different sites and the presence or absence of the instructor.

Westbrook, T. S., & Moon, D. K. (1997). Lessons learned from the delivery of a graduate business degree program utilizing interactive television. **Journal of Continuing Higher Education, 45** (2), 25-33. Interviews with three distance education administrators, nine faculty, and 24 students who used the Iowa Communications Network for graduate study identified the following: need for well-articulated policy, value of financial incentives, benefits of institutional cooperation, importance of a student orientation program and faculty training, and use of norms for remote classrooms.

Zajkowski, M. E. (1997). Price and persistence in distance education. **Open Learning, 12** (1), 12-23. Examines student reactions to new fee levels for distance education courses in order to understand how fees, and their possible reimbursement by employers, impact student persistence at the Open Polytechnic of New Zealand. Discusses completion rates, attrition in distance learning, employer support, and financial assistance.

EDUCATIONAL RESEARCH

American Educational Research Journal. American Educational Research Association, 1230 17th St. NW, Washington, DC 20036-3078. [Q., $41 indiv., $56 inst.]. Reports original research, both empirical and theoretical, and brief synopses of research.

Collis, B., & Knezek, G. (1997). **Teaching and learning in the digital age: Research into practice with telecommunications in educational settings**. [Book, 230pp., $36]. ISTE, 480 Charnelton St., Eugene, OR 97401-2626, (800)336-5191, fax (541)302-3887. Contains 14 expanded articles from the Tel-Ed '97 Conference, focusing on integrated technology practice, resource development, learner interaction and communication, and new dynamics in teacher education.

Current Index to Journals in Education (CIJE). Oryx Press, 4041 N. Central at Indian School Rd., Phoenix, AZ 85012-3397, [Mo., $245 ($280 outside North America); semi-ann. cumulations $250 ($285 foreign); combination $475]. A guide to articles published in some 830 education and education-related journals. Includes complete bibliographic information, annotations, and indexes. Semiannual cumulations available. Contents are produced by the ERIC (Educational Resources Information Center) system, Office of Educational Research and Improvement, and the US Department of Education.

Education Index. H. W. Wilson, 950 University Ave., Bronx, NY 10452. [Mo., except July and August; $1,295 for CD-ROM, including accumulations]. Author-subject index to educational publications in the English language. Cumulated quarterly and annually.

Educational Research. Routledge, 11 Fetter Ln., London EC4P 4EE, England. [3/yr., £30 indiv. ($62 US and Canada)]. Reports on current educational research, evaluation, and applications.

Educational Researcher. American Educational Research Association, 1230 17th St. NW, Washington, DC 20036-3078. [9/yr., $39 indiv., $56 inst.]. Contains news and features of general significance in educational research.

Fulop, M. P., & others. (1997). Using the World Wide Web to conduct a needs assessment. **Performance Improvement, 36** (6), 22-27. Demonstrates how electronic mail and the World Wide Web are effective tools for focus group research and programmatic decision-making by highlighting how an electronic needs assessment survey was conducted on participants' use of the Web. Sidebars contain the four-step focus group methodology, sample questions and responses, and a comparison of real time and e-mail focus groups.

Research in Science & Technological Education. Carfax Publishing Co., 875-81 Massachusetts Ave., Cambridge, MA 02139. [2/yr., $134 indiv., $432 inst.]. Publication of original research in the science and technological fields. Includes articles on psychological, sociological, economic, and organizational aspects.

Resources in Education (RIE). Superintendent of Documents, US Government Printing Office, P.O. Box 371954, Pittsburgh, PA 15250-7954. [Mo., $77 US, $96.25 elsewhere]. Announcement of research reports and other documents in education, including abstracts and indexes by subject, author, and institution. Contents produced by the ERIC (Educational Resources Information Center) system, Office of Educational Research and Improvement, and the US Department of Education.

Ross, S. M., & Morrison, G. R. (1997). **Getting started in instructional technology research**. 2nd ed. [Monograph, 31pp., $9.95]. AECT, 1025 Vermont Ave. NW, Suite 820, Washington, DC 20005-3547. Summarizes authors' ideas and experiences related to performing research in the field. Seeks to motivate new professionals to begin an active research program, and to guide experienced researchers in refining their skills.

EDUCATIONAL TECHNOLOGY

Appropriate Technology. Intermediate Technology Publications, Ltd., 103-105 Southampton Row, London, WC1B 4HH, England. [Q., $28 indiv., $37 inst.]. Articles on less technologically advanced, but more environmentally sustainable, solutions to problems in developing countries.

Barron, A. E., & Orwig, G. W. (1997). **New technologies for education: A beginner's guide**. 3rd ed. [Book, 295pp., $32.50]. Libraries Unlimited, P.O. Box 6633, Englewood, CO 80155-6633, (800)237-6124, fax (303)220-8843, lu-books@lu.com, http://www.lu.com. Offers an updated look at the technologies that are affecting education, including LANs, the Internet, and multimedia.

Baule, S. M. (1997). **Technology planning**. [Book, 100pp., $29.95]. Linworth Publishing, 480 E. Wilson Bridge Rd., Suite L, Worthington, OH 43085-2372, (800)786-5017, fax (614)436-9490, orders@linworth.com, http://linworth.com. Focuses on technology application to authentic curricular problems and situations, considering present and future needs.

Bazeli, M. J., & Heintz, J. L. (1997). **Technology across the curriculum: Activities and ideas**. [Book, 207pp., $24.50]. Libraries Unlimited, P.O. Box 6633, Englewood, CO 80155-6633, (800)237-6124, fax (303)220-8843, lu-books@lu.com, http://www.lu.com. Contains 75 activities focusing on curriculum application and integration.

Bodily, S., & Mitchell, K. J. (1997). **Evaluating challenge grants for technology in education: A sourcebook**. [Book, 206pp., $9]. Rand, Santa Monica, CA. Provides strategies for the evaluation of grant programs and addresses evaluation issues. Contains instruments.

British Journal of Educational Technology. National Council for Educational Technology, Millburn Hill Rd., Science Park, Coventry CV4 7JJ, England. [3/yr., £82 inst. UK, £95 overseas air, personal subscriptions £32 UK, £42 overseas]. Published by the National Council for Educational Technology, this journal includes articles on education and training, especially theory, applications, and development of educational technology and communications.

C®LL Journal. ISTE, University of Oregon, 1787 Agate St., Eugene, OR 97403-1923, (800)336-5191, cust_svc@ccmail.uoregon.edu. [Q., $35, $48.15 Canada, $45 intl., $51 intl. air]. Focuses on current issues facing computer-using language teachers; covers trends, products, applications, research, and program evaluation.

Canadian Journal of Educational Communication. Association for Media and Technology in Education in Canada, AMTEC-CJEC Subscription, 3-1750 The Queensway, Suite 1318, Etobicoke, ON M9C 5H5, Canada. [3/yr., $80.25 Canada, $101.65 foreign]. Articles, research reports, and literature reviews on all areas of educational communication and technology.

Casey, J. M. (1997). **Early literacy: The empowerment of technology**. [Book, 178pp., $24]. Libraries Unlimited, P.O. Box 6633, Englewood, CO 80155-6633, (800)237-6124, fax (303)220-8843, lu-books@lu.com, http://www.lu.com. Discusses the use of technology to provide stimulating media-rich environments for the promotion of reading in young learners.

Children's Software Review. Active Learning Associates, Inc., 44 Main St., Flemington, NJ 08822, http://www.childrenssoftware.com. [6/yr., $29]. Provides reviews and other information about software to help parents and educators more effectively use computers with children.

Cifuentes, L. (1997). From sages to guides: A professional development study. **Journal of Technology and Teacher Education, 5** (1), 67-77. The educational technology course for preservice teachers at Texas A&M University incorporates a constructivist model for professional development. A study of this model examined how it helps teachers change from disseminators of information to facilitators of learning and how it underscores differences between preservice and inservice teachers' choices of teaching methods.

Clariana, R. B. (1997). Considering learning style in computer-assisted learning. **British Journal of Educational Technology, 28** (1), 66-68. In a study involving three diverse computer assisted learning (CAL) experiences and different learner populations (13- and 14-year olds, 19 to 21 year olds, and adult education majors), a general shift in learning style (Kolb) was observed. The magnitude of the shift appeared to vary with learner ability and exposure to CAL.

Cohen, V. L. (1997). Learning styles in a technology-rich environment. **Journal of Research on Computing in Education, 29** (4), 338-50. Describes a study of gifted freshmen in a magnet high school that investigated whether learning style would change after a year in a technology-rich educational environment using constructivist learning techniques. Conclusions regarding learning style were inconclusive, but results showing effects on the curriculum and the social context are discussed.

Cradler, J., & Cordon-Cradler, R. (1997). **The technology planning and funding guide**. [Book, 155pp., $39]. Educational Support Systems; available through ISTE, University of Oregon, 1787 Agate St., Eugene, OR 97403-1923. Designed for teachers and administrators who want a practical step-by-step guide for developing grant proposals.

Dickey, E., & Roblyer, M. D. (1997). Technology, NAEP, and TIMSS: How does technology influence our national and international report cards? **Learning & Leading with Technology, 25** (3), 55-57. Disputes the assumption that the National Assessment of Educational Progress and the Third International Mathematics and Science Study adequately assess skills enhanced by technology.

Educational Technology. Educational Technology Publications, Inc., 700 Palisade Ave., Englewood Cliffs, NJ 07632-0564. [Bi-mo., $119 US, $139 elsewhere]. Covers telecommunications, computer-aided instruction, information retrieval, educational television, and electronic media in the classroom.

Educational Technology Abstracts. Carfax Publishing Co., 875-81 Massachusetts Ave., Cambridge, MA 02139. [6/yr., $218 indiv., $582 inst.]. An international publication of abstracts of recently published material in the field of educational and training technology.

Education Technology News. Business Publishers, Inc. 951 Pershing Dr., Silver Spring, MD 20910-9973, (800)274-6737, fax (301)589-8493, bpinews@bpinews.com, http://www.bpinews.com. [Bi-w., $270 per 25 issues]. Newsletter containing news, product reviews, funding sources, useful Internet sites, and case studies for technology coordinators, administrators, and teachers.

Educational Technology Research and Development. AECT, 1025 Vermont Ave., NW, Suite 820, Washington, DC 20005. [Q., $55 US, $63 foreign]. Focuses on research and instructional development in the field of educational technology.

Electronic School. NSBA Distribution Center, P.O. Box 161, Annapolis Jct., MD 20701-0161, (800)706-6722, fax (301)604-0158, http://www.nsba.org/itte. [Q., $5 per issue]. Provides resource for all school personnel covering school technology trends, staff development, funding, telecommunications, and restructuring.

Enghagen, L., ed. (1997). **Technology and higher education**. [Book, 208pp., $21.95]. NEA Professional Library, P.O. Box 509, West Haven, CT 06516, (800)229-4200, fax (203)933-5276. Addresses issues including access, copyright law, software choice, distance learning, and the underrepresentation of women and minorities in technical fields, and many other pressing concerns. Contributing authors include Carol Baroudi, John R. Levine, Kenneth Salomon, Michael Pierce, Steven W. Gilbert, Kenneth C. Green, C. Dianne Martin, Thomas E. Duston, Eric P. Healy, J. N. Musto, Donald C. Savage, Patricia A. Finn, and Gene Aitken.

Escalada, L. T., & Zollman, D. A. (1997). An investigation on the effects of using interactive digital video in a physics classroom on student learning and attitudes. **Journal of Research in Science Teaching, 34** (5), 467-89. Examines the effects of using interactive digital video on student learning and attitudes in an introductory physics course. Results indicate that sophisticated instructional video software can be perceived by students as easy to use and effective. The software can also be used to promote active learning.

Forman, D. W. (1997). How does using technology affect student attitudes about teachers? **Computers in the Schools, 13** (1-2), 53-60. Describes how a version of the Tuckman Teacher Feedback Form (TTFF) was used to measure teachers' "personality" factors as perceived by students. The instrument included 28 sets of bipolar adjectives to use in describing the teacher. Findings revealed that the application of technology to instruction improved students' perceptions of teacher creativity and originality.

Gottfried, J., & McFeely, M. G. (1997-1998). Learning all over the place: Integrating laptop computers into the classroom. **Learning & Leading with Technology, 25** (4), 6-11. Describes two case studies conducted during a project sponsored by corporations and a private foundation to provide laptop computers to middle school students. The case studies focus on student and teacher reactions.

Haugland, S. W., & Wright, J. L. (1997). **Young children and computers: A world of discovery**. [Book, 304pp.]. Allyn & Bacon, 160 Gould St., Needham Heights, MA 02194-2315. Considers educational computing from an early childhood perspective.

Hayes, J. (1997). Educational technology trends, 1987-1996. **ERS Spectrum, 15** (2), 3-6. Based on Quality Education Data's ninth annual Educational Technology Trends Survey of 2,501 school districts and 5,000 public schools, this article reviews findings concerning technology expenditures, uses, and effects. Districts spent an estimated $4.1 billion on instructional technology during 1996–1997. Schools have a 10 to 1 student/computer ratio, are acquiring multimedia computers, and are spending more to train teachers.

Hemmer, J. (1998). Melissa's year in sixth grade: A technology integration vignette. **Learning & Leading with Technology, 25** (5), 11-14. Demonstrates how technology can be integrated into the middle school curriculum, replacing exploratory computer classes.

Hoffman, R., & Rossett, A. (1997). **School technology planner (STP) software**. [Software: dual platform CD-ROM]. Allyn & Bacon, 160 Gould St., Needham Heights, MA 02194-2315. Assists school technology leaders in drafting Technology Use Plans (TUPs); reviews literature on success factors for technology integration.

Holsbrink-Engels, G. A. (1997). Computer-based role-playing for interpersonal skills training. **Simulation & Gaming, 28** (2), 164-80. Examines design and evaluation of computer-based role-playing. University students (n=41) were divided into two groups to use instructional programs with and without computer-based role-playing. Findings indicated that computer-based role-playing enhanced interpersonal skill development by employing a conversational model, offering opportunities for reflection, performing protagonist roles, and capturing individual contribution and learning.

HomePC. CMP Media Inc., (800)829-0119, hpc-order@palmcoastd.com, http://www.homepcmag. com. [Mo., $21.97]. Consumer computer magazine that reviews selected children's software each month.

Innovations in Education and Training International (formerly *Educational and Training Technology International*). Kogan Page, FREEPOST 1, 120 Pentonville Rd., London N1 9JN. [Q., £61, $102 US]. The international journal of the Association for Educational and Training Technology emphasizes developing trends in and the efficient use of educational technology. It is now extending its interest to include the field of staff and educational development.

Insight Media. (1997). **School technology planner**. [CD-ROM, Mac/Windows, $129]. Insight Media, 2162 Broadway, New York, NY 10024, (800)233,9910, fax (212)799-5309, http://www.insight-media.com. Assists school personnel in assessing needs and drafting a technology plan. Includes a recent literature survey of relevant issues.

International Journal of Technology and Design Education. Kluwer Academic Publishers, Order Dept., P.O. Box 358, Accor Station, Hingham, MA 02018-0358, (617)871-6600, fax (617)871-6528, kluwer@wkap.com. [3/yr., $154]. Publishes research reports and scholarly writing about aspects of technology and design education.

Jackson, D. F. (1997). Case studies of microcomputer and interactive video simulations in middle school earth science teaching. **Journal of Science Education and Technology, 6** (2), 127-41. Synthesizes the results of three case studies of middle school classrooms in which computer and video materials were used to teach topics in earth and space sciences through interactive simulations. Describes specific instances in which common current practice is problematic. Suggests improved design principles for such materials.

Journal of Instruction Delivery Systems. Learning Technology Institute, 50 Culpeper St., Warrenton, VA 22186. [Q., $60 US, $75 elsewhere]. Devoted to the issues and applications of technology to enhance productivity in education, training, and job performance.

Journal of Science Education and Technology. Plenum Publishing Corporation, 233 Spring St., New York, NY 10013-1578, (212)620-8000, (800)221-9369, info@plenum.com, http://www.plenum.com. [Q., $56 indiv., $195 inst.]. Publishes studies aimed at improving science education at all levels in the US.

Kimball, C., & Sibley, P. H. R. (1997-1998). Am I on the mark? Technology planning for the E-Rate. **Learning & Leading with Technology, 25** (4), 52-57. Describes components of sound technology and their functions. Includes rubric for technology plan analysis.

Kimbell, R. (1997). **Assessing technology: International trends in curriculum and assessment**. [Book, 192pp., $26.95]. Open University Press, Bristol, PA. Applies assessment of existing installations to planning. Draws upon examples from the UK, USA, Germany, Taiwan, and Australia.

King, T., ed. (1997). **Technology in the classroom: A collection of articles**. [Book, 143pp., $22.95]. IRI/Skylight Training & Publishing, 2626 Clearbrook Dr., Arlington Heights, IL 60005, (847)290-6600, (800)348-4474, fax (847)290-6609, info@iriskylight.com. Discusses trends and developments in educational technology, including the Web, curricular integration, innovation, case studies of successful implementations, and support for multiple intelligences. Authors include Curman L. Gaines, Willie Johnson, D. Thomas King, Boris Berenfeld, Michael Hopkins, Lani M. Van Dusen, Blaine R. Worthen, Elizabeth M. Riddle, Hilary McLellan, Dawn L. Morden, Marlene Scardamalia, Carl Bereiter, David A. Bennett, and Susan W. Hixson.

Land, M., & Turner, S. (1997). **Tools for schools**. 2nd ed. [Book, 320pp.]. International Thomson Publishing. Details specific uses for various computer applications for teachers.

Lloyd, L. (1997). **Technology and teaching**. [Book, 366 pp., $42.50]. Information Today, 143 Old Marlton Pike, Medford, NJ 08055, (800)300-9868. Presents a selection of case studies focused on computer and multimedia applications in college-level courses. Discusses selection, teaching strategies, and adapting and designing software for individual courses.

Logo Exchange. ISTE, University of Oregon, 1787 Agate St., Eugene, OR 97403-1923, (800)336-5191, cust_svc@ccmail.uoregon.edu. [Q., $34, $47.08 Canada, $44 intl., $51 intl. air]. Brings ideas from Logo educators throughout the world, with current information on Logo research, resources, and methods.

Lu, C. R., & others. (1997). The effect of a microcomputer-based biology study center on learning in high school biology students. **American Biology Teacher, 59** (5), 270-78. Describes a computer-assisted instruction (CAI) package covering biology concepts for an entire school year and evaluates the effect of this CAI on learning. Findings indicate positive effects of CAI on achievement and attitude.

Maddux, C. D., Johnson, D. L., & Willis, J. W. (1997). **Educational computing: Learning with tomorrow's technologies**. 2nd ed. [Book, 351pp.]. Allyn & Bacon, 160 Gould St., Needham Heights, MA 02194-2315. Covers theory, applications, and evaluation of educational computing. Targeted at courses for educators with basic computing skills.

Moberly, D. L. (1997). ASBO responds to technology's impact: A report on the Technology Task Force. **School Business Affairs, 63** (2), 22-25. Summarizes the action plan and final recommendations of the Association of School Business Officials International's (ASBO) Technology Task Force. Also highlights the findings of surveys completed by all ASBO Committee leaders, a sample of general members, and the officers of ASBO's affiliates. A list of task force members is included.

Moursand, D. (1997). **Obtaining resources for technology in education: A how-to guide for writing proposals, forming partnerships, and raising funds.** 2nd ed. [Book, 199pp., $34.95]. ISTE, University of Oregon, 1787 Agate St., Eugene, OR 97403-1923, (800)336-5191, cust_svc@ccmail.uoregon.edu. Contains updated information on obtaining money, hardware, software, staff development, curriculum materials, and consulting for educational technology.

National School Boards Association. (1997). **Investing in school technology: Strategies to meet the funding challenge.** [Book, 80pp., $25]. NSBA Distribution Center, P.O. Box 161, Annapolis Jct., MD 20701-0161, (800)706-6722, fax (301)604-0158, http://www.nsba.org/itte. Provides costing and budgeting strategies to help administrators improve technology funding practices.

Ravel, S., & Layte, M. (1997). **Technology-based training.** [Book, $39.95]. Gulf Publishing Company, 3301 Allen Pkwy., Houston, TX 77019, (713)529-4301, fax (713)520-4433, http://www.gulfpub.com. Describes technology-based training as support for workers in training, ranging from audiotape to virtual reality.

Reynolds, K. E., & Barba, R. H. (1997). **Technology for the teaching and learning of science.** [Book, 269pp.]. Allyn & Bacon, 160 Gould St., Needham Heights, MA 02194-2315. Consolidates information about current issues such as systemic reform, multiculturalism, and National Standards for Science Education into a text for preservice and inservice teachers. Uses reflectivism as a learning technique.

Roblyer, M. D., Edwards, J., & Havriluk, M. A. (1997). **Integrating educational technology into teaching.** [Book, 503pp.]. Merrill/Prentice Hall, 445 Hutchinson Ave., Columbus, OH 43235-5677. Provides strategies, examples, and leading-edge developments for use in junior to graduate-level methods classes.

Sandholtz, J. H., Ringstaff, C., & Dwyer, D. C. (1997). **Teaching with technology: Creating student-centered classrooms.** [Book, 240pp., $18.95]. Teachers College Press, Columbia University, 1234 Amsterdam Ave., New York, NY 10027-6694. Based on 20,000 cases described in the Apple Classrooms of Tomorrow database.

Saye, J. (1997). Technology and educational empowerment: Students' perspectives. **Educational Technology Research and Development, 45** (2), 5-25. Interviews with high school seniors and teachers explored perceptions of technology's role in schooling. Most preferred to adapt technology to traditional, teacher-centered instruction. A minority valued technology as a facilitator of student-centered inquiry and differed in beliefs about schooling and in dispositional tolerance for uncertainty.

Science Communication (formerly *Knowledge: Creation, Diffusion, Utilization*). Sage Publications, Inc., 2455 Teller Rd., Thousand Oaks, CA 91320. [Q., $189 inst.]. An international, interdisciplinary journal examining the nature of expertise and the translation of knowledge into practice and policy.

Scrogan, L. (1997). **Tools for change—Restructuring technology in our schools.** 2nd ed. [Book, 130pp., $34.95]. Institute for Effective Educational Practice; available from ISTE, University of Oregon, 1787 Agate St., Eugene, OR 97403-1923, (800)336-5191, cust_svc@ccmail. uoregon.edu. Helps educational decision-makers ask the right questions about technology in classrooms, better use available resources, and realize the benefits of technology in learning.

SIGTC Connections. ISTE, University of Oregon, 1787 Agate St., Eugene, OR 97403-1923, (800)336-5191, cust_svc@ccmail.uoregon.edu. [Q., $29 US, $41.73 Canada, $39 intl., $42 intl. air]. Provides forum to identify problems and solutions, and to share information on issues facing technology coordinators.

Somekh, B., & Davis, N., eds. (1997). **Using information technology effectively in teaching and learning**. [Book, 288pp., $22.95]. Routledge, 29 West 35th St., New York, NY 10001-2299, http://www.routledge.com/routledge.html. Explores differences in learning quality afforded by information technology, and considers professional development in this regard.

Strickland, J. (1997). **From disk to hard copy: Teaching writing with computers**. [Book, 136pp., $18.50]. Heinemann, Portsmouth, NH, (800)541-2086. Takes advantage of the word processor's affordances for the writing process and explains how to implement them educationally.

Tan, S. B. (1998). Making one-computer teaching fun. **Learning & Leading with Technology, 25** (5), 6-10. Demonstrates how a single computer can serve in the classroom by projecting instructional materials, recording information, accessing the Internet, and conducting quizzes.

Technology and Learning. Peter Li Education Group, P.O. Box 49727, Dayton, OH 45449-0727. [8/yr., $24 US, $32 foreign]. Publishes features, reviews, news, and announcements of educational activities and opportunities in programming, software development, and hardware configurations.

Technology Leadership News. NSBA Distribution Center, P.O. Box 161, Annapolis Jct., MD 20701-0161, (800)706-6722, fax (301)604-0158, http://www.nsba.org/itte. [9/yr., $75]. Official newsletter of the National School Boards Association Institute for the Transfer of Technology to Education. Updates issues, trends, products, programs, applications, district profiles, case studies, government initiatives, funding, and videoconferences in layman's terms.

TECHNOS. Agency for Instructional Technology, Box A, 1111 W. 17th St., Bloomington, IN 47402-0120. [Q., $28 indiv., $24 libr., $32 foreign]. A forum for discussion of ideas about the use of technology in education, with a focus on reform.

TechTrends. Association for Educational Communications and Technology, 1025 Vermont Ave., NW, Suite 820, Washington, DC 20005-3516. [6/yr., $40 US, $44 elsewhere, $6 single copy]. Features authoritative, practical articles about technology and its integration into the learning environment.

T.H.E. Journal (Technological Horizons in Education). T.H.E., 150 El Camino Real, Suite 112, Tustin, CA 92680-3670. [11/yr., $29 US, $95 elsewhere]. For educators of all levels. Focuses on a specific topic for each issue, as well as technological innovations as they apply to education.

Viau, E. A. (1998). Color me a writer: Teaching students to think critically. **Learning & Leading with Technology, 25** (5), 17-20. Discusses how teachers can use color coding and a color printer to teach students to analyze texts for argumentation, emotion, and persuasion.

Woolsey, K., & Bellamy, R. (1997). Science education and technology: Opportunities to enhance student learning. **Elementary School Journal, 97** (4), 385-99. Describes how technological capabilities such as calculation, imaging, networking, and portability support a range of pedagogical approaches, such as inquiry-based science and dynamic modeling. Includes as examples software products created at Apple Computer and others available in the marketplace.

Wright, C. R. (1997). Educational technology consulting in developing countries. **TechTrends, 42** (1), 35-40. Describes the jobs of the international educational technology consultant, including challenges, media selection, and distance education. Includes a Code of Conduct for International Consultants.

INFORMATION SCIENCE AND TECHNOLOGY

Breivik, P. S. (1997). **Student learning in the information age**. [Book, 240pp., $34.95]. Oryx Press, P.O. Box 33889, Phoenix, AZ 85067-3889, (800)279-6799, http://www.oryxpress.com. Examines and promotes resource-based learning for higher education, which requires that students assume responsibility for their own learning from the information around them.

Canadian Journal of Information and Library Science/Revue canadienne des sciences de l'information et de bibliothèconomie. CAIS, University of Toronto Press, Journals Dept., 5201 Dufferin St., Downsview, ON M3H 5T8, Canada. [Q., nonmembers $95, $110 inst.]. Published by the Canadian Association for Information Science to contribute to the advancement of library and information science in Canada.

CD-ROM Databases. Worldwide Videotex, Box 3273, Boynton Beach, FL 33424-3273. [Mo., $150 US, $190 elsewhere]. Descriptive listing of all databases being marketed on CD-ROM with vendor and system information.

CD-ROM Professional. Online, Inc., 462 Danbury Rd., Wilton, CT 06897. [Bi-mo., $55 indiv. and school libr., $98 inst., $148 foreign]. Assists publishers, librarians, and other information professionals in the selection, evaluation, purchase, and operation of CD-ROM systems and titles.

Coyle, K. (1997). **Coyle's information highway handbook**. [Book, 272pp., $30]. American Library Association, ALA Editions, 50 East Huron St., Chicago, IL 60611-2795, (800)545-2433, fax (312)836-9958. Analytical view of the Internet considering copyright, access, privacy, censorship, and the information marketplace.

Crawford, R. (1997). **Managing information technology**. [Book, 272pp., $22.95 US, $31.95 Canada]. Routledge, 11 Fetter Ln., London EC4P 4EE, England. Discusses multiple aspects of information technology in secondary school contexts.

Data Sources. Ziff-Davis Publishing Co., One Park Ave., New York, NY 10016. [2/yr., $440]. Comprehensive guide to the information processing industry. Covers equipment, software, services, and systems, and includes profiles of 10,000 companies.

Database. Online, Inc., 462 Danbury Rd., Wilton, CT 06897. [Bi-mo., $110 online]. Features articles on topics of interest to online database users; includes database search aids.

Datamation. Cahners Publishing Co., 8773 S. Ridgeline Blvd., Highlands Ranch, CO 80126. [24/yr., $75 US, $110 Canada, Mexico, $195 Japan, Australia, New Zealand, $165 elsewhere (free to qualified personnel)]. Covers semitechnical news and views on hardware, software, and databases, for data- and information processing professionals.

Fitzgerald, M. A. (1997). Misinformation on the Internet: Applying evaluation skills to online information. **Emergency Librarian, 24** (3), 9-14. Describes online misinformation: incomplete, out-of-date, biased information; pranks; contradictions; improperly translated data; software incompatibilities; unauthorized revisions; factual errors; and scholarly misconduct. Suggests online searchers should be skeptical, establish prior knowledge, distinguish between fact and opinion, evaluate arguments, compare related information from different sources, evaluate source reliability, identify bias, learn the conventions of the Internet, and examine assumptions.

Gale Directory of Databases (in 2 vols: Vol. 1, **Online Databases**; Vol 2, **CD-ROM, Diskette, Magnetic Tape Batch Access, and Handheld Database Products**). Gale Research Inc., 835 Penobscot Building, Detroit, MI 48226. [Ann. plus semi-ann. update $280, Vol. 1 $199, Vol. 2 $119]. Contains information on database selection and database descriptions, including producers and their addresses.

Information Processing and Management. Pergamon Journals, Inc., 660 White Plains Rd., Tarrytown, NY 10591-5153. [Bi-mo., $152 indiv. whose inst. subscribes, $811 inst.]. International journal covering data processing, database building, and retrieval.

Information Retrieval and Library Automation. Lomond Publications, Inc., Box 88, Mt. Airy, MD 21771. [Mo., $66 US, foreign $79.50]. News, articles, and announcements on new techniques, equipment, and software in information services.

Information Services & Use. I.O.S. Press, Box 10558, Burke, VA 22009-0558. [4/yr., $254]. An international journal for those in the information management field. Includes online and offline systems, library automation, micrographics, videotex, and telecommunications.

The Information Society. Taylor and Francis, 1900 Frost Rd., Suite 101, Bristol, PA 19007-1598. [Q., $140, $168 with online edition]. Provides a forum for discussion of the world of information, including transborder data flow, regulatory issues, and the impact of the information industry.

Information Technology and Libraries. American Library Association, ALA Editions, 50 East Huron St., Chicago, IL 60611-2795, (800)545-2433, fax (312)836-9958. [Q., $50 US, $55 Canada, Mexico, $60 elsewhere]. Articles on library automation, communication technology, cable systems, computerized information processing, and video technologies.

Information Today. Information Today, 143 Old Marlton Pike, Medford, NJ 08055, (800)300-9868. [11/yr., $49.95 US, $63 Canada and Mexico, $68 outside North America]. Newspaper for users and producers of electronic information services. Articles and news about the industry, calendar of events, and product information.

Journal of Database Management. Idea Group Publishing, 4811 Jonestown Rd., Suite 230, Harrisburg, PA 17109-1751. [Q., $65 indiv., $110 inst.]. Provides state-of-the-art research to those who design, develop, and administer DBMS-based information systems.

Journal of Documentation. Association for Information Management, Learned Information, 143 Old Marlton Pike, Medford, NJ 08055-8750. [5/yr., £118 ($200) members , £148 ($252) nonmembers]. Describes how technical, scientific, and other specialized knowledge is recorded, organized, and disseminated.

Library & Information Science Research. Ablex Publishing Corp., 55 Old Post Rd., No. 2, P.O. Box 5297, Greenwich, CT 06831-0504, (203)661-7602, fax (203)661-0792. [Q., $45 indiv., $135 inst.]. Reports library-related research to practicing librarians, emphasizing planning and application.

Losee, R. M. (1997). A discipline independent definition of information. **Journal of the American Society for Information Science, 48** (3), 254-69. Examines definitions of information and highlights a definition that is independent of any specific discipline. Topics include processes; a hierarchical model of information transmission; information representation; information theory; belief and knowledge; and errors, misinformation, and bad data.

Marcovitz, D. M. (1997). I read it on the computer, it must be true: Evaluating information from the Web. **Learning & Leading with Technology, 25** (3), 18-21. Presents an activity to build awareness in K-12 students of the need to evaluate information.

Maze, S., Moxley, D., & Smith, D. J. (1997). **Neal-Schuman authoritative guide to Web search engines**. [Book, 225pp., $49.95]. Neal-Schuman Publishers, 100 Varick St., New York, NY 10013-1506, (212)925-8650, fax (800)584-2414, orders@neal-schuman.com. Describes and evaluates various search engines, explains how they work, and compares various features.

Microcomputers for Information Management. Ablex Publishing Corp., 55 Old Post Rd., No. 2, P.O. Box 5297, Greenwich, CT 06831-0504, (203)661-7602, fax (203)661-0792. [Q., $45 indiv., $135 inst.]. Addresses information networking issues for libraries.

Moursand, D. (1997). **The future of information technology**. [Book, 135pp., $17.95]. ISTE, University of Oregon, 1787 Agate St., Eugene, OR 97403-1923, (800)336-5191, cust_svc@ccmail. uoregon.edu. Discusses the complex questions and challenges facing education, offering conclusions and recommendations for school leaders at each stage of the technology planning process.

Nelson, B. R. (1997). **OPAC directory: An annual guide to Internet-accessible online public access catalogs**. [Book, 500pp., $70]. Information Today, 143 Old Marlton Pike, Medford, NJ 08055, (800)300-9868. Lists Internet addresses of 1300 worldwide online catalogs with dialup and logon instructions. Also provides descriptive information about the indexed libraries.

Online and CD-ROM Review. Information Today, 143 Old Marlton Pike, Medford, NJ 08055, (800)300-9868. [Bi-mo., $130, Canada and Mexico, $140]. An international journal of online information systems featuring articles on using and managing online and optical information systems, training and educating online users, developing search aids, creating and marketing databases, policy affecting the continued development of systems and networks, and the development of new professional standards.

Resource Sharing and Information Networks. Haworth Press, 10 Alice St., Binghamton, NY 13904-1580, (800)HAWORTH, fax (800)895-0582. getinfo@haworth.com, http://www.haworth. com. [2/yr., $42 indiv., $160 inst. and libraries]. A forum for ideas on the basic theoretical and practical problems faced by planners, practitioners, and users of network services.

Snyder, H., & Davenport, E. (1997). **Costing and pricing in the digital age: A practical guide for information services**. [Book, 175pp., $45]. Neal-Schuman Publishers, 100 Varick St., New York, NY, 10013-1506, (212)925-8650, fax (800)584-2414, orders@neal-schuman.com. Guide to common accounting practices for electronic information systems and services; includes models, worksheets, scenarios, and exercises. Topics include fixed and variable costs, life costs of systems, cost pooling and allocation across integrated systems, and internal auditing procedures.

Somekh, B., & Davis, N. (1997). **Using information technology effectively in teaching and learning: Studies in pre-service and in-service teacher education**. [Book, 288pp., $22.95 US, $31.95 Canada]. Routledge, 11 Fetter Ln., London EC4P 4EE, England. Incorporates information technology into instructional strategies.

Vickery, B. (1997). Knowledge discovery from databases: An introductory review. **Journal of Documentation, 53** (2), 107-122. Introduces new procedures being used to extract knowledge from databases and discusses rationales for developing knowledge discovery methods. Methods are described for such techniques as classification, clustering, and the detection of deviations from pre-established norms. Examines potential uses of knowledge discovery in the information field.

Web Feet. Rock Hill Press, 14 Rock Hill Road, Bala Cynwyd, PA 19004, fax (610)667-2291, http://www.rockhillpress.com. [12/yr., $66.50]. Indexes Web sites for general interest, classroom use, and research; reviews Web sites for quality, curricular relevance, timeliness, and interest.

INNOVATION

Briscoe, C., & Peters, J. (1997). Teacher collaboration across and within schools: Supporting individual change in elementary science teaching. **Science Education, 81** (1), 51-65. Explores how collaboration among teachers from several schools and with university researchers facilitates attempts to change practices. Analysis indicates that collaboration facilitates change because it provides opportunities for teachers to learn new content and pedagogical knowledge, encourages them to be risk-takers in implementing new ideas, and supports and sustains the processes of individual change.

Dochy, F. J. (1997). A line of argument for innovation in teaching and assessment starting from students' conceptions and misconceptions in learning processes. **European Journal of Agricultural Education and Extension, 3** (4), 231-239. A task related to knowledge and beliefs was completed by 154 researchers, graduate students, and undergraduates. Greater expertise led to more varied views. Common beliefs and misconceptions can be made explicit through appropriate formative assessment and a focus on transformative learning.

Gbomita, V. (1997). The adoption of microcomputers for instruction: Implications for emerging instructional media implementation. **British Journal of Educational Technology, 28** (2), 87-101. Examined the behavior of 203 secondary school business education teachers with reference to selected social system factors, relative to their adoption of microcomputers for delivering instruction. Findings suggest that the individual's attitude, the characteristics of the innovation, and the critical threshold mark influence microcomputer adoption behavior.

Hargreaves, A., Lieberman, A., Fullan, M., & Hopkins, D., eds. (1997). **International handbook of educational change**. [Book, 1200pp., $395]. Kluwer Academic Publishers, Order Dept., P.O. Box 358, Accor Station, Hingham, MA 02018-0358, (617)871-6600, fax (617)871-6528, kluwer@wkap.com. Addresses issues such as educational innovation, reform, restructuring, change management, and resistance to change. Examines social, economic, cultural, and political forces driving educational change.

Kraus, C., & Volk, D. (1997). A case study of teacher/facilitator collaboration. **School Community Journal, 7** (1), 73-100. Based on a case study of two elementary teachers, this article describes a conceptual framework for teacher/facilitator collaboration that accounts for individual teachers' stages of development and their stages of concern for adopting an innovation. Teachers passed through a certain sequence of stages, but their movement was not always linear. Implications for professional development are discussed.

Lewis, L. K. (1997). Users' individual communicative responses to intraorganizationally implemented innovations and other planned changes. **Management Communication Quarterly, 10** (4), 455-90. Reports on results of an empirical study of users' communicative responses regarding intraorganizationally implemented innovations and other planned changes. A list of users' individual communicative responses was developed and analyzed by means of multidimensional scaling to reveal the conceptual structure underlying the responses.

INSTRUCTIONAL DESIGN AND DEVELOPMENT

Branch, R. M. (1997). Educational technology frameworks that facilitate culturally pluralistic instruction. **Educational Technology, 37** (2), 38-41. Suggests ways in which the domains of instructional technology (design, development, evaluation, management, and diffusion), the systematic design of instruction, and the nine events of instruction can facilitate intentional learning episodes that are culturally sensitive. Discusses cultural pluralism and explains the use of pluralism rather than diversity.

Brooks, D. W. (1997). **Web-teaching: A guide to designing interactive teaching for the World Wide Web**. [Book, 236pp., $25]. Plenum Publishing Corporation, 233 Spring St., New York, NY 10013-1578, (212)620-8000, (800)221-9369, info@plenum.com, http://www.plenum.com. Discusses the integration of Web tools and discussions into instructional designs.

Brush, T. A. (1997). The effects on student achievement and attitudes when using integrated learning systems with cooperative pairs. **Educational Technology Research and Development, 45** (1), 51-64. Describes a study that determined whether combining cooperative learning strategies with instruction delivered using an integrated learning system (ILS) produced academic and attitudinal gains in fifth-grade students. Results revealed that students using an ILS in cooperative groups for mathematics instruction performed better and were more positive toward math.

Carnine, D. (1997). Instructional design in mathematics for students with learning disabilities. **Journal of Learning Disabilities, 30** (2), 130-41. Describes and illustrates five areas of instructional design in mathematics well suited to students with learning disabilities. Suggested learning strategies for teachers to incorporate include using big ideas and conspicuous strategies; teaching efficient use of time; giving clear, explicit instruction on strategies; and taking time for appropriate practice and review.

Dijkstra, S. (1997). The integration of instructional systems design models and constructivistic design principles. **Instructional Science, 25** (1), 1-13. Constructivist theory argues that students construct knowledge for themselves and that each knows the world in a different way. The problem for education is how students can construct an "objectified" knowledge. Outlines an integrative framework for the description of information and problem-solving procedures and a problem-solving approach for the acquisition of knowledge and skills.

Dijkstra, S., Schott, F., Seel, N., & Tennyson, R. D., eds. (1997). **Instructional design: International perspectives**. 2 vols. [Books, 456pp. & 376pp.]. Lawrence Erlbaum, 10 Industrial Ave., Mahwah, NJ 07430-2262, orders@erlbaum.com. Strives to bridge the gap between instructional design principles and practice and define theoretical foundations.

Dills, C. R., & Romiszowski, A. J., eds. (1997). **Instructional development paradigms**. [Book, 882pp.] Englewood Cliffs, NJ: Educational Technology Publications. Contains sections on the philosophy of instructional development, cultural perspectives, theory, development macro-strategies, development micro-strategies, and technology-based paradigms.

El-Tigi, M., & Branch, R. M. (1997). Designing for interaction, learner control, and feedback during Web-based learning. **Educational Technology, 37** (3), 23-29. Combining concepts of instructional design with the attributes of Web technology is one way to maximize Web-based learning. Highlights the applications, limitations, and cognitive implications of Web-based organizational techniques such as frames, image maps, and tables, and outlines a two-phase Web-based learning design model.

Evaluation Practice. JAI Press, 55 Old Post Rd., No. 2, P.O. Box 1678, Greenwich CT 06836-1678. [Tri-ann., $80 indiv., $180 inst.]. Interdisciplinary journal aimed at helping evaluators improve practice in their disciplines, develop skills, and foster dialogue.

Frank, D. (1997). **Terrific training materials**. [Book, 200pp., $39.95]. Training Express, 11358 Aurora Ave., Des Moines, IA 50322. Provides hands-on, business-perspective approach to graphic design of manuals, handouts, and job aids.

Fripp, J. (1997). A future for business simulations? **Journal of European Industrial Training, 21** (4), 138-42. Although technical developments have occurred in the design and use of business simulations for management training, other changes are needed to keep them relevant. Design of simulations should address current and future trends in the workplace and skills that will be needed by managers.

Gros, B., & others. (1997). Instructional design and the authoring of multimedia and hypermedia systems: Does a marriage make sense? **Educational Technology, 37** (1), 48-56. Examines the relationship between instructional design (ID) and courseware development, especially for multimedia and hypermedia systems. Discusses ID models; external and internal reasons for the neglect of models; characteristics of models suitable for multimedia and hypermedia development; and models integrating those characteristics: Guided Approach to Instructional Design Advising (GAIDA) and Guidance for Open-Ended Learning Designs for Instructional Environments (GOLDIE).

Hashim, Y., & Tik, C. C. (1997). Use of instructional design with mastery learning. **Educational Technology, 37** (2), 61-63. Explains the use of instructional design with a mastery learning strategy (IDML) in teaching mathematics. The IDML model, a combination of other theories including Gagné's instructional events, has been used to improve mathematics instruction in Malaysian schools, and includes developing test items, the teachers' development of learning materials, and evaluation.

Human-Computer Interaction. Lawrence Erlbaum Associates, 365 Broadway, Hillsdale, NJ 07642. [Q., $39 indiv. US and Canada, $69 elsewhere, $230 inst., $260 elsewhere]. A journal of theoretical, empirical, and methodological issues of user science and of system design.

Instructional Science. Kluwer Academic Publishers, Order Dept., P.O. Box 358, Accor Station, Hingham, MA 02018-0358, (617)871-6600, fax (617)871-6528, kluwer@wkap.com. [Bi-mo., $345 inst.]. Promotes a deeper understanding of the nature, theory, and practice of the instructional process and the learning resulting from this process.

Jonassen, D. H. (1997). Instructional design models for well-structured and ill-structured problem-solving learning outcomes. **Educational Technology Research and Development, 45** (1), 65-94. Considers well-structured problems versus ill-structured problems and presents models for how learners solve them, as well as models for designing instruction to support problem-solving skill development. Information processing theories of learning, an emerging theory of ill-structured problem solving, constructivist learning, and situated cognition are discussed.

Jonassen, D. H., & others. (1997). Certainty, determinism, and predictability in theories of instructional design: Lessons from science. **Educational Technology, 37** (1), 27-34. The strongly positivist beliefs on which traditional conceptions of instructional design (ID) are based derive from Aristotelian logic and oversimplify the world, reducing human learning and performance to a repertoire of manipulatable behaviors. Reviews the cases against deterministic predictability and discusses hermeneutic, fuzzy logic, and chaos theory perspectives and their implications for ID.

Journal of Educational Technology Systems. Baywood Publishing Co., 26 Austin Ave., Box 337, Amityville, NY 11701. [Q., $136]. In-depth articles on completed and ongoing research in all phases of educational technology and its application and future within the teaching profession.

Journal of Interactive Instruction Development. Learning Technology Institute, Society for Applied Learning Technology, 50 Culpeper St., Warrenton, VA 22186. [Q., $60 indiv., $75 inst., add $15 postage outside North America]. A showcase of successful programs that will heighten awareness of innovative, creative, and effective approaches to courseware development for interactive technology.

Journal of Technical Writing and Communication. Baywood Publishing Co., 26 Austin Ave., Box 337, Amityville, NY 11701. [Q., $130 inst.]. Essays on oral and written communication, for purposes ranging from pure research to needs of business and industry.

Journal of Visual Literacy. International Visual Literacy Association, c/o John C. Belland, 122 Ramseyer Hall, 29 West Woodruff Ave., Ohio State University, Columbus, OH 43210. [Semi-ann., $18 US, $26 foreign]. Interdisciplinary forum on all aspects of visual/verbal languaging.

Kimczak, A. K., & Wedman, J. F. (1997). Instructional design project success factors: An empirical basis. **Educational Technology Research and Development, 45** (2), 75-83. A study of four stakeholder groups identified 23 instructional design and development (ID) project success factors and grouped them into four categories: tangible resources, curriculum development, training strategies, and implementation support. Data analysis revealed differences in the importance attached to the factors by the stakeholder groups and in the importance of success factor categories to ID project success.

Kincaid, T. M., & Horner, E. R. (1997). Designing, developing, and implementing diversity training: Guidelines for practitioners. **Educational Technology, 37** (2), 19-26. Discusses diversity in the workplace and offers guidelines for practitioners in designing, developing, and implementing diversity training. Highlights include linking the diversity initiative to the organization's mission, cultural climate assessments, reviewing policies and procedures, needs assessment, learner analysis, establishing objectives, using the nine events of instruction, and formative evaluation.

Kirby, A. (1997). **A compendium of icebreakers, energizers, and introductions**. [Book, 196pp., $69.95]. Training Express, 11358 Aurora Ave., Des Mones, IA 50322. Contains 75 activities designed to capture attention, motivate participants, and prepare participants for training.

Knupfer, N. N. (1997). Gendered by design. **Educational Technology, 37** (2), 31-37. Examines the relationship between gender equity and instructional design. Topics include stereotypes of men's and women's roles, perpetuating old assumptions and practices, inequities from instructional design, differing expectations, gender bias, and how instructional designers can help by being sensitive to these issues.

Layng, J. (1997). Parallels between project management and instructional design. **Performance Improvement, 36** (6), 16-20. Describes the stages of project management and instructional design. Outlines and compares the roles of project managers and instructional designers, and discusses how designers need to use a systematic approach that combines the stages of each process to remain detail-oriented while being cognizant of the entire project.

Liang, C. C., & Schwen, T. (1997). A framework for instructional development in corporate education. **Educational Technology, 37** (4), 42-45. Examines the gap between instructional development (ID) theory and practice and proposes a conceptual framework to describe how expert ID practitioners work in the corporate world. The framework consists of cultural context, situation analysis and synthesis, client and other stakeholders, performance capacities, and competitive advantages.

Lohman, M. C. (1997). Effects of an inductive versus a deductive instructional approach on the constructive feedback and problem-solving skills of supervisors. **Performance Improvement Quarterly, 10** (3), 37-55. Investigates the effects of an inductive versus a deductive instructional approach on the constructive feedback and problem-solving skills of supervisors. Assesses 16 supervisors' acquisition and transfer of skill in giving instructional feedback, facilitating of subordinate problem-solving skill, and attitudes toward training. Discusses implications for instructional design theory, research, and practice.

Mager, R. F. (1997). **Analyzing performance problems**. 3rd ed. [Book, $19.95]. Center for Effective Performance, 4250 Perimeter Park South, Suite 131, Atlanta, GA 30341, (800) 558-4237, fax (770)458-9109. Describes a systematic process for determining why desired results are not being achieved.

Mager, R. F. (1997). **Goal analysis**. 3rd ed. [Book, $19.95]. Center for Effective Performance, 4250 Perimeter Park South, Suite 131, Atlanta, GA 30341, (800)558-4237, fax (770)458-9109. Discusses all aspects of goal recognition, definition, and achievement so that appropriate instruction can be designed.

Mager, R. F. (1997). **Making instruction work**. 2nd ed. [Book, $19.95]. Center for Effective Performance, 4250 Perimeter Park South, Suite 131, Atlanta, GA 30341, (800)558-4237, fax (770)458-9109. A step-by-step guide to designing and developing effective instruction.

Mager, R. F. (1997). **Measuring instructional results**. 3rd ed. [Book, $19.95]. Center for Effective Performance, 4250 Perimeter Park South, Suite 131, Atlanta, GA 30341, (800)558-4237, fax (770)458-9109. Updated text with four revised chapters and practice exercises. Describes methods for determining when instructional objectives have been achieved.

Mager, R. F. (1997). **Preparing instructional objectives**. 3rd ed. [Book, $19.95]. Center for Effective Performance, 4250 Perimeter Park South, Suite 131, Atlanta, GA 30341, (800)558-4237, fax (770)458-9109. The new edition of this classic contains practice exercises, an objectives effectiveness checklist, a new chapter discussing objective origination, and a new index.

Means, T. B., Jonassen, D. H., & Dwyer, F. (1997). Enhancing relevance: Embedded ARCs strategies vs. purpose. **Educational Technology Research and Development, 45** (1), 5-17. This study compared the effects of intrinsic relevance with embedded, extrinsic relevance-enhancing strategies based on the ARCS (attention, relevance, confidence, and satisfaction) model of instruction on perceived motivation and the learning outcomes of identification, terminology, comprehension, and drawing. Both intrinsic and extrinsic strategies enhanced the motivation of the college learners.

Merrill, M. D. (1997). Learning-oriented instructional development tools. **Performance Improvement, 36** (3), 51-55. Discusses design requirements, and advantages and disadvantages of the following learner-centered instructional development tools: information containers; authoring systems; templates, models, or widgets; learning-oriented instructional development tools; and adaptive learning-oriented systems.

Milheim, W. (1997). Instructional design issues for electronic performance support systems. **British Journal of Educational Technology, 28** (2), 103-10. Reviews instructional design issues for electronic performance support systems and outlines strategies for developing an effective system for a given work setting. Discusses overall design, the information database, the advisory and instructional components, and access to applications software.

Muldner, T., & others. (1997). Experience from the design of an authoring environment. **Journal of Educational Multimedia and Hypermedia, 6** (1), 115-32. Computer-based teaching is ineffective when instructional systems are designed emphasizing technology rather than course information. In view of this, the development of NEAT (Integrated Environment for Authoring in

ToolBook) at Acadia University (Nova Scotia) is discussed. Other topics include intelligent tutoring systems, a question repository and student models, and pros and cons of ToolBook.

Performance and Instruction. International Society for Performance Improvement, 1300 L St. NW, Suite 1250, Washington, DC 20005. [10/yr., $69]. Journal of ISPI; promotes performance science and technology. Contains articles, research, and case studies relating to improving human performance.

Performance Improvement Quarterly. International Society for Performance Improvement, 1300 L St. NW, Suite 1250, Washington, DC 20005. [Q., $20]. Presents the cutting edge in research and theory in performance technology.

Persico, D. (1997). Methodological constants in courseware design. **British Journal of Educational Technology, 28** (2), 111-23. Examines the methodological common denominator among several models for courseware development and discusses in detail both the design and the validation phases. Emphasizes the need for a systematic approach in which multiple authors' skills are exploited and the cost-benefit ratio is kept at an acceptable level.

Powell, G. C. (1997). On being a culturally sensitive instructional designer and educator. **Educational Technology, 37** (2), 6-14. Discusses the need for instructional designers, trainers, and educators to have cultural sensitivity, or a cross-cultural perspective and awareness. Considers learning environment, classroom rituals, intelligence assessment instruments, cultural background, teacher-student relationship, nonverbal behavior, discipline, locus of control, rewards, and student attitudes. A cultural sensitivity quiz is also included.

Reigeluth, C. M., ed. (1997). Instructional theory, practitioner needs, and new directions: Some reflections. **Educational Technology, 37** (1), 42-47. Examines issues related to theory and instructional systems design: the utility of theory; differences between descriptive (scientific) and design (goal-oriented) theories; the value of multiple theoretical perspectives; the inadequacy of current instructional design theories; and new directions needed in instructional theory, emphasizing the effects of a shift from industry to information.

Shambaugh, R. N., & Magliaro, S. G. (1997). **Mastering the possibilities: A process approach to instructional design**. [Book, 308pp., instructor's manual available]. Allyn & Bacon, 160 Gould St., Needham Heights, MA 02194-2315. Uses learner-centered approach in designing instruction with integrated experiences.

Stamps, D. (1997). Communities of practice: Learning is social, training is irrelevant? **Training, 34** (2), 34-42. Some training failures may be attributed to lack of recognition that learning is a social activity and that collective learning results in communities of practice. The experiences of Dede Miller at Xerox Corporation and the gap that separates learning theory and common training practice show how hard it is to apply new approaches to workplace training.

Starr, R. M. (1997). Delivering instruction on the World Wide Web: Overview and basic design principles. **Educational Technology, 37** (3), 7-15. This paper presents a history of the Internet and the World Wide Web, describes benefits and disadvantages of the Web for instructional programs, makes recommendations for Web-based instructional design, and provides technical information for Web-based learning. A glossary of terms is also included.

Sugrue, B., & Kobus, R. C. (1997). Beyond information: Increasing the range of instructional resources on the World Wide Web. **TechTrends, 42** (2), 38-42. Describes a prototype for a World Wide Web site that supports as many student and instructor needs as possible and was developed for a graduate course on instructional design. Topics include roles of the instructor and of the webmaster, student perspectives, technical design issues, user interface, and graphics.

Tessmer, M., & Richey, R. C. (1997). The role of context in learning and instructional design. **Educational Technology Research and Development, 45** (2), 85-115. Although context is a potent force in learning, instructional design models contain little guidance in accommodating contextual elements to improve learning and transfer. Defines context, outlines levels and types, specifies contextual factors within the types, suggests methods for conducting contextual analysis for instructional design, and outlines future issues for context-based instructional design.

Training. Lakewood Publications, Inc., 50 S. Ninth, Minneapolis, MN 55402. [Mo., $78 US, $88 Canada, $99 elsewhere]. Covers all aspects of training, management, and organizational development, motivation, and performance improvement.

Winn, W., ed. (1997). Advantages of a theory-based curriculum in instructional technology. **Educational Technology, 37** (1), 34-41. Discusses the current state of instructional technology programs, highlighting two problems with a prescriptive approach to instructional design (ID): making ID entirely empirical by assuming finite and knowable instructional principles and the ultimate impossibility of using prescriptions in any procedural way. Explores why and what theory is needed and the role of the university in preparing instructional technologists.

Wright, C. R. (1997). Educational technology consulting in developing countries. **TechTrends, 42** (1), 35-40. Provides information for educational technologists who are considering work as consultants in developing countries. Discusses cultural, societal, and political differences; issues of personnel, funding, and power and telecommunications systems; and selecting media. Suggests guidelines for selecting instructional materials and designing distance education systems, and includes the code of conduct for international consultants.

INTERACTIVE MULTIMEDIA

Brett, P. (1997). A comparative study of the effects of the use of multimedia on listening comprehension. **System, 25** (1), 39-53. Investigates listening performance in a computer-based multimedia environment. Learner success rates were compared on comprehension of English as a Second Language and language recall tasks while using audio, video, and multimedia. Results of performance on tasks reveal more effective comprehension and recall while using multimedia than either audio or video plus pen and paper.

Catenazzi, N., & others. (1997). The evaluation of electronic book guidelines from two practical experiences. **Journal of Educational Multimedia and Hypermedia, 6** (1), 91-114. This study applied evaluation techniques to "Cesar" (a hypermedia learning environment for deaf children based on electronic stories) and "Hyper-Book" (an electronic book based on the paper book metaphor and designed to be part of an electronic library). It also identifies steps that can be used in evaluating electronic books regardless of application domain.

Cates, W. M., & Goodling, S. C. (1997). The relative effectiveness of learning options in multimedia computer-based fifth-grade spelling instruction. **Educational Technology Research and Development, 45** (2), 27-46. A study of 38 fifth-grade students investigated the effectiveness of two interactive multimedia instructional spelling programs, one offering behaviorist-visual learning options and the other offering cognitivist-phonological learning options. Both groups showed increased spelling ability, though neither program outperformed the other, suggesting computer-based spelling instruction can be an effective instructional tool.

CD-ROM World. PC World Communication Inc., 501 Second St., Suite 600, San Francisco, CA 94107. [10/yr., $29]. Articles and reviews for CD-ROM users.

Chen, P. W., & Chang, S. K. (1997). Knowledge-based multimedia information retrieval in hyperspace. **Telematics and Information, 14** (1), 27-50. Presents a World Wide Web page model that reacts to predefined events and performs actions like "prefetching" automatically. Discusses the active index, conceptual page model, design of the client system, status of the current implementation, prefetching algorithm, an experiment of the algorithm, experimental results of the active index system, and future work. Includes the active index specification.

Cockerton, T., & Shimell, R. (1997). Evaluation of a hypermedia document as a learning tool. **Journal of Computer Assisted Learning, 13** (2), 133-44. To evaluate the effectiveness of a hypermedia learning package about the Middle Ages, two groups of seventh-graders completed either instructional worksheets with a book or a hypermedia package. No differences were found between the two groups in the number of questions completed, questions answered correctly, interest in material, or task difficulty.

Deadman, G. (1997). An analysis of pupils' reflective writing within a hypermedia framework. **Journal of Computer Assisted Learning, 13** (1), 16-25. Describes a study of 24 secondary school students in London (England) that explored ways in which reflective writing supported pupils' learning. Writing with support from the teacher was compared with support from the teacher and from a hypermedia framework, and results showed improvement in pupils' ability to reason with the hypermedia support.

Fitzgerald, G. E., & others. (1997). An interactive multimedia program to enhance teacher problem-solving skills based on cognitive flexibility theory: Design and outcomes. **Journal of Education Multimedia and Hypermedia, 6** (1), 47-76. Cognitive flexibility theory is a constructivist learning paradigm emphasizing real-world complexity and the ill-structured nature of knowledge. This article discusses the design of a multimedia program (Perspectives on Emotional and Behavioral Disorders) based on cognitive flexibility theory and presents quantitative and qualitative results of two field tests of the materials in graduate education courses.

Galas, C. (1997-1998). From presentation to programming: Doing something different, not the same thing differently. **Learning & Leading with Technology, 25** (4), 18-21. Describes student use of *MicroWorlds* to simulate an ocean ecosystem containing dolphins.

Gillham, M., & Buckner, K. (1997). User evaluation of hypermedia encyclopedias. **Journal of Educational Multimedia and Hypermedia, 6** (1), 77-90. To establish evaluation criteria for home multimedia products, this study examined 13 case studies of experienced users of CD-ROM encyclopedias aimed at the home consumer. Findings ranked seven features from most to least important: searching; textual content; browsing; multimedia; aesthetics; interactivity; and system performance. Results suggest that users employed the material inefficiently, especially in search strategies.

Handler, M. G., & Dana, A. S. (1998). **Hypermedia as a student tool: A guide for teachers**. 2nd ed. [Book, 350pp., $30]. Libraries Unlimited, P.O. Box 6633, Englewood, CO 80155-6633, (800)237-6124, fax (303)220-8843, lu-books@lu.com, http://www.lu.com. Demonstrates a variety of hypermedia programs, provides instructional strategies, and describes hypermedia learning environments conducive to collaboration.

Ivers, K. S., & Barron, A. E. (1997). **Multimedia projects in education: Designing, producing, and assessing**. [Book, 200pp., $25]. Libraries Unlimited, P.O. Box 6633, Englewood, CO 80155-6633, (800)237-6124, fax (303)220-8843, lu-books@lu.com, http://www.lu.com. Describes a model that takes fourth- through twelfth-grade students through the entire design process, including evaluation. Includes black line masters for guides, organizers, and assessment tools, as well as ideas and implementation strategies.

Journal of Educational Multimedia and Hypermedia. Association for the Advancement of Computing in Education, Box 2966, Charlottesville, VA 22902-2966. [Q., $65 indiv., $75 foreign, $93 inst., $103 foreign]. A multidisciplinary information source presenting research about and applications for multimedia and hypermedia tools.

Journal of Hypermedia and Multimedia Studies. ISTE, University of Oregon, 1787 Agate St., Eugene, OR 97403-1923, (800)336-5191, cust_svc@ccmail.uoregon.edu. [Q., $29 US, $41.73 Canada, $39 intl., $42 intl. air]. Features articles on projects, lesson plans, and theoretical issues, as well as reviews of products, software, and books.

Korolenko, M. (1997). **Writing for multimedia: A guide and source book for the digital writer**. [Book, 400pp.]. Integrated Media Group, Belmont, CA. Covers the style of writing required for nonlinear text.

Luna, C. J., & McKenzie, J. (1997). Testing multimedia in the community college classroom. **T.H.E. Journal, 24** (7), 78-81. The efficacy of multimedia in community college instruction is examined, with a focus on how students with different cognitive styles respond. The majority of students agreed that using the CD-ROM was a positive experience. Qualitative data provide a stronger case (than the quantitative data) that student performance improved, especially in the case of underrepresented students.

Peck, D. D. (1997). **Multimedia: A hands-on introduction**. [Book with CD-ROM, 320pp.]. Thomson. Written for multimedia and graphics arts courses; covers history, technique, current technology, and resources.

Phillips, R. (1997). **The developer's handbook to interactive multimedia: A practical guide for education applications**. [Book, 224pp., $35]. Cassell/Stylus, P.O. Box 605, Herndon, VA 20172-0605, (800)232-0223, fax (703)661-1510, styluspub@aol.com. Describes the design of multimedia support for education. Discusses technical aspects; includes examples and case studies.

Rojo, A., & Ragsdale, R. G. (1997). Participation in electronic forums: Implications for the design and implementation of collaborative distributed multimedia. **Telematics and Informatics, 14** (1), 83-96. Describes participation patterns in scholarly mailing lists; analyzes their implications for the design and implementation of collaborative distributed multimedia, particularly systems intended for academic and professional settings; and suggests that participant reluctance to invest time in reading or contributing messages could be amplified when participation involves the composition of multimedia messages.

Simpson, C. (1997). How much, how many and when? Copyright and multimedia. **Book Report, 16** (1), 25-26, 65. Discusses new guidelines for fair use as it impacts student multimedia projects and other educational uses.

Smith, I., & Yoder, S. (1998). **On the Web or off: Hypermedia design basics**. [Book, 151pp., $18.95]. ISTE, 480 Charnelton St., Eugene, OR 97401-2626, (800)336-5191, fax (541)302-3887. From the Instant Success Series. Presents clear instructions and basic guidelines for designing media, supplemented by a discussion of design elements added by hypermedia.

Welsh, T. (1997). From multimedia to multiple-media: Designing computer-based course materials for the Information Age. **TechTrends, 42** (1), 17-23. Suggests a strategy for designing course materials for use in multiple digital formats.

White, S. H., & Kuhn, T. (1997). A comparison of elementary students' information recall on text documents, oral reading, and multimedia. **Journal of Computing in Childhood Education, 8** (1), 15-21. This study examined the effect of different modes of presentation on the amount of information elementary students (n=38) in mixed-age classrooms can recall about historical figures. Assessment of information recall followed a pre-test/post-test format. Analysis showed no significant difference in recall due to the varied modes of presentation.

LIBRARIES AND MEDIA CENTERS

Albaugh, P. R., & others. (1997). Using a CD-ROM encyclopedia: Interaction of teachers, middle school students, library media specialists, and the technology. **Research in Middle Level Education Quarterly, 20** (3), 43-55. Observed sixth-grade students and their ways of gathering information for a science report from *Encarta 94*, a CD-ROM encyclopedia. Developed recommendations for collaboration between the classroom teacher and the school library media specialist during the implementation of CD-ROM technology for information gathering, as well as ways to manage a CD-ROM-based project.

Barber, P. (1997). Computers, technology, books—Yes, but literacy must come first. **American Libraries, 28** (5), 42-43. Argues that librarians have five reasons to give literacy building top mission priority.

Benson, A. C. (1997). **Neal-Schuman complete Internet companion for librarians**. 2nd ed. [Book, 500pp., $65]. Neal-Schuman Publishers, 100 Varick St., New York, NY 10013-1506, (212)925-8650, fax (800)584-2414, orders@neal-schuman.com. Offers instructions and explanations of Internet tools and protocols, using library illustrations.

Benson, A. C. (1998). **Securing library PCs and data: A handbook with menuing, anti-virus, and other protective software**. [Book and CD-ROM, 250pp., $125]. Neal-Schuman Publishers, 100 Varick St., New York, NY 10013-1506, (212)925-8650, fax (800)584-2414, orders@neal-schuman.com. Discusses Windows security problems for library application. Topics include blocking unauthorized access, viruses, hacking, theft, usage policies, backup procedures, disaster recovery, and hard-drive maintenance.

Book Report. Linworth Publishing, 480 E. Wilson Bridge Rd., Suite L, Worthington, OH 43085-2372, (800)786-5017, fax (614)436-9490, orders@linworth.com, http://linworth.com. [5/school yr., $44 US, $9 single copy]. Journal for junior and senior high school librarians provides articles, tips, and ideas for day-to-day school library management, as well as reviews of audiovisuals and software, all written by school librarians.

Bosman, E., & Rusinek, C. (1997). Creating the user-friendly library by evaluating patron perception of signage. **RSR: Reference Services Review, 25** (1), 71-82. Librarians at Indiana University Northwest Library surveyed patrons on how to make the library's collection and services more accessible by improving signage. Examines the effectiveness of signage to instruct users, reduce difficulties and fears, ameliorate negative experiences, and contribute to a user-friendly environment.

Boss, R. (1997). **The library administrator's automation handbook**. [Book, 226pp., $39.50]. Information Today, 143 Old Marlton Pike, Medford, NJ 08055, (800)300-9868. Covers the automation process, including updated information of current hardware, system architecture, software, standards, and data communication. Includes related and often linked technologies such as CD-ROM, remote database services, and the Internet.

Burks, F. (1997). Faculty use of school library media centers in selected high schools in Greater Dallas-Fort Worth, Texas. **School Library Media Quarterly, 25** (3), 143-49. This is the second part of a descriptive survey that analyzed the behavior of students and faculty in three high school library media centers in the Dallas-Fort Worth (Texas) area. It reports on the nature and extent of faculty use of library media centers and describes their perceptions of service, and compares data with an earlier study.

Burt, D. (1997). In defense of filtering. **American Libraries, 28** (7), 46, 48. Responds to 10 common arguments commonly used against the practice of filtering the Internet in libraries.

Byerly, G., & Brodie, C. S. (1997). **Children's reference and information services**. [Book, 352pp., $49]. Oryx Press, 4041 North Central Ave., Suite 700, Phoenix, AZ 85012-3397, (800)279-6799, fax (800)279-4663. Annotates and recommends over 500 reference sources for K-8 students.

Byrne, D. J. (1997). **MARC manual: Understanding and using MARC records**. [Book, 270pp., $34]. Libraries Unlimited, P.O. Box 6633, Englewood, CO 80155-6633, (800)237-6124, fax (303)220-8843, lu-books@lu.com, http://www.lu.com. Explains the three types of MARC records, along with considerations and specifications for MARC database processing.

California Media & Library Education Association. (1997). **From library skills to information literacy: A handbook for the 21st century**. 2nd ed. Hi Willow Research & Publishing, Castle Rock, CO. Covers information skills through curricular integration; provides models and strategies. Outlines the adaptation of these principles for ESL students.

Callison, D., & Grover, R. (1997). **The AASL electronic library, 1997 ed**. [Book, $40]. ALA Order Fulfillment, 50 East Huron St., Chicago, IL 60611, (800)545-2433. Contains documents pertaining to school library issues, including 100 new ones, National Library Power Program information, Department of Education activities, and selected articles from *School Library Media Quarterly*.

Champelli, L., & Rosenbaum, H. (1997). **Neal-Schuman Webmaster**. [Book & CD-ROM, 160pp., $175]. Neal-Schuman Publishers, 100 Varick St., New York, NY 10013-1506, (212)925-8650, fax (800)584-2414, orders@neal-schuman.com. Provides templates, icons, training modules, and design principles for library Web page construction.

Cibbarelli, P. (1997). **Directory of library automation software, systems, and services**. [Book, $89]. Information Today, 143 Old Marlton Pike, Medford, NJ 08055, (800)300-9868. Indexes resources, distributors, and automation packages for micro, mini, and mainframe computers.

Cibbarelli, P. (1997). **IOLS '97: Proceedings of the 12th integrated online library systems meeting, May 14-15, 1997.** [Book, 175pp., $30]. Information Today, 143 Old Marlton Pike, Medford, NJ 08055, (800)300-9868. Contains 21 papers addressing a variety of automation topics, including Internet connectivity, system design, and document delivery from the user's perspective.

Cohn, J. M., Kelsey, A. L., & Fiels, K. M. (1997). **Planning for automation**. [Book, 150pp., $49.95]. Neal-Schuman Publishers, 100 Varick St., New York, NY 10013-1506, (212)925-8650, fax (800)584-2414, orders@neal-schuman.com. Targets the automation procedure for small- to medium-sized libraries.

Collection Building. M.C.B. University Press Ltd., 60-62 Toller Ln., Bradford, W. Yorks BD8 9BY, England. [Q., $89]. Focuses on all aspects of collection building, ranging from microcomputers to business collections to popular topics and censorship.

Computers in Libraries. Information Today, 143 Old Marlton Pike, Medford, NJ 08055, (800)300-9868. [10/yr., $89.95 US, $41.95 indiv./K-12, $51.95 Canada, Mexico, $59.95 outside North America]. Covers practical applications of microcomputers to library situations and recent news items.

Daugherty, T. K., & Carter, E. W. (1997). Assessment of outcome-focused library instruction in psychology. **Journal of Instructional Psychology, 24** (1), 29-33. A sample of 49 nonpsychology majors taking a course integrating library research skills with social science research showed increases in skill level, efficiency, and positive attitudes toward the library after a semester of outcome-focused instruction. The results suggest that codevelopment between course and library faculty can be an effective approach to library instruction.

Dewey, P. R. (1997). **303 software programs to use in your library: Descriptions, evaluations, and practical advice**. [Book, 304pp., $36]. American Library Association, ALA Editions, 50 East Huron St., Chicago, IL 60611-2795; (800)545-2433; fax (312)836-9958. Reviews currently available software with specialized library needs in mind.

Dillon, K. (1997). Serving the professional information needs of rural secondary-school teachers in New South Wales, Australia. **School Library Media Quarterly, 25** (3), 171-76. Describes a study that examined the professional information needs of rural secondary school teachers in New South Wales (Australia). Concludes that teacher librarians have a pivotal role in meeting information needs, and that computer networks provide a means of overcoming the teachers' professional and geographical isolation.

The Electronic Library. Information Today, 143 Old Marlton Pike, Medford, NJ 08055, (800)300-9868. [Bi-mo., $127 US, $137 Canada/Mexico]. International journal for minicomputer, microcomputer, and software applications in libraries; independently assesses current and forthcoming information technologies.

Emergency Librarian. Box 34069, Dept. 284, Seattle, WA 98124-1069, eml@rockland.com. [Bi-mo. except July-Aug., $49]. Articles, review columns, and critical analyses of management and programming issues for children's and young adult librarians.

Ensor, P., ed. (1997). **The cybrarian's manual**. [Book, 472pp., $42]. American Library Association, ALA Editions, 50 East Huron St., Chicago, IL 60611-2795, (800)545-2433, fax (312)836-9958. Extensive librarian's access guide to Internet service, including OPACs, SGML, HTML, client/server architecture, multimedia, network standards, and intellectual freedom.

Foote, J. B., & others. (1997). Electronic library resources: Navigating the maze. **Resource Sharing & Information Networks, 12** (2), 5-17. A review of statistics on CD-ROM usage on the Southern Illinois University at Carbondale's library network revealed patron difficulty in utilizing electronic indexes. Appropriate database selection and searching problems are identified, and introductory workshops on electronic library resources are suggested to assist students in making better choices among the available CD-ROM databases.

Fritz, D. A. (1997). **Cataloging with AACR2 and MARC**. [Book, 608pp., $60]. American Library Association, ALA Editions, 50 East Huron St., Chicago, IL 60611-2795, (800)545-2433, fax (312)836-9958. Provides essential cataloging authority for libraries of all types and sizes; organized by media type.

Gerhardt, L., ed. (1997). **School Library Journal's best: A reader for children's, young adult and school librarians**. [Book, 474pp., $39.95]. Neal-Schuman Publishers, 100 Varick St., New York, NY 10013-1506, (212)925-8650, fax (800)584-2414, orders@neal-schuman.com. Contains over 200 articles published over 40 years in *SLJ*.

Government Information Quarterly. JAI Press, 55 Old Post Rd., No. 2, P.O. Box 1678, Greenwich, CT 06836-1678. [Q., $80 indiv., $100 foreign; $205 inst., $225 foreign]. International journal of resources, services, policies, and practices.

Gross, M. (1997). Pilot study on the prevalence of imposed queries in a school library media center. **School Library Media Quarterly, 25** (3), 157-59. Discussion of information-seeking behavior focuses on a study of the imposed query, as opposed to self-generated queries, in an elementary school library media center in order to quantify its presence, to record characteristics of the users that carry them, and to identify the persons imposing them.

Heath, J. A. (1997). The combined school/community library: An enhanced sense of community through shared public services. **ERS Spectrum, 15** (2), 28-34. Discusses a study of combined school/community libraries in eight small communities in South Dakota and Minnesota. Students get more time to use the library, enhanced collections and research opportunities, and improved technological access. The community gets longer operating hours, a better reference section, access to technology, and a cost-sharing benefit. Generally, a combined library seems best suited to small communities of 5,000 or less.

Heller, N. (1998). **Technology connections for grades 3-5: Research projects and activities**. [Book, 210pp., $24]. Libraries Unlimited, P.O. Box 6633, Englewood, CO 80155-6633, (800)237-6124, fax (303)220-8843, lu-books@lu.com, http://www.lu.com. Presents practical projects connecting information literacy, technology skills, and the elementary curriculum through collaboration between teachers and media specialists.

Howden, N. (1997). **Local area networking for the small library: A how-to-do-it manual for librarians**. 2nd ed. [Book, 150pp., $39.95]. Neal-Schuman Publishers, 100 Varick St., New York, NY 10013-1506, (212)925-8650, fax (800)584-2414, orders@neal-schuman.com. Describes all aspects of LAN networking for small libraries, including TCP/IP, Novell, Internet hardware, Web equipment issues, Windows NT and Windows for Workgroups, and LINUX.

Information Outlook (formerly *Special Libraries*). Special Libraries Association, 1700 18th St., NW, Washington, DC 20009-2508. [Q., $65 nonmembers (foreign $75), $10 single copy]. Discusses administration, organization, and operations. Includes reports on research, technology, and professional standards.

Information Services and Use. Elsevier Science Publishers, Box 10558, Burke, VA 22009-0558. [4/yr., $254]. Contains data on international developments in information management and its applications. Articles cover online systems, library automation, word processing, micrographics, videotex, and telecommunications.

Jacso, P. (1997). The hardware helper II: Finding the right sytem for accessing the Web. **School Library Journal, 43** (1), 30-33. Recommends providing two computers for Web access, one for text-based sites and a faster one for graphics-heavy sites.

Journal of Academic Librarianship. JAI Press, 55 Old Post Rd., No. 2, Box 1678, Greenwich, CT 06836-1678. [Bi-mo., $60 indiv., $80 foreign, $160 inst., $185 foreign inst.]. Results of significant research, issues and problems facing academic libraries, book reviews, and innovations in academic libraries.

Journal of Government Information (formerly *Government Publications Review*). Elsevier Science Ltd., Journals Division, 660 White Plains Rd., Tarrytown, NY 10591-5153. [Bi-mo., £251, $472 US]. An international journal covering production, distribution, bibliographic control, accessibility, and use of government information in all formats and at all levels.

Journal of Librarianship and Information Science. Worldwide Subscription Service Ltd., Unit 4, Gibbs Reed Farm, Ticehurst, E. Sussex TN5 7HE, England. [Q., $155]. Deals with all aspects of library and information work in the United Kingdom and reviews literature from international sources.

Journal of Library Administration. Haworth Press, 10 Alice St., Binghamton, NY 13904-1580, (800)HAWORTH, fax (800)895-0582, getinfo@haworth.com, http://www.haworth.com. [Q., $40 indiv., $115 inst.]. Provides information on all aspects of effective library management, with emphasis on practical applications.

Kafai, Y., & Bates, M. F. (1997). Internet Web-searching instruction in the elementary classroom: Building a foundation for information literacy. **School Library Media Quarterly, 25** (2), 103-11. Describes a preliminary study of six elementary classrooms examining Web searching instruction and relates findings regarding management, skill development, and critical thinking.

Kennedy, S., ed. (1997). **Reference sources for small and medium-sized libraries**. 6th ed. [Book, 448pp., $50]. American Library Association, ALA Editions, 50 East Huron St., Chicago, IL 60611-2795, (800)545-2433, fax (312)836-9958. Describes useful reference sources for small and medium-sized public or academic libraries and their users; has over 2,000 entries.

Koechley, R. (1997). **Libraries and the Internet**. [Book, 104pp., $15]. Highsmith Press, P.O. Box 800, Fort Atkinson, WI 53538-0800. Concise survey of Internet issues, including safety, reference, and home page development.

Kovacs, D., & Kovacs, M. (1997). **The cybrarian's guide to developing successful Internet programs and services**. [Book, 225pp., $59.95]. Neal-Schuman Publishers, 100 Varick St., New York, NY 10013-1506, (212)925-8650, fax (800)584-2414, orders@neal-schuman.com. Discusses Internet use as a library service. Topics include electronic journals, using the Internet as a support medium for coursework and distance education, traditional library services, and electronic archives.

Library and Information Science Research. Ablex Publishing Corp., 55 Old Post Rd., No. 2, P.O. Box 5297, Greenwich, CT 06831-0504. [Q., $70 indiv., $170 inst.]. Research articles, dissertation reviews, and book reviews on issues concerning information resources management.

Library Hi Tech. Pierian Press, Box 1808, Ann Arbor, MI 48106, (800)678-2435. [Q., $45 indiv., $75 inst.]. Concentrates on reporting on the selection, installation, maintenance, and integration of systems and hardware.

Library Journal. Box 59690, Boulder, CO 80322-9690, (800)677-6694, fax (800)604-7455. [22/yr., $94.50 US, $116 Canada, $159 elsewhere]. A professional periodical for librarians, with current issues and news, professional reading, a lengthy book review section, and classified advertisements.

Library Quarterly. University of Chicago Press, Journals Division, Box 37005, Chicago, IL 60637. [Q., $34 indiv., $64 inst.]. Scholarly articles of interest to librarians.

Library Resources and Technical Services. Association for Library Collections and Technical Services, 50 E. Huron St., Chicago, IL 60611-2795. [Q., $55 nonmembers]. Scholarly papers on bibliographic access and control, preservation, conservation, and reproduction of library materials.

Library Software Review. Sage Publications, Inc., 2455 Teller Rd., Thousand Oaks, CA 91320. [Q., $49 indiv., $170 US inst., foreign add $8]. Emphasizes practical aspects of library computing for libraries of all types, including reviews of automated systems ranging from large-scale mainframe-based systems to microcomputer-based systems, and both library-specific and general-purpose software used in libraries.

Library Trends. University of Illinois Press, Journals Dept., 1325 S. Oak St., Champaign, IL 61820. [Q., $50 indiv., $75 inst., add $7 elsewhere]. Each issue is concerned with one aspect of library and information science, analyzing current thought and practice and examining ideas that hold the greatest potential for the field.

LISA: Library and Information Science Abstracts. Bowker-Saur Ltd., Maypole House, Maypole Rd., E. Grinsted, W. Sussex RH19 1HH, England. [Mo., $785 US, £380 elsewhere]. More than 500 abstracts per issue from more than 500 periodicals, reports, books, and conference proceedings.

MacDonald, R. M. (1997). **The Internet and the school library media specialist**. [Book, 224pp., $39.95]. Greenwood Publishing Group, 88 Post Rd. W., P.O. Box 5007, Westport, CT 06881-5007, (203)226-3571, fax (203)222-1502. Introduces media specialists with little or no experience to the Internet, including resource identification and learning activities.

Mather, B. R. (1997). **Creating a local area network in the school library media center**. [Book, 160pp., $39.95]. Greenwood Publishing Group, 88 Post Rd. W., P.O. Box 5007, Westport, CT 06881-5007, (203)226-3571, fax (203)222-1502. Provides practical information for planning, funding, creating, and maintaining media LANs.

Maxymuk, J. (1997). **Using desktop publishing to create newsletter, library guides, and Web pages: A how-to-do-it manual for librarians**. [Book, 221pp., $49.95]. Neal-Schuman Publishers, 100 Varick St., New York, NY 10013-1506, (212)925-8650, fax (800)584-2414, orders @neal-schuman.com. Describes the creation of library materials with desktop publishing software, including design rules, newsletters, library guides, and Web pages.

Meghabghab, D. B. (1997). **Automating media centers and small libraries**. [Book, 200pp., $30]. Libraries Unlimited, P.O. Box 6633, Englewood, CO 80155-6633, (800)237-6124, fax (303)220-8843, lu-books@lu.com, http://www.lu.com. Covers the entire spectrum of activities involved in automating media centers and small libraries.

Microcomputers for Information Management. Ablex Publishing, 355 Chestnut St., Norwood, NJ 07648. [Q., $40 indiv., $120 inst.]. Focuses on new developments with microcomputer technology in libraries and in information science in the US and abroad.

Morrison, H. (1997). Information literacy skills: An exploratory focus group study of student perceptions. **Research Strategies, 15** (1), 4-17. Reports the results of an information literacy research study in which focus group methodology was used. A small focus group of undergraduates discussed the concept of information literacy and the role of the undergraduate library in developing information literacy skills. Information needs, information seeking, and further research are also discussed.

Naumer, J. N., & Thurman, G. B. (1998). **The Works for library and media center management**. [Book, 200pp., Dos/Windows disk, $32.50]. Libraries Unlimited, P.O. Box 6633, Englewood, CO 80155-6633, (800)237-6124, fax (303)220-8843, lu-books@lu.com, http://www.lu.com. Demonstrates how media specialists can use integrated software packages to analyze and meet management needs. Disk contains templates. [See Thurman & Naumer for similar book in Macintosh version.]

Ogg, H.C. (1997). **Introduction to the use of computers in libraries**. [Book, 324pp., $42.50]. Information Today, 143 Old Marlton Pike, Medford, NJ 08055, (800)300-9868. Surveys uses of a variety of applications for library purposes. Also discusses automation systems and selection issues.

Peck, R. (1997). From strawberry statements to censorship. **School Library Journal, 43** (1), 28-29. A well-known children's author offers his opinions on the censorship controversy.

The Public-Access Computer Systems Review. An electronic journal published on an irregular basis by the University Libraries, University of Houston, Houston, TX 77204-2091, Lthompson @uh.edu. Free to libraries. Contains articles about all types of computer systems that libraries make available to their patrons and technologies to implement these systems.

Public Libraries. Public Library Association, American Library Association, ALA Editions, 50 East Huron St., Chicago, IL 60611-2795, (800)545-2433, fax (312)836-9958. [Bi-mo., $50 US nonmembers, $60 elsewhere, $10 single copy]. News and articles of interest to public librarians.

Public Library Quarterly. Haworth Press, 10 Alice St., Binghamton, NY 13904-1580, (800)HAWORTH, fax (800)895-0582, getinfo@haworth.com, http://www.haworth.com. [Q., $40 indiv., $140 inst.]. Addresses the major administrative challenges and opportunities that face the nation's public libraries.

Reference Librarian. Haworth Press, 10 Alice St., Binghamton, NY 13904-1580, (800)HAWORTH, fax (800)895-0582, getinfo@haworth.com, http://www.haworth.com. [2/yr., $60 indiv., $160 inst.]. Each issue focuses on a topic of current concern, interest, or practical value to reference librarians.

RQ. Reference and Adult Services Association, American Library Association, ALA Editions, 50 East Huron St., Chicago, IL 60611-2795, (800)545-2433, fax (312)836-9958. [Q., $50 nonmembers, $55 nonmembers Canada/Mexico, $60 elsewhere, $15 single copy]. Disseminates information of interest to reference librarians, bibliographers, adult services librarians, those in collection development and selection, and others interested in public services; double-blind refereed.

Schmidt, W. D., & Rieck, D. A. (1998). **Managing media services: Theory and practice**. 2nd ed. [Book, 475pp., $45]. Libraries Unlimited, P.O. Box 6633, Englewood, CO 80155-6633, (800)237-6124, fax (303)220-8843, lu-books@lu.com, http://www.lu.com. Serves as a text for graduate students in technology management courses. Covers all aspects of the media management role.

Schneider, K. G. (1997). **A practical guide to Internet filters**. [Book, 75pp., $49.95]. Neal-Schuman Publishers, 100 Varick St., New York, NY 10013-1506, (212)925-8650, fax (800)584-2414, orders@neal-schuman.com. Defines and describes filters, and assesses commercially available ones for effectiveness.

School Library Journal. Box 57559, Boulder, CO 80322-7559, (800)456-9409, fax (800)824-4746. [Mo., $79.50 US, $105 Canada, $125 elsewhere]. For school and youth service librarians. Reviews about 4,000 children's books and 1,000 educational media titles annually.

School Library Media Activities Monthly. LMS Associates LLC, 17 E. Henrietta St., Baltimore, MD 21230-3190. [10/yr., $49 US, $54 elsewhere]. A vehicle for distributing ideas for teaching library media skills and for the development and implementation of library media skills programs.

School Library Media Quarterly. American Association of School Librarians, American Library Association, ALA Editions, 50 East Huron St., Chicago, IL 60611-2795, (800)545-2433, fax (312)836-9958. [Online, http://www.ala.org/aasl/SLMQ]. For library media specialists, district supervisors, and others concerned with the selection and purchase of print and nonprint media and with the development of programs and services for preschool through high school libraries.

Siess, J. A. (1997). **The SOLO librarian's sourcebook**. [Book, 256pp., $39.50]. Information Today, 143 Old Marlton Pike, Medford, NJ 08055, (800)300-9868. Covers library management issues with the one-person staff in mind.

Simpson, C. (1997). **Copyright for schools: A practical guide**. 2nd ed. [Book, 128pp., $29.95]. Linworth Publishing, 480 E. Wilson Bridge Rd., Suite L, Worthington, OH 43085-2372, (800)786-5017, fax (614)436-9490, orders@linworth.com, http://linworth.com. Adds practical "real life" examples to updated information from the first edition. Emphasizes importance of holistic school involvement.

Smallwood, C. (1997). **Insider's guide to school libraries: tips and resources**. [Book, 200pp., $32.95]. Linworth Publishing, 480 E. Wilson Bridge Rd., Suite L, Worthington, OH 43085-2372, (800)786-5017, fax (614)436-9490, orders@linworth.com, http://linworth.com. Describes common problems, complexities, and challenges confronted in day-to-day operations of media centers.

Stewart, B. (1997). **Neal-Schuman directory of library technical services home pages**. [Book, 250pp., $55]. Neal-Schuman Publishers, 100 Varick St., New York, NY 10013-1506, (212)925-8650, fax (800)584-2414, orders@neal-schuman.com. Assists librarians in completing technical tasks through professional services available on the Web.

Still, J. (1997). **The library Web**. [Book, 230pp., $39.50]. Information Today, 143 Old Marlton Pike, Medford, NJ 08055, (800)300-9868. Contains articles on Web topics including instructional materials, resources, commercial design, Web page creation software, and design.

Summers, S. L. (1997). **Media alert!: 200 activities to create media-savvy kids**. [Book, $15]. Hi Willow Research & Publishing, Castle Rock, CO. Contains an updated approach to media literacy, including such concepts as reality vs. fantasy, fact vs. opinion, violence, and commercialism.

Sykes, J. A. (1997). **Library centers: Teaching information literacy in elementary schools**. [Book, 280pp., $30]. Libraries Unlimited, P.O. Box 6633, Englewood, CO 80155-6633, (800)237-6124, fax (303)220-8843, lu-books@lu.com, http://www.lu.com. Documents a continuous library center program with a series of mini-lessons covering a variety of curricular topics.

Tastad, S. A., & Collins, N. D. (1997). Teaching the information skills process and the writing process: Bridging the gap. **School Library Media Quarterly, 25** (3), 167-69. Discusses research conducted in a middle school writing center that showed the necessity of a constructivist philosophy for the curriculum and the teaching process if information-seeking skills or writing is taught as a process. Problems with the teachers' use and understanding of the writing center are described.

Truett, C. (1997). Censorship and the Internet: A stand for school librarians. **School Library Media Quarterly, 25** (4), 223-27. Outlines recent legislative and Supreme Court action concerning the Communications Decency Act and ALA's official stance on these issues. Argues that school librarians are obligated to protect free speech.

Truett, C. (1997). Technology use in North Carolina public schools: The school library media specialist plays a major role. **North Carolina Libraries, 55** (1), 32-37. This report on teachers and technology in North Carolina schools continues an earlier report based on a survey of North Carolina schools that focused on media specialists. Highlights include how teachers incorporate CD-ROM and videodisk technologies, school library media specialists as technology instructors, and teacher expectations of media specialists.

The Unabashed Librarian. Box 2631, New York, NY 10116. [Q., $40 US, $48 elsewhere]. Down-to-earth library items: procedures, forms, programs, cataloging, booklists, software reviews.

Valenza, J. K. (1997). **Power tools: 100 + essential forms and presentations for your school library information program**. [Book & CD-ROM, 272pp., $45]. American Library Association, ALA Editions, 50 East Huron St., Chicago, IL 60611-2795, (800)545-2433, fax (312)836-9958. Contains presentations and copier-ready forms for research skills, critical thinking, the Internet, and public relations.

Voice of Youth Advocates. Scarecrow Press, 52 Liberty St., Box 4167, Metuchen, NJ 08840. [Bi-mo., $38.50 US, $43.50 elsewhere]. Contains articles, bibliographies, and media reviews of materials for or about adolescents.

Wakiji, E., & Thomas, J. (1997). MTV to the rescue: Changing library attitudes through video. **College & Research Libraries, 58** (3), 211-16. "Liberspace" is an eight-minute video demonstrating library use and practices for new students at California State University, Long Beach. An analysis of responses from 1,879 students about library use and attitudes suggests that viewing the video will increase undergraduate and graduate use of the library and consultations with librarians during research.

Wilson Library Bulletin. H. W. Wilson Co., 950 University Ave., Bronx, NY 10452, http://www.hwwilson.com/default.html; also available in microform from UMI, PMC. Significant articles on librarianship, news, and reviews of films, books, and professional literature.

Wynar, B. S., ed. (1998). **Recommended reference books for small and medium-sized libraries and media centers 1998**. [Book, 300pp., $50]. Libraries Unlimited, P.O. Box 6633, Englewood, CO 80155-6633, (800)237-6124, fax (303)220-8843, lu-books@lu.com, http://www.lu.com. Selects over 600 books from the same publishers' *American Reference Books Annual* as most appropriate and valuable for smaller collections. Provides titles by subject, citations for other reviews, designations of suitable library type, and comparisons between similar titles.

Yesner, B. L., & Jay, H. L. (1997). **Operating and evaluating school library media programs: A handbook for administrators and librarians**. [Book, 280pp., $39.95]. Neal-Schuman Publishers, 100 Varick St., New York, NY 10013-1506, (212)925-8650, fax (800)584-2414, orders @neal-schuman.com. Comprehensive evaluation tool to assess effectiveness of school library media programs.

Zuiderveld, S., ed. (1997). **Cataloging correctly for kids: An introduction to the tools**. 3rd ed. [Book, 88pp., $20]. American Library Association, ALA Editions, 50 East Huron St., Chicago, IL 60611-2795, (800)545-2433, fax (312)836-9958. Describes cataloging designed to provide children easy access to the resources they want while maintaining detailed records.

MEDIA TECHNOLOGIES

A-V ONLINE. Knight-Ridder Information (formerly *Dialog*), 2440 El Camino Real, Mountain View, CA 94040, DIALOG File 46, customer@corp.dialog.com. Updated quarterly, this NICEM database provides information on nonprint media covering all levels of education and instruction. Nonprint formats covered are 16mm films, videos, audiocassettes, CD-ROMs, software, laserdiscs, filmstrips, slides, transparencies, motion cartridges, kits, models, and realia. Entries date from 1964 to the present, with over 425,000 records.

Beadle, M. E., & Stephenson, A. (1997). Frieda Hennock: Leader for educational television. **TechTrends, 42** (6), 45-50. Outlines Hennock's influence during the early years of educational television.

Beasley, A. E. (1997). Fun with video editing: Creating the illusion of reality. **School Library Media Activities Monthly, 13** (6), 27-29. Discusses how students and teachers can produce more creative and technically proficient videotapes with an inexpensive editing system. Describes the basics of creating different shots, steps to follow in the editing process, and how to avoid mistakes.

Bielefeld, A., & Cheeseman, L. (1997). **Technology and copyright law: A guidebook for the library, research, and teaching professions**. [Book, 213pp., $49.95]. Neal-Schuman Publishers, 100 Varick St., New York, NY 10013-1506, (212)925-8650, fax (800)584-2414, orders @neal-schuman.com. Addresses copyright controversies brought about by technology, including software copying, Internet document reproduction and distribution, distance learning dilemmas, and graphics scanning.

Broadcasting and Cable. Box 6399, Torrence, CA 90504, http://www.broadcastingcable.com. [W., $129 US, $169 Canada, $199 elsewhere, $350 foreign air, $7.95 single copy]. All-inclusive newsweekly for radio, television, cable, and allied business.

Brown, S. A. (1997). Ten questions to ask when selecting a scientific information service or product. **Online User, 3** (1), 44-45. Lists 10 questions that should be asked when evaluating a new scientific information provider, and discusses how to make a decision after the questions are answered.

CableVision. Chilton Co./ABC Publishing Group, Box 10727, Riverton, NJ 08076-0727, http://www.cvmag.com. [Semi-mo., $59 US surface, $89 US air, $165 elsewhere]. A newsmagazine for the cable television industry. Covers programming, marketing, advertising, business, and other topics.

California Instructional Technology Clearinghouse. (1997). **Guidelines for the evaluation of instructional technology resources**. [Book, $12]. ISTE, 480 Charnelton St., Eugene, OR 97401-2626, (800)336-5191, fax (541)302-3887. Contains rubrics for the evaluation of each type of instructional technology resource, focusing on curricular content, instructional design, and learner needs.

Communication Abstracts. Sage Publications, Inc., 2455 Teller Rd., Thousand Oaks, CA 91320. [Bi-mo., $498 inst.]. Abstracts communication-related articles, reports, and books. Cumulated annually.

Communication Booknotes. C. H. Sterling, 4507 Airlie Way, Annandale VA 22003, (202) 994-6211, Cbooknotes@aol.com, http://members.aol.com/Cbooknotes/index.html. [Bi-mo., $45 indiv., $95 inst., $80 foreign air, $130 foreign air inst.]. Newsletter that reviews books and periodicals about mass media, telecommunications, and information policy for academic, research, and library readership.

Communications News. Nelson Publishing Co., 2504 N. Tamiami Trail, Nokomis, FL 34275. [Mo.]. Up-to-date information from around the world regarding voice, video, and data communications.

Curchy, C., & Kyker, K. (1997). **Educator's survival guide to TV production equipment and setup**. [Book, 150pp., $22.50]. Libraries Unlimited, P.O. Box 6633, Englewood, CO 80155-6633, (800)237-6124, fax (303)220-8843, lu-books@lu.com, http://www.lu.com. Helps educators assess, select, connect, and use audio and video production equipment for school projects.

Document and Image Automation (formerly *Optical Information Systems Magazine*). Meckler Publishing Corp., 11 Ferry Lane W., Westport, CT 06880-5808. [Bi-mo., $125]. Features articles on the applications of videodisc, optical disc, and teletext systems; future implications; system and software compatibilities; and cost comparisons. Also tracks videodisc projects and covers world news.

Document and Image Automation Update (formerly *Optical Information Systems Update*). Meckler Publishing Corp., 11 Ferry Lane W., Westport, CT 06880-5808. [12/yr., $297]. News and facts about technology, software, courseware developments, calendar, conference reports, and job listings.

Educational Media International. Turpin Distribution Centre, Blackhorse Road, Letchworth, Herts SG6 1HN, England, http://www.cndp.fr./icem/. [Q., $95 US, $29 single copy]. The official journal of the International Council for Educational Media.

Federal Communications Commission Reports. Superintendent of Documents, Government Printing Office, Box 371954, Pittsburgh, PA 15250-7954. [Irreg., price varies]. Decisions, public notices, and other documents pertaining to FCC activities.

Heeren, E., & Lewis, R. (1997). Selecting communication media for distributed communities. **Journal of Computer Assisted Learning, 13** (2), 85-98. Presents insights gained by studying media use in existing distributed research communities. Describes the "Virtual Mobility and

Distributed Laboratories" research project and three naturalistic case studies, highlights the concepts of activity theory and media-richness theory and suggests an integration of the two, and addresses the applicability of these theories to distributed learning.

Historical Journal of Film, Radio, and Television. Carfax Publishing Limited in association with the International Association for Media and History, 875-81 Massachusetts Ave., Cambridge, MA 02139. [Q., $144 North America, $398 inst.]. Articles by international experts in the field, news and notices, and book reviews concerning the impact of mass communications on political and social history of the twentieth century.

International Journal of Instructional Media. Westwood Press, Inc., 24 E. 22nd St., New York, NY 10010. [Q., $125 per vol., $30 single issue]. Focuses on quality research and ongoing programs in instructional media for education, distance learning, computer technology, instructional media and technology, telecommunications, interactive video, management, media research and evaluation, and utilization.

Journal of Broadcasting and Electronic Media. Broadcast Education Association, 1771 N St., NW, Washington, DC 20036-2891. [Q., $40 US, $25 student, $50 elsewhere]. Includes articles, book reviews, research reports, and analyses. Provides a forum for research relating to telecommunications and related fields.

Journal of Educational Media (formerly *Journal of Educational Television*). Carfax Publishing Co., 875-81 Massachusetts Ave., Cambridge, MA 02139. [3/yr., $148 indiv., $438 inst.]. This journal of the Educational Television Association serves as an international forum for discussions and reports on developments in the field of television and related media in teaching, learning, and training.

Journal of Educational Media and Library Sciences (formerly *Journal of Educational Media*). Carfax Publishing Co., 875-81 Massachusetts Ave., Cambridge, MA 02139. [3/yr., $30 indiv., $360 inst.]. Forum for discussion of issues concerning educational television and related media.

Journal of Popular Film and Television. Heldref Publications, 1319 Eighteenth St., NW, Washington, DC 20036-1802, (800)365-9753. [Q., $34 indiv., $66 inst., $9 single copy]. Articles on film and television, book reviews, and theory. Dedicated to popular film and television in the broadest sense. Concentrates on commercial cinema and television, film and television theory or criticism, filmographies, and bibliographies. Edited at the College of Arts and Sciences of Northern Michigan University and the Department of Popular Culture, Bowling Green State University.

Kurtz, A. (1997). To preserve and enjoy the past: Recreating "Our Town." **MultiMedia Schools, 4** (3), 44-46, 48-49. Describes a project where students in an Iowa City, Iowa, middle school recreated their town at the turn of the century using electronic and manipulative media. Discusses initial studies of structures, construction principles, and architectural terminology; student research of primary source documents and interviews with local architects; and student presentations.

Media International. Reed Business Information, Publisher. Oakfield House, Perrymount Rd., W. Sussex RH16 3DH, England. [Mo., £42 Europe, £76 elsewhere]. Contains features on the major media developments and regional news reports from the international media scene and global intelligence on media and advertising.

Multimedia Monitor (formerly *Multimedia and Videodisc Monitor*). Phillips Business Information, Inc., 1201 Seven Locks Rd., Potomac, MD 20854, (301)424-3338, fax (301)309-3847, pbi@phillips.com. [Mo., $395 indiv., $425 foreign]. Describes current events in the worldwide interactive multimedia marketplace and in training and development, including regulatory and legal issues.

Multimedia Schools. Information Today, 143 Old Marlton Pike, Medford, NJ 08055, (800)300-9868. [5/yr., $38 US, $41.75 Canada/Mexico, $60 elsewhere]. Reviews new titles, evaluates hardware and software, offers technical advice and troubleshooting tips, and profiles high-tech installations.

NICEM (National Information Center for Educational Media) EZ. NICEM, P.O. Box 8640, Albuquerque, NM 87198-8640, (505) 265-3591, (800)926-8328, fax (505)256-1080, nicem @nicem.com. A custom search service to help those without access to the existing NICEM products. Taps the resources of this specialized database. Fees are $50 per hour search time plus $.20 for each unit identified.

NICEM (National Information Center for Educational Media) NlightN. Contact NlightN, The Library Corp, 1807 Michael Faraday Ct., Reston, VA 20190, (800)654-4486, fax (703)904-8238, help@nlightn.com, http://www.nlightn.com. [Subscription service]. NlightN, an Internet online service, widens the accessibility of information in the NICEM database to users of the Internet. The NICEM database of 425,000 records, updated quarterly, provides information on nonprint media for all levels of education and instruction in all academic areas.

Rose, S. A., & Fernlund, P. M. (1997). Using technology for powerful social studies learning. **Social Education, 61** (3), 160-66. Identifies and outlines key considerations that should influence the selection of instructional technology. Provides specific questions to ask about hardware, multimedia use, computer assisted instruction, and the Internet. Considers specific applications (and limitations) of these technologies with regard to specific social studies standards and objectives.

Rostad, J. (1997). Produce live news broadcasts using standard AV equipment: A success story from the Le Center High School in Minnesota. **TechTrends, 42** (3), 21-24. Describes a student-produced news programming project, including equipment and management issues.

Salomon, G. (1997). Of mind and media. **Phi Delta Kappan, 78** (5), 375-80. Explores mind/ media relationships and discusses how culture's symbolic forms affect learning and thinking. The socially held and communicated views of various media appear to affect the way children handle them, the depth of their information processing, and what they actually learn from them. Media's symbolic forms of representation have both positive and negative effects on children's cognitive apparatus.

Taack, D. L., & others. (1997). The Perkins Farm: A video-enhanced decision case for extension education. **Journal of Natural Resources and Life Sciences Education, 26** (1), 15-19. Presents and discusses a video-enhanced decision case developed for use in a single learning session with little or no preparation beforehand. The content of the case is well suited to introducing and analyzing issues affecting the sustainability of farming operations. A lesson plan for using the case with extension audiences is described. Includes discussion questions and issues.

Talab, R. S. (1997). An educational use checklist for copyright and multimedia. **TechTrends, 42** (1), 9-11. Discusses copyright considerations in multimedia development, and provides a checklist for teachers and students based on the U.S. House of Representative's "Fair Use Guidelines for Educational Multimedia" (1996) and the Association for Computing Machinery's "Interim Copyright Policies." Describes three copyright use scenarios: open house, classroom instruction, and remote instruction.

Technology Connection. Linworth Publishing, 480 E. Wilson Bridge Rd., Suite L, Worthington, OH 43085-2372, (800)786-5017, fax (614)436-9490, orders@linworth.com, http://linworth.com. [9/yr., $43 US, $7 single copy]. A forum for K-12 educators who use technology as an educational resource, this journal includes information on what works and what does not, new product reviews, tips and pointers, and emerging technology.

Telematics and Informatics. Elsevier Science Regional Sales Office, Customer Support Department, P.O. Box 945, New York, NY 10159-0945, (888)4ES-INFO, usinfo-f@elsevier.com. [Q., £395]. Publishes research and review articles in applied telecommunications and information sciences in business, industry, government, and educational establishments. Focuses on important current technologies including microelectronics, computer graphics, speech synthesis and voice recognition, database management, data encryption, satellite television, artificial intelligence, and the ongoing computer revolution. Contributors and readers include professionals in business and industry, as well as in government and academia, who need to keep abreast of current technologies and their diverse applications.

Treadway, G., & Stein, B. (1998). **Finding and using educational videos: A how-to-do-it manual**. [Book, 150pp., $35]. Neal-Schuman Publishers, 100 Varick St., New York, NY 10013-1506, (212)925-8650, fax (800)584-2414, orders@neal-schuman.com. Assists elementary and middle school library media specialists and teachers look for subject-specific educational videos.

Video Systems. Intertec Publishing Corp., 9800 Metcalf, Overland Park, KS 66212-2215. [Mo., $45, free to qualified professionals]. For video professionals. Contains state-of-the-art audio and video technology reports. Official publication of the International Television Association.

Videography. Miller Freeman, PSN Publications, 2 Park Ave., 18th floor, New York, NY 10016. [Mo., $30]. For the video professional; covers techniques, applications, equipment, technology, and video art.

PROFESSIONAL DEVELOPMENT

Brown, R. (1997). The Center for Innovation in Instruction at Valley City State University: Improving teaching with technology. **Cause/Effect, 20** (1), 54-56. The Valley City State University (North Dakota) Center for Innovation in Instruction serves the entire state as an educational, informational, and support center for use of emerging technologies in education. The center supports instructional innovation, provides professional development opportunities for teachers and administrators, promotes partnerships, develops products and disseminates technology information, and assists school districts in technology implementation.

Brownell, K. (1997). Technology in teacher education: Where are we and where do we go from here? **Journal of Technology and Teacher Education, 5** (2/3), 117-38. Reviews research on the application of educational technology in teacher education from 1990 to 1995.

Cifuentes, L. (1997). From sages to guides: A professional development study. **Journal of Technology and Teacher Education, 5** (1), 67-77. The educational technology course for preservice teachers at Texas A&M University incorporates a constructivist model for professional development. A study of this model examined how it helps teachers change from disseminators of information to facilitators of learning and how it underscores differences between preservice and inservice teachers' choices of teaching methods.

Corcoran, M., & Jones, R. (1997). Chief knowledge officers? Perceptions, pitfalls, and potential. **Information Outlook, 1** (6), 30-31, 35-36. Argues that few librarians possess the needed competencies to fill the role of "chief knowledge officer" or "knowledge executive." Outlines executive competencies required: communications, leadership, experience, financial management, customer focus, entrepreneurial insight, and information technology grounding; and examines gaps in these competencies reported by librarians.

Ellery, P. J. (1997). Using the World Wide Web in physical education. **Strategies, 10** (3), 5-8. Describes World Wide Web capabilities and services of interest to physical education teachers in the areas of professional development (e.g., communicating with colleagues and accessing professional organizations and publications) and class activities (e.g., finding facts, distributing class materials, and using bulletin boards).

Fisher, M. M. (1997). The voice of experience: Inservice teacher technology competency recommendations for preservice teacher preparation programs. **Journal of Technology and Teacher Education, 5** (2/3), 139-47. Reports the results of a survey study of K-12 teachers in Colorado. Provides 10 technology competency recommendations and describes an assessment instrument.

Harrington, H. L. (1997). Technology's second-level effects: Fostering democratic communities. **Journal of Technology and Teacher Education, 5** (2/3), 203-22. Examines electronic dialogs in an introductory teacher education class for characteristics of democratic communities.

Hoelscher, K. (1997). The road ahead: Pre-service educators' ideas for using technology in K-6 classrooms. **Computers in the Schools, 13** (1-2), 69-75. Describes a new model of elementary teacher training at Western Washington University. Guided by college and public school faculty and students, preservice teachers learn how to use technology. This full-time certification program emphasizes current technology and intensive experience. A final project features students producing useful projects and mastering multimedia skills to use as future teachers.

ISTE Accreditation and Standards Committee. (1998). **Curriculum guidelines for accreditation of educational computing and technology programs: A folio preparation manual**. 3rd ed. [Book, 55pp., $20]. ISTE, 480 Charnelton St., Eugene, OR 97401-2626, (800)336-5191, fax (541)302-3887. Updates NCATE-approved guidelines for technology teacher preparation programs.

Johnson, D. (1997). Extending the educational community: Using electronic dialoguing to connect theory and practice in preservice teacher education. **Journal of Technology and Teacher Education, 5** (2/3), 163-70. Describes a project modeling the incorporation of facilitative technology into the curriculum in a preservice reading methods class.

Journal of Computing in Teacher Education. ISTE, University of Oregon, 1787 Agate St., Eugene, OR 97403-1923, (800)336-5191, cust_svc@ccmail.uoregon.edu. [Q., $29 US, $41.73 Canada, $39 intl., $42 intl. air]. Contains refereed articles on preservice and inservice training, research in computer education and certification issues, and reviews of training materials and texts.

Journal of Technology and Teacher Education. Association for the Advancement of Computing in Education (AACE), P.O. Box 2966, Charlottesville, VA 22902, AACE@virginia.edu, http://www.aace.org. [Q., $65 indiv. US, $93, US inst., $20 single copy]. Serves as an international forum to report research and applications of technology in preservice, inservice, and graduate teacher education.

Lambdin, D. V., Duffy, T. M., & Moore, J. A. (1997). Using an interactive information system to expand preservice teachers' visions of effective mathematics teaching. **Journal of Technology and Teacher Education, 5** (2/3), 171-202. Investigates how using an interactive videodisk information system helps preservice teachers expand and enact their visions of teaching, learning, and assessment in mathematics instruction.

Marx, R. W., & others. (1997). Enacting project-based science. **Elementary School Journal, 97** (4), 341-58. Discusses changes in ideas about learning underlying reforms in science education. Highlights experiences with project-based science, which focuses on student-designed inquiry organized by investigations to answer driving questions, including collaboration among learners, new technology, and the creation of authentic artifacts that represent student understanding. Illustrates challenges of project-based science for classroom practice, professional development, and policy.

Nicol, M. P. (1997). How one physics teacher changed his algebraic thinking. **Mathematics Teacher, 90** (2), 86-89. Describes the study of a physics teacher whose teaching changed as his beliefs about mathematics changed. Following a week-long institute on using graphing calculators, the teacher became an advocate of calculator use, and his algebraic thinking progressed as he realized the importance of functions.

Norton, P., & Sprague, D. (1997). On-line collaborative lesson planning: An experiment in teacher education. **Journal of Technology and Teacher Education, 5** (2/3), 149-62. Describes the results of a study of online collaborative lesson planning. Reports no significant difference in lesson quality but an improvement of teacher attitudes toward the educational usefulness of telecommunications and collaboration.

Parker, D. R. (1997). Increasing faculty use of technology in teaching the teacher education. **Journal of Technology and Teacher Education, 5** (2/3), 105-15. Reports results of a faculty self-study exploring faculty use of technology, required student use, obstacles to increased use, and faculty interest in professional development concerning technology.

Salas, A. A., & Anderson, M. B. (1997). Introducing information technologies into medical education: Activities of the AAMC. **Academic Medicine, 72** (3), 191-93. Outlines ways in which the Association of American Medical Colleges (AAMC) is working to support introduction of new technologies into medical education and facilitate dialogue on information technology and curriculum issues. Describes six AAMC initiatives related to computing in education, including projects concerning educational objectives, medical curricula, instructional development, professional development, information systems, and a staff interest group.

Skolnik, R. (1997). "Miss T" and the new old technology. **TECHNOS, 6** (2), 15-18. Discussion of the use of classroom television focuses on the need for effective instruction rather than sophisticated technology. Highlights include math activities developed by teacher Kay Toliver; a PBS (Public Broadcasting Service) series for elementary math students; integrated learning, with an interdisciplinary approach; and teacher training and professional development.

Smith, R. A. (1997). Find the perfect technology coordinator: Interviewing to the fullest. **Learning and Leading with Technology, 24** (6), 56-58. The most important step in recruiting a school technology coordinator is the interview. Examines the candidate interview, concentrating on four areas: technical expertise, understanding technology use in instructional environments, professional development, and Internet knowledge and experience.

Solomon, D. L. (1997). Entering the consulting relationship: A guide for instructional technologists. **Performance Improvement, 36** (4), 24-28. Emphasizes the importance of effective communication at the outset of the instructional technologist/training client relationship. Discusses using the basic taxonomy of client types and entry strategies for the following different types of clients: theorist, expert, novice, practitioner, and generalist. Includes a sample self-assessment form.

Stafford, D. J. (1997). PowerPointing the way. **Technology Connection, 4** (1), 16-17. Describes instructional uses of Microsoft PowerPoint software as demonstrated in a summer workshop for educators. Notes three uses: open house-type presentations, tutorials, and student-produced projects. Discusses how PowerPoint was used to present general information about the school and gives examples of uses in science and music history instruction. A sidebar details how PowerPoint was introduced in the workshop.

Wiburg, K. M. (1997). The dance of chance: Integrating technology in classrooms. **Computers in the Schools, 13** (1-2), 171-84. Describes a two-year university/public school grant-funded collaborative research project designed to help teachers learn to use multimedia and telecommunications in the classroom and to develop culturally relevant curricula for students in a primarily Hispanic, lower-income community. Goals were developed in four areas: collaborative design, multimedia-assisted learning, staff development, and teacher education.

Zellner, L. J., & Erlandson, D. A. (1997). Leadership laboratories: Professional development for the 21st century. **NASSP Bulletin, 81** (585), 45-50. In 1992, Texas A&M University's College of Education established the Texas Education Collaborative, a center for professional development and technology, to redesign teacher preparation and staff development programs. In 1996, the TEC joined with the university's Principal's Center to focus on principals' development in schools reconceived as leadership laboratories. The program is described.

SIMULATION, GAMING, AND VIRTUAL REALITY

Aspects of Educational and Training Technology Series. Kogan Page Ltd., 120 Pentonville Rd., London N1 9JN, England. [Ann., £35]. Covers the proceedings of the annual conference of the Association of Educational and Training Technology.

Baker, A. C., & others. (1997). In conversation: Transforming experience into learning. **Simulation & Gaming, 28** (1), 6-12. Simulations and games are designed to provide participants with an experiential context for reflection and learning in classrooms, corporate training centers, and community-based organizations. A conversational approach to debriefing sessions is one way to more deeply involve participants in exploring the meaning of their experience from multiple perspectives.

Barua, A., & others. (1997). Effective intra-organizational information exchange. **Journal of Information Science, 23** (3), 239-48. A game theory approach to illustrating elements of organizational culture can help to achieve desirable information exchange by aligning individual and organizational goals. The game approach should involve the values of permanence, trust, teamwork, and credibility and should be combined with appropriate reward systems and parity in information technology capabilities.

Bigelow, B. (1997). On the road to cultural bias: A critique of "The Oregon Trail" CD-ROM. **Language Arts, 74** (2), 84-93. Presents a critical review of "The Oregon Trail" CD-ROMs. Argues that "The Oregon Trail" is sexist, racist, culturally insensitive, and contemptuous of the earth, imparting bad values and errant history. Suggests questions teachers can ask before choosing to use these materials, and offers classroom activities to develop students' critical computer literacy.

Cook, S. (1997). Get ready, get set, go read! Motivation through competition. **Emergency Librarian, 24** (5), 29-30. Illustrates how teachers and librarians can use competitive activities to motivate children to read and to encourage personal achievement and group cooperation. Discusses computer games and the group-oriented bees, bowls, circles, and quiz contests. Notes the benefits in terms of social interaction, communication, resource center use, and recognition.

Edward, N. S. (1997). Computer based simulation of laboratory experiments. **British Journal of Educational Technology, 28** (1), 51-63. Examines computer-based simulations of practical laboratory experiments in engineering. Discusses the aims and achievements of lab work (cognitive, process, psychomotor, and affective); types of simulations (model building and behavioral); and the strengths and weaknesses of simulations. Describes the development of a centrifugal pump simulation, and assesses its effectiveness with a test group of 28 students.

Galas, C. (1997-1998). From presentation to programming: Doing something different, not the same thing differently. **Learning & Leading with Technology, 25** (4), 18-21. Describes student use of MicroWorlds to simulate an ocean ecosystem containing dolphins.

Hoenack, S. A. (1997). An application of a structural model of school demand and supply to evaluate alternative designs of voucher education systems. **Economics of Education Review, 16** (1), 1-14. Presents a structural supply/demand model for enrollment practices in parochial schools and uses it to evaluate alternative voucher policy designs. Uses the model's estimated parameters to simulate effects of differently sized and targeted vouchers on public and private school attendance, districts' fiscal status, and public educational costs. Vouchers could displace donors' support for private schools.

Holsbrink-Engels, G. A. (1997). Computer-based role-playing for interpersonal skills training. **Simulation & Gaming, 28** (2), 164-80. Examines design and evaluation of computer-based role-playing. University students (n=41) were divided into two groups to use instructional programs with and without computer-based role-playing. Findings indicated that computer-based role-playing enhanced interpersonal skills development by employing a conversational model, offering opportunities for reflection, performing protagonist roles, and capturing individual contribution and learning.

Jackson, D. F. (1997). Case studies of microcomputer and interactive video simulations in middle school earth science teaching. **Journal of Science Education and Technology, 6** (2), 127-41. Synthesizes the results of three case studies of middle school classrooms in which computer and video materials were used to teach topics in earth and space sciences through interactive simulations. Describes specific instances in which common current practice is problematic. Suggests improved design principles for such materials.

Kaplan, M. A. (1997). Learning to converse in a foreign language: The Reception Game. **Simulation & Gaming, 28** (2), 149-63. The Reception Game teaches conversation skills to adult foreign-language learners with positions in international business and diplomacy. The design combines elements of simulation and experiential learning and takes into account conversation's rapport-building function, turn-taking mechanisms, open-ended structure, listening demands for following topic shifts, and ways to display understanding and involvement.

Kirby, A. (1997). **The encyclopedia of games for trainers**. [Book, 444pp., $99.95]. Training Express, 11358 Aurora Ave., Des Moines, IA 50322. Contains over 145 group games to encourage participation, motivation, and enjoyment for adults in business training contexts.

Kirby, A. (1997). **Great games for trainers**. [Book, 200pp., $69.95]. Training Express, 11358 Aurora Ave., Des Moines, IA 50322. Contains over 75 educational adult games on topics such as team building, stress management, leadership, creativity, assertiveness, and corporate ethics.

Land, S. M., & Hannafin, M. J. (1997). Patterns of understanding with open-ended learning environments: A qualitative study. **Educational Technology Research and Development, 45** (2), 47-73. A study of four seventh-graders using an open-ended learning environment (OELE) on mechanical physics combining computer-generated graphics, computer simulations, video, and print-based materials indicated that while learners built and formalized scientific theories, in some cases, they assimilated new data into existing theories, ignored inconsistent data, or derived independent theories to account for contradictory evidence.

Liu, L., & others. (1997). The effectiveness of using simulated patients versus videotapes of simulated patients to teach clinical skills to occupational and physical therapy students. **Occupational Therapy Journal of Research, 17** (3), 159-72. In one seminar, 39 occupational and 34 physical therapy students interacted with a simulated patient; in another, they viewed a videotape of a simulated patient and clinician. Student identification of patient problems tended to agree with experts in the first seminar; more student treatment plans agreed with experts in the video seminar.

Newstrom, J. W., & Scannell, E. E. (1997). **Games trainers play**. [Book, 301pp., $29.95]. Training Express, 11358 Aurora Ave., Des Moines, IA 50322. Contains games to develop leadership ability, self-confidence, problem solving, cooperation, and communication in business training contexts.

Opheim, C., & Stouffer, W. B. (1997). Using "Capitol Hill" CD-ROM to teach undergraduate political science courses. **Political Science and Politics, 30** (1), 68-70. Describes a CD-ROM product that simulates introducing a freshman congressman to Washington, D.C. The member is briefed on duties and responsibilities (including a historical overview) and given a tour of the Capitol. Interactive components include hiring staffers and acquiring leadership positions. Includes suggestions for integrating the product into class instruction.

Ploetzner, R., & VanLehn, K. (1997). The acquisition of qualitative physics knowledge during textbook-based physics training. **Cognition and Instruction, 15** (2), 169-205. Used computerized simulation models of qualitative, conceptual problem solving and quantitative problem solving to examine qualitative physics knowledge acquisition during textbook-based physics training. Found that qualitative knowledge was acquired on the basis of explicit textbook information, but there were also cases of qualitative learning on the basis of implicit information that led to less frequent use of incorrect qualitative preknowledge.

Ramnarayan, S., & others. (1997). Trappings of expertise and the pursuit of failure. **Simulation & Gaming, 28** (1), 28-43. Analyzes how 20 groups of management specialists in charge of a computer-simulated company behaved when confronted with complex problems that arose. Difficulties stemmed from an incorrect use of available knowledge, a tendency to avoid risks and reduce uncertainty, and a motivational process that sheltered the subjective sense of competence.

Sanger, J., with Wilson, J., Davies, B., & Whittaker, R. (1997). **Young children, videos and computer games: Issues for teachers and parents**. [Book, 192pp.]. Falmer Press, c/o Taylor & Francis, 1900 Frost Rd., Suite 101, Bristol, PA 19007-1598. Frames debate over effects on young children of computer games, video games, and videos.

Saunders, P., & Cox, B. (1997). **International simulation and gaming yearbook, Vol. 5**. [Book, 224pp., $65]. Cassell/Stylus, P.O. Box 605, Herndon, VA 20172-0605, (800)232-0223, fax (703)661-1510, styluspub@aol.com. Contains timely articles related to educational gaming. Sample topics include adventure multimedia distance education games, eco-ethological simulations, multimedia presentation techniques, case approach simulations, and others.

Scannell, E. E., & Newstrom, J. W. (1997). **More games trainers play**. [Book, 302pp., $29.95]. Training Express, 11358 Aurora Ave., Des Moines, IA 50322. Second volume in series that contains games, activities, and exercises deigned to help trainers teach vital business skills.

Scannell, E. E., & Newstrom, J. W. (1997). **Still more games trainers play**. [Book, 311pp., $29.95]. Training Express, 11358 Aurora Ave., Des Moines, IA 50322. Third volume in series in business through games.

Simulation and Gaming. Sage Publications, Inc., 2455 Teller Rd., Thousand Oaks, CA 91320. [Q., $64 indiv., $244 inst., $18 single issue]. An international journal of theory, design, and research focusing on issues in simulation, gaming, modeling, role-play, and experiential learning.

Valenza, J. K. (1997). Girls + technology = turnoff? **Technology Connection, 3** (10), 20-21, 29. Examines gender differences in computer use, citing male-oriented software as a possible reason girls are turned off, and highlights traditionally feminine and gender-neutral games. Describes ways of encouraging females: all-female computer and math classes, pairing students, mentoring, integrating technology into content areas, early introduction, placement of home computers, and providing software that encourages creation and collaboration.

Windschitl, M. (1997). Student epistemological beliefs and conceptual change activities: How do pair members affect each other? **Journal of Science Education and Technology, 6** (1), 37-47. Describes a study that examined the relationships in achievement between members of dyads who were paired according to epistemological maturity. Each dyad engaged in a photosynthesis simulation exercise. Also examines the relationship between individual students' epistemological maturity and their understanding of photosynthesis.

Yerushalmy, M. (1997). Mathematizing verbal descriptions of situations: A language to support modeling. **Cognition and Instruction, 15** (2), 207-64. Used software environment to examine algebra students' attempts to reformulate narratives using verbal and iconic lexical sets. Described how natural language text turns into a script of events and processes, how the qualitative graphic description of the script is sketched using iconic notations, and how the graph turns into a subject for qualitative analysis of rate of change.

SPECIAL EDUCATION AND DISABILITIES

Blackhurst, A. E. (1997). Perspectives on technology in special education. **Teaching Exceptional Children, 29** (5), 41-48. A special educator reviews his experiences with technology and offers his perspectives on the technology continuum (high-tech, medium-tech, low-tech, and no-tech); types of technology (teaching, medical, instructional, and assistive); a functional model of technology; federal initiatives; and the Council for Exceptional Children's role in technology applications.

Carnine, D. (1997). Instructional design in mathematics for students with learning disabilities. **Journal of Learning Disabilities, 30** (2), 130-41. Describes and illustrates five areas of instructional design in mathematics well suited to students with learning disabilities. Suggested learning strategies for teachers to incorporate include using big ideas and conspicuous strategies; teaching efficient use of time; giving clear, explicit instruction on strategies; and taking time for appropriate practice and review.

Cunningham, C., & Coombs, N. (1997). **Information access and adaptive technology**. [Book, 192pp., $34.95]. Oryx Press, 4041 North Central Ave., Suite 700, Phoenix, AZ 85012-3397, (800)279-6799, fax (800)279-4663. Surveys available adaptive technologies for disabled students in computer labs, libraries, and classrooms from access and compensation perspectives.

Fitzgerald, G. E., Semrau, L. P., & Deasy, G. S. (1997). Interactive multimedia training materials for assessment of students with behavioral problems: Design and outcomes. **Journal of Technology and Teacher Education, 5** (2/3), 231-50. Describes the effects of a case-based MicroWorlds simulation program in a preservice behavior disorders course.

Higgins, K., & Boone, R. (1997). **Technology for students with learning disabilities: Educational applications**. [Monograph with CD-ROM, 288pp., $49]. Synthesizes research in the technology for learning disabled individuals area, including hardware, software, and applications.

Kaufman, C. C. (1997). Technology as a tool in achieving the mandates of inclusion. **Journal of Technology and Teacher Education, 5** (2/3), 223-29. Proposes that the current reforms in technology and inclusion can work together to increase instruction effectiveness.

Male, M. (1997). **Technology for inclusion: Meeting the special needs of all students**. 3rd ed. [Book, 198pp., $46]. Allyn & Bacon; available from ISTE, University of Oregon, 1787 Agate St., Eugene, OR 97403-1923, (800)336-5191, cust_svc@ccmail.uoregon.edu. Targets practitioners (either novice or advanced technology users) and suggests affordances of technology for special populations. Topics include mainstreaming, cooperative learning, multiple intelligences, and access.

Montague, M. (1997). Cognitive strategy instruction in mathematics for students with learning disabilities. **Journal of Learning Disabilities, 30** (2), 164-77. Discusses the use of cognitive strategy instruction to improve students' performance in mathematics. The theoretical and research base for strategy instruction is reviewed, and developmental characteristics of students who have difficulties in mathematics are examined. A practical example of cognitive strategy instruction illustrates assessment and teaching of mathematical problem solving to middle school students with learning disabilities.

National School Boards Association. (1997). **Technology for students with disabilities: A decision maker's resource guide**. [Book, 106pp., $25]. NSBA Distribution Center, P.O. Box 161, Annapolis Jct., MD 20701-0161, (800)706-6722, fax (301)604-0158, http://www.nsba.org/itte. Provides resources enabling educational leaders to understand the use of technology in special education.

Rodriguez, J. (1997). Building an adaptive information system. **School Administrator, 54** (4), 22-25. When a special-education student in the Tucson (Arizona) Unified School District moves to a new address, that information is communicated quickly and efficiently to every office needing to know. School community members have discovered the value of a well-planned information management system. Specifics about line speed, vendor reliability, standardization, software integration, and system managers are discussed.

TELECOMMUNICATIONS AND NETWORKING

Anderson, S. E., & Harris, J. B. (1997). Factors associated with amount of use and benefits obtained by users of a statewide educational telecomputing network. **Educational Technology Research and Development, 45** (1), 19-50. This study identified factors that best predicted the amount and perceived benefits of network use based on TENET (Texas Education Network) use. A 70-item electronic mail survey measured five categories of variables, and findings suggest that network facilitators should try to increase interactions among potential and current network users.

Barkhouse, N. (1997). Grasping the thread: Web page development in the elementary classroom. **Emergency Librarian, 24** (3), 24-25. Overviews simple Web page development.

Barron, A. E. (1997). **How to create great school Web pages**. [Binder with CD-ROM, 350pp., $79]. Classroom Connect, 1866 Colonial Village Ln., P.O Box 10488, Lancaster, PA 17605-0488, (800) 638-1639, fax (717) 393-1507, connect@classroom.net. Offers complete beginning-to-advanced instruction for K-12 Web authoring, with examples.

Berge, Z. L. (1997). Computer conferencing and the on-line classroom. **International Journal of Educational Telecommunications, 3** (1), 3-21. Summarizes the characteristics and advantages of computer conferencing systems and translates these affordances into educational features.

Berge, Z. L., & Collins, M. P., eds. (1997). **Wired together: The online classroom in K-12**. Vol. 1: **Perspectives and instructional design**. Vol. 2: **Case studies**. Vol. 3: **Teacher education and**

professional development. Vol. 4: **Writing, reading and language acquisition**. [Set of books, approx. 300 pages each, $22.95 each]. Hampton Press, Inc., Cresskill, NJ. Collection of articles addressing models for implementation, perspectives, and instructional design; examples of networked education for curricular subject areas, special education, and library media centers; CMC use with preservice teachers, changing classroom roles, and professional development; and writing, reading, student publishing, correspondence projects, foreign-language learning, and audiographics in second-language learning.

Bigelow, J. D. (1997). Developing a World Wide Web section of a management course: Transporting learning premises across media. **International Journal of Educational Telecommunications, 3** (2/3), 131-48. Identifies six learning premises and integrates them into a learning model implemented into a Web course.

Biner, P., & Dean, R. S. (1997). Profiling the successful tele-education student. **Distance Education Report, 1** (2), 1, 3. Results of a personality assessment questionnaire revealed three basic personality characteristics that are predictive of student achievement in telecourses: 1) high performers were the most self-sufficient; 2) the least compulsive students earned the highest grades in their courses; and 3) telecourse students who performed at the highest levels tend to be highly expedient in their daily lives.

Bos, N., & UMDL Teaching and Learning Group. (1997). Analysis of feedback from an "authentic" outside-the-classroom audience on high school fiction writing: Validation of a theoretical model. **International Journal of Educational Telecommunications, 3** (1), 83-98. Describes study testing a model for analyzing distant audiences and its implementation.

Bratina, T. A., & Bosnick, J. (1997). Better than sliced bread? This is the question! **TechTrends, 42** (3), 35-37. Explores the preparation of mathematics teachers to incorporate Internet information into lessons.

Buchanan, L. (1997). Tune in the Net with RealAudio. **MultiMedia Schools, 4** (2), 38-39. Describes how to utilize a new streaming audio technology to provide Web page sound.

Bull, G., Bull, G., & Sigmon, T. (1997). Internet discussion groups. **Learning & Leading with Technology, 25** (3), 12-17. Explains newsgroups, listservs, and Web-based discussions.

Cafolla, R., Kauffman, D., & Knee, R. (1997). **World Wide Web for teachers: An interactive guide**. [Book, 231pp.]. Allyn & Bacon, 160 Gould St., Needham Heights, MA 02194-2315. Features four interactive tutorials and a Website for updating resources mentioned in the book.

Canadian Journal of Educational Communication. Association for Media and Technology in Education in Canada, 3-1750 The Queensway, Suite 1318, Etobicoke, ON M9C 5H5, Canada. [3/yr., $75]. Concerned with all aspects of educational systems and technology.

Chinowsky, P. S., & Goodman, R. E. (1997). The World Wide Web in engineering team projects. **International Journal of Educational Telecommunications, 3** (2/3), 149-62. Explores the remote interaction of teams in an engineering course environment.

Cifuentes, L., Sivo, S., & Reynolds, T. (1997). Building partnerships between preservice and inservice teachers: A project facilitated by interactive videoconferencing. **International Journal of Educational Telecommunications, 3** (1), 61-82. Describes participants' reactions to a school-university partnership facilitated by two-way interactive video and identifies influencing variables.

Classroom Connect. (1997). **The educator's Internet companion**. [Book with video & CD-ROM, 290pp., $34.95]. Classroom Connect, 1866 Colonial Village Ln., P.O Box 10488, Lancaster, PA 17605-0488, (800) 638-1639, fax (717) 393-1507, connect@classroom.net. Contains lesson plans, site tours, and explains Internet basics.

Classroom Connect. Classroom Connect, 1866 Colonial Village Ln., P.O Box 10488, Lancaster, PA 17605-0488, (800)638-1639, fax (717)393-1507, connect@classroom.net. [9/yr., $39]. Provides pointers to sources of lesson plans for K-12 educators as well as descriptions of new

Websites, addresses for online "keypals," Internet basics for new users, classroom management tips for using the Internet, and online global projects. Each issue offers Internet adventures for every grade and subject.

Cohen, K. C., ed. (1997). **Internet links for science education: Student-scientist partnerships**. [Book, 250pp., $33]. Plenum Publishing Corporation, 233 Spring St., New York, NY 10013-1578, (212)620-8000, (800)221-9369, info@plenum.com, http://www.plenum.com. Describes the use of student-scientist partnerships for learning via the Internet.

Collis, B., Andernach, T., & Van Diepen, N. (1997). Web environments for group-based project work in higher education. **International Journal of Educational Telecommunications, 3** (2/3), 109-30. Analyzes transcripts from two online courses for cohesion, motivation, collaboration, communication, "group memory," evaluation, and learning.

Computer Communications. Elsevier Science, Inc., P.O. Box 882, Madison Square Station, New York, NY 10159-0882. [14/yr., $1,136]. Focuses on networking and distributed computing techniques, communications hardware and software, and standardization.

Cooper, G., & Cooper, G. (1997). **Virtual field trips**. [Book, 168pp., $24]. Libraries Unlimited, P.O. Box 6633, Englewood, CO 80155-6633, (800)237-6124, fax (303)220-8843, lu-books@lu.com, http://www.lu.com. Lists Internet resources by subject; cross-referenced.

Cotton, E. G. (1997). **The online classroom**. 2nd ed. [Book with CD/ROM, 247pp., $29.95]. Classroom Connect, 1866 Colonial Village Ln., P.O Box 10488, Lancaster, PA 17605-0488, (800)638-1639, fax (717)393-1507, connect@classroom.net. Explains the Internet, searching, Web page development, online correspondence and projects, and lists recommended Websites.

Crotchett, K. R. (1997). **A teacher's project guide to the Internet**. [Book, 184pp., $26.50]. Heinemann, Portsmouth, NH, (800)541-2086. Guides teachers through the Internet with suggestions for student projects.

Data Communications. Box 473, Hightstown, NJ 08520. [Mo., $160]. Provides users with news and analysis of changing technology for the networking of computers.

Davis, B. H., & Brewer, J. P. (1997). **Electronic discourse: Linguistic individuals in virtual space**. [Book, 217 pp., $16.95]. State University of New York Press, c/o CUP Services, P.O. Box 6525, Ithaca, NY 14851, (607)277-2211, fax (800)688-2877, orderbook@cupserv.org. Examines electronic discourse as language. Describes a naturalistic longitudinal study of undergraduates involved in computer conferencing.

De Bra, P. M. E. (1977). Teaching through adaptive hypertext on the WWW. **International Journal of Educational Telecommunications, 3** (2/3), 163-79. Describes the evolution of an online course in hypermedia from its beginnings as a hypertext document to current Web technology.

EDUCOM Review. EDUCOM, 1112 Sixteenth St., NW, Suite 600, Washington, DC 20036-4823, (800)254-4770, offer@educom.edu. [Bi-mo., $18 US, $24 Canada, $43 elsewhere]. Features articles on current issues and applications of computing and communications technology in higher education. Reports of EDUCOM consortium activities.

Ellsworth, J. B. (1997). Curricular integration of the World Wide Web. **TechTrends, 42** (2), 24-30. Provides a model for K-12 Internet use, including dissemination of the products of learning, global awareness, pedagogy design and evaluation, online collaboration, and assessment of learning.

EMMS (Electronic Mail & Micro Systems). Telecommunications Reports, 1333 H Street NW, 11th Floor-W, Washington, DC 20005. [Semi-mo., $657 US, $816 elsewhere]. Covers technology, user, product, and legislative trends in graphic, record, and microcomputer applications.

Follansbee, S., & others. (1997). Can online communications improve student performance? Results of a controlled study. **ERS Spectrum, 15** (1), 15-26. Describes a 1995-1996 CAST- (Center for Applied Special Technology) controlled study conducted in seven major U.S. cities that measured the effects of online usage (via Internet and Scholastic Network) on student learning. Results show that online use can increase student performance. Students in experimental classes produced better results on a civil rights unit than those in control classes.

Forsyth, I. (1997). **Teaching and learning materials and the Internet**. [Book, 190pp., $25]. Cassell/Stylus, P.O. Box 605, Herndon, VA 20172-0605, (800)232-0223, fax (703)661-1510, styluspub @aol.com. Concerns Internet college-level course design, development, and assessment.

French, D., Hale, C., & Johnson, C. (1997). **Internet based learning**. [Book, 288pp., $25]. Cassell/Stylus, P.O. Box 605, Herndon, VA 20172-0605, (800)232-0223, fax (703)661-1510, styluspub @aol.com. Suggests a framework for altering teaching styles for courses using the Internet for a range of instruction-enhancing activities.

Gannoun, L., Dubois, P., & Labetoulle, J. (1997). Asynchronous interaction method for a remote teleteaching session. **International Journal of Educational Telecommunications, 3** (1), 41-59. Presents a method for asynchronous interaction during a remote instruction session.

Gomes, M. P., & others. (1997). Promoting exploitation of university research by SMEs: On evaluating technology dissemination on the World Wide Web. **Industry and Higher Education, 11** (1), 21-27. Describes a Web-based technology bank that provides examples of university research of interest to businesses. Addresses the use of electronic communications for dissemination, highlighting potential problems: considerable database maintenance, the volume of information and number of links, and appropriateness of links.

Hack, L., & Smey, S. (1997). A survey of Internet use by teachers in three urban Connecticut schools. **School Library Media Quarterly, 25** (3), 151-55. Discusses effective use of the Internet when integrated into the curriculum as an information resource, and describes the current lack of access in many schools.

Hall, B. (1997). **Web-based training cookbook**. [Book, 482pp., $39.99]. John Wiley & Sons, Distribution Center, 1 Wiley Dr., Somerset, NJ 08875-1272. Explains the use of the Web for supplemental or principal training in business contexts.

Hill, J. R., Tharp, D., Sindt, K., Jennings, M., & Tharp, M. (1997). Collaborative Web site design from a distance: Challenges and rewards. **TechTrends, 42** (2), 31-37. Explores issues associated with developing Websites for large organizations, including audience appraisal, design, development challenges, and practical issues dealing with distance collaboration.

International Journal of Educational Telecommunications. Association for the Advancement of Computing in Education, P.O. Box 2966, Charlottesville, VA 22901, (804)973-3987, fax (804)978-7449, AACE@virginia.edu, http://www.aace.org. [Q., $65 indiv., $93 inst., $20 single copy]. Reports on current theory, research, development, and practice of telecommunications in education at all levels.

The Internet and Higher Education. JAI Press, 55 Old Post Rd., No. 2, P.O. Box 1678, Greenwich CT 06836-1678, order@jaipress.com. [Q., $50 indiv., $175 inst.]. Designed to reach faculty, staff, and administrators responsible for enhancing instructional practices and productivity via the use of information technology and the Internet in their institutions.

Internet Reference Services Quarterly. Haworth Press, 10 Alice St., Binghamton, NY 13904-1580, (800)HAWORTH, fax (800)895-0582, getinfo@haworth.com, http://www.haworth. com. [Q., $36 indiv., $48 inst., $48 libr.]. Describes innovative information practice, technologies, and practice. For librarians of all kinds.

Internet Research (previously Electronic Networking: Research, Applications, and Policy). MCB University Press Ltd., 60-62 Toller Ln., Bradford, W. Yorks BD8 9BY, England. [Q., $499 US, $619 elsewhere]. A cross-disciplinary journal presenting research findings related to electronic networks, analyses of policy issues related to networking, and descriptions of current and potential applications of electronic networking for communication, computation, and provision of information services.

Internet World. Mecklermedia Corporation. Orders for North and South America, Internet World, P.O. Box 713, Mt. Morris, IL 61054; elsewhere, Mecklermedia Ltd., Artillery House, Artillery Row, London SW1P 1RT, England. [Mo., $29 US]. Analyzes development with National Research and Education Network, Internet, electronic networking, publishing, and scholarly communication, as well as other network issues of interest to a wide range of network users.

Ivers, K. S., & Barron, A. E. (1997). Training for telecommunications: Examining the effects of video- and computer-based instruction on preservice teachers' achievement, near-transfer performance, and perception of instruction. **Journal of Computing in Teacher Education, 13** (3), 23-29. Discusses the results of two different delivery methods (video and computer-based instruction) for teaching preservice educators how to use an electronic mail system. Analysis of student questionnaires and achievement found significant differences between the methods on students' perceptions of instruction and near-transfer performance (favoring the computer-based instruction group).

Jensen, C. (1997). **Internet lesson plans for teachers: Bridging the gap between education and technology**. [Book, 80pp., $29.95]. ISTE, 480 Charnelton St., Eugene, OR 97401-2626, (800)336-5191, fax (541)302-3887. Contains 15 complete lesson plans covering several subject areas.

John, N. R., & Valauskas, E. J. (1997). **World Wide Web troubleshooter**. [Book, 192pp., $36]. American Library Association, ALA Editions, 50 East Huron St., Chicago, IL 60611-2795, (800)545-2433, fax (312)836-9958. Explains HTML, Web publishing, and Web use for librarians.

Jones, D. (1997). **Exploring the Internet using critical thinking skills**. [Book, 90pp., $35]. Neal-Schuman Publishers, 100 Varick St., New York, NY 10013-1506, (212)925-8650, fax (800)584-2414, orders@neal-schuman.com. Discusses critical thinking applied to online information, Web searching, and information evaluation.

Journal of Online Learning. ISTE, University of Oregon, 1787 Agate St., Eugene, OR 97403-1923, (800)336-5191, cust_svc@ccmail.uoregon.edu. [Q., $29 US, $41.73 Canada, $39 intl., $42 intl. air]. Reports activities in the areas of communications, projects, research, publications, international connections, and training.

Junion-Metz, G. (1997). **K-12 resources on the Internet: An instructional guide**. 2nd ed. [Book with disk, $54]. Library Solutions Press, Berkeley, CA, http://www.library-solutions.com. Introduces the Internet to teachers and librarians with an emphasis on time efficiency.

Junion-Metz, G. (1997). **K-12 resources on the Internet plus: Instructor's supplement**. [Book, $30]. Library Solutions Press, Berkeley, CA, http://www.library-solutions.com. Provides resources, including transparencies in paper and electronic forms, to help trainers implement the material from the *Guide* [see above].

Kennedy, S. D. (1997). **Best bet Internet: Reference and research when you don't have time to mess around**. [Book, 264pp., $35]. American Library Association, ALA Editions, 50 East Huron St., Chicago, IL 60611-2795, (800)545-2433, fax (312)836-9958. Lists and profiles over 500 reference sites.

Kurland, D. J., Sharp, R. M., & Sharp, V. F. (1997). **Internet guide for education**. [Book, 128pp.]. Wadsworth Publishing Co., 10 Davis Dr., Belmont, CA 94002-3098. Introductory educational telecommunications guide, with list of top Internet sites.

Lamb, A. (1997). **Creating Internet resources**. [Video, 60min., $59.95]. AECT Publication Sales, 1025 Vermont Ave., NW, Suite 820, Washington, DC 20005. Explores Websites created by students and teachers; explains Web authoring.

Lamb, A. (1997). **Exploring Internet resources**. [Video, 60min., $59.95]. AECT Publication Sales, 1025 Vermont Ave., NW, Suite 820, Washington, DC 20005. Explores implications for teachers and students using the Web; examines basics of utilization.

Lamb, A. (1997). **Integrating Internet resources**. [Video, 60min., $59.95]. AECT Publication Sales, 1025 Vermont Ave., NW, Suite 820, Washington, DC 20005. Illustrates the evaluation, selection, and integration of Internet resources into the classroom.

Leshin, C. B. (1997). **Internet adventures: Step-by-step guide to finding and using educational resources, version 1.2**. [Book, 321pp., $24.95]. Allyn & Bacon; available through ISTE, University of Oregon, 1787 Agate St., Eugene, OR 97403-1923. Written for educators; directs readers to substantial educational resources.

Leu, D. J., & Leu, D. D. (1997). **Teaching with the Internet: Lessons from the classroom**. [Book, 200pp., $24.95]. Christopher-Gordon Publishers, Inc., 480 Washington St., Norwood, MA 02062. Explains in teacher-friendly terms how to integrate telecommunications experiences into classroom learning.

Link-Up. Information Today, 143 Old Marlton Pike, Medford, NJ 08055, (800)300-9868. [Bimo., $29.95 US, $36 Canada/Mexico, $54 elsewhere]. Newsmagazine for individuals interested in small computer communications; covers hardware, software, communications services, and search methods.

Merlic, C. A., & Walker, M. J. (1997). Virtual office hours: Facilitating faculty-student communication. **International Journal of Educational Telecommunications, 3** (2/3), 261-78. Describes a successful, large-scale project providing instructional materials and question-answer facilitation.

Milheim, W. D. (1997). Instructional utilization of the Internet in public school settings. **TechTrends, 42** (2), 19-23. Focuses on providing information to K-12 personnel to heighten awareness of utilization of the Internet for educational purposes.

Miller, E. B. (1997). **The Internet resource directory for K-12 teachers and librarians, 97/98 edition**. [Book, 322pp., $25]. Libraries Unlimited, P.O. Box 6633, Englewood, CO 80155-6633, (800)237-6124, fax (303)220-8843, lu-books@lu.com, http://www.lu.com. Designed for educators who are beginners on the Internet; specifies available materials and demonstrates how to find them.

Miller, G. (1997). Agricultural education at a distance: Attitudes and perceptions of secondary teachers. **Journal of Agricultural Education, 38** (1), 54-60. Responses from 102 of 140 Iowa secondary agriculture teachers revealed attitudes toward the interactive communications network (ICN), a two-way fiber-optic telecommunications system. Teachers were concerned about such obstacles as scheduling ICN use and managing laboratory and supervised agricultural experience activities. They were undecided about ICN's usefulness as a teaching tool.

Miller, S. (1998). **Searching the World Wide Web: An introductory curriculum for using search engines**. [Book, 55pp., $12.95]. ISTE, 480 Charnelton St., Eugene, OR 97401-2626, (800)336-5191, fax (541)302-3887. Presents a sequenced, time-efficient approach to skills and concepts for Web navigation and searching. Includes adaptations for individual students, small groups, and entire classes, as well as exceptional students.

Montgomerie, T. C., & Harapnuik, D. (1997). Observations on Web-based course development and delivery. **International Journal of Educational Telecommunications, 3** (2/3), 181-203. Describes the implementation of an online course about the Internet, and provides recommendations for future course design.

Muffoletto, R. (1997). Reflections on designing and producing an Internet-based course. **TechTrends, 42** (2), 50-53. Details several social issues involved in online course delivery, including interactivity, student voice, and equity.

Murray, L. K. (1997). **Basic Internet for busy librarians**. [Book, 192pp., $26]. American Library Association, ALA Editions, 50 East Huron St., Chicago, IL 60611-2795, (800)545-2433, fax (312)836-9958. Designed for novice Internet librarians in all kinds of libraries.

Oliver, K. (1997). Getting online with K-12 Internet projects. **Tech Trends, 42** (6), 33-40. Analyzes Web K-12 projects for meaning, context, procedures, and problems.

Oliver, W. C., & Nelson, T. (1997). Un Meurtre à Cinet (Un homicidio en Toluca): A Web and email whodunit to develop writing competence in intermediate-level language courses. **International Journal of Educational Telecommunications, 3** (2/3), 205-17. Describes a course using problem solving, E-mail, role-playing, listserv, and the Web as tools to teach language.

Online. Online, Inc., 462 Danbury Rd., Wilton, CT 06897. [6/yr., $110]. For online information system users. Articles cover a variety of online applications for general and business use.

Online-Offline. Rock Hill Press, 14 Rock Hill Rd., Bala Cynwyd, PA 19004, (888)ROCK HILL, fax (610)667-2291, http://www.rockhillpress.com. [9/yr., $66.50]. Examines classroom resources, linking curricular themes with Websites and other media.

Owston, R. D. (1997). The World Wide Web: A technology to enhance teaching and learning? **Educational Researcher, 26** (2), 27-33. Considers whether or not the Web can increase access to learning, improve learning, and help contain costs.

Price, S., & others. (1997). The MARBLE Project: A collaborative approach to producing educational material for the Web. **International Journal of Educational Telecommunications, 3** (2/3), 293-320. Describes a Scottish collaborative project to provide learning materials, including a peer tutoring module.

Provenzo, E. F. (1997). **The educator's brief guide to the Internet and the World Wide Web.** [Book, 200pp., $29.95]. Eye on Education, 6 Depot Way W., Suite 106, Larchmont, NY 10538. Demonstrates access, integration, planning, and resources for the beginning educational telecommunicator.

Ritchey, A. C. (1997). Academic skills and cultural awareness through GlobaLearn. **TechTrends, 42** (6), 41-44. Discusses a popular Web learning site from an action research perspective.

Robertson, J. E., & Solomon, C. (1997). Frames-based, image-oriented instruction. **International Journal of Educational Telecommunications, 3** (2/3), 237-59. Describes the development of a frames-based, image-oriented instructional template with examples.

Robin, B., Keeler, E., & Miller, R. (1997). **Educator's guide to the Web.** [Book, 409pp., $19.95]. International Society for Technology in Education, University of Oregon, 1787 Agate St., Eugene, OR 97403-1923, (800)336-5191, cust_svc@ccmail.uoregon.edu. Covers concepts needed to understand the issues involved in teaching with telecommunications, beginning with basic principles.

Rogan, J. M. (1997). Online mentoring: Reflections and suggestions. **Journal of Computing in Teacher Education, 13** (3), 5-13. Reports a study of "Reach for the Sky," a telecommunications project offering rural teachers access to the Internet and online courses. Teachers received Internet training, then became mentors for other teachers enrolled in online courses. Interviews and analysis of E-mail messages highlighted lessons learned about mentoring and online education.

Royer, R. (1997). Teaching on the Internet: Creating a collaborative project. **Learning & Leading with Technology, 25** (3), 6-11. Touts Internet collaborative projects as able to give K-12 students authentic learning experiences; presents appropriate methods.

Ryder, R. J., & Hughes, T. (1997). **Internet for educators.** [Book, 240pp.]. Merrill/Prentice Hall, 445 Hutchinson Ave., Columbus, OH 43235-5677. Guides teachers through Internet explorations with an interactive approach. Contains appendices with sample Acceptable Use Policies (AUPs).

Schrum, L., & Berenfeld, B. (1997). **Teaching and learning in the information age: A guide to educational telecommunications.** [Book, 179pp., $34]. Allyn & Bacon; available from ISTE, University of Oregon, 1787 Agate St., Eugene, OR 97403-1923, (800)336-5191, cust_svc@ccmail.uoregon.edu. Offers introduction to using telecommunications for educators and others within authentic curricular activities in educational settings, placed in the context of professional development, research, and compelling issues.

Sener, J. (1997). Creating asynchronous learning networks in mathematics, science, and engineering courses for home-based learners. **International Journal of Educational Telecommunications, 3** (1), 23-39. Describes courses developed for community college learners.

Sharp, R. M., Levine, M. G., & Sharp, V. F. (1997). **The best math and science Web sites for teachers**. [Book, 125pp., $18.95]. ISTE, University of Oregon, 1787 Agate St., Eugene, OR 97403-1923. Lists and describes appropriate Websites alphabetically, and by curriculum area and grade level.

Shearer, R. (1997). The Internet: How fast can you download? **TechTrends, 42** (2), 47-49. Analyzes and describes trends in telecommunications technology, including ADSL modems and Internet II.

Sheekey, A. (1997). **Education and telecommunications: Critical issues and resources**. [Book, $29.95]. Information Gatekeepers Inc., 214 Harvard Ave., Boston, MA 02134, (800)323-1088, fax (617)734-8562, igiboston@aol.com, http://www.igigroup.com. References issues and information sources detailing how schools can benefit from the universal service fund established by the Telecommunications Act of 1996.

Sheekey, A. D. (1997). Public and private interests in networking educational services for schools, households, communities. **TechTrends, 42** (3), 26-31. Describes the implications of new networking technologies for place- and time-independent schooling and information services, including roles for public and private entities.

Simpson, C., & McElmeel, S. L. (1997). **Internet for schools**. 2nd ed. [Book, 175pp., $29.95]. Linworth Publishing, 480 E. Wilson Bridge Rd., Suite L, Worthington, OH 43085-2372, (800)786-5017, fax (614)436-9490, orders@linworth.com, http://linworth.com. Contains improvements and additions to the original edition; discusses searching, filtering, and other topics for novices and more experienced users.

Skomars, N. (1997). **Educating with the Internet: Using net resources at school and home**. [Book with CD-ROM, $29.95]. Charles River Media, 403 VFW Dr., P.O. Box 417, Rockland, MA 02370, (800) 382-8505, fax (781)871-4376, chrivmedia@aol.com, http://www.charlesriver.com. Instructs educators of all levels about how Web incorporates into the learning process. Includes directory of over 1,300 education-related sites.

Sugrue, B., & Kobus, R. C. (1997). Beyond information: Increasing the range of instructional resources on the World Wide Web. **TechTrends, 42** (2), 38-42. Describes the development of a prototype of an instructional site designed to support a large number of students enrolled in a beginning graduate instructional design course.

Telecommunications. (North American Edition). Horizon House Publications, Inc., 685 Canton St., Norwood, MA 02062. [Mo., $75 US, $135 elsewhere, free to qualified individuals]. Feature articles and news for the field of telecommunications.

T.I.E. News (Telecommunications in Education). ISTE, 1787 Agate St., Eugene, OR 97403-1923. [Q., $20 members, $29 nonmembers, $39 foreign]. Contains articles on all aspects of educational telecommunications.

Van Gorp, M. J., & Boysen, P. (1997). ClassNet: Managing the virtual classroom. **International Journal of Educational Telecommunications, 3** (2/3), 279-91. Describes ClassNet, which automates many of the administrative tasks associated with global Internet classes through a simple Web interface.

Wenrich, J. (1997). Making the connection: A high-speed Internet link for rural schools. **Learning & Leading with Technology, 25** (3), 52-54. Describes a wireless networking system, which provides a solution for the high cost of connecting rural schools.

Williams, B. (1997). **Web publishing for teachers**. [Book with CD-ROM, 384pp., $24.99]. IDG Books, http://www.idgbooks.com. Demonstrates Web page creation and organization, graphics, and interactivity. Discusses authoring software and professional collaboration.

Wolcott, J. R., & Robertson, J. E. (1997). The World Wide Web as an environment for collaborative research: An experiment in graduate education. **International Journal of Educational Tele-communications, 3** (2/3), 219-36. Examines the result when a group of researchers attack a single problem from different perspectives, working in a collaborative environment.

Index

AACC. *See* American Association of Community Colleges (AACC)

AACE. *See* Association for the Advancement of Computing in Education (AACE)

AAP. *See* Association of American Publishers (AAP)

AASCU. *See* American Association of State Colleges and Universities (AASCU)

AASL. *See* American Association of School Librarians (AASL)

The AASL electronic library, 1997 ed., 226

Abramovich, S., 199

"Academic skills and cultural awareness through GlobaLearn," 249

Academy of Motion Picture Arts and Sciences (AMPAS), 104

ACCESS ERIC, 119

ACCESS NETWORK, 152

ACEI. *See* Association for Childhood Education International (ACEI)

ACHE. *See* Association for Continuing Higher Education (ACHE)

"Achievement-related expectations and aspirations in college women," 26

"The acquisition of qualitative physics knowledge during textbook-based physics training," 241

ACRL. *See* Association of College and Research Libraries (ACRL)

Addressing vocational training and retraining through educational technology, 12

ADJ/CC. *See* Adjunct ERIC Clearinghouse for Child Care (ADJ/CC)

ADJ/CL. *See* Adjunct ERIC Clearinghouse on Clinical Schools (ADJ/CL)

ADJ/CN. *See* Adjunct ERIC Clearinghouse for Consumer Education (ADJ/CN)

ADJ/JS. *See* Adjunct ERIC Clearinghouse for United States-Japan Studies (ADJ/JS)

ADJ/LE. *See* Adjunct ERIC Clearinghouse for ESL Literacy Education (ADJ/LE)

ADJ/LR. *See* Adjunct ERIC Clearinghouse for Law-Related Education (ADJ/LR)

Adjunct ERIC Clearinghouse for Art Education, 120

Adjunct ERIC Clearinghouse for Child Care (ADJ/CC), 122

Adjunct ERIC Clearinghouse for Consumer Education (ADJ/CN), 121

Adjunct ERIC Clearinghouse for ESL Literacy Education (ADJ/LE), 123

Adjunct ERIC Clearinghouse for Law-Related Education (ADJ/LR), 120

Adjunct ERIC Clearinghouse for United States–Japan Studies (ADJ/JS), 120

Adjunct ERIC Clearinghouse on Clinical Schools (ADJ/CL), 124

"The adoption of microcomputers for instruction: Implications for emerging instructional media implementation," 217

Adult education and vocational education: Implications for research on distance delivery, 12

"Advantages of a theory-based curriculum in instructional technology," 223

AECT. *See* Association for Educational Communications and Technology (AECT)

AECT Archives, 111

AEE. *See* Association for Experiential Education (AEE)

AEL. *See* Appalachia Educational Laboratory, Inc. (AEL)

AERA. *See* American Educational Research Association (AERA)

AETT. *See* Association for Educational & Training Technology (AETT)

AFB. *See* American Foundation for the Blind (AFB)

AFC. *See* Anthropology Film Center (AFC)

Agency for Instructional Technology (AIT), 104

"Agricultural education at a distance: Attitudes and perceptions of secondary teachers," 206, 248

Aisenberg, N., 26

AIT. *See* Agency for Instructional Technology (AIT)

AIVF/FIVF. *See* Association of Independent Video and Filmmakers/Foundation for Independent Video and Film (AIVF/FIVF)

ALA. *See* American Library Association (ALA)

Alabama

    graduate programs in instructional technology, 161

Alabama State University, 161

Albaugh, P. R., 225

ALCTS. *See* Association for Library Collections and Technical Services (ALCTS)

Alexander, N., 47

ALISE. *See* Association for Library and Information Science Education (ALISE)

ALS. *See* PBS Adult Learning Service (ALS)

ALSC. *See* Association for Library Service to Children (ALSC)

ALTA. *See* American Library Trustee Association (ALTA)

"Am I on the mark? Technology planning for the E-Rate," 212

"From multimedia to multiple-media: Designing computer-based course materials for the Information Age," 225

"From presentation to programming: Doing something different, not the same thing differently," 224, 240

"From sages to guides: A professional development study," 209, 237

"From strawberry statements to censorship," 231

Fullan, M., 3, 218

Fulop, M. P., 208

"Fun with video editing: Creating the illusion of reality," 233

"Fundamental dimensional properties of the operant," 95

"A future for business simulations?," 219

The future of information technology, 216

FWL. *See* Far West Laboratory for Educationa Research and Development (FWL)

Gagné, Robert M., 95
   The conditions of learning, 95
   Instructional technology: Foundations, 72
Galas, C., 224, 240
Gale directory of databases, 215
Games trainers play, 241
Gannoun, L., 246
Garrison, D. R., 11
GATF. *See* Graphic Arts Technical Foundation (GATF)
Gbomita, V., 217
Gender advertisements, 25
Gender and instructional design, 22–29
   advertising, images in, 25–26
   background, 22
   increasing gender equity, 26–28
   schooling, 24–25
   and society, 23
   stereotypes, 23–24
"Gender DiVisions across technology advertisements and the WWW: Implications for educational equity," 22, 25, 26
Gender equity and classroom experiences: A review of research, 24
"Gender equity on-line: Messages portrayed with and about the new technologies," 23
"Gender roles and women's achievement-related decisions," 26
"Gender stereotyped computer clip-art images as an implicit influence in instructional message design," 26
"Gender, Technology, and Instructional Design: Balancing the Picture," 22–29
Gender-responsible leadership: Do your teaching methods empower women?, 24
"Gendered by design," 24, 27, 220
Gentry, C. G., 87
George Eastman House, 126
The George Lucas Educational Foundation, 126
George Mason University, 193

George Washington University, 166
Georgia
   graduate programs in instructional technology, 169
Georgia Southern University, 169
Georgia State University, 169
Geralien, A., 201
Gerhardt, L., 228
Gerlach, V. S., 86
"Get ready, get set, go read! Motivation through competition," 240
"Getting online with K–12 Internet projects," 249
Getting started in instructional technology research (2nd ed.), 208
Gilbert, Thomas F.
   "gap," concept of, 96
   profile, 94–97
   writings
      "An early approximation to the principles of programming continuous discourse, self-instructional materials," 95
      "Fundamental dimensional properties of the operant," 95
      Human competence: Engineering worthy performance, 96
      Human competence: Engineering worthy performance, tribute edition, 96
      Journal of Mathetics, 95
      "Mathetics: The technology of education," 95
Gillham, M., 224
Gimblett, R. R., 8
"Girls + technology = turnoff?," 242
Goal analysis (3rd ed.), 221
Goffman, E., 25
Gomes, M. P., 246
Goodling, S. C., 200, 223
Goodman, R. E., 244
Gornick, V.
   Woman in sexist society: Studies in power and powerlessness, 26, 27
   Women in science: 100 journeys into the territory, 26–27
Gottfried, J., 211
Government Information Quarterly, 228
Governors State University, 171
Gowin, D. B., 82
GPN. *See* Great Plains National ITV Library (GPN)
Graphic Arts Technical Foundation (GATF), 127
"Grasping the thread: Web page development in the elementary classroom," 243
Great games for trainers, 241
Great Plains National ITV Library (GPN), 127
Gros, B., 219
Gross, M., 228
"Groupware for collaborative learning: A research perspective on processes, opportunities, and obstacles," 13
Grover, R., 226
Grunwald, K. A., 62
Guidelines for the evaluation of instructional technology resources, 234

Library Resources and Technical Services, 229
Library Software Review, 230
Library Trends, 230
The library Web, 232
Lieberman, A., 218
"A line of argument for innovation in teaching and assessment starting from students' conceptions and misconceptions in learning processes," 217
Link-Up, 248
LISA: Library and Information Science Abstracts, 230
Lister Hill National Center for Biomedical Communications, 133
LITA. *See* Library and Information Technology Association (LITA)
Liu, L., 241
Lloyd, L., 212
Local area networking for the small library: A how-to-do-it manual for librarians, (2nd ed.), 228
Lockee, Barbara B., 64–71
Logo Exchange, 212
Lohman, M. C., 221
Losee, R. M., 216
Louisiana
 graduate programs in instructional technology, 175
Louisiana State University, 175
Lovdal, L. T., 23
Lu, C. R., 202, 212
Luetkehans, L., 207
Lumsdaine, A., 37
Luna, C. J., 224
Lyons, C. M., 12

MacArthur, C. A., 8
MacBrayne, P., 12
Maccoby, N., 25
MacDonald, R. M., 230
MacIntosh, J., 204
Macklin, M. C., 23
MacWorld, 202
Maddux, C. D., 212
Magazine Publishers of America (MPA), 133
Mager, R. F., 37, 41n. 2, 221
The magic carpet ride—Integrating technology into the K–12 classroom, 202
Magliaro, S. G., 222
Mahmoud, E., 26
Mahoney, J. E., 23
Making instruction work (2nd ed.), 221
"Making one-computer teaching fun," 214
"Making sense of our motivation: A systematic model to consolidate motivational constructs across theories," 89
"Making the connection: A high-speed Internet link for rural schools," 250
Male, M., 243
Managerial attitudes and performance, 89

Managing information technology, 215
Managing interactive video/multimedia projects, 86
Managing media services: Theory and practice (2nd ed.), 231
Managing open systems, 205
Mankato State University, 180
"The MARBLE Project: A collaborative approach to producing educational material for the Web," 249
MARC manual: Understanding and using MARC records, 226
Marcovitz, D. M., 216
"The marginal media man. Part 1: The great paradox," 35
Markham, W. T., 24
Markwood, R., 64
Marland, P., 205
Martin, B., 206
Martin, D. C., 26
Marx, R. W., 238
Maryland
 graduate programs in instructional technology, 175
Maslow, A. H., 51
Massachusetts
 graduate programs in instructional technology, 177
"Master's degree and six year programs in instructional technology," 73
Mastering the possibilities: A process approach to instructional design, 222
"Mathematizing verbal descriptions of situations: A language to support modeling," 242
Mather, B. R., 230
"Mathetics: The technology of education," 95
Maxymuk, J., 230
Maze, S., 216
McAleese, Ray, 75
McAlister, K., 58
McBeath, R. J., 40
McClelland, J., 12
McCormick, T. M., 26, 27
McCulloch, K. H., 205
McDevitt, M., 12
McElmeel, S. L., 250
McFeely, M. G., 211
McHenry, L., 206
McIsaac, M., 64
McKavanagh, C., 207
McKenzie, J., 224
McLoughlin, C., 206
MCN. *See* Museum Computer Network (MCN)
McREL. *See* Mid-continent Regional Educational Laboratory (McREL)
MDPD. *See* Media Design and Production Division (MDPD)
Means, T. B., 221
Measuring instructional results (3rd ed.), 221

Multimedia Monitor, 235
Multimedia projects in education: Designing, producing, and assessing, 224
Multimedia Schools, 235
Munby, H., 83
Munroe, J. P., 33, 34, 37
Murphy, K. L., 206
Murray, L. K., 248
Museum Computer Network (MCN), 134
Museum of Modern Art, Circulating Film and Video Library, 135

Nabors, W., 199
NAEYC. *See* National Association for the Education of Young Children (NAEYC)
NAMAC. *See* National Alliance for Media Arts and Culture (NAMAC)
NAPT. *See* Native American Public Telecommunications (NAPT)
NARMC. *See* National Association of Regional Media Centers (NARMC)
NASA. *See* National Aeronautics and Space Administration (NASA)
NASTA. *See* National Association of State Textbook Administrators (NASTA)
Natal Mercury (South Africa)
"Seeking the big African link-up," 46
"Still no stationery or books for pupils," 46
A nation at risk: A report to the nation from the secretary of education, 2
National Aeronautics and Space Administration (NASA), 135
National Alliance for Media Arts and Culture (NAMAC), 135
National Association for the Education of Young Children (NAEYC), 135
National Association for Visually Handicapped (NAVH), 135
National Association of Regional Media Centers (NARMC), 136
National Association of State Textbook Administrators (NASTA), 136
The National Cable Television Institute (NCTI), 136
The National Center for Improving Science Education, 136
National Center to Improve Practice (NCIP), 137
National Clearinghouse for Bilingual Education (NCBE), 137
National Commission on Libraries and Information Science (NCLIS), 137
National Communication Association (NCA), 138
National Council for Accreditation of Teacher Education (NCATE), 138
National Council for Educational Technology, 74
National Council of Teachers of English (NCTE), Commission on Media, 138
National Council of the Churches of Christ in the USA, 138
National Education Knowledge Industry Association (NEKIA), 139

National Education Telecommunications Organization & EDSAT Institute (NETO/EDSAT), 139
National Endowment for the Humanities (NEH), 139
National Federation of Community Broadcasters (NFCB), 139
National Film Board of Canada (NFBC), 140, 153
National Film Information Service, 140
National Gallery of Art (NGA), 140
National Information Center for Educational Media (NICEM), 140
National ITFS Association (NIA), 140
National Press Photographers Association, Inc. (NPPA), 141
National PTA, 141
National Public Broadcasting Archives (NPBA), 141
National Religious Broadcasters (NRB), 141
National School Boards Association, 213, 243
National School Boards Association (NSBA) Institute for the Transfer of Technology to Education (ITTE), 142
National School Supply and Equipment Association (NSSEA), 142
National Science Foundation (NSF), 142
National Special Media Institute, 87
National Telemedia Council Inc. (NTC), 142
Native American Public Telecommunications (NAPT), 142
Naumer, J. N., 230
NAVH. *See* National Association for Visually Handicapped (NAVH)
NCA. *See* National Communication Association (NCA)
NCATE. *See* National Council for Accreditation of Teacher Education (NCATE)
NCBE. *See* National Clearinghouse for Bilingual Education (NCBE)
NCIP. *See* National Center to Improve Practice (NCIP)
NCLIS. *See* National Commission on Libraries and Information Science (NCLIS)
NCME. *See* Network for Continuing Medical Education (NCME)
NCREL. *See* North Central Regional Educational Laboratory (NCREL)
NCTE. *See* National Council of Teachers of English, Commission on Media (NCTE)
NCTI. *See* The National Cable Television Institute (NCTI)
Neal-Schuman authoritative guide to Web search engines, 216
Neal-Schuman complete Internet companion for librarians (2nd ed.), 225
Neal-Schuman directory of library technical services home pages, 232
Neal-Schuman Webmaster, 226
Nebraska
graduate programs in instructional technology, 181
NEEMA. *See* New England Educational Media Association (NEEMA)